# GLANCES BACKWARD

# GLANCES BACKWARD
## AN ANTHOLOGY OF AMERICAN HOMOSEXUAL WRITING 1830–1920

EDITED BY

JAMES J. GIFFORD

broadview press

**Canadian Cataloguing in Publication Data**

Glances backward : an anthology of American homosexual writing, 1830-1920 / edited by James J. Gifford

Includes bibliographical references.
ISBN-13: 978-1-55111-728-7
ISBN-10: 1-55111-728-2

1. Gay men's writings, American.   2. Gays' writings, American.   3. Homosexuality—Literary collections.   4. American literature—19th century.   5. American literature—20th century.   I. Gifford, James J., 1946-

PS509.H57G53  2006     810.8'0920664    C2006-903347-1

Broadview Press is an independent, international publishing house, incorporated in 1985. Broadview believes in shared ownership, both with its employees and with the general public; since the year 2000 Broadview shares have traded publicly on the Toronto Venture Exchange under the symbol BDP.

We welcome comments and suggestions regarding any aspect of our publications- please feel free to contact us at the addresses below or at broadview@broadviewpress.com.

North America
PO Box 1243, Peterborough, Ontario, Canada K9J 7H5
PO Box 1015, 3576 California Road, Orchard Park, NY, USA 14127
Tel: (705) 743-8990; Fax: (705) 743-8353
email: customerservice@broadviewpress.com

UK, Ireland, and continental Europe
NBN International, Estover Road, Plymouth, UK PL6 7PY
Tel: 44 (0) 1752 202300; Fax: 44 (0) 1752 202330
email: enquiries@nbninternational.com

Australia and New Zealand
UNIREPS, University of New South Wales
Sydney, NSW, Australia 2052
Tel: 61 2 9664 0999; Fax: 61 2 9664 5420
email: info.press@unsw.edu.au

www.broadviewpress.com

Typesetting and assembly: True to Type Inc., Mississauga, Canada.

PRINTED IN CANADA

FOR BARBARA, JACK, DICK, ROB, AND TOMMY

*Dec 24th 1887.*

*Dear Ernest.*

*What ever betide,*
  *No change of time*
*Can our true hearts divide*
*If thou in me,*
  *and I in thee*
*Shall trustingly confide.*

  *your friend*

    *Bernard.*

Christmas card, 1887, discovered in a Syracuse, New York antiques shop in the 1970s. See page 372.

"However displeasing to the reader, let it be affirmed that all real friendships between men have a sexual germ."
THE INTERSEXES (1908), Edward Prime-Stevenson

From childhood's hour I have not been
As others were; I have not seen
As others saw; I could not bring
My passions from a common spring.
ALONE (1830), Edgar Allan Poe

Upon waking next morning about daylight, I found Queequeg's arm thrown over me in the most loving and affectionate manner. You had almost thought I had been his wife.
MOBY-DICK (1851), Herman Melville

"Ay," said Pathie. "That has had more to do with it. I hope he will overtake and win, for I love the boy. I keep my oldish heart pretty well locked against strangers; but there is a warm cell in it, and in that cell he has, sleeping and waking, made himself a home."

"Ah, Doctor," said Ruby, "you and I, for want of women to love, have to content ourselves with poetic rovers like Brent. He and Biddulph were balls, operas, champagne on tap, new novels, flirtations, and cigars to me last winter."
JOHN BRENT (1861), Theodore Winthrop

"Oh, where is it? Don't let me see it!" screamed Molly. And at this deeply feminine remark, the Virginian looked at her with such a smile that, had I been a woman, it would have made me his to do what he pleased with on the spot. Upon the lady, however, it seemed to make less impression.
THE VIRGINIAN (1902), Owen Wister

"He is dead," he said simply.
Dead!
In a dazed way I walked up to the chair and coldly glanced at the face, which, white and expressionless, looked to me unlike that which I had known as my husband's. The proprietor quietly went from the room and left me alone with Arthur. On the mantel-piece my staring eyes saw a small bottle, on which a label marked "laudanum" stood out with fearful clearness. Then I realized it all. With an agonized cry I flung myself into the unresisting arms of my husband. I kissed his cold, dead lips, his face, and the open, unseeing eyes, as I would have kissed him in life, had he willed it so. Ah! he could not ward me off now. He was mine, and I would cherish him forever.
Suddenly I sprang back, a horrible feeling of repulsion creeping over me.

Just above Arthur's head, on the wall, I saw two portraits, placed together in a single frame. One represented my husband, happy and smiling; the other showed the hateful features of Captain Dillington. My grief gave place to a violent, overpowering sense of anger. Tearing the frame from the wall, I threw it roughly to the floor. The glass broke with a crisp, short noise; but with my feet I crushed it into atoms. Then stooping down, I picked up the photographs, and tore them into smallest pieces. In the same frenzied manner, I went to the window, opened it, and gathering up the bits of glass—regardless of the fact that they cut my hands until the blood flowed freely—I flung them with the torn photographs from the window and looked from it until I saw them scatter in all directions. Then turning away, and without another look at the dead form in the chair, I left the room and the hotel.

A MARRIAGE BELOW ZERO (1889), Alan Dale [Alfred J. Cohen]

The story starts in the Running-Pitch Place or Jah-dokonth. Hashjeshjim, the son of the Fire, whose mother is a Comet, and Etsay-Hasteen, the first man, who is the son of Night and whose father is Nah-doklizh, which is the blue above the place where the Sun has set, were there; also Estsa-assun, who is the first woman, whose mother is the Daybreak and whose father is Nahtsoi which is the yellow light after the Sun has set; also Etsay-hashkeh or Coyote Man, whose mother is Yah-zheh-kih, or the Dawn Light. The fifth who is there is Begochiddy, the blue-eyed and yellow-haired god, the great god, whose mother is a Ray of Sunlight, Shah-bekloth, and whose father is the Daylight, Shundeen; also Asheen-assun, the Salt Woman, whose mother was Tohe-estan, or Water Woman, and whose father was Tsilth-tsa-assun, or Mountain Man. (He looks like a woman but is a man.) These are the six people who were living on the dark earth or first world, Jah-dokonth.

NAVAJO ORIGIN MYTH (1942), Hastiin Klah

# CONTENTS

## PART X: OF HEARTS THROWN OPEN

## PART XI: DOCTORS, CASE STUDIES, AND EROTOPATHS

# Acknowledgements

Thanks to Jennie Rubio, Brian A. Dominick, John W. Crowley, Sherry Day, Raimondo Biffi, Tom Sargant, Jean-Claude Féray, John Seelye, Kevin Killian, Michael Williams, Dawn Fisk Thomsen, Sandra Engel, Will Roscoe, Burton Weiss, Jay Salsberg, Timothy Drew, Coy Ludwig, Charles N. Watson, Alan Pickrell, and of course Paul D. Stern.

With special thanks to a friend who left the party too early: Fred Harbeck (1958-2006).

# INTRODUCTION

THE PAST IS A FOREIGN COUNTRY, it is said. It never seems so much so as when we explore the American writings that impact on homosexuality during the period 1830 to 1920.

Melville begins *Moby-Dick* with page after page of quotations—extracts, as he calls them—which attempt to capture some sense of what "the whale" is all about. In a similar manner, this book begins with quotations where the notion of sexual "difference" tentatively surfaces in early American literature. As it unfolds, *Glances Backward* includes a considerable range of different voices which make up a so-called literature of "homosexuality." Because the past in question is not so very long ago, we are sometimes lulled into thinking that our knowledge of it is quite complete. Even a brief glance at works collected here reveals the assortment of expression—some overt, some far more indirect—which confront a modern reader. Do these passages deal with same-sex affection, or simply "difference"? Are these conscious, subconscious, or unconscious examples, and to what extent must the author's intentionality affect our reading? The selections in this collection come from a time and cultural position distinctly different from our own, very different from what would be found in an anthology of contemporary gay literature.

For one thing, a twenty-first-century understanding of homosexuality challenges the prevailing understanding of the nineteenth century. The last four decades have seen many changes in attitudes towards homosexuality. Today, Belgium, the Netherlands, Spain, and Canada all allow same-sex unions; *Brokeback Mountain*, a movie about gay cowboys, wins the Venice Film Festival; and Americans watch *Will & Grace* and *Queer as Folk* on television—while Iran executes homosexual men. Many contemporary gay men and women can recall hiding the very impulses that now find their way into mainstream expression in television, novels, and the news. Why, then, should a look at the past prove so difficult? Indeed, why look back at all?

The past serves as a prologue to who we are now. Each minority eventually glances backward to trace their historical trajectory. Just as many adopted children seek their biological parents, we demand a knowledge of the past, to allow us better to understand the present. No one is like the goddess Athena, leaping fully formed into existence from the forehead of Zeus. We study the faces of our parents to trace our own features. Alice Walker had to discover the grave of Zora Neale Hurston, both literally and figuratively, to understand her own position in African-American literature. The same holds true for modern gay men, and especially for their literature.

One difficulty is that nineteenth-century views on same-sex desire were not as clear-cut as we feel they are in modern-day Western culture, though essentialists argue that same-sex-attracted people have existed since the dawn of humanity. Doubtless they have, but the social construction of what we call "the homosexual" is a more recent phenomenon. It was Darwin, standing on the shoulders of the great taxonomist Carl Linnaeus (1708–78), who compelled the nineteenth century to categorize, sort, and label, and suddenly human beings found themselves joining plants and animals in various "groups" as well. But it is Michel Foucault (1926–84) who provides us with the fundamental insight that sexuality itself—when seen as a possible human "category"—is actually a set of discursive practices (i.e., ways of establishing orders of truth, or what is accepted as "reality" in a given society) that *shifts with history and culture.* Foucault, gay himself, tells us that it is inaccurate to believe that a particular sexual category preceded the word "homosexuality." The early nineteenth century, not aware of the word (which was coined about 1870), was therefore unaware of sexual orientation as a grouping for human differentiation. The term, with all its implications and assumptions, simply did not exist in peoples' minds for most of the nineteenth century—something we should not forget while reading this anthology.

It is interesting to trace the development of sex-preference categorization in nineteenth-century America. While Native Americans often respected the bisexuality of their "berdaches" (see pp. 9–14), European immigrants imported certain cultural prohibitions and biases towards same-sex-loving people. Writers like John Tanner and George Catlin, for example, are the result of such confrontation between cultures in their inability to grasp such "bisexual" beings as any sort of norm. In nineteenth-century America we witness the increasing visibility of homosexuality, as it emerges from religious proscription to the bright (if equally unforgiving) light of medical scrutiny and scientific description. A person's sexual preference began to take on a new meaning: the "sodomite" was identified by certain sexual *acts*, but the homosexual became an *identity*, a new sexual category. David Halperin argues that this period saw the development of the homosexual as a "heavily psychologized model of sexual subjectivity—which knits up desire, its objects, sexual behavior, gender identity, reproductive function, mental health, erotic sensibility, personal style, and degrees of normality or deviance" as a new category we now label "sexual orientation."[1]

In other words, the category of "gay person" did not exist as such in the nineteenth century. As awareness grew, however, an oversaturated brew of possibilities had to eventually precipitate forth a cultural formation of the homosexual. This anthology exists to examine that "mix," and to understand better where it finally led. And though there were many names for same-sex-loving people floating about ("uranians," "sodomites," "fairies," "catamites," "inverts," "perverts," "mollies," "pansies," "fruits," "queers," and so on), in another sense there were none at all. What Oscar Wilde called "the love that dare not speak its name" had not even identified what that name *was*.

**Victorian America**

Unless we place this anthology's readings into some kind of historical context, it is difficult to understand them.

The post-Civil War era that we now call the "Gilded Age" witnessed the birth of "Clubland"—men's groups and fraternal organizations like the Knights of Damon and Pythias, the scouts, and the YMCA. It also saw a growing obsession with imperialistic military strength, team sports, and the modern Olympics—and caught up in these was a fascination with the male body itself. A cult of manliness and physicality emerged, influenced by the Darwinian notion of the "improvement of the race,"[2] until it blossomed into such phenomena as Teddy Roosevelt's concept of "The Strenuous Life"[3] and "Sandow the Great,"[4] the world's first modern muscleman. Alongside America's industrial growth, urban centers increased in population; YMCAs, men's clubs and fraternal organizations, and the growth of athletics (both teams and fans) served as connecting points for men, especially homosexual men; for into such settings that glorified maleness it was only logical that same-sex-loving men would meet and flourish as well. As such institutions arose, so did a certain eroticization of masculinity.

The cult of romantic friendship was strong during the nineteenth century, between men as well as women. But as Eve Kosofsky Sedgwick points out in *Between Men* (1985), close friendships gradually came to be viewed with some suspicion, as developing (and sometimes conflicting) notions of homosexuality invited closer scrutiny of such relationships. This collection highlights aspects of this development: Leatherstocking and Chingachgook, along with Huck and Jim (suspicious pairs themselves), led to "Joseph and His Friend," Delaney and Flemming ("Marjorie Daw"), and Gifford and Weigell ("The Striding Place"), and Ned and Tom (*Two College Friends*).

In addition, the gradual shift in American literature from Romanticism to Realism signaled the new appeal of representing life "as it was." The idealized characters and plots of a Leatherstocking Tale gradually gave way to the nitty-gritty detail of everyday life and the believable people of *Huckleberry Finn*. Another influence on American literature of this period was the growing interest in "dynamic psychology." Doctors and scientists were formulating new rules about what constituted "normal" behavior. In literature, realism provided ample opportunity to accommodate homosexuality within its various discourses, and the fascinating entries that various genres provide is one of the chief interests in this anthology. How did homosexual sensibility, repressed and often hidden as it was, find its way into public discourse? This anthology suggests an answer.

Homosexual writing, as this book sees it, is a literary production that concerns itself with the experience of men who love men. The authors here are not necessarily all homosexual; what makes them interesting is how their writing looks behind the mask that many homosexuals were forced or chose to wear (no surprise that masks are a recurring image for these writers), and provide some expression—not always positive—for what society labeled "aberrant."

## The Medical Establishment Invents Homosexuality

Richard von Krafft-Ebing's *Psychopathia Sexualis* appeared in 1886, and Havelock Ellis and John Addington Symonds' *Sexual Inversion* in 1897. Both these weighty psychological treatises, along with many others, served as the genesis of the medical establishment's "invention" of the homosexual—and eventually the heterosexual (for without homosexuality, the notion of heterosexuality had not been necessary). With the rise of psychology, same-sex-loving people became a new class of human beings—a new pathology that demanded examination and explanation. Under the medical gaze, "inverts'" stories were told through case studies, where there could never be too much probing or detail as to heritage, suspected "causes," and actual practices. According to Bert Hansen, "Even though some of the medical writings were not supposed to be distributed to the public, they were eagerly sought out—and found—by individuals searching for clues to their own nature."[5]

Although science would control the definition of homosexuality for many decades, there was also input from homosexuals themselves. For every article written by a Dr. William Lee Howard (warning insurance companies that homosexuals were poor risks in one memorable instance; see below, 329–33), there were counter-appeals appearing even in pathological studies, such as the eloquent testimony of "Professor X" (James Mills Peirce) in *Sexual Inversion* (1897), defending homosexuals as part of Nature's plan. Indeed, the homosexual John Addington Symonds would adumbrate the scientific Havelock Ellis in co-writing *Sexual Inversion* (although significantly, Symonds would be erased as author from later editions[6]). Using the model of the case study, Claude Hartland and Earl Lind would tell their own stories directly, without the intervention of doctors, using "scientific" formats but transforming them into something more human and sympathetic than the doctors would generally permit. Taking his cue directly from Krafft-Ebing (indeed, dedicating his book to him), the homosexual Edward Prime-Stevenson would lead a counter-attack in an equally weighty tome called *The Intersexes* (1908), where the medical establishment was called into question over the validity of their many negative assertions. ("Subjective and scarcely scientific," Ellis would later sneeringly retort.[7])

## The Whitman/Wilde Dialectic

Two major models for homosexuals had presented themselves by the close of the nineteenth century, and each was exemplified by a single man: American poet Walt Whitman was one; British writer/playwright Oscar Wilde the other. Beyond their literary contributions, each consciously created public person-ae which grew into representations that probably neither intended.

If one circumstance could be singled out for its overwhelming significance for the American homosexual during this period, it would have to be a non-American event: the 1895 trials of Oscar Wilde, which suddenly catapulted homosexuals onto a public stage and into the modern age, and found deep resonance in the United States as well as Great Britain.

Wilde was arguably the most notorious exponent of the cult of aestheti-cism, and lily-in-hand, his bohemian style of dressing became an integral part of his pursuit of Beauty.[8] Aestheticism found deep resonance by the end of the nineteenth century in continental Europe, as well as Great Britain and the United States. It espoused art as an end in itself, the greatest aspect of life finding precedence even over society, culture, and morality. The decadence of the *fin-de-siècle* was well served by figures like Algernon Swinburne (1837–1909), Walter Pater (1839–94), James McNeil Whistler (1834–1903), the Pre-Raphaelites, and Aubrey Beardsley (1872–98). If the cult and its fig-ure were much parodied—and none more so than Wilde, it meant that they were well-known; and Wilde's wit and ripostes were beyond attack. Indeed, Wilde's career as a flamboyant *poseur* occasionally overshadowed such major works as *The Importance of Being Earnest* (1895) and *The Picture of Dorian Gray* (1891). But it was his confrontation with British law in 1895 that suddenly cast aestheticism as an avatar of homosexuality. For his eloquent defense of "the love that dare not speak its name," Wilde served two years at hard labor, which in effect destroyed him. Significantly, his condemnation as a homo-sexual meant that, to the public, anything associated with him—particularly the accoutrements of his aestheticism—was also branded "homosexual." A very specific model of the "invert" was born. His British manners, his cloth-ing, his posing and pronouncements appeared "precious" and effeminized to American eyes, and he was vilified as the very model of deviation.[9] Wilde would become the public figure of homosexuality for decades to come, and any traits identified with him became "homosexual" by association.

Although no single catastrophic event would similarly underline Walt Whitman's emergence as homosexual in the public eye, one might argue that Whitman's view of same-sex-loving men finds its apex in the 1860 *Calamus* poems, which celebrate male "adhesiveness" along with a more liberating view of human sexuality in general. He was shocking to his generation ("I heard he was disgraceful" said Emily Dickinson) but his identification with the common man, the blue-collar worker, the fellow soldier, created images whose very roughness was part of this new openness. Under his pen, fraternal feelings between men apotheosed into something deeper and more importantly, something unashamed: the love between comrades. This representation of manly attachment is defined in his essay *Democratic Vistas* (1871) as "Intense and loving comradeship, the personal and passionate attachment of man to man." Further, Whitman explained, "It is to the development, identification, and general prevalence of that fervid comradeship, (the adhesive love, at least rivaling the amative love hitherto possessing imaginative literature, if not going beyond it,) that I look for the counterbalance and offset of our materialistic and vulgar American democracy, and for the spiritualization thereof."[10] Whitman's own bachelor life, with his many attachments to younger men,[11] allied with his public persona of the American blue-collar worker, untutored, rough-hewn, and natural, created an image of the same-sex-loving man that stood in opposition to Oscar Wilde. After Whitman's death in 1891, George Santayana introduced Whitman's writings to the academic establishment at Harvard, and this served to legitimize more than his poetry by suggesting a new prototype for homosexuality as well.

These two great writers of this period, then, exemplify for many the two ends of an emerging homosexual spectrum: the American Walt Whitman and the British Oscar Wilde—two "types" of homosexuals—seemingly opposed to each other, but united in offering the new century two contrasting ways to view the same-sex-loving man.

### Codes of Mutual Recognition

Gay writing in this period often presents us with a mysterious text, because we are not always sure how to read it. Detection becomes a game whereby the author invites us to reconfigure an ambiguous text. It offers an opening, we suppose, to certain sympathetic readers, men "in the know." Such radical destabilization directed them as it now instructs us to uncover, or recover, love-stories between two males, often embedded in "acceptable" fiction; but the way is not always clear. Invitations to hidden subtexts shimmer at the boundaries of visibility.

The nineteenth century had its homosexual markers, ways for men to seek each other out, just as nowadays we talk about "gaydar." We know some of them; there were doubtless others. George Chauncey and Edward Prime-Stevenson discuss places where homosexual men could meet in the flesh; but this anthology concentrates on literary codes, where the meetings took place on paper. When were author and reader talking the same language? In their letters, Frank Millet referred to his "other self" and Clyde Fitch referred to his "private life": we can assume that many of their readers knew there was a submerged meaning here. But might a homosexual man see his likeness in the more public writing of this period? When they found access to the case studies of the medical establishment in particular, homosexuals must have felt a sense of relief, to find that there were others like themselves. But were there markers of recognition in popular literature that might have reached out in the same way? As we have seen, Prime-Stevenson, describing the library of a homosexual in "Out of the Sun," suggests there were; and he confirms it in the excerpt from *The Intersexes* below. To the "sympathetic reader" certain situations or sentiments suggested alternative readings of texts.

The revival in Greek studies, begun in the mid-eighteenth century and still flourishing throughout the nineteenth, is significant here.[12] Universities found themselves in a tricky position. In extolling the wonders of classic culture—the plays, the philosophy, the arts and architecture, the civilizing notions of democracy—they also had to deal with "the despicable vice of the Greeks" (as a professor in Forster's *Maurice* [written 1913–14, pub. 1971] puts it). They could hardly ignore the poetry of Sappho, the comedies of Aristophanes, the passionate attachment of Achilles and Patroclus (so central to the *Iliad*), Plato's *Symposium* and *Phaedrus*, the myth of Zeus and Ganymede, with their images of male-male love. John Addington Symonds' essay, privately printed but apparently much circulated, *A Problem in Greek Ethics* (1873, pub. 1883) makes plain that the Greeks were more liberal in their understanding of human sexuality than the Victorians were willing to accept. He also suggests that the figure of Socrates in Plato's *Symposium* represents a more understanding time.[13] While it would be an overstatement to say that all things Greek were signposts of homosexuality, references to the Greeks and Hellenism in general were often markers for same-sex love.[14] In the present day, Tom Stoppard's play *The Invention of Love* (1997) is a wonderful introduction to the role classics and the university arena might play in the conflicting sexual dynamics of a homosexual man during this period, by examining the life of poet A.E. Housman (1859–1936). Both Prime-Stevenson's *Imre: A Memorandum* (1906) and E.M. Forster's *Maurice* (1913–14), novels which with their positive portrayals of homosexual men and their unprecedented happy endings, are harbingers of shifting twentieth-century attitudes, make frequent erudite references to the Greeks. The heroes of both books are upper-class well-educated men who are all too aware of ancient Hellenic times as models for an acceptance that their era denies them.

Literature itself, including the Bible, provided many models of/for homosexual couples, and the very mention of David and Jonathan, Damon and Pythias, Ruth and Naomi, Hadrian and Antinous, Achilles and Patroclus, Nisus and Euryalus, Edward II and Gaveston, even Jesus and St. John, were enough to turn on the light of mutual recognition in some people.[15] Such figures as Michelangelo or Shakespeare (as sonneteer) or bachelor-composers like Brahms or Tchaikovsky—not to mention a love of music and opera itself[16]—might be enough to raise a knowing eyebrow. Even the names of Whitman and Wilde "dropped" into conversation (the latter only with care after the trials of 1895) might serve as markers for "those in the know."

In art, St. Sebastian and his namesakes were suspicious. This martyr gave artists an excuse to idolize the male torso in writhing *contrapposto*[17] and the young soldier-saint or at least his name could serve as a signal. Prime-Stevenson uses the name frequently and consciously in his writings, including "*Aquae Multae Non—*" (239–55 below).

Décor could also serve as a signal. The baroque fussiness of surroundings in Prime-Stevenson's magazine story "Mrs. Dee's Encore" (213–26) suggests that its owner is homosexual, just as the details of the college rooms in *Cult of the Purple Rose* (62–66) and *Harvard Episodes* (59–61) imply that ornate aesthetics go beyond mere college-boy pranks in defining their inhabitants. Indeed, the "purpleness" of the rose is just as damning as the red clothing of Will Scarlet in *Robin Hood* (33–40). Even the smells of "Our Aromatic Uncle" (202–12) prove to be nasal markers! Charles Warren Stoddard identifies his hero as homosexual in describing his rooms in his autobiographical novel *For the Pleasure of His Company*, just as Willa Cather suggests that Paul's obsession with décor reflects his sexuality in her short story "Paul's Case" (311–26). For the late nineteenth century, even the wearing of certain colors could be a cue.[18] Indeed, the gilding of the page in Viereck's "The Ballad of the Golden Boy" (169–70) carries aesthetic marking to a fatal extreme.

**Networking**

This is the least-understood aspect of the rise of homosexuality in the late nineteenth century; very little is known about networking given that it operated on a very private level. How far and wide pertinent manuscripts or books or writings were circulated among homosexuals is only gradually becoming clear to us. Mark Mitchell and David Leavitt convincingly discuss such "Pages Passed from Hand to Hand"—"pertinent" texts which would be distributed in homosexual circles.[19] Today, bookstores often have a separate shelf for "gay writing"; a hundred years ago, the distribution of a homosexual text was not so easily accomplished.

Did homosexual writers know each other? We know they did. (Charles Warren Stoddard even claimed that Jack London was one of his "Kids."[20]) Edward Prime-Stevenson wrote to George Woodberry, as did George Sylvester Viereck. Whitman wrote to Stoddard who in turn wrote to Francis Millet. DeWitt Miller wrote both to Stoddard and to Clyde Fitch; and we know that Miller sent scores of books of a "certain hue" to several others, such as Stoddard—who in turn was a friend of Woodberry ... and so on.[21] Prime-Stevenson would often recommend or secure books for interested friends, and the preface to his collection of short stories *Her Enemy, Some Friends, and Other Personages* contains a list of continental bookstores where certain "lavender" titles must have been available, possibly "under the counter." Such networking must have been more common than we realize, for even books of limited circulation found their way into appreciative hands. The bookplates of homosexual-themed texts now in library collections often reveal not only ownership but networking paths as well. The circulation of these texts, not to mention how homosexual authors and readers would influence and support each other, is not yet fully understood.

**Invasion of the Genres**

This anthology shows that no genre of writing was exempt from homosexual cooptation. The expression of same-sex-loving feelings and figures crop up in short stories, novels, general fiction, poetry, drama, personal correspondence, historical writing, nonfiction of every kind—even Christmas cards. We can now appreciate how subtly homosexual writers could daringly insert their concerns into texts meant for a general public; and we can also appreciate how revealingly they might express themselves in more personal writings. Some of the latter, as to be expected, can be strikingly overt; or, occasionally subtexts are so subtle as to make us ask whether they are there at all. Some of the pieces here may require a second look.

Boys' books provide a surprising arena for the display of same-sex feelings. A plethora of tales were available to would-be Tom Sawyers and "Little Men," whether as history, Westerns, adventures, or dime novels. Into this area authors such as Horatio Alger and Edward Prime-Stevenson both couch a homosexual dynamic in their writings for juveniles; Prime-Stevenson was quite conscious, in fact, of doing so. Others appear more innocent. Was Howard Pyle aware, for example, of how certain sections of his tale of Robin Hood might be read? Or was Harry Enton's *Young Sleuth* series quite innocent? Often it seems impossible to tell.

It seems that readers were willing to forgive all kinds of behavior, so long as it took place in schools. Howard Overing Sturgis's early novel *Tim: A Story of Eton* (1891) with its pathetic depiction of a schoolboy crush seems—to modern readers at least—as blatant as Frederick Loring's *Two College Friends* (1871) (see below, pp. 43–50), who are clearly in love with each other. Harvard in the 1890s appears in retrospect as a hotbed of homosexual sensibility, with authors such as Loring, Flandrau, and Shirley Everton Johnson roiling the literary waters with their reminiscences, no matter how exaggerated. Alongside such writing, there was still the heavy subtlety of George Santayana, George Cabot Lodge, Trumbull Stickney, Bliss Carman, and Richard Hovey, poeticizing their love for their own gender.

The nineteenth century's fascination with death, so well lampooned in *Huckleberry Finn* (1885), found at least one homosexual outlet, in the permission poetic elegies gave a man to express his love for another (safely dead).

Alfred Lord Tennyson's long series of poems on the death of his friend Arthur Hallam in his book *In Memoriam* (1850) was the most well-known during this period, but it inspired many American authors to carry the genre one step further. Fitz-Greene Halleck, Trumbull Stickney, and especially George Cabot Lodge all found the elegy suited to feelings perhaps not otherwise expressible.

In like manner, a "man's tale" provides an acceptable landscape for feelings between men in "The White Silence" (227–34), "Tennessee's Partner" (177–84), and "Good-Bye Jim" (267–69) (though here we must recognize that not all the authors would be pleased to know that they are included in this anthology; would they perhaps resent their "covers" being divulged?).

### Landmark Books: What's Included and What's Not

Homosexual writing of this period has its classics, and this anthology makes no pretense about gathering them all. Such seminal writings as Whitman's Calamus poems are widely available in many editions, so they are given short but respectful treatment here. Bayard Taylor's 1870 novel *Joseph and His Friend* deserves to be reread but, alas, remains hard to find. Edward Prime-Stevenson published *Imre: A Memorandum* in 1906, and its important status as arguably the first American novel with a happy ending for its homosexual protagonists requires a reading by any serious scholar in this field (and it is fortunately available in Broadview's catalogue). Several Melville and James titles now seem "tinged with lavender," but Melville's *Billy Budd* (1889, pub. 1922) and James' "The Pupil" (1891) are easy to come by. Thanks to modern reprints, complete versions of *A Marriage Below Zero* (1889) and *Two College Friends* (1871) can now be easily found.[22] But Prime-Stevenson's seminal *Intersexes* is only available in a hard-to-read reprint. A new edition of Henry Blake Fuller's homosexual college novel *Bertram Cope's Year* (1919) is on the way, but interested readers still have to scrounge limited resources to read Viereck's *House of the Vampire* (1907) or an unedited version of Grierson's *The Valley of Shadows* (1909). Gay literary studies from this period are hampered by an inaccessibility of texts—some swallowed up by history (such as Prime-Stevenson's tantalizing—and lost—*Sebastian au Plus Bel Age*[23]), but some are simply not available due to the subtle censorship of falling out of print.

And what of the correspondence, the diaries, the unnamed other works of the past that would give us a completer picture of gay people's forefathers? Who knows what documents lie waiting to be discovered?[24]

### How this Book is Organized

Most anthologies offer works in chronological order. Although there is a loose chronological framework here, some selections have been grouped together in order to highlight trends, contrasts, and themes. Certain selections are better appreciated by being observed in counterpoint to others. I have organized some genres together, such as boys' books, popular magazine fiction, case studies, verse, or correspondence. Other writing, however, has been assembled according to subject matter, such as school/college life, imaginary landscapes or arcadias, or homosocial institutions. Instead of locating contextual material in appendices, I have instead placed this material within relevant categories. It is my hope that these selections represent a broad spectrum of genres rather than being restricted to a few formal literary modes. This variety reflects, ironically, the broadness of forums for homosexual expression during this period.

Most importantly, such grouping allows for more enjoyable reading while providing food for thought.

## Notes

1  *How to Do the History of Homosexuality*, 29. We should also remember that this was the age that constructed modern notions of heterosexuality as well. (See Jonathan Ned Katz's *The Invention of Heterosexuality*.)
2  The principle of sexual selection, that both sexes should avoid marriage if they are defective either physically or mentally.
3  Roosevelt introduced the term in an 1899 speech, calling for "the doctrine of the strenuous life, the life of toil and effort, of labor and strife; to preach that highest form of success which comes … to the man who does not shrink from danger, from hardship, or from bitter toil.…"
4  Eugen Sandow (1867–1925) was a famous Victorian strongman and the father of modern-day bodybuilding. For further discussion of this idea see Ann Douglas's *The Femininization of American Culture* and Jackson Lears' *No Place of Grace: Antimodernism and the Transformation of American Culture 1880–1920*.
5  Hansen, 111.
6  See Wayne Koestenbaum's discussion in *Double Talk*, 43–67.
7  Havelock Ellis, *Studies in the Psychology of Sex: Part Two: Sexual Inversion*, 3rd ed. (New York: Random House, 1936), 72.
8  See Richard Ellmann's compelling biography *Oscar Wilde* (New York: Vintage, 1987).
9  Ed Cohen's remarkable examination of this phenomenon is explored in depth in his *Talk on the Wilde Side* (1993). Another compelling discussion is found in Alan Sinfield's *The Wilde Century* (1994).
10  *Leaves of Grass and Other Writings* (2002), edited by Michael Moon, 770.
11  Ed Folsom's striking essay "Whitman's Calamus Photographs" (193-219) is only one introduction to Whitman's homosexuality. See *Breaking Bounds: Whitman and American Cultural Studies*, ed. Betsy Erkkila and Jay Grossman (New York: Oxford UP, 1996) (which contains Folsom's essay), as well as *Calamus Lovers:*

*Walt Whitman's Working-class Camerados*, ed. Charley Shively (San Francisco: Gay Sunshine P, 1987), and Michael Moon's *Disseminating Whitman: Revision and Corporeality in* Leaves of Grass (Cambridge: Harvard UP, 1991).

12  See Louis Crompton, *Byron and Greek Love*, especially pp. 85–86.

13  For further discussion of this idea, see Louis Compton's informative essay "Ancient Greek Literature" in *Gay and Lesbian Literary Heritage* (ed. Claude J. Summers), 342–48; Kenneth Dover's seminal study *Greek Homosexuality* (Cambridge: Harvard UP, 1978); and David Halperin's *One Hundred Years of Homosexuality and Other Essays on Greek Love* (New York: Routledge, 1990), among others.

14  Richard Dellamora provides an insightful discussion on Hellenism as a euphemism for homosexuality in his book, *Masculine Desire: The Sexual Politics of Victorian Aestheticism* (Chapel Hill: U of North Carolina P, 1990), 33.

15  In Summers' aforementioned *Gay and Lesbian Literary Heritage*, Raymond-Jean Frontain's essay on "The Bible" (92–100) provides an illuminating discussion of homosexual figures in both Old and New Testaments.

16  See Wayne Koestenbaum's witty and informative *The Queen's Throat: Opera, Homosexuality and the Mystery of Desire* (New York: Poseidon, 1993) for further discussion of this idea.

17  I.e., counterpoise [Italian]; the position of a figure in painting or sculpture in which the hips and legs are turned in a different direction from the shoulders and head.

18  See Judy Grahn's comments in this regard in *Another Mother Tongue: Gay Words, Gay Worlds* (Boston: Beacon, 1984), 3–8, 76–79.

19  See their learned and provocative Introduction in *Pages Passed from Hand to Hand* (Boston: Mariner, 1997).

20  Roger Austen's *Genteel Pagan* (ed. John W. Crowley), 165.

21  *Genteel Pagan* 154, 166.

22  *A Marriage Below Zero* is reprinted in Mitchell and Leavitt's *Pages Passed from Hand to Hand*, while *Two College Friends* is in Nissen's *Romantic Friendship Reader*. Both novels appear in their entirety.

23  This tantalizing homosexual tale, self-referenced in Edward Prime-Stevenson's short story "Out of the Sun" (1913) has never been located, and is presumed lost.

24  For an example of such continuing unearthing of such homosexual documents, see the remarkable story of the discovery of two remarkably explicit 1826 letters from ante-bellum South Carolina (Martin Bauml Duberman, "'Writhing Bedfellows,'" printed in Duberman et al., *Hidden from History*).

# PART ONE

# THE INTERSEXES

*Though American-born and in the midst of a successful career as a professional writer for such publications as* Harper's *and* The Independent, *Edward Prime-Stevenson left it all and fled to Europe permanently after 1900. Here he devoted much of his time to writing several works dealing explicitly with homosexuality, published under the name "Xavier Mayne." At his own expense and through a private press in Italy, he printed his best work,* Imre: A Memorandum *(1906).[1] This novel was remarkable for its straightforward and honest depiction of two men who through a series of mutual revelations about their homosexuality fall in love and wind up happily with each other—an ending quite unprecedented for its time. In his short story "Out of the Sun" (1913) the main character Dayneford's homosexuality is revealed by the catalogue of certain titles in his library—works that reveal to a modern reader how a same-sex-loving man of his day saw himself both defined and reflected in contemporary literature. Many of the titles remain obscure, but our eye catches the names of four American authors in the list: Woodberry, Whitman, Overing-Sturgis (the anonymous author of* Tim), *and Mayne (Prime-Stevenson himself). The pseudonymous signature and pen-name catch our eye, and remind us that such ruses were necessary in this period to write about same-sex-loving men (we shall encounter more of them in this anthology). In 1908 Prime-Stevenson's monumental defense of homosexuality,* The Intersexes, *was published (again, at his own expense and through a private Italian press with only 125 copies). At the urging of Krafft-Ebing (as he claimed in the book's dedication to that pioneer of modern sexual studies), he compiled hundreds of examples of homosexuality through history up to the present and explored their implications in a well-reasoned and passionate defense from what he felt was a growing attack by the contemporary medical community. The excerpts below provide a fitting introduction to this anthology of literary works that possess a homoerotic dynamic.*

# FROM "OUT OF THE SUN" (1913)

Ah, his books! The library of almost every man of like making-up, whose life has been largely solitary, so concentratedly from the inside, is companioned from youth up by innermost literary sympathies of his type. Dayneford stood now before his bookcase, reading over mechanically the titles of a special group of volumes—mostly small ones. They were crowded into a few lower shelves, as if they sought to avoid other literary society, to keep themselves to themselves, to shun all unsympathetic observation. Tibullus, Propertius and the Greek Antologists [sic] pressed against Al Nafsaweh and Chakani and

Hafiz. A little further along stood Shakespeare's Sonnets, and those by Buonarrotti; along with Tennyson's "In Memoriam," Woodberry's "The North-Shore Watch," and Walt Whitman. Back of Platen's bulky "Tagebuch" lay his poems. Next to them came Wilbrandt's "Fridolins Heimliche Ehe," beside Rachilde's "Les Hors-Nature;" then Pernauhm's "Die Infamen," Emil Vacano's "Humbug," and a group of psychologic works by Krafft-Ebing and Ellis and Moll. There was a thin book in which were bound together, in a rich-ly-decorated arabesque cover, some six or seven stories from Mardrus' French translation of "The Thousand Nights And A Night"—remorsely [sic] separat-ed from their original companions. On a lower shelf, rested David Christie Murray's "Val Strange" and one or two other old novels; along with Dickens' "David Copperfield," the anonymous "Tim," and Vachell's "The Hill," com-panioned by Mayne's "Intersexes," "Imre" and "Sebastian au Plus Bel Age."

## FROM *THE INTERSEXES* (1908)

### American Philarrhenic Literature[2]

[...] The North-American (by such term indicating particularly the United States) with his nervosity, his impressionability, his complex fusion of bloods and of racial traits, even when of directly British stocks, is usually far more "temperamental" than the English. He has offered interesting excursions at least towards, if not always into, the homosexual library. His novels, verses and essays have pointed out a racial uranianism. In the United States and adjacent British possessions, the prejudices and restrictions as to literature philar-rhenic in accent, are quite as positive as in Great Britain. The authour [sic] or publisher of a homosexual book, even if scientific, not to speak of a belles-lettres work,[3] will not readily escape troublesome consequences. Even psy-chiatric works from medical publishers are hedged about with conditions as to their publication and sale. Nevertheless, similisexualism is far from being an unknown note in American belles-lettres, and has even achieved its clas-sics.

### Walt Whitman

An American poet, who has assumed an international significance and cult—well-deserved—Walt Whitman, can be regarded through a large proportion of his most characteristic verse, as one of the prophets and priests of homo-sexuality. Its atmosphere pervades Whitman's poems: being indeed an almost inevitable concurrent of the neohellenic, platonic democracy of Whitman's philosophic muse. One series of Whitman's earlier poetic utterances, at once psychologic and lyric, the famous "Calamus" group in "Leaves of Grass," out of dispute stands as among the most openly homosexual matters of the sort, by idealizing (but sensually idealizing) man-to-man love, psychic and physical, that modern literature knows: in virility far beyond the verse of Platen;[4] while Whitman much exceeds Platen in giving physical expressiveness to what he sings. Of Whitman's own personal homosexualism there can be no question, if anyone be acquainted with the intimate story of the "good gray poet's long life." Episodes in his reminiscences called "Hospital Sketches," (many others were never put into print) are personally significant enough. Whitman's choice of intimates too was significant. The tie with the young Irish tram-driver, Peter Doyle, was only one of the Whitmanian divagations of the kind. To women, Whitman was sexually quite indifferent: philosophically contemptuous of them. In physical type the magnificent manly beauty of Whitman, and its endurance, even late in his life, are in key with his philarrhenic nature. [...]

## American Verse of the Day

Several contemporary poets of the United States, older and younger, have interjected the accent of at least psychic uranianism in their verses, though none known to the present writer approach Whitman in loftiness, directness and clarity. Professor George E. Woodberry, of Columbia University, is the authour of a long elegy, giving title to a volume, "The North-Shore Watch": a retrospect and lament inspired by the death of a lad—a poem hellenically passional, and of superiour poetic quality. Noticeable, *passim*,[5] is also the poetry frequently tending to the sort of psychology here in question (though unequal in inspiration) by the Canadian-American, Bliss Carman.

## Suggestions in American Prose

In prose, as in verse, of American origin, the connection between the addresses of ardent and absorbing friendship and a stronger emotion is not one to be taken for granted, any more than in belles-lettres not in English. In Emerson's neo-grecian attitude to friendship, in his essays and his poetry, there is no clear uranian suggestion. To read uranianism between even such Emersonian lines as those that say that only through the friend is the sky blue, the rose red, the fountains of hidden life fair, is not by warrant. The same reserve applies to numerous contemporaries, including many in minor letters. Here and there, however, in current American periodicals, occur tales or poems of at least a two-coloured psychic suggestion. In the chapter on military uranianism, was mentioned a recent volume, "The Spirit of Old West-Point," a charming series of reminiscences of cadet-days, by General Morris Schaff.[6] In certain sketches of the late H.C. Bunner[7] something of the uranian strain occasionally echoes. An openly homosexual novelette, apparently unique in such an explicit category in America, came many years ago from a New York journalist—"A Marriage Below Zero," signed with the pen-name "Alan Dale."[8] The story, not one of any artistic development, narrates (in the person of a neglected wife) her marriage with an uranian, apparently a passivist, who cannot shake off his sexual bondage to an older and coarser man, an officer. The story ends in the young husband's suicide in Paris, after an homosexual scandal has ostracised him.

In the charming "South-Sea Idyls" of Charles Warren Stoddard,[9] a Californian writer and university-professor, occur episodes and suggestions of uranian complexion: though in case of a book so light-heartedly fantastic it is difficult to say where the personal and absolutely reminiscent are to be understood. […]

## Notes

1   Available in a Broadview Press edition.
2   "Philarrhenic" was an uncommon term for homosexual [Greek].
3   Light, elegant, refined literature [French].
4   August von Platen (1796–1835), a German writer whose published diary revealed his "uranianism." Prime-Stevenson appended a critical study of Platen to *The Intersexes.*
5   "In passing" [Latin].
6   See pp. 348–50, below.
7   See pp. 202–12, below.
8   See pp. vii.
9   See pp. 93–103, below.

# PART TWO

# TWO-SPIRIT PEOPLE

*The literature of native Americans is as varied as the many different tribes. It is fundamentally an oral tradition, which did not take written form until the twentieth century. The androgynous figure of the "berdache" or "nádleehí" (in Navajo) was held sacred, and as such represents the acceptance of men who displayed "feminine" characteristics. They were revered as being spiritual and touched by the divine, and as such were highly respected by their cultures. This Navajo myth introduces the divine berdache named Begochidi, a complex two-spirit being who contains both male and female sides. The story, typical of the native American oral tradition, was dictated by the elderly Navajo Slim Curly to the sociologist Berard Haile in 1930–31, but it was not published in written form until 1978. The figure of Begochidi here is seen in his earlier incarnation as the great trickster hero, though he is later depicted as sympathetic.*

# FROM "THE MOTHWAY MYTH" (RECORDED 1930)

[...] This, it seems, (happened) also at the same Riverward Knoll. Along its sunny side, in swampy places, (there are) beautiful flowers which are white in season. There it seems that White Butterfly (Moth) originated, and red moths of various colors had originated there, they say. Along its slope, the plants were large and their tips (blossoms were) white. As they were of both sexes, I suppose, it happened that the Sun looked at them time and again. At their (flowery) tips, it seems, their female organ happened to be, and at the tips (of others were) their male organs. Here, after these (plants) were put in this condition, the Begochidi-to-be was born.

This one, it seems, began to go about here. When those Butterfly People had been born, a number of whom I suppose were of the same parents, he began to stay among them taking them in his care. Some of these were boys, some girls, (and) he would put his hand to their crotches saying "be-go be-go"—as he was a berdache. Right there, it seems, he raised the Butterfly People, young men and young women in large numbers, taking care of them, encircling them all the time and never letting them out of his sight. It seems that he knew of a report that somewhere along the mountain range, people were hunting, (because) he traveled there with the haze, they say. So immediately he traveled by haze. There, it seems, whenever they would crawl upon deer and at the moment they wanted to shoot, he would feel their lower parts from behind and say "Bego" to them. On that account, the game would be missed and it was unpleasant (hunting).

Then too, when marrying was done and the two would lie down and were about to have intercourse, he would touch the lower parts of both parties and say "Bego." It was simply everywhere that he did this, they say. Even if a woman wanted to urinate and would squat for that, he would touch her lower parts and say "Bego." And even to men he did likewise. So it seems that Bego did this and, according to this saying that he has touched somebody's crotch, he was called Bego-chidi. By a change of colors, the (same) haze moved about with him, they say. The same person they called "Bego-who-touches," "Bego-who-is-white," "Bego-who-is-black," "Bego-who-is yellow," they say.

In this manner it seems that he appeared everywhere, along the mountain ranges, along the water courses, or wherever Holy People dwelt. He had in his possession the so-called "earth mirage (stone)," they say, (also) rock mirage, tree mirage, plant mirage and rising haze (heat waves). So it seems that large numbers of maidens, as said, were raised at that place. If from various places it were said, "Let him be married to her," he would say "No, no," as he would shake his finger and refuse to part from her. Neither would he part from the young men. So whenever it was said concerning maidens of different places: "Let him be married to her," he would say: "No, no." And whenever it was said of a youth, "He shall marry at this and that place," he would say "No," as he walked in their protection. Only he himself would go among them when they would lie down to sleep, saying "Bego bego" as he put his hands to their crotches.

# JOHN TANNER (1780–?)

*Captured by Indians at the age of nine, John Tanner spent much of his adult life among the Ojibwa; he eventually chose to remain with them, rather than return to a life among white people. This excerpt from his* Adventures *describes his encounter with a berdache (or here A-go-kwa)—who wants to marry him.*

## FROM *A NARRATIVE OF THE CAPTIVITY AND ADVENTURES OF JOHN TANNER* (1830)

[...] Some time in the course of this winter, there came to our lodge one of the sons of the celebrated Ojibbeway chief, called Wesh-ko-bug, (the sweet,) who lived at Leech Lake. This man was one of those who make themselves women, and are called women by the Indians. There are several of this sort among most, if not all the Indian tribes. They are commonly called A-go-kwa, a word which is expressive of their condition. This creature, called Ozaw-wen-dib, (the yellow head,) was now near fifty years old and had lived with many husbands. I do not know whether she had seen me, or only heard of me, but she soon let me know she had come a long distance to see me, and with the hope of living with me. She often offered herself to me, but not being discouraged with one refusal, she repeated her disgusting advances until I was almost driven from the lodge. Old Net-no-kwa was perfectly well acquainted with her character, and only laughed at the embarrassment and shame which I evinced whenever she addressed me. She seemed rather to countenance and encourage the Yellow Head in remaining at our lodge. The latter was very expert in the various employments of the women, to which all her time was given. At length, despairing of success in her addresses to me, or being too much pinched by hunger, which was commonly felt in our lodge, she disappeared, and was absent three or four days. I began to hope I should be no more troubled with her, when she came back loaded with dry meat. She stated that she had found the band of Wa-ge-to-tah-gun, and that that chief had sent by her an invitation for us to join him. He had heard of the niggardly conduct of Waw-zhe-kwaw-maish-koon towards us, and had sent the A-go-kwa to say to me, "my nephew, I do not wish you to stay there to look at the meat that another kills, but is too mean to give you. Come to me, and neither you nor my sister shall want any thing it is in my power to give you." I was glad enough of this invitation, and started immediately. At the first encampment, as I was doing something by the fire, I heard the A-go-kwa at no great distance in the woods, whistling to call me. Approaching the place, I found she had her eyes on game of some kind, and presently I discovered a moose. I shot him twice in succession, and twice he fell at the report of the gun, but it is probable I shot too high, for at last he escaped. The old woman reproved me severely for this, telling me she feared I should never be a good hunter. But before night the next day, we arrived at Wa-ge-tote's lodge, where we ate as much as we wished. Here, also, I found myself relieved from the persecutions of the A-go-kwa, which had become intolerable. Wa-ge-tote, who had two wives, married her. This introduction of a new inmate into the family of Wa-ge-tote, occasioned some laughter, and produced some ludicrous incidents, but was attended with less uneasiness and quarreling than would have been the bringing in of a new wife of the female sex.

*For eight years, artist George Catlin traveled among the natives of the North
American Plains, and attempted to capture their lives in words and pictures. He
provided one of the earliest glimpses (for Westerners) of the "two-spirit" person, the
berdache, who was seen from early childhood as special: a man with a woman's
soul, embodying a third gender (women with men's souls were the fourth).
Berdaches dressed and did the work of the opposite gender, were seen as spiritual-
ly gifted, and were highly respected by their tribes—something that does not quite
register with the ethnocentric Catlin in his description below.*

## "DANCE TO THE BERDASHE" (1844)

[From Letters and Notes on the Manners, Customs, and Conditions of
North American Indians (1832–39).]

[...] Dance to the Berdashe is a very funny and amusing scene, which happens once a year or oftener, as they choose, when a feast is given to the
"Berdashe," as he is called in French, (or *I-coo-coo-a*, in their own language),
who is a man dressed in woman's clothes, as he is known to be all his life, and
for extraordinary privileges which he is known to possess, he is driven to the
most servile and degrading duties, which he is not allowed to escape; and he
being the only one of the tribe submitting to this disgraceful degradation, is
looked upon as *medicine* and sacred, and a feast is given to him annually; and
initiatory to it, a dance by those few young men of the tribe who can, as in the
sketch, dance forward and publicly make their boast (without the denial of
the Berdashe), that Ahg-whi-ee-choose-cum-me hi-anh-dwax-cumme-ke on-
daig-nun-ehow ixt. Che-ne-a'hkt ah-pex-ian I-coo-coo-a wi-an-gurotst whow-
itcht-ne-axt-ar-rah, ne-axt-gun-he h'dow-k's dow-on-daig-o-ewhict nun-go-was-
see.

   Such, and such only, are allowed to enter the dance and partake of the
feast, and as there are but a precious few in the tribe who have legitimately
gained this singular privilege, or willing to make a public confession of it,
it will be seen that the society consists of quite a limited number of "odd
fellows."

   This is one of the most unaccountable and disgusting customs, that I have
ever met in the Indian country, and so far as I have been able to learn,
belongs only to the Sioux and Sacs and Foxes—perhaps it is practiced by

other tribes, but I did not meet with it; and for further account of it I am constrained to refer the reader to the country where it is practiced, and where I should wish that it might be extinguished before it be more fully recorded.

## PART THREE

# LUCK, PLUCK, AND A KINDLY MENTOR

# WALT WHITMAN (1819–92)

*Known primarily as a poet, Walt Whitman's early prose laid the groundwork for themes he would later develop more fully in his verse. Later revisions of this story emphasized its temperance theme and played down the feelings of the young man for the boy; but the earliest version printed here seems to modern readers surprisingly direct in its depiction of same-sex love (made all the more complex by the ages of its subjects). Certainly the affection of an older for a younger boy was a tradition that would later be found in the boys' books of Horatio Alger and Edward Prime-Stevenson (*White Cockades *[1887] and* Left to Themselves *[1891]*[1] *among others). Of particular interest is this early appearance of the Whitmanian hero, who would be further developed in Whitman's* Calamus *(1860) poems and* Specimen Days *(1882). This heroic figure served for many as an early homosexual model. Many readers came to associate it with Whitman's own persona: a man of the people, close to nature and aware and unashamed of his feelings and desires. Often rough on the outside, Whitman had a soft heart, and believed in "adhesiveness," or passional social bonding, between men. Such attraction often bordered on the erotic, particularly in* Calamus. *Such a homosexual model would become, by the end of the nineteenth century, dialectically opposed to the "Oscar Wilde aesthete" (see below, 69–81).*

## "THE CHILD'S CHAMPION" (1841)[2]
### AND SELECTED POEMS

Just after sunset one evening in summer—that pleasant hour when the air is balmy, the light loses its glare, and all around is imbued with soothing quiet—on the door-step of a house there sat an elderly woman waiting the arrival of her son. The house was in a straggling village some fifty miles from the great city, whose spires and ceaseless clang rise up, where the Hudson pours forth its waters. She who sat on the door-step was a widow; her neat white cap covered locks of gray, and her dress though clean, was patched and exceeding homely. Her house, for the tenement she occupied was her own, was very little, and very old. Trees clustered around it so thickly as almost to hide its color—that blackish gray color which belongs to old wooden houses that have never been painted; and to get to it, you had to enter a little rickety gate, and walk through a short path, bordered by carrot-beds, and beets, and other vegetables. The son whom she was expecting was her only child. About a year before, he had been bound apprentice to a rich farmer in the place, and after finishing his daily tasks, he was in the habit of spending half an hour at his mother's. On the present occasion, the shadows of the night had settled heavily before the youth made his appearance; when he did, his walk was slow and dragging, and all his motions were languid, as if from great weariness. He opened the gate, came through the path, and sat down by his mother in silence.

"You are sullen, to-night, Charley," said the widow, after a minute's pause, when she found that he returned no answer to her greetings. As she spoke, she put her hand fondly on his head; it was as wet as if it had been dipped in the water. His shirt, too, was soaked; and as she passed her fingers down his shoulder, she felt a sharp twinge in her heart, for she knew that moisture to be hard wrung sweat of severe toil, exacted from her young child, (he was but twelve years old,) by an unyielding task-master.

"You have worked hard to-day, my son."

"I've been mowing."

The widow's heart felt another pang. "Not all day, Charley?" she said in a low voice, and there was a slight quiver in it.

"Yes, mother, all day," replied the boy; "Mr. Ellis said he couldn't afford to hire men, for wages is so high. I've swung the scythe ever since an hour before sunrise. Feel of my hands." There were blisters on them like great lumps.

Tears started in the widow's eyes. She dared not trust herself with a reply, though her heart was bursting with the thought that she could not better his condition. There was no earthly means of support on which she had dependence enough to encourage her child in the wish she knew was coming; the wish—not uttered for the first time—to be freed from his bondage.

"Mother," at length said the boy, "I can stand it no longer. I cannot and will not stay at Mr. Ellis's. Ever since the day I first went into his house, I've been a slave, and if I have to work there much longer, I know I shall run away, and go to sea, or somewhere else. I'd as lieve[3] be in my grave as there." And the child burst into a passionate fit of weeping.

His mother was silent, for she was in deep grief herself. After some minutes had flown, however, she gathered sufficient self-possession to speak to her son in a soothing tone, endeavoring to win him from his sorrows, and cheer up his heart. She told him that time was swift; that in the course of years he would be his own master; that all people had their troubles; with other ready arguments, which though they had little effect in calming her own distress, she hoped would act as a solace on the disturbed temper of the boy. And as the half hour to which he was limited had now elapsed, she took him by the hand and led him to the gate to set forth on his return. The child seemed pacified, though occasionally one of those convulsive sighs that remain after a fit of weeping, would break from his throat. At the gate, he threw his arms round his mother's neck; each pressed a long kiss on the lips of the other, and the youngster bent his steps toward his master's house.

As her child passed out of sight, the widow returned, shut the gate, and entered her lonesome room. There was no light in the old cottage that night; the heart of its occupant was dark and cheerless. Sore agony, and grief, and tears, and convulsive wrestlings were there. The thought of a beloved son condemned to labor—labor that would bend down a man— struggling from day to day under the hard rule of a soulless gold-worshipper; the knowledge that years must pass thus; the sickening idea of her own poverty, and of living mainly on the grudged charity of neighbors—these racked the widow's heart, and made her bed a sleepless one. O, you, who, living in plenty and peace, fret at some little misfortune or some trifling disappointment—behold this spectacle, and blush at your unmanliness! Little do you know of the dark trials (compared to yours as night's great veil to a daylight cloud) that are still going on around you; the pangs of hunger—the faintness of the soul at seeing those we love trampled down, without our having the power to aid them—the wasting away of the body in sickness incurable—and those dull achings of the heart when the consciousness comes upon the poor man's mind, that while he lives he will in all probability live in want and wretchedness.

The boy bent his steps to his employer's as has been said. In his way down the village street, he had to pass a public house, the only one the place contained; and when he came off against it, he heard the sound of a fiddle, drowned however at intervals by much laughter and talking. The windows were up; and, the house standing close to the road, Charles thought it would be no harm to take a look and see what was going on within. Half-a-dozen footsteps brought him to the low casement, on which he leaned his elbow, and where he had a full view of the room and its occupants. In one corner was an old man known in the village as Black Dave; he it was whose musical performances had a moment before drawn Charles's attention to the tavern; and he it was who now exerted himself in a most violent manner to give with divers flourishes and extra twangs, a tune popular among that thick-lipped race whose fondness for melody is so well known. In the middle of the room were five or six sailors, some of them quite drunk, and others in the earlier stages of that process; while on benches around were more sailors, and here and there a person dressed in landsmen's attire, but hardly behind the sea-gentlemen in uproariousness and mirth. The individuals in the middle of the room were dancing—that is, they were going through certain contortions and shufflings, varied occasionally by exceeding hearty stamps upon the sanded floor. In short, the whole party were engaged in a drunken frolic, which was in no respect different from a thousand other drunken frolics, except perhaps that there was less than the ordinary amount of anger and quarrelling. Indeed, every one seemed in remarkably good humor. But what excited the boy's attention more than any other object, was an individual seated on one of the benches opposite, who though evidently enjoying the spree as much as if he were an old hand at such business, seemed in every other particular to be far out of his element. His appearance was youthful; he might have been twenty-one or two. His countenance was intelligent—and had the air of city life and society. He was dressed not gaudily, but in all respects fashionably, his coat being of the finest black broadcloth, his linen delicate and spotless as snow, and his whole aspect a counterpart to those which may be nightly seen in the dress circles of our most respectable theatres. He laughed and talked with the rest; and it must be confessed his jokes, like the most of those that passed current there, were by no means distinguished for their refinement or purity. Near the door, was a small table covered with decanters, and with glasses, some of which had been used but were used again indiscriminately, and a box of very thick and long cigars.

"Come, boys," said one of the sailors, taking advantage of a momentary pause in the hubbub to rap his enormous knuckles on the table, and call attention to himself; the gentleman in question had but one eye, and two most extensive whiskers. "Come, boys, let's take a drink, I know you're all a getting dry, so curse me if you shan't have a suck at my expense."

This polite invitation was responded to by a general moving of the company toward the little table, holding the before-mentioned decanters and glasses. Clustering there around, each gentleman helped himself to a very respectable portion of that particular liquor which suited his fancy; and steadiness and accuracy being at that time by no means distinguishing traits of the arms and legs of the party, a goodly amount of fluid was spilled upon the floor. This piece of extravagance excited the ire of the personage who was treating; and his anger was still further increased when he discovered two or three loiterers who seemed disposed to slight his civil request to drink.

"Walk up boys, walk up. Don't let there be any skulkers among us, or blast my eyes if he shan't go down on his marrow bones and gobble up the rum we've spilt. Hallo!" he exclaimed, as he spied Charles, "Hallo! You chap in the window, come here and take a sup."

As he spoke, he stepped to the open casement, put his brawny hands under the boy's armpits, and lifted him into the room bodily.

"There, my lads," he said to his companions, "there's a new recruit for you. Not so coarse a one either," he added as he took a fair view of the boy, who, though not what is called pretty, was fresh, and manly looking, and large for his age.

"Come youngster, take a glass," he continued; and he poured one nearly full of strong brandy.

Now Charles was not exactly frightened, for he was a lively fellow and had often been at the country merry-makings, and with the young men of the place who were very fond of him; but he was certainly rather abashed at his abrupt introduction to the midst of strangers. So, putting the glass aside, he looked up with a pleasant smile in his new acquaintance's face.

"I've no need of any thing now," he said, "but I'm just as much obliged to you as if I was."

"Poh! Man, drink it down," rejoined the sailor; "drink it down, it won't hurt you." And by way of showing its excellence, the one-eyed worthy drained it himself to the very last drop. Then filling it again he renewed his hospitable efforts to make the lad go through the same operation.

"I've no occasion; beside, it makes my head ache, and I have promised my mother not to drink any," was the boy's answer.

A little irritated by his continued refusals, the sailor, with a loud oath, declared that Charles should swallow the brandy whether he would or no. Placing one of his tremendous paws on the back of the boy's head, with the other he thrust the edge of the glass to his lips, swearing at the same time, that if he shook it so as to spill its contents, the consequences would be of a nature by no means agreeable to his back and shoulders. Disliking the liquor, and angry at the attempt to overbear him, the undaunted child lifted his hand and struck the arm of the sailor with a blow so sudden, that the glass fell and was smashed to pieces on the floor, while the liquid was about equally divided between the face of Charles, the clothes of the sailor, and the sand. By this time the whole of the company had their attention drawn to the scene. Some of them laughed when they saw Charles's undisguised antipathy to the drink; but they laughed still more heartily when he discomfited the sailor. All of them, however, were content to let the matter go as chance would have it— all but the young man of the black coat, who had before been spoken of. Why was it that from the first moment of seeing him, the young man's heart had moved with a strange feeling of kindness toward the boy? He felt anxious to know more of him—he felt that he should love him. O, it is passing wondrous, how in the hurried walks of life and business, we meet with young beings, strangers, who seem to touch the fountains of our love, and draw forth their swelling waters. The wish to love and to be beloved, which the forms of custom, and the engrossing anxiety for gain, so generally smother, will sometimes burst forth in spite of all obstacles; and, kindled by one, who, till the hour was unknown to us, will burn with a lovely and a pure brightness. No scrap is this of sentimental fiction; ask your own heart, reader, and your own memory, for endorsement to its truth.

Charles stood, his cheek flushed and his heart throbbing, wiping the trickling drops from his face with a handkerchief. At first, the sailor, between his drunkenness and his surprise, was pretty much in the condition of one who is suddenly awakened out of a deep sleep, and cannot call his consciousness about him. When he saw the state of things, however, and heard the jeering laugh of his companions, his dull eye, lighting up with anger, fell upon the boy who had withstood him. He seized the child with a grip of iron; he bent Charles half way over, and with the side of his heavy foot, gave him a sharp and solid kick. He was about repeating the performance, for the child hung like a rag in his grasp; but all of a sudden his ears rung as if pistols had snapped close to them; lights of various hues flickered in his eye, (he had but one, it must be remembered,) and a strong propelling power caused him to move from his position, and keep moving until he was brought up by the wall. A blow—a cuff, given in such a scientific and effectual manner, that the hand from which it came was evidently no stranger to the pugilistic art—had been suddenly planted on the ear of the sailor. It was planted by the young stranger of the black coat. He had watched with interest the proceedings of the sailor and the boy: two or three times he was on the points of interfering, but when he witnessed the kick, his rage was uncontrollable. He sprung from his seat like a mad tiger. Assuming, unconsciously, however, the attitude of a boxer, he struck the sailor in a manner to cause those unpleasant sensations just described; and he would probably have followed up his attack in a method by no means consistent with the sailor's personal case, had not Charles, now thoroughly terrified, clung round his leg, and prevented his advancing. The scene was a strange one, and for a moment quite a silent one. The company had started from their seats and held startled but quiet positions; in the middle of the room stood the young man, in his not at all ungraceful posture, every nerve strained, and his eyes flashing very brilliantly. He seemed to be rooted like a rock, and clasping him with an appearance of confidence in his protection, hung the boy.

"Dare! You scoundrel!" cried the young man, his voice thick with agitation; "dare to touch this boy again, and I'll batter you till no sense is left in your body."

The sailor, now partially recovered, made some gestures from which it might be inferred that he resented this ungenteel treatment.

"Come on, drunken brute!" continued the angry youth; "I wish you would—you've not had half what you deserve."

Upon sobriety and sense more fully taking their seats in the brain of the one-eyed mariner, however, that worthy determined in his own mind, that it would be most prudent to let the matter drop. Expressing, therefore, his conviction to that effect, adding certain remarks to the purport that he "meant no harm to the lad," that he was surprised at such a gentleman getting so "up about a little piece of fun," and so forth. He proposed that the company should go on with their jollity just as if nothing had happened. In truth, he of the single eye was not a bad hearted fellow; the fiery enemy, whose advances he had so often courted that night, had stolen away his good feelings, and set busy devils at work within him, that might have made his hands do some dreadful deed, had not the stranger interfered.

In a few minutes the frolic of the party was upon its former footing. The young man sat down on one of the benches, with the boy by his side; and, while the rest were loudly laughing and talking, the two held communion together. The stranger learned from Charles all the particulars of his simple story—how his father had died years since—how his mother had worked hard for a bare living, and how he himself for many dreary months had been the bond-child of a hard hearted, avaricious master. More and more interested, drawing the child close to his side, the young man listened to his plainly told history; and thus an hour passed away. It was now past midnight. The young man told Charles that on the morrow he would take steps to have him liberated from his servitude; for the present night, he said, it would perhaps be best for the boy to stay and share his bed at the inn; and little persuading did the child need to do so.[4] As they retired to sleep, very pleasant thoughts filled the mind of the young man; thoughts of a worthy action performed; of unsullied affection; thoughts, too—newly awakened ones—of walking in a steadier and wiser path than formerly. All his imaginings seemed to be interwoven with the youth who lay by his side; he folded his arms around him, and, while he slept, the boy's cheek rested on his bosom. Fair were those two creatures in their unconscious beauty—glorious, but yet how differently glorious! One of them was innocent and sinless of all wrong; the other—O to that other, what evil had not been present, either in action or to his desires!

Who was the stranger? To those who, from ties of relationship or otherwise, felt an interest in him, the answer to such a question was not a pleasant theme to dwell upon. His name was Lankton—parentless—a dissipated young man—a brawler—one whose too frequent companions were rowdies, blacklegs, and swindlers. The New-York police officers were not altogether strangers to his countenance; and certain reporters who note the transactions there, had more than once received gratuities for leaving out his name from the disgraceful notoriety of their columns. He had been bred to the profession of medicine: beside that, he had a very respectable income, and his house was in a pleasant street on the west side of the city. Little of his time, however, did Mr. John Lankton spend at his domestic hearth; and the elderly lady who officiated as housekeeper was by no means surprised to have him gone for a week or a month at a time, and she knowing nothing of his whereabout. Living as he did, the young man was an unhappy being. It was not so much that his associates were below his own capacity, for Lankton, though sensible and well-bred, was by no means talented or refined—but that he lived without any steady purpose—that he had no one to attract him to his home—that he too easily allowed himself to be tempted—which caused his life to be of late one continued scene of dissatisfaction. This dissatisfaction he sought to drive away (ah! Foolish youth!) by mixing in all kinds of parties and places where the object was pleasure. On the present occasion, he had left the city a few days before, and was passing the time at a place near the village where Charles and his mother lived. He had that day fallen in with those who were his companions in the tavern spree—and thus it happened that they were all together: for Lankton hesitated not to make himself at home with any associates that suited his fancy.

The next morning, the poor widow rose from her sleepless cot, and from that lucky trait in our nature which makes one extreme follow another, she set about her daily toil with a lightened heart. Ellis, the farmer, rose too, short as the nights were, an hour before day; for his God was gain, and a prime article of his creed was to get as much work as possible from every one around him. He roused up all his people, and finding that Charles had not been home the preceding night, he muttered threats against him, and calling a messenger, to whom he hinted that any minutes which he stayed beyond a most exceeding short period, would be subtracted from his breakfast time, dispatched him to the widow's to find what was her son about.

What was he about? With one of the brightest and earliest rays of the warm sun a gentle angel entered his apartment, and hovering over the sleepers on invisible winds, looked down with a pleasant smile and blessed them. Then noiselessly taking a stand by the bed, the angel bent over the boy's face, and whispered strange words into his ear: thus it came that he had beautiful visions. No sound was heard but the slight breathing of those who slumbered there in each other's arms; and the angel paused a moment, and smiled another and a doubly sweet smile as he drank in the scene with his large soft eyes. Bending over again to the boy's lips, he touched them with a kiss, as the languid wind touches a flower. He seemed to be going now—and yet he lingered. Twice or thrice he bent over the brow of the young man—and went not. Now the angel was troubled; for he would have pressed the young man's forehead with a kiss, as he did the child's; but a spirit from the Pure Country, who touches anything tainted by evil thoughts, does it at the risk of having his breast pierced with pain, as with a barbed arrow. At that moment a very pale bright ray of sunlight darted through the window and settled on the young man's features. Then the beautiful spirit knew that permission was granted him: so he softly touched the young man's face with his, and silently and swiftly wafted himself away on the unseen air.

In the course of the day Ellis was called upon by young Lankton, and never perhaps in his life was the farmer more puzzled than at the young man's proposals—his desire to provide for a boy who could do him no pecuniary good—and his willingness to disburse money for that purpose. In that department of Ellis's structure where the mind was, or ought to have been situated, there never had entered the slightest thought assimilating to those which actuated the young man in his proceedings in this business. Yet Ellis was a church member and a county officer.

The widow, too, was called upon, not only that day, but the next and the next.

It needs not to particularize the subsequent events of Lankton's and the boy's history: how the reformation of the profligate might be dated to begin from that time; how he gradually severed the guilty ties that had so long galled him—how he enjoyed his own home, and loved to be there, and why he loved to be there; how the close knit love of the boy and him grew not slack with time; and how, when at length he became head of a family of his own, he would shudder when he thought of his early danger and escape.

Loved reader, own you the moral of this simple story? Draw it forth—pause a moment, ere your eye wanders to a more bright and eloquent page—and dwell upon it.

## SELECTED POEMS

### Hours Continuing Long[5] (1860)

Hours continuing long, sore and heavy-hearted,
  Hours of the dusk, when I withdraw to a lonesome and unfrequent-
  ed spot, seating myself, leaning my face in my hands;
Hours sleepless, deep in the night, when I go forth,
  speeding swiftly the country roads, or through the city streets, or
  pacing miles and miles, stifling plaintive cries;
Hours discouraged, distracted—for the one I cannot content
  myself without, soon I saw him content himself without me;
Hours when I am forgotten, (O weeks and months are passing,
  but I believe I am never to forget!)
Sullen and suffering hours! (I am ashamed—but it is
  useless—I am what I am;)
Hours of my torment—I wonder if other men ever have the
  like, out of the like feelings?
Is there even one other like me—distracted—his friend,
  his lover, lost to him?
Is he too as I am now? Does he still rise in the morning,
  dejected, thinking who is lost to him? and at night, awaking, think
  who is lost?
Does he too harbor his friendship silent and endless?
  harbor his anguish and passion?
Does some stray reminder, or the casual mention of a name,
  bring the fit back upon him, taciturn and deprest?
Does he see himself reflected in me? In these hours, does
  he see the face of his hours reflected?

### Now Lift Me Close (1860)

Now lift me close to your face till I whisper,
What you are holding is in reality no book, nor part of a
  book;
It is a man, flush'd and full-blooded—it is I—*So long!*
—We must separate awhile—Here! take from my lips this
  kiss;
Whoever you are, I give it especially to you;
*So long!*—And I hope we shall meet again.

# HORATIO ALGER, JR. (1832–99)

*Horatio Alger's books were as much a historical as a literary phenomenon, for they taught nineteenth-century boys the basics of the American Dream and the Protestant Ethic by recycling the example of Benjamin Franklin, whose* Autobiography *(1791) recounted his own rise from poverty to fame, becoming the first real account of the American success story. In Alger's world, hard work always secures worldly success for sturdy youths. Title after title (suggestive perhaps for their unconscious phallocentrism)* —Risen from the Ranks *(1874),* Bound to Rise *(1873),* Struggling Upward *(1890),* Strong and Steady *(1871),* Charlie Codman's Cruise, *and especially his most popular book* Ragged Dick *(1868)—testify to the trajectory of his boy-heroes' rise in a homosocial community (i.e., a man's world run by and for males). Less well known is Alger's own trajectory: prior to his own success, he had been a Harvard-educated pastor who was expelled by his Unitarian parish in Brewster, Massachusetts, for the "abominable and revolting crime of unnatural familiarity with boys."*[6] *Modern readers often detect a gay subtext in his tales of boys who make their way by pluck and luck and—without fail—the help of kindly older men.*

*The following excerpt has an unusual setting for an Alger novel: the ship onto which our young hero has been impressed to serve, and where he now faces unjust punishment. But its depiction of a homosocial group with its pecking order, and the intervention of the "kindly older man," are typical of Alger's boys' books.*

## FROM *CHARLIE CODMAN'S CRUISE; OR, A YOUNG SAILOR'S PLUCK* (1866)

Chapter XXVII

THE LASH.

"Pipe all hands to see punishment inflicted," ordered Captain Brace.

Charlie and Bill Sturdy looked at each other, uncertain where the blow was to fall.

"It must be Antonio," thought Charlie.

Evidently Antonio was of the same opinion, for over his swarthy face there stole a pallor which showed his apprehension.

Such was the understanding of the crew, also, as they could think of no other wrongdoer. Little pity was excited in behalf of the supposed sufferer. He had so abused his position when champion of the crew, that he had forfeited the good-will of all; and even if this had not been the case, his treacherous and mean attempt to bring Charlie into trouble would have been sufficient to bring him into disfavor.

The uncertainty as to the victim was dissipated by the captain's next words. "Jack Randall, come here!"

Charlie came forward.

"Boy," said Captain Brace sternly, "you were guilty of insolence to me this morning. This shall never go unpunished while I am in command of a vessel. As to the ring, you may or may not have stolen it. It rests between you and Antonio. As it cannot be proved of either, neither will be punished on this account."

Antonio's sallow face lighted up with joy at this unexpected escape, a joy which was not reflected on the faces of the crew.

"It is for insolence, therefore, and not on account of theft," pursued the captain, "that I sentence you, Jack Randall, to a dozen lashes on the bare back. Off with your jacket!"

Charlie was a brave boy, but the prospect of this ignominious punishment caused his cheek to pale and his voice to tremble as he exclaimed:

"Captain Brace, if I have been guilty of insolence or want of proper respect to you, it was not intentional. Do not compel me to submit to this disgraceful punishment."

There was a movement of sympathy among the crew, and more than one heart softened at the sight of Charlie's manly front, though his lips quivered, and pride alone kept back the tears from his eyes. Bill Sturdy started, but checked himself, to hear what the captain would say in response.

"It is too late," he said coldly. "You should have thought of all that before you indulged in insolence."

"But—"

"It is too late, I say," roared the captain, irritated. "Strip, you young rascal, or you shall have some help about it, and that of a rough kind."

It seemed as if all chance of escape was over for poor Charlie. But at that moment Bill Sturdy pressed forward, and, hitching up his trousers, as he was wont to do preparatory to speaking, said, in a distinct tone of voice: "Captain Brace."

"Well?" said the captain. "What have you to say?"

"I should like to make a proposal to you, sir."

"A proposal," repeated the captain, mystified. "What am I to understand by that?"

"It's just this, Captain Brace. You're the captain of this vessel, and you've got a right to flog that boy, I suppose, according to the law."

"Of course I have," said the captain fiercely. "Do you presume to question that right?"

"I don't think proper to question it just now," said Bill; "but, Captain Brace, just look at that boy. Look at his bright, honest face, and you can't have the heart to abuse him."

"Abuse him!" exclaimed the captain, stamping on the deck in his fury; "say that again, and I'll have you flogged with him."

"It was something of that kind that I was going to propose," said Bill Sturdy.

Captain Brace stared at him in astonishment, a feeling which was shared by the crew.

"If you want to be flogged," said the captain grimly, "we will try to accommodate you."

"It is in this way that I mean," exclaimed Bill. "I've taken a liking to that lad, and I've promised him I'll stand his friend. Now, Captain Brace, if somebody must be flogged, spare him, and flog me in his place."

Surprise was depicted on every face, and the sun-burned and rough-visaged men about him felt an involuntary thrill of respect and admiration, as Sturdy manfully came forward and offered his own back to the punishment, which is properly regarded as an insult to manhood, though the disgrace attaches not to the one who endures, but to the one who inflicts it.

Charlie was the first to speak. His generous heart revolted at the idea of escaping punishment at the expense of his friend.

"No, Bill Sturdy," said he manfully, "I don't want you to suffer in my place. It'll be hard to bear it," and his lip quivered; "but it would be weak and cowardly for me to let anybody else suffer in my place."

Charlie began to take off his jacket.

There was a murmuring among the crew, testifying to the excitement which they felt.

"Put on your jacket, my lad," said Bill. "I'm older and tougher than you, and I can bear it better."

And the stout seaman pulled off his shirt, and displayed his brawny shoulders, and a chest whose breadth and depth betokened a strength which could not be styled less than Herculean.

Antonio looked on, his eyes blazing with vindictive joy. Whichever was flogged, his satisfaction would be equal.

"Hark you!" exclaimed Captain Brace, interfering at this juncture. "I think that I shall choose to have a voice in this matter. So you wish," turning to Sturdy, "to relieve this boy of his punishment, do you?"

"I do," said the old seaman.

"I don't want him to," interrupted Charlie. "It is mine, and I will bear it."

"It seems the parties are not agreed," said the captain sardonically.

"Spare him," said Bill Sturdy, his eyes resting affectionately on Charlie. "He is so young."

"Perhaps the best way in which I can please you both is to divide the punishment between you. I had sentenced this lad to receive twelve lashes. Since you wish to do him a service, you shall receive six, and he the other six."

"I do not consent," said Sturdy, comprehending the captain's purpose to humiliate both. "If his back is to receive a single lash, my offer will not save him from the disgrace, and that is worse than the pain."

At this juncture the mate whispered something in the captain's ear. The face of the latter lighted up with satisfaction, and his next words revealed the nature of the mate's suggestion.

"I consent to the substitution," he said, and then paused.

Bill Sturdy's face glowed with generous satisfaction, and with heroic forgetfulness of self, he began to strip for punishment.

A moment, and his back, broad and ample, was bared, and the thick, corded muscles could be seen.

"Antonio, come forward," said Captain Brace.

Antonio advanced amid the general surprise of the crew, and somewhat to his own, and stood still, awaiting orders.

"Now," said Captain Brace, his tone showing his malignant satisfaction, "I appoint you as my deputy to administer twelve lashes to this man; mind that you don't spare him."

Antonio did not need this injunction. His eyes were full of fiendish triumph, as he seized the instrument of torture, and flourished it above his head.

As for Bill Sturdy, when he knew that Antonio was to be employed to inflict punishment upon him, this refinement of torture shook his resolution for a moment. It was, indeed, the bitterest drop in the cup. But not for an instant did his resolution falter. He would save Charlie at all hazards. He quickly recovered himself, and said in a firm voice:

"I am ready."

Instantly the lash was whirled aloft, and buried itself in his flesh.

There was a quiver, and that was all.

One—two—three—four—

In fast succession the blows fell upon his flesh, he meanwhile standing firmly braced, though his cheek was paler than its wont.

Charlie's heart sickened, and he closed his eyes to shut out the fearful spectacle.

As for Antonio, he seemed to revel in the task which had been assigned him. His eyes fairly danced with baleful light, and he seemed almost beside himself. It was this, perhaps, that led him to exceed by one the strokes which he had been ordered to administer.

A moment after and the lash was wrested from him by Bill Sturdy, who threw him to the deck, and with one powerful grasp tore the covering from his back, and buried the lash which had seared his own back in the flesh of his late executioner, who, with face distorted with fright and pain, roared for mercy.

"That is to pay for the blow you struck on your own account, you scoundrel," exclaimed Sturdy. "And now," as the lash descended once more with prodigious force, and the victim fairly writhed under it, "you are one in my debt." […]

# HARRY ENTON (1854–1927)

*Pulp fiction for boys, whether in magazine or book form, was very popular in the last quarter of the nineteenth century. Occasionally these dime-novel boy detectives would adopt strange disguises to pursue criminals, but none with quite so strange a result as appears the extract below. The following novel was published under the pseudonym "Police Captain Howard" (Enton used numerous assumed names for his many publication outlets), and like much of his writing, uses humor to lighten his darker tales. But is the effect here simply humorous, or does it suggest a darker slant?*

## FROM *YOUNG SLEUTH, THE KEEN DETECTIVE; OR, THE SHARPEST BOY IN NEW YORK* (1877)

Chapter III: The Sharpest Boy in New York

[...] In the meantime little Jack had grown and developed, and we now see in him a lad of about eighteen, lithe and slender, small arms and delicate hands and feet, that had many times been the envy of the weaker sex; his face was rather small and very fair; his eyes were blue, and hair light in color; in general his appearance was as much feminine as masculine, and, presuming on this, various youths, at divers times had sought to play pranks upon Jack, but they speedily found that his femininity was only in appearance, for those slight hands when tightly clenched were hard as bullets; and in case his antagonist was larger than he, his feet had a queer knack of rising with lightning-like rapidity, and stopping suddenly beneath his antagonist's chin.

Jack had been enabled to go to school, and, being quick to learn, made rapid strides in the department of knowledge which he studied.

If he had any one peculiarity it was a passionate desire to trace up the outlaws of society, and any case which came to his knowledge displaying shrewdness on the part of the detective, was to him a perfect feast.

It was not odd, therefore, that Jack should spend much of his time about the station-house with which his father was connected.

Captain Corney sat behind the desk one day when Jack entered.

While they were talking, a friend of the captain's a detective named Dick Blood, came in, and approached the desk.

"How are you, Blood?" said Captain Corney.

"First-rate. How goes it with you?"

"Middling. Do you want to see me on business?"

"Yes."

Captain Corney glanced at Jack, and the lad at once betook himself away.

The captain's eyes followed the retreating figure fondly, and with a tone imbued with pride, he said:

"Blood, there goes the sharpest boy in New York."

"Nonsense," said Blood, with a light laugh. "That's saying too much. But whose boy is he?"

"Mine."

"Ah! That accounts for it. Of course, then, he's the sharpest boy in New York." […]

## Chapter IV: The Captain's Mistake

Hastily locking the store the jeweler had hurried after the blonde, and seeing the men arrested had followed them to the station-house, where the blonde, having gone by another route, arrived first.

She retired to a back room, and through the crack of the partially-open door, saw the men brought in.

The jeweler made a charge against the thieves, and a close search brought the stolen diamond to light, after which the quartet were sent below stairs.

The sergeant had taken down the charge while the captain stood by; finishing the entry, after the thieves had gone below, he said:

"Captain, there is a lady in the back room to see you."

"Is there? Who is it?"

"A devilish handsome blonde."

With considerable alacrity the captain stepped toward the back room, and entering found the blonde seated near a window, demurely reading an open letter which she held in her hand.

She glanced at him, as he crossed the threshold, and rising, extending her hand, saying:

"Well, captain, you have made a good capture."

"Yes, by your assistance. You have been playing a sharp game on those fellows, most charming of your sex," said the captain, warmly.

"Please don't compliment me, captain," said the blonde, a merry twinkle in her eyes.

"Not a bit of compliment, I assure you, but absolute truth," and the captain gently squeezed the hand she allowed him to retain. "You are the most handsome woman"—

"Oh! Captain, what would your wife say?"

"Hang my wife, just now, anyhow. My dear, I'm going to kiss you," and assuming a lover-like air, he advanced a step nearer the blonde.

"No, no, you must not," she said. "I wouldn't object, only that it would not be right."

She would not object.

Ah! The words made the gallant captain's heart beat high, and throwing right or wrong to the winds, he implanted a kiss on the lips of the dazzling creature.

"My dear," he said, a minute or so later, "who are you? What is your name?"

"Don't you know me?" and there was a wicked, mischievous twinkling in her eyes as she spoke.

"No."

"Do you know me now?"

As she spoke, the blonde stepped back a pace, took off her jaunty hat, gave a twitch at her hair, which turned out to be a wig, and spat into her hand several plumpers which had been used to distend and make her cheeks more plump.

For an instant after the transformation the captain gazed at her, then gasped out in an agony that was comical to hear:

"Young Sleuth!"

"Correct! It is Young Sleuth. Would you like to kiss me, my dear?" laughingly said the lad.

The good captain was completely nonplussed, and his agitation of manner was mirth-provoking to behold.

Taking pity on him at last, Sleuth said in a tone of condolence:

"Never mind, I won't tell anybody. And now, what think you of 'the sharpest boy in New York?'"

"That he deserves the title," replied the captain, recovering his equanimity to an extent. "But, Sleuth, why did you fool me so?"

"I didn't fool you," retorted Sleuth. "You wanted to kiss me and did so, even when I told you it was wrong."

"You're a sad dog," laughed the captain. "But, Sleuth, you'll not say anything to your mother."

"Certainly not, I'll never breathe a word about your mistake."

"Of course you wouldn't, Sleuth, you always were a considerate lad," said the captain, in a tone of relief.

"But the capture," said Sleuth. "Is it really an important one?"

"Yes, but it is only a beginning, for the gang must number at least a dozen."

"If this is but a beginning I shall certainly make an ending," replied Sleuth, confidently.

# HOWARD PYLE (1853–1911)

*The story of Robin Hood, the man who steals from the rich to give to the poor, is over 600 years old, and has been told many times since its origin in fifteenth-century ballads. Artist Howard Pyle found success in retelling and illustrating several medieval legends (including his King Arthur stories [1903]). It is no surprise that many boys' books are inhabited exclusively by male characters; Pyle's popular version of the famed British outlaw is no exception. But other readings of this genre can yield suggestive alternatives. Graham Robb, for example, singles out Pyle's interpretation of the Robin Hood story to explore these implications, pointing out that for generations of readers, such narratives provided an initial exposure to a form of male difference for many boys.[7] The stranger, "a mincing fellow," dressed in a foppish color, offends Robin's notions of manliness. But our hero must be educated—presumably along with boyish readers—to discover that the transgressor is really "family," and as such deserves to be a member of Robin's band.*

## FROM *THE MERRY ADVENTURES OF ROBIN HOOD* (1883)

Part Third, Chapter Two

Thus they traveled along the sunny road, three stout fellows such as you could hardly match anywhere else in all merry England. Many stopped to gaze after them as they strode along, so broad were their shoulders and so sturdy their gait.

Quoth Robin Hood to Little John, "Why didst thou not go straight to Ancaster, yesterday, as I told thee? Thou hadst not gotten thyself into such a coil hadst thou done as I ordered."

"I feared the rain that threatened," said Little John in a sullen tone, for he was vexed at being so chaffed by Robin with what had happened to him.

"The rain!" cried Robin, stopping of a sudden in the middle of the road, and looking at Little John in wonder. "Why, thou great oaf! not a drop of rain has fallen these three days, neither has any threatened, nor hath there been a sign of foul weather in earth or sky or water."

"Nevertheless," growled Little John, "the holy Saint Swithin holdeth the waters of the heavens in his pewter pot, and he could have poured them out, had he chosen, even from a clear sky; and wouldst thou have had me wet to the skin?"

At this Robin Hood burst into a roar of laughter. "O Little John!" said he, "what better wits hast thou in that head of thine! Who could hold anger against such a one as thou art?"

So saying, they all stepped out once more, with the right foot foremost, as the saying is.

After they had traveled some distance, the day being warm and the road dusty, Robin Hood waxed thirsty; so, there being a fountain of water as cold as ice, just behind the hedgerow, they crossed the stile and came to where the water bubbled up from beneath a mossy stone. Here, kneeling and making cups of the palms of their hands, they drank their fill, and then, the spot being cool and shady, they stretched their limbs and rested them for a space.

In front of them, over beyond the hedge, the dusty road stretched away across the plain; behind them the meadow lands and bright green fields of tender young corn lay broadly in the sun, and overhead spread the shade of the cool, rustling leaves of the beechen tree. Pleasantly to their nostrils came the tender fragrance of the purple violets and wild thyme that grew within the dewy moisture of the edge of the little fountain, and pleasantly came the soft gurgle of the water. All was so pleasant and so full of the gentle joy of the bright Maytime, that for a long time no one of the three cared to speak, but each lay on his back, gazing up through the trembling leaves of the trees to the bright sky overhead. At last, Robin, whose thoughts were not quite so busy wool-gathering as those of the others, and who had been gazing around him now and then, broke the silence.

"Heyday!" quoth he, "yon is a gaily feathered bird, I take my vow."

The others looked and saw a young man walking slowly down the highway. Gay was he, indeed, as Robin had said, and a fine figure he cut, for his doublet was of scarlet silk and his stockings also; a handsome sword hung by his side, the embossed leathern scabbard being picked out with fine threads of gold; his cap was of scarlet velvet, and a broad feather hung down behind and back of one ear. His hair was long and yellow and curled upon his shoulders, and in his hand he bore an early rose, which he smelled at daintily now and then.

"By my life!" quoth Robin Hood, laughing, "saw ye e'er such a pretty, mincing fellow?"

"Truly, his clothes have overmuch prettiness for my taste," quoth Arthur a Bland, "but, ne'ertheless, his shoulders are broad and his loins are narrow, and seest thou, good master, how that his arms hang from his body? They dangle not down like spindles, but hang stiff and bend at the elbow. I take my vow, there be no bread and milk limbs in those fine clothes, but stiff joints and tough thews."[8]

"Methinks thou art right, friend Arthur," said Little John. "I do verily think that yon is no such roseleaf and whipped-cream gallant as he would have one take him to be."

"Pah!" quoth Robin Hood, "the sight of such a fellow doth put a nasty taste into my mouth! Look how he doth hold that fair flower betwixt his thumb and finger, as he would say, 'Good rose, I like thee not so ill but I can bear thy odor for a little while.' I take it ye are both wrong, and verily believe that were a furious mouse to run across his path, he would cry, 'La!' or 'Alack-a-day!' and fall straightway into a swoon. I wonder who he may be."

"Some great baron's son, I doubt not," answered Little John, "with good and true men's money lining his purse."

"Ay, marry, that is true, I make no doubt," quoth Robin. "What a pity that such men as he, that have no thought but to go abroad in gay clothes, should have good fellows, whose shoes they are not fit to tie, dancing at their bidding. By Saint Dunstan, Saint Alfred, Saint Withold, and all the good men in the Saxon calendar, it doth make me mad to see such gay lordlings from over the sea go stepping on the necks of good Saxons who owned this land before ever their great-grandsires chewed rind of brawn! By the bright bow of Heaven, I will have their ill-gotten gains from them, even though I hang for it as high as e'er a forest tree in Sherwood!"

"Why, how now, master," quoth Little John, "what heat is this? Thou dost set thy pot a-boiling, and mayhap no bacon to cook! Methinks yon fellow's hair is overlight for Norman locks. He may be a good man and true for aught thou knowest."

"Nay," said Robin, "my head against a leaden farthing, he is what I say. So, lie ye both here, I say, till I show you how I drub this fellow." So saying, Robin Hood stepped forth from the shade of the beech tree, crossed the stile, and stood in the middle of the road, with his hands on his hips, in the stranger's path.

Meantime the stranger, who had been walking so slowly that all this talk was held before he came opposite the place where they were, neither quickened his pace nor seemed to see that such a man as Robin Hood was in the world. So Robin stood in the middle of the road, waiting while the other walked slowly forward, smelling his rose, and looking this way and that, and everywhere except at Robin.

"Hold!" cried Robin, when at last the other had come close to him. "Hold! Stand where thou art!"

"Wherefore should I hold, good fellow?" said the stranger in soft and gentle voice. "And wherefore should I stand where I am? Ne'ertheless, as thou dost desire that I should stay, I will abide for a short time, that I may hear what thou mayst have to say to me."

"Then," quoth Robin, "as thou dost so fairly do as I tell thee, and dost give me such soft speech, I will also treat thee with all due courtesy. I would have thee know, fair friend, that I am, as it were, a votary at the shrine of Saint Wilfred who, thou mayst know, took, willy-nilly, all their gold from the heathen, and melted it up into candlesticks. Wherefore, upon such as come hereabouts, I levy a certain toll, which I use for a better purpose, I hope, than to make candlesticks withal. Therefore, sweet chuck, I would have thee deliver to me thy purse, that I may look into it, and judge, to the best of my poor powers, whether thou hast more wealth about thee than our law allows. For, as our good Gaffer Swanthold sayeth, 'He who is fat from overliving must needs lose blood.'"

All this time the youth had been sniffing at the rose that he held betwixt his thumb and finger. "Nay," said he with a gentle smile, when Robin Hood had done, "I do love to hear thee talk, thou pretty fellow, and if, haply, thou art not yet done, finish, I beseech thee. I have yet some little time to stay."

"I have said all," quoth Robin, "and now, if thou wilt give me thy purse, I will let thee go thy way without let or hindrance so soon as I shall see what it may hold. I will take none from thee if thou hast but little."

"Alas! It doth grieve me much," said the other, "that I cannot do as thou dost wish. I have nothing to give thee. Let me go my way, I prythee. I have done thee no harm."

"Nay, thou goest not," quoth Robin, "till thou hast shown me thy purse."

"Good friend," said the other gently, "I have business elsewhere. I have given thee much time and have heard thee patiently. Prythee, let me depart in peace."

"I have spoken to thee, friend," said Robin sternly, "and I now tell thee again, that thou goest not one step forward till thou hast done as I bid thee." So saying, he raised his quarterstaff above his head in a threatening way.

"Alas!" said the stranger sadly, "it doth grieve me that this thing must be. I fear much that I must slay thee, thou poor fellow!" So saying, he drew his sword.

"Put by thy weapon," quoth Robin. "I would take no vantage of thee. Thy sword cannot stand against an oaken staff such as mine. I could snap it like a barley straw. Yonder is a good oaken thicket by the roadside; take thee a cudgel thence and defend thyself fairly, if thou hast a taste for a sound drubbing."

First the stranger measured Robin with his eye, and then he measured the oaken staff. "Thou art right, good fellow," said he presently, "truly, my sword is no match for that cudgel of thine. Bide thee awhile till I get me a staff." So saying, he threw aside the rose that he had been holding all this time, thrust his sword back into the scabbard, and, with a more hasty step than he had yet used, stepped to the roadside where grew the little clump of ground oaks Robin had spoken of. Choosing among them, he presently found a sapling to his liking. He did not cut it, but, rolling up his sleeves a little way, he laid hold of it, placed his heel against the ground, and, with one mighty pull, plucked the young tree up by the roots from out the very earth. Then he came back, trimming away the roots and tender stems with his sword as quietly as if he had done nought to speak of.

Little John and the Tanner had been watching all that passed, but when they saw the stranger drag the sapling up from the earth, and heard the rending and snapping of its roots, the Tanner pursed his lips together, drawing his breath between them in a long inward whistle.

"By the breath of my body!" said Little John, as soon as he could gather his wits from their wonder, "sawest thou that, Arthur? Marry, I think our poor master will stand but an ill chance with yon fellow. By Our Lady, he plucked up yon green tree as it were a barley straw."

Whatever Robin Hood thought, he stood his ground, and now he and the stranger in scarlet stood face to face.

Well did Robin Hood hold his own that day as a mid-country yeoman. This way and that they fought, and back and forth, Robin's skill against the stranger's strength. The dust of the highway rose up around them like a cloud, so that at times Little John and the Tanner could see nothing, but only hear the rattle of the staves against one another. Thrice Robin Hood struck the stranger; once upon the arm and twice upon the ribs, and yet had he warded all the other's blows, only one of which, had it met its mark, would have laid stout Robin lower in the dust than he had ever gone before. At last the stranger struck Robin's cudgel so fairly in the middle that he could hardly hold his staff in his hand; again he struck, and Robin bent beneath the blow; a third time he struck, and now not only fairly beat down Robin's guard, but gave him such a rap, also, that down he tumbled into the dusty road.

"Hold!" cried Robin Hood, when he saw the stranger raising his staff once more. "I yield me!"

"Hold!" cried Little John, bursting from his cover, with the Tanner at his heels. "Hold! give over, I say!"

"Nay," answered the stranger quietly, "if there be two more of you, and each as stout as this good fellow, I am like to have my hands full. Nevertheless, come on, and I will strive my best to serve you all."

"Stop!" cried Robin Hood, "we will fight no more. I take my vow, this is an ill day for thee and me, Little John. I do verily believe that my wrist, and eke my arm, are palsied by the jar of the blow that this stranger struck me."

Then Little John turned to Robin Hood. "Why, how now, good master," said he. "Alas! Thou art in an ill plight. Marry, thy jerkin is all befouled with the dust of the road. Let me help thee to arise."

"A plague on thy aid!" cried Robin angrily. "I can get to my feet without thy help, good fellow."

"Nay, but let me at least dust thy coat for thee. I fear thy poor bones are mightily sore," quoth Little John soberly, but with a sly twinkle in his eyes.

"Give over, I say!" quoth Robin in a fume. "My coat hath been dusted enough already, without aid of thine." Then, turning to the stranger, he said, "What may be thy name, good fellow?"

"My name is Gamwell," answered the other.

"Ha!" cried Robin, "is it even so? I have near kin of that name. Whence camest thou, fair friend?"

"From Maxfield Town I come," answered the stranger. "There was I born and bred, and thence I come to seek my mother's young brother, whom men call Robin Hood. So, if perchance thou mayst direct me—"

"Ha! Will Gamwell!" cried Robin, placing both hands upon the other's shoulders and holding him off at arm's length. "Surely, it can be none other! I might have known thee by that pretty maiden air of thine—that dainty, finicking manner of gait. Dost thou not know me, lad? Look upon me well."

"Now, by the breath of my body!" cried the other, "I do believe from my heart that thou art mine own Uncle Robin. Nay, certain it is so!" And each flung his arms around the other, kissing him upon the cheek. Then once more Robin held his kinsman off at arm's length and scanned him keenly from top to toe. "Why, how now," quoth he, "what change is here? Verily, some eight or ten years ago I left thee a stripling lad, with great joints and ill-hung limbs, and lo! here thou art, as tight a fellow as e'er I set mine eyes upon. Dost thou not remember, lad, how I showed thee the proper way to nip the goose feather betwixt thy fingers and throw out thy bow arm steadily? Thou gavest great promise of being a keen archer. And dost thou not mind how I taught thee to fend and parry with the cudgel?"

"Yea," said young Gamwell, "and I did so look up to thee, and thought thee so above all other men that, I make my vow, had I known who thou wert, I would never have dared to lift hand against thee this day. I trust I did thee no great harm."

"No, no," quoth Robin hastily, and looking sideways at Little John, "thou didst not harm me. But say no more of that, I prythee. Yet I will say, lad, that I hope I may never feel again such a blow as thou didst give me. By'r Lady, my arm doth tingle yet from fingernail to elbow. Truly, I thought that I was palsied for life. I tell thee, coz, that thou art the strongest man that ever I laid mine eyes upon. I take my vow, I felt my stomach quake when I beheld thee pluck up yon green tree as thou didst. But tell me, how camest thou to leave Sir Edward and thy mother?"

"Alas!" answered young Gamwell, "it is an ill story, uncle, that I have to tell thee. My father's steward, who came to us after old Giles Crookleg died, was ever a saucy varlet, and I know not why my father kept him, saying that he did oversee with great judgment. It used to gall me to hear him speak up so boldly to my father, who, thou knowest, was ever a patient man to those about him, and slow to anger and harsh words. Well, one day—and an ill day it was for that saucy fellow—he sought to berate my father, I standing by. I could stand it no longer, good uncle, so, stepping forth, I gave him a box o' the ear, and—wouldst thou believe it?—the fellow straightway died o't. I think they said I broke his neck, or something o' the like. So off they packed me to seek thee and escape the law. I was on my way when thou sawest me, and here I am."

"Well, by the faith of my heart," quoth Robin Hood, "for anyone escaping the law, thou wast taking it the most easily that ever I beheld in all my life.

Whenever did anyone in all the world see one who had slain a man, and was escaping because of it, tripping along the highway like a dainty court damsel, sniffing at a rose the while?"

"Nay, uncle," answered Will Gamwell, "overhaste never churned good butter, as the old saying hath it. Moreover, I do verily believe that this overstrength of my body hath taken the nimbleness out of my heels. Why, thou didst but just now rap me thrice, and I thee never a once, save by overbearing thee by my strength."

"Nay," quoth Robin, "let us say no more on that score. I am right glad to see thee, Will, and thou wilt add great honor and credit to my band of merry fellows. But thou must change thy name, for warrants will be out presently against thee; so, because of thy gay clothes, thou shalt henceforth and for aye be called Will Scarlet."

"Will Scarlet," quoth Little John, stepping forward and reaching out his great palm, which the other took, "Will Scarlet, the name fitteth thee well. Right glad am I to welcome thee among us. I am called Little John; and this is a new member who has just joined us, a stout tanner named Arthur a Bland. Thou art like to achieve fame, Will, let me tell thee, for there will be many a merry ballad sung about the country, and many a merry story told in Sherwood of how Robin Hood taught Little John and Arthur a Bland the proper way to use the quarterstaff; likewise, as it were, how our good master bit off so large a piece of cake that he choked on it."

"Nay, good Little John," quoth Robin gently, for he liked ill to have such a jest told of him. "Why should we speak of this little matter? Prythee, let us keep this day's doings among ourselves."

"With all my heart," quoth Little John. "But, good master, I thought that thou didst love a merry story, because thou hast so often made a jest about a certain increase of fatness on my joints, of flesh gathered by my abiding with the Sheriff of—"

"Nay, good Little John," said Robin hastily, "I do bethink me I have said full enough on that score."

"It is well," quoth Little John, "for in truth I myself have tired of it somewhat. But now I bethink me, thou didst also seem minded to make a jest of the rain that threatened last night; so—"

"Nay, then," said Robin Hood testily, "I was mistaken. I remember me now it did seem to threaten rain."

"Truly, I did think so myself," quoth Little John, "therefore, no doubt, thou dost think it was wise of me to abide all night at the Blue Boar Inn, instead of venturing forth in such stormy weather; dost thou not?"

"A plague of thee and thy doings!" cried Robin Hood. "If thou wilt have it so, thou wert right to abide wherever thou didst choose."

"Once more, it is well," quoth Little John. "As for myself, I have been blind this day. I did not see thee drubbed; I did not see thee tumbled heels over

head in the dust; and if any man says that thou wert, I can with a clear conscience rattle his lying tongue betwixt his teeth."

"Come," cried Robin, biting his nether lip, while the others could not for-
bear laughing. "We will go no farther today, but will return to Sherwood, and
thou shalt go to Ancaster another time, Little John."

So said Robin, for now that his bones were sore, he felt as though a long
journey would be an ill thing for him. So, turning their backs, they retraced
their steps whence they came.

## Notes

1  For further information on Prime-Stevenson's boys' books see my essay "Left to
Themselves: The Subversive Boys Books of Edward Prime-Stevenson
(1858–1942)," in *Journal of American and Comparative Cultures* 24 (Fall/Winter
2001): 113–16.

2  "The Child's Champion" was originally published in the tabloid *New World* in
1841 and reprinted many times after that, most notably revised as a temperance
tale in *Columbian Magazine* (1844) as "The Child and the Profligate." For a full
history see *The Collected Writings of Walt Whitman: The Early Poems and the Fiction*,
edited by Thomas L. Brasher (New York: New York UP, 1963), 68–69.

3  Willing, disposed [obsolete].

4  The bed-sharing scene predates that of *Moby-Dick* (1851) by a decade, yet they
both puzzle contemporary eyes as to what degree of intimacy is being depicted:
certainly "adhesiveness," or close attraction between men, as Whitman would
attest, but what further? Bed-sharing was common in the nineteenth century and
did not necessarily imply sexuality. But it also clearly presented easy opportunity.
For a remarkable discussion and examples, see Martin Bauml Duberman's
"'Writhing Bedfellows' in Antebellum South Carolina: Historical Interpretation
and the Politics of Evidence" in Duberman et al. *Hidden from History: Reclaiming
the Gay and Lesbian Past*, 153–68.

5  For a concentrated selection of Whitman's poems of "adhesive love," i.e., the
love between comrades, see the entire *Calamus* section of his *Leaves of Grass*. This
poem was originally published as part of the *Calamus* cluster, but not reprinted
in later editions of *Leaves of Grass*.

6  Qtd. in Gary Scharnhorst, *The Lost Life of Horatio Alger, Jr.* (Bloomington: Indiana
UP, 1985) 67.

7  See his *Strangers: Homosexual Love in the Nineteenth Century*, 217–18.

8  Muscles; i.e., physical strength. Robin (and Pyle) often discuss the width of
men's shoulders and the leanness of their loins; this subtext recurs throughout
the story.

PART FOUR

SCHOOLDAYS

# Frederick Wadsworth Loring (1848–71)

*Boston-born, Fred Loring showed great promise as a writer, and upon graduation from Harvard contributed to several newspapers and popular magazines such as* The Atlantic Monthly *and* The Independent. *In addition to a book of poetry and many sketches of the South and Southwest, it is his single novel that has resurrected interest in his name today. Was* Two College Friends *a thinly disguised reminiscence of his years at Harvard? The dedication suggests this possibility: the novel was inscribed to a favorite professor who had recently died, as well as to college friend William Chamberlin who, with "a few others [who] will know what I mean by it." Ostensibly this is a Civil War novel: the heroes will shortly go off to war together. But at the same time,* Two College Friends *extols a romantic friendship to a degree which modern readers might find suspicious (although it was perhaps then quite innocent). It was first published in the theological journal* Old and New *(April/July 1871), edited by Edward Everett Hale; it was published as a book later that same year. How the audience in 1871 read this story of romantic friendship is another question, but Loring never lived to find out. Late that same year he was killed in an Indian raid while returning from a West Coast assignment.*[1]

## From *Two College Friends* (1871)

"'At dawn,' he said, 'I bid them all farewell,
   To go where bugles blow and rifles gleam;'
   And with the waking thought asleep he fell,
And wandered into dream."[2]

I. The Lecture on Domestic Arts

It was quarter after two in the afternoon, and the professor was sitting at his desk, engaged in arranging the notes of his lecture, when there came a knock on the door.

"Come in," said the Professor. "Ah, Ned! is it you?" This to a graceful boy of twenty, who entered the room.

"Yes, it is Ned," said the boy; "and he particularly wishes to see you for a few minutes."

"Every moment is precious," said the Professor, "until my lecture is in order. What is the matter? Are you in trouble?"

"Yes," said Ned, "I am in trouble."

"Then let me read to you," said the Professor, "the concluding paragraph of my lecture on Domestic Arts."[3]

"Oh, don't!" said Ned; "I really am in trouble."

"Are you the insulter or the insulted, this time?" asked the Professor.

"Neither," said Ned, shortly; "and I'm not in trouble on my own account."

"Ah!" said the Professor; "then you have got into some difficulty in your explorations in low life; or you have spent more than your income; or it's the perpetual Tom."

"It's the perpetual Tom," said Ned.

"I supposed so," observed the Professor. "What has that youth been doing now? Drinking, swearing, gambling, bad company, theft, murder?—out with it! I am prepared for anything, from the expression of your face; for anything, that is to say, except my lecture on Domestic Arts, which comes at three."

"Well, if you choose to make fun of me," said Ned, "I can go; but I thought you would advise me."

"And so I will, you ridiculous creature, when you need it," said the Professor; "only at such times you generally act for yourself. But, come; my advice and sympathy are yours; so what has Tom done?"

"He has fallen in love," said Ned.

"Oh, no!" said the Professor.

"Yes, sir," repeated Ned, more firmly, "he has fallen in love."

"'Tis the way of all flesh," said the Professor; "But I don't think Tom can fall in love. He never even dislikes any one without a cause."

"That's all very well, sir," said Ned; "but when a fellow has a girl's picture, and looks at it when he thinks he isn't watched; and when he receives notes, and keeps them, instead of throwing them around, as usual; and when he takes to being blue,—what do you say?"

"Please state your propositions separately," said the Professor, "and I will endeavor to form an opinion. When a fellow has a girl's picture,—what was the rest?"

"I wish you wouldn't make fun of me," said Ned.

"Well, in Heaven's name, what is there to trouble you, if Tom is in love?" asked the Professor.

"Because he hasn't told me," said Ned.

"Oh! you are jealous then," rejoined the Professor. "You are the most selfish person, for one who is so generous, that I have ever seen. You are morbid upon the subject of Tom, I believe."

"Well, look here," said Ned; "I have neither father nor mother; I have no one except Tom. I care more for him than for any one else in the world, as you know; but you never will know how much I care for him; and it does seem hard that he should shut me out of his confidence when I have done nothing to forfeit it. There's some girl at the bottom of all this. He and that big Western friend of his, the Blush Rose, whom I never liked, have been off together two or three times; and, as I say, Tom has got this picture; and the Blush Rose knows it, and knows who she is. I've seen them looking at it, and admiring it.

I'm afraid, from Tom's not telling me about it, that he's doing something out of the way."

"In that case," said the Professor, "you had better let me read you the closing paragraph of my lecture on Domestic Arts."

"No, I thank you," said Ned; "I shall have to hear it, any way, this afternoon."

"So you will," said the Professor; "and, by the way, I shall give you a private[4] if you behave to-day as you did in my last lecture. I have told your class-tutor to warn you."

"Well, that is pleasant," said Ned.

"I meant it to be," replied the Professor. "Good-by. I may call at your room tonight,—to see Tom."

And, as Ned was heard going down the stairs, the Professor, seeing that he had still twenty-five minutes to spare, took his lecture, and sat down before the fire, which flickered slightly, and just served to destroy the dampness of that April day.

## II. The Picture over the Fireplace

Whether the Professor would have made any alterations or amendments in his lecture, it is difficult to say; that he did not is due to the fact that his eye fell upon a little photograph, which hung over his fireplace. As he sits there, thinking over what Ned has told him, and laughing at the idea of Tom's being really in love, he gazes on this little photograph, and smiles. The Professor has one or two real art treasures, but nothing that he values quite as much as this fading picture. This is the only copy in existence; and this hangs there, and will hang there until the Professor dies. How well he remembers the morning when the two boys, whom he loves so well, rushed into his room, and left it there! As he looks at it now, there is an expression of tenderness on his plain but strongly cut features that would greatly astonish those of his pupils who only know him as a crusty instructor.

The Professor is somewhat crusty, it must be owned. It is, however, an acquired and not a natural crustiness. Cause, the fact that at thirty years of age he discovered that he cared more for a certain Miss Spencer than for all the world beside. On intimating this fact to her, she told him that she should always value his friendship; and that she hoped soon to introduce to him her cousin Hugh, "who is," she added quietly, "to become my husband." After this the Professor withdrew almost entirely from society, and plunged deeper and deeper into study. Before many years his reputation was cosmopolitan, his head bald, and his life a matter of routine. Boys came and went; and at intervals he repeated before them much of what he knew. It is to these two boys, of whom he thinks now, as he gazes on the picture over the mantel, that he owes his rescue from this lethargic life.

What does he see in the picture? He sees behind a chair, in which a boy is sitting, another boy with soft, curling brown hair, deep blue eyes, and dazzling complexion. His features are delicately cut; but the especial beauty of his face is the brilliancy of color in his hair, eyes, and complexion. There is the freshness of youth on his features; and his whole attitude, as he leans over his companion, is full of that quaint grace of boyish tenderness so indefinable and so transitory. The boy in the chair has a face full of strength and weakness. The photograph makes him appear the more striking of the two, though the less handsome. The sunny sweetness of the first face, though it never alters, never becomes wearisome; but the second face is now all love, now disfigured by scorn and hatred, now full of intellect, and glowing with animation, now sullen and morose. The complexion is olive, the eyes brown, the lips strongly cut, yet so mobile as to be capable of every variety of earnest and sneering expression. The face is always, in all its varying phases, the face of one who is not dissatisfied but unsatisfied. This is what the Professor sees, as the firelight throws its glimmer over the room, making grotesque shadows waver fitfully on the pictures and books around him, as well as on the heavy curtains that hide the rays of afternoon light which struggle through the leafy boughs of the old elms in the yard without.

As the Professor sits there thinking, he seems to recall again the first visit of Tom and Ned to his room. Tom is a lovely boy,—the original of the standing figure in the photograph; and the Professor had been attracted by his face once or twice when he had met him in the yard, soon after his entrance into college. Still he is surprised, one evening, when he hears a knock at his door, and this Freshman enters half shyly. The Professor asks him to be seated, and then looks at him inquiringly.

"I was awfully homesick," says Tom, with perfect trustfulness; "and mother told me that you were once a very dear friend of hers; so I thought I would come up and see you." The Professor is bewildered. Still he is a gentleman; so he smiles, and says to Tom:—

"Pray be seated. Your mother is well, I trust."

"Oh, yes!" says Tom. "Perhaps, as she hasn't seen you since before I was born, I ought to have said who she was. Her name was Spencer."

The Professor turns quickly. Tom proceeds with entire unconsciousness:—

"She often speaks of you, sir, and always in a way that has made me want to know you."

"I am very glad, Tom," said the Professor. "You must excuse my calling you by your first name; but then you are the son of—your mother."

Any one but Tom, who never noticed anything, would have seen here that the Professor's manner was peculiar. But Tom is always so brightly ignorant of what is before his eyes, that the Professor recovers his self-possession, and says calmly:—

"And your mother is well, I hope?"

"Oh, yes!" said Tom; "very well, but a little sad at my leaving home. She is very fond of me, sir."

"Strange fact!" said the Professor, dryly. "and I see that you are equally fond of her. I am not given to moralizing; but I think that college life will not decay you, if you don't forget how much you are to your mother,—how unhappy you can make her."

"Forget her?" said Tom; "not I! When I am at home, I make love to her all the time."

"Then," said the Professor, "it is well that you have left home; for it will soon be time for you to make love to some one else."

As the Professor makes this observation, there is another knock at the door, and Ned enters. Who is Ned? Ned is the original of the sitting figure in the little picture over the fireplace. He is despotic in character, and has therefore many sincere friends and enemies. He is fearless when indignant, and is indignant easily. He is not handsome as Tom is,—for Tom's beauty charms you immediately, and the charm is never broken; but he has a curious grace and fascination of manner when he is not perverse; but then, he often is perverse.

The Professor cannot tell whether he likes Ned, or not. He has been giving Ned private tuition, to fit him for college, for nearly a year. All their acquaintance hitherto has been one of business, all their conversation confined to an occasional dry remark on either side. Now, when their contract is fulfilled, the Professor cannot imagine why Ned should take advantage of his general invitation, and visit him. Still he asks Ned to be seated, and then enters into conversation with him.

Ned talks. His keen eye has noted everything ludicrous and everything interesting among his instructors, among his classmates, among all the persons and things with which college life has brought him in contact. He is full of animation; he tells stories, all of which have a point; he sparkles with wit, which is none the less brilliant for having a certain boyish freshness about it. All this is a new revelation to the Professor. He laughs, and in his turn becomes entertaining; and, finally, going to his sideboard, produces three quaint glasses, which he fills with some of that rare and wonderful old Madeira, which many of his acquaintances have heard of, but which few have ever seen.

Tom, in the mean time, sits listening, radiant with enjoyment, with the firelight tinting his lovely face. "Such a jolly old fellow as this Professor is!" he says to himself; "and such a being as Ned!" He is happier than he has been since he left home; and he wishes his mother could look in upon them now; and he drains his glass to her health. He is puzzled because Ned will address his remarks only to the Professor, and seems shy whenever he speaks. Finally, conscious that it is growing late, he bids the Professor farewell, and Ned rises to accompany him. The Professor says then, with a courteous and quiet dignity:—

"Tom, you must give my regards to your mother, when you write. Tell her that her boy will be always an object of especial interest to her old friend." Then, turning to Ned, the Professor adds, as Tom disappears in the entry:—

"I have to thank you for a very pleasant evening. You will come again, my boy, will you not? Why have you never before shown me what you really are?"

"It wasn't for you, sir," said Ned, with a certain frankness that was not discourteous. "It was for Tom, sir; though I like you, and hope we shall be friends. But the moment I saw Tom, I felt drawn towards him; and, as I saw him come up here, I felt that here was a chance to get acquainted with him. Good-night, sir."

And Ned joined Tom at the foot of the stairs, leaving the Professor in a state of complete bewilderment. The Professor laughs now, as he recalls that evening, and looks again at the picture over the fireplace.

"They are an interesting pair,—a sunbeam and a volcano," he says; and, throwing on his cloak, just as the bell begins to ring, he starts for his lecture-room.

III. He Moved with a Vast Crowd

It was just after supper; and the Professor, with his thoughts still occupied by Tom and Ned, walked slowly toward his room through the dimly-lighted yard, where the twilight was half dispelled by the gleams of gas-light that stole from the windows around. He sauntered along, enjoying the sweet spring air of the evening, and touching his hat to one boy after another until he came by Ned's entry, when he turned, and took his way to the room of his boys. He had stopped, as he passed through the square, for his paper, and had noticed that a crowd seemed to be eagerly and excitedly discussing the news of the evening around the post-office. Pausing an instant in the entry to look at his paper, before ascending the stairs, his eye fell on an announcement which caused him to utter an exclamation of surprise; and he rushed eagerly into the room, with the words:—

"Boys, have you heard the news?"

Ned turned from the glass, where he was tying his cravat, and Tom raised himself from his lounge; but before either of them had an opportunity to answer, the Professor said:—

"There has been a quarrel here. Now, boys, I must know all about it. See, I'm going to spring the lock, and have you clear your minds at once."

"There's nothing to clear," said Tom.

"Speak for yourself, if you please," said the Professor. "You may not have a mind at all; but I know that Ned has, to a limited extent. Doubtless you are both wrong; so let me see which will be gentleman enough to apologize first. Come, boys, this matter must be set right. 'Let not the sun go down upon your wrath' is one of the best pieces of advice ever given."

"It is after sunset now," said Ned; "and we are not both wrong. I am right."

"Cheerful self-confidence," said the Professor. "Please let me understand the cause of wrath."

"Simply because I object to the Blush Rose," said Ned. "I say that he has come between us."

"And I say"—broke in Tom.

"Hush, Tom!" said the Professor, "until Ned has finished."

"I have nothing more to say," said Ned, "except that Tom must, once for all, choose between us."

"Very well," said Tom; "as you please; only, while I don't care for any fellow as I do for you, I'm not going to submit to dictation."

"You're entangled with some woman, through Blodgett," said Ned. "He's a nice associate for a gentleman, he is."

"I entangled with a woman!" repeated Tom. "Why, Ned! you're crazy."

"Whose picture is it that you are carrying?" asked Ned.

"Oh, thunder!" said Tom; "is that what all this row is about?"

"I suppose you've fallen in love, and in Junior year too!" continued Ned, wrathfully and contemptuously.

"Juniors have done such things before," observed the Professor.

"Fallen in love!" said Tom; "as if I'd do that! Look here, old fellow, if you knew about that picture, you'd ask my pardon."

"Well, as I don't, I shan't," said Ned.

"Come, boys," said the Professor, "this ridiculous quarrel, worthy only of a couple of little children, has gone quite far enough. Ned, I think you are petulant and absurd; but if you will go out for a few minutes, and take a short walk, Tom will unbosom himself to me, I am sure."

"Well, I call that cheek, to turn a man out of his own room," said Ned.

"Correct that sentence, please, Ned," said the Professor. "You would call it cheek if it were not done by a member of the Faculty. There, be off with you. And now, Tom, tell your story."

"I haven't any," said Tom; "only Ned is in one of his moods."

"Then you are not in love," said the Professor.

"Why, no!" said Tom, "how could I be?"

"I don't know," replied the Professor; "but people are sometimes. And have you a secret connected with that fat, red-faced brute, Blodgett, whom you call the Blush Rose?"

"Well, yes," said Tom: "it's about a photograph."

"Let us see this photograph," said the Professor. "Explain!"

"Why, it's a surprise for Ned, don't you see?" said Tom. "It's the proof picture of me in the last theatricals. See, there I am as Marton, the Pride of the Market."

"What a mistake nature made about your sex, Tom!"[5] said the Professor. "You dear little peasant girl, put yourself away directly; and now take my advice: show it to Ned; it will make him ashamed of his folly, and will prevent any further angry words between you. It is hard to quarrel, and so you will think some day, though now you find it so easy. There, put it away; for I hear Ned's footsteps on the stairs! Come in, Ned! Why! what has happened?"

For Ned, standing in the open doorway, his perverse moodiness all gone, wore an expression the Professor had never seen before.

"Happened!" said Ned. "Something to live for, something to die for. We know now that we have a country. Haven't you heard the news?"

"Dear me!" said the Professor, "that's what I came to tell you; but your quarrel drove it out of my head."

"How could anything else come into your head?" said Ned.

"Tell me what it is," asked Tom, impatiently.

"The President has called the people to arms, to aid him in saving the country," said Ned, fairly glowing as he spoke.

"Yes," said the Professor, "is it not grand to think that we are aroused at last?"

"Well," said Ned, "I have still more to tell you. I have enlisted."

There was a pause of a few moments; then the Professor grasped Ned's hand, and said simply:—

"My noble boy!"

"What do you say, Tom?" asked Ned.

"I'm going with you, old fellow," said Tom; and he threw his arm over Ned's shoulder, and smiled at the Professor.

# Henry Blake Fuller (1857–1929)

*In this hitherto unpublished selection, written only several years after the events it recounts, Henry Blake Fuller gives us a rare look at the sensitivity and isolation of a nineteenth-century, decidedly "different," high-school student. As an outsider he effectively describes what many homosexuals then and now must have felt in their teens. The friends who form the heterosexual "Quartette" with their "male" symbols of oysters and cigars are all too clearly a paradigm for the straight world he cannot enter. Fuller's somewhat jealous description of his more popular roommate resonates with the only revenge he feels able to exact: that of the campy distance of the "superior observer."*

## From *The Allisonian Classical Academy, 1873–74: A School Boy's Own Recollections of a Year at Boarding School* (1876)

### I

[…] One of the peculiar institutions of the Cottage, one which beyond our walls, had, I believe, no existence, was the Jolly Quartette.

The gentle reader will perhaps suppose that it comprised Paul, Frank, Charles and myself. The gentle reader is mistaken. The Quartette was composed of Paul, Frank, Charles and Ernest. Gentle reader, allow me to present Ernest Thompson. Ernie, as the boys called him, Ernestus, as I called him; Ernestine, as I call him now, was a "town feller," who attended the A.C.A. as a day scholar. Toward the latter part of November, he began dropping in occasionally, to see Frank and Paul, with whom, I suppose, he had become acquainted the year before. I never felt at all acquainted with him until after the first debate. We were on the same side, and in the exultation which followed our victory, we became a little more familiar. After this he came more frequently, and the quartette became one of our institutions.

I was the spectre at the banquet. I played cards rather indifferently, and couldn't tolerate raw oysters. P.S. And didn't smoke.

The dissipations of the Quartette, though somewhat frequent, were not of a very wild and exciting character. A can of oysters, a pound of crackers, a few cigars and a pack of cards were the only contributions of an evening entertainment. Our soirées were very select in character; outside barbarians were seldom admitted. George and Will considered the toleration of their presence as the greatest possible favor.

The entertainment, to which no formal invitation was considered necessary, generally began about half past 8, or 9 p.m. with the arrival of Ernestus and the oysters from his father's store. Paul produced the *arma Cerealia*[6] from his ancient ark, and Frank, dispatched for vinegar and pepper, performed his raid on the Allisonian storeroom with the swiftness and cunning of a Mercury. Mr. Norris, after his first failure, never again essayed a stew, and the oysters, after a just and impartial division among the four bowls were eaten raw. As I could never summon up enough resolution to swallow a raw oyster, I was graciously permitted free access to the cracker bag. I sat on the bed munching crackers during the whole entertainment, and my appetite for crackers became a standing joke. It "still lives"; as witness: "We have succeeded in keeping up, to a certain extent," he (Ern) wrote last October, "our fashionable and brilliant card and supper parties....We certainly miss your smiling countenance at our nocturnal gatherings, but we did not miss as 'many crackers.' *Coz why? Coz we don't!*"

Cruel!

After the craving of the inner man was satisfied, cigars were produced. I ate crackers. Cigars were lighted and cards were produced. Almost stifled by tobacco smoke, and bored to death by their interminable games of euchre, I sat at the foot of the bed, made saucy remarks on the game, which tried Mr. Norris's patience dreadfully, and—ate crackers. How I lived through so many soirees, I fail to comprehend even at this late day. In the consumption of crackers I followed and gratified a natural desire; but the amount of tobacco smoke I withstood, passes all belief. Our door was shut and rigidly guarded; no light must reach the hall. My only hope lay in the window, [which] invaluable convenience, I firmly believe, carried me through the ordeal.

The entertainment closed with a slap-bang anywhere from 11 p.m. to 1 a.m. I breathed a sigh of relief, pushed up the window further, and showed with the utmost plainness and impoliteness that I rejoiced in the departure of our guests. We went to bed at once; and in the morning I dressed and ate crackers among unwashed stew-pans, scattered packs of cards and old cigar stumps. Going to breakfast I closed the door on a room full of disordered furniture, paper bags, oyster cans, and a multitude of other interesting commodities.

Writing now, I can think of the Quartette meetings only with pleasure, and regret that they are forever passed. But of my whole school life at the Allison these convivial nocturnes were my greatest trial. Quiet and privacy were invaded, study was entirely prevented, bedtime and sleep thoughtlessly disregarded. A room full of stifling heat, and boys, and smoke, and noise. How vividly I can recall my sufferings! One night I indulged in a Terrible Revenge! Before I departed for an evening at the Draper, Will and I hid their eatables—the crackers behind the woodbox, the oysters under the mattress. Will escaped to bed; I to the Draper. I returned at 11:30. Had totally forgotten the episode of the oysters. I innocently entered the room. High words. I draw a veil.

## II

We, Us, & Co.—Mr. Norris and myself.

I am ashamed to find how few pages of my Recollections refer to Mr. Norris, my dear roommate at the A.C.A. I now gird up my loins for a full exposition of the domestic relations of "we twain;" for a full account of our year's bed and board together.

For some days before my grand entrée I had understood that Mrs. Allison designed "Mr. Norris" and "Mr. Fuller" for roommates. Inasmuch as Mrs. A. informed me that Mr. Norris had gone through the High School in Chicago, I concluded that he must be a most aged young person—19 or 20 at least. Inasmuch as he had chosen the south-west room for the fine sunset views discernible from that point, I set him down as a youth of poetic temperament. Out of this material I constructed a young man, tall and slender, with dark wavy hair and dreamy eyes, a lover of Nature and Art. The result of my labor threw me into the greatest consternation. Righteous indig. against Mrs. Allison reigned in my bosom. I regretted the want of tact which had brought us together as roommates. In the firm conviction that Mrs. A. had made a ridiculous blunder, I began my first day at the Allison. In Mrs. Allison's recitation room, I was introduced to most of the older scholars, with whom I should meet in my classes. Boys and girls, young men and maidens returned my bow, and no Mr. Norris. To the right of me, to the left of me, to the front of me, volleyed and thundered, "Mr. Fuller," and Mr. N. tarried. Last of all, his name greeted my expectant ears, and from the back seat rose my roommate. Alas! For my poetic imagery! Alas! For all my conceptions of my loving mate! Alas, for the slimness! Alas, for the eyes! Alas, for the hair! "*Mr. Norris*" produced a "young man," a year or more younger than myself, and a trifle shorter; a regular strawberry blonde, with very light hair, and very light blue eyes—just like myself, only blond-ier, and whiter, and bluer. My idol was shattered; but to this day I call my dear child, "Mr. Norris."

What my darling thought of me, I wist not. As he had been alarmed by a report that I had gone through the High School, he may have held in some degree, the same idea of me, as I had of him.

My indig. against Mrs. Allison died within me, and I acknowledged that she had mated us pretty well after all.

Of our few days, in number 20 in the main building, I remember little. We dovetailed very well, and until my dear child was led astray, bid fair to rival Dawn; we were very careful to have the lights out at 10 in the evening, and to rise at the first bell in the morning—how sadly we afterwards degenerated; we were very persistent in our persecution of Harkness, and improved the wee small hours by making up such impossible words as bedstead-a, wall-paper-a, or bowl-and-pitcher-a. Every evening we paid the inevitable penalty of a residence in the upper hall—we regularly entertained a promiscuous crowd of—

oh, well—bummers! Paul and Frank roomed opposite us, and Paul's first appearance in our room, was accompanied by the request of a light for his cigar. I failed to be impressed.

I have already said that Paul and Frank, on the renting of the Cottage were the first to change their quarters. We followed. I was quite indifferent at that time on the subject of removal, and perhaps Mr. N.'s and Paul's affinity of spirits, then just manifesting itself, settled the question.

A few boys, set apart from the rest, will, of course, clique. Paul and Charlie cliqued excessively, in the course of a few weeks. But Mr. Norris and I, let me say, did not quarrel, for al' that; we were very kind and forbearing, indeed. Let us exult.

Charles and I really got on very well together—for roommates. I hardly know if we were held up as models for the school; but we were one of the very few couples who stuck firm to the last; nominally, of course. It would have been a miracle, indeed, if the close of school had found two roommates bound up in each other, heart and soul. A toleration of each other ought to be considered as almost verging on the incredible. Mr. Norris was bound up on Paul; I in my books; each of us pursued the even tenor of his way, and followed his own sweet will. If Paul and Charles indulged in a little boating or hunting excursions, Frank was sometime included; I never. If Charles ran up home to North Lake for a day or two, Paul almost invariably accompanied him, sometimes Frank; sometimes, even barbarians from the main building; I never. Though we drifted so curiously apart, we still roomed together, and continued to be very good friends. I sometimes wondered why I regarded Mr. Norris' neglect and his sometimes very perceptible attempts at snubbing, with such indifference. I didn't care as much—a quarter as much—as propriety demanded. But if I had been tormented to whatever extent, by indignation at Charles and jealousy of Paul, I never would have shown my true feelings as did poor Frank. That Paul should have confided all his nice little secrets to *my*, instead of *his* roommate, was a dreadful trial to him; but his sufferings, when Paul slept there three or four nights in succession with Mr. Norris, and with him whiled away the night in sweet love prattle, passed all bounds. Poor boy! I, however, took the matter quite calmly, and whether George or Will was quartered off on me, or whether I slept alone, with "a mind, conscious to itself of rectitude," I slept the sleep of the just, and the sleep of the righteous. Paul's and Charles' nocturnal confidences, given and received under cover of darkness and privacy, I regarded with supreme indifference; their diurnal whisperings, from rosy morn till dewy eve, their sweet little chatterings under breath in the farthest corner of the room, I could not tolerate. Alas! I was never able to fully break my dear young friends of this most disagreeable and ridiculous habit.

As time passed on, Messrs. Norris and Weil became quite pronounced in their demonstration of affection, and of the disposition they would like to make of me. When, about the middle of January, I spoke of leaving at the end of the term, they expressed, very properly and prettily, the regret they would feel on losing me, and then, in my presence, coolly proceeded to perfect a plan whose carrying out, would fill the aching void in Mr. Norris' heart, and would deprive Frank of a roommate. After keeping them on the ragged edge of suspense for some days, I relieved them by the intelligence that I had concluded to remain in Coonie.[7] I rejoice to say that no unseemly manifestations of joy were exhibited by the young gentlemen.

A month later, Mr. Norris most heartlessly and cruelly, snubbed me. Naturally obtuse, I did not discover till sometime after, that a snub was intended. I am sure of it now.

One Saturday (Feb. 21) Mr. Norris, with Paul and Frank, departed to North Lake, to pass that day, and the following Sunday, and to return on Monday. This visit had been talked of continually in my presence for the three or four days previous. In my hearing, their plans had been fully discussed and elaborated; and never, in all this time, did I receive the slightest intimation, that my company would be desired, or that my presence would add to the pleasure of the trip. I was entirely ignored. Ah, me. Yet, Saturday morning when the trio set off, I viewed their departure with real indifference. I fear that I was utterly devoid of sensibility. I spent the morning, most contently in study, and Paul's return about noon, found me still engaged with my books.

Of the results of this excursion, among the most vivid of my recollections Allisonian, I write farther on. I shed a tear—here it is to think that Mr. Norris' last night in the College was spent with Paul. O, ye tears!

Though the thermometer of our affection seldom rose above "temperate," upon one occasion only did it fall below zero. Once, Mr. Norris and I actually quarreled. My mortification on account of the bare fact of a quarrel, was aggravated by the way in which my dear child showed how big a fool he could be when occasion required. Any thought of "Besser's watch," is always accompanied by a smile for the whole affair, and a deep, deep blush for my poor darling's foolishness.

*Summa sequart fastigna resum:*[8] A propensity for filching from his true love handkerchief, pencils, knives, and other little articles, for the purpose of teasing and tantalizing his own true love, had obtained among the amorous Allisonians. Paul and Charles, who were especially smitten by this mild form of lunacy, invaded neutral territory, and surreptitiously gained possession of Bessie Harrison's watch. Mr. N., who took charge of the "swag," boldly wagered that Bessie would not obtain her time-piece within a specified time. Stakes, a pound of candy.

"Besser" accepted the wager, and engaged Mr. Norris' roommate as a most useful ally, and Mr. Norris's roommate, bound by a solemn promise to secure the watch, darkly plotted to gain possession of the same.

No; we didn't quarrel; Mr. Norris quarreled.

To resume: when we retired to rest that night—that is, went to bed—I carefully noticed the position of the furniture, and my dear child's pants. While engaged in moving his apparel so as to the better suit my convenience in my midnight proceedings, I shoved his panties, with the watch, from the chair, upon the floor. Mr. Norris, *miserabile dictu*,[9] picked up the watch and put it under his pillow—more,—under the mattress. I breathed curses, not loud, but deep. Charles was an immense time in dropping into the arms of Morpheus. From the persistency with which he resisted the benevolent old party's soothing influence, one might well have supposed that he was most perseveringly bent upon churchyards yawn, and upon witnessing all the phenomena attendant upon the "witching hour." When, at last Mr. N. yielded to "tired Nature's sweet restorer," my patience and wide-awakeativeness were alike nearly exhausted. When fully assured that Mr. N. slumbered and slept, I began operations. I silenced the little squeams of a tender conscience, and I took the initial step in an unquenchable feud. Unsoftened by my victim's state of innocent unconsciousness, I worked his destruction. For an hour, at the least, I burrowed in the bedclothes, and finally grappled the watch. Securing it under my pillow, I fell into a troubled sleep. Strange to say, I was not in the least tormented with uncomfortable visions of my terrible crime. No Mr. Norris brained me with "Besser's watch"; no Mr. Weil pelted me with gumdrops.

Next morning, in order to avoid the questioning, which Mr. N., on the discovery, that the watch was *non est inventus*,[10] would surely institute, I arose by a Herculean effort at least an hour before my usual time. Just before breakfast, I placed the watch in Bessie's hands. Mr. Norris entered the dining room unusually late, even for him, and viewing me with a suspicious smile, remarked that I had it. He smiled, poor child, ignorant of the terrible depths of my treachery. But when, after breakfast, Bessie dangled the watch before his very eyes, my crime was disclosed to him in all its terrible deformity. He bowed beneath the blast. Fortunately, I was not present, and no scene ensued.

That a.m. we were gathered, as was our wont, before the ringing of the bell in Mrs. A.'s recitation room. I was somewhat excited, and can only recollect the moving spectacle of my dear child in tears, and surrounded by sympathizing friends. I have a faint impression that Mr. A. made some remark about treachery or duplicity, or something of the sort. Paul, I believe, echoed the remarks—I don't remember.

At the morning recess, Bessie showed me a note which she had received from Mr. Norris. She was informed that I had lost my room, and that she would discover her loss when she returned to the house at noon. We laughed. My dear child was threatening Bessie, and was angry at me. But the idea of his ousting me from our room, was too ridiculous, and I declared to Bessie, that at noon, I should haul Mr. Norris over the coals. She begged me not to inform

Mr. N. that I had seen his note, and announced her intention to see Mr. N. at noon, and to smooth his ruffled front. I told her that I should speak with my dear child first, and make things generally salubrious. It had been my intention to give Mr. Norris, figuratively speaking, a breeze; but Besser's pleading voice compelled me to relinquish the design. If Mr. Norris wondered at my excessive softness and humility, he is informed that Bessie was his salvation.

On returning to Mr. Norris' room, I found assembled there, the proprietor, Paul, and the usual crowd. Paul was bitterly, cruelly sarcastic—or intended to be—and was loud in his denunciations of my baseness. Mr. N. did not trust himself to say much, but feelingly attended to the pound of candy. The relative effects on his constitution, of the discovery of my treachery, and of the loss of the candy, I never learned.

After the mob had withdrawn, I ventured to humbly approach Mr. N. He was at the washstand, and his back was turned to me. When I began my oration, he paused in the operation of washing his hands, and listened *auribus arrectitus.*[11] I was exceedingly humble, and delivered my apology with most heroic meekness. When in the conclusion, I asked if I was to consider myself pardoned, Mr. N. without turning around—for he might have burst into tears, had he done so—gave utterance to a very hesitating "ye-e-s," as if he had not yet fully resolved to forgive my offense. "Ye-e-s"! It was too ridiculous! I am afraid that I almost smiled. Mr. N.'s gracious condescension touched my heart, and I never afterwards could sufficiently admire the rare magnanimity that could forgive such dark treachery and such base duplicity.

Crossing to the house, we found in the parlor Bessie and Susie Curran—Bessie's second, as Paul had been Mr. Norris'. Bessie and Mr. Norris straightway "made up," and we all went into the dining room with the utmost serenity and amicability.

This, then, was my only serious rupture with Mr. Norris. After this we continued to live in peace and harmony to the end of the chapter.

Early in the year, Charles bestowed upon me the name of Mentor; by this name both he and Paul called me, as long as we remained at school. Mentor is still one of my dear child's "modes of address." The other day, in answer to my intelligence that I contemplated a visit to Coonie, he wrote: "Come and let Telemachus"[12]—for so I frequently address him—"come, and let Telemachus once more hear wise precepts fall from the mouth of the revered Mentor." It will thus be seen that I held the position of adviser-at-large to the Cottage, and Mentor-like, attempted to govern the minds and restrain the passions of the Cottage youth. I regret to say that I was not always appreciated.

I have written at some length on our relations at school; as they were. I rejoice to say, that, at the present time, things are much improved. Mr. Norris has been separated from his bosom friend Paul, and from Totten, Paul's successor in his affections; he has fallen back on his old and reliable *quon-*

*dam*[13] roommate, and on this bosom, yearning for him with love unutterable, he has at last found rest. (How touching!) We correspond rather regularly, and Mr. Norris has deigned to express his pleasure on learning of my intended visit to Coonie. In the sweet vales of beloved Coonie, will we bind still more firmly together, the friendships of early days; amid the scenes hallowed by dear association, will we bring to its perfection, a love pure and sacred, a love which shall cease to exist only when our hands are palsied and our eyes closed in Death. (Extremely affecting!) [...]

# CHARLES MACOMB FLANDRAU (1871–1938)

*Some people never progress past their college years, and Charles Flandrau was one of them. Like canonical American writer F. Scott Fitzgerald (also from St. Paul, MN), he could not get "the Ivy League" out of his blood. When* Harvard Episodes *became a surprising bestseller, he continued to write articles about college antics; these were collected in a sequel,* The Diary of a Freshman *(1900). A good friend of "Bay" Lodge (pp. 290–93, below), Flandrau's arch and witty memoir pointedly excluded women while pointedly including Oscar Wildean posturing (the Wildean model is discussed below, 62, 71–80). Like the contemporary* Cult of the Purple Rose *(see below, 62–66),* Harvard Episodes *paints a stylized and comical picture of undergraduate "hauteur"—a certain Ivy League arrogance—and aestheticism then in vogue among undergraduates.*

# FROM *HARVARD EPISODES* (1897)

[…] Dickey called, "Come in!" to a doubting knock at the door, and Mrs. Dawson advanced two steps into the study and then stopped.

For a moment no one, with the exception of Dawson, grasped the situation. He had grasped it and was wrestling with it as he threw off the rug that covered him where he lay on the sofa—as he stepped across the room—as he placed his hands on his mother's shoulders and kissed her lightly on the cheek. He had grasped the situation, but he was utterly at a loss to know what to do with it.

"Didn't you get my telegram?" his mother was saying; "why, that's funny— I sent one from the hotel quite a time ago, 'Am worried about sore throat will come to see you'—just ten words exactly."

Then he found himself introducing his three friends to her: Tommy first, Charlie Bolo second, and Bigelow last, and as he pronounced their names slowly and distinctly, he tried to look ahead and discover what he should do next.

On realizing that the impassive Tommy was being presented to her, Mrs. Dawson began to extend her hand toward him; but her impulse collapsed for some reason or other and the movement resulted in nothing more definite than the disclosure of her silk mits.

The three men were so completely outside of any calculations she had made before knocking on her son's door, that she had nothing to say to them just then, so she turned once more to Dickey with frank adoration and said,—

"I *was* worried about your throat."

"I suppose, like the rest of us, Mrs. Dawson, you have found out how seriously he objects to the serious," ventured Charlie Bolo airily. The smile Mrs. Dawson gave him did not lack sweetness, for she had been looking at Dickey; but it was desperately vague, and Bolo felt that he had made a false start.

"They are taking pretty good care of me, don't you think?" There was something pallid and heroic about Dickey's playfulness.

"Oh, this college life!" began Mrs. Dawson, forgetfully. She was trying to recollect a clipping she had once made from a newspaper.

"There's a lack of woman's sweeping, without doubt," grumbled Bigelow jocosely—the music books he had been examining had dirtied his hands.

"Richard, what was that piece I cut from the 'Weekly' and sent you last year?" Mrs. Dawson sat down in the chair Dickey pushed toward her. It was a heavy chair of dark wood, and gave Tommy a vicious desire to look at the picture on the mantelpiece. Dickey elaborated the little anecdote to which his mother referred and made the most of it—it was nearly dinner time; the fellows would certainly go soon.

"You have so many books, Richard," said Mrs. Dawson, looking about the room for the first time.

"Aren't his shelves attractive," assented Tommy with enthusiasm. "I think you would approve of everything there too, Mrs. Dawson, with the possible exception of this, which you undoubtedly know enough about to disapprove of." He laughingly handed her a volume of "Degeneration"[14] from the table. Dawson could have slain him had he not realized that all three fellows must be somewhat bewildered.

"Isn't it—isn't it—thick—" faltered Mrs. Dawson.

"What *is* one to think of a creature like Nordau?" asked Bigelow, theatrically; "that is to say, of course, beyond his exquisitely unconscious sense of humour." He had made this remark on several previous occasions, and its technique was, in consequence, becoming quite perfect. Mrs. Dawson looked helplessly at Dickey and said nothing. She was at least displaying what Charlie Bolo called "admirable *savoir taire.*"[15]

When she opened the volume and leaned over to examine the title-page, Tommy gave the photograph on the mantelpiece a surreptitious glance. There was a more or less grotesque resemblance in it to the almost portly, middle-aged original, who was dressed with a quiet absence of taste and answered in a general way Tommy's description of a superior woman. It was very embarrassing and inexplicable and altogether impossible. Tommy did not understand it—he did not understand anything any more, and only wished to get outside and pinch himself and Charlie Bolo and Bigelow.

Dickey Dawson did most of the talking, and achieved thereby a dismal sort of success. His mother had introduced—or rather stumbled on—fallen over—the subject of books, and for a time it was as if Dawson had said to himself,—

"Books! books! what can I say of the origin, development, history, and present condition of books?" For he chattered incessantly about them—his own—Tommy's—anybody's. He told funny stories that were not in the least funny, about book agents, and was in the midst of a detailed description of a book-case when he realized he was making a fool of himself and stopped.

"I like reading," mused Mrs. Dawson, as she mechanically turned the leaves of "Degeneration." "I think it cultivates the observation."

"I feel sometimes that it would be more advisable to cultivate blindness than observation," answered Tommy. He was becoming reckless and got up to go.

Mrs. Dawson's lips parted to say something, but Dickey broke in with,—

"I wish one of you fellows would kindly stop at the stable and send round a cab. It is too late for my mother to go back to town in the car."

A protest from Mrs. Dawson seemed imminent, but she apparently thought better of it and returned to the book.

The getting away was difficult, but not nearly so difficult as staying any longer would have been. They chirped "good-byes," and "get well soons," and "so glad to have met yous," galore, and Bigelow felt waxing within him a new and passionate love for his own family, who were all decently dead. Then they echoed off through a long corridor. After they had gone Mrs. Dawson said nothing for several minutes, and Dickey made a noise with the fire.

"They're queer young men," she finally reflected aloud. "Do you like them very much, Richard?"

"Oh, yes," answered Dickey, indifferently, "you get to like people you see a great deal, I imagine." He sat on the arm of his mother's chair and held one of his mother's hands and kissed it.

"I wonder if you get to *dis*like people you *don't* see much of," said Mrs. Dawson. She was turning the leaves of her book without stopping to look at them.

"Not if you ever truly loved them," answered Dickey, tenderly drawing nearer to her and laying his cheek against hers. He was almost overdoing the thing.

"Not if you ever truly loved them, I suppose," thoughtfully repeated his mother with more intelligence than Dickey had ever given her credit for.

Then she began to turn the leaves of the book all over again. [...]

# SHIRLEY EVERTON JOHNSON (1871–1911)

*Did Harvard have a "gay alliance" in the 1890s? We can never be certain; however, some very suggestive writing emerged from Harvard graduates during this period. Shirley Everton Johnson is one of them: his reminiscence is an amusing spoof of the aesthetic movement (see above, xix). Students congregating in an unusual clique, making every effort to outquip one another à la Oscar Wilde, can be compared to Flandrau's contemporary* Harvard Episodes *(see above, 59–61). Was this book entirely fictional? Maybe not. Johnson ends his Preface with a toast "To the men who, on one occasion, at least, wore the purple rose, and to their successors, this book is modestly tendered with the hope that it may perpetuate the memory of The Cult of the Purple Rose." Although Oscar Wilde is never directly mentioned in* Cult, *the Wildean connection is unmistakable—the students strive for "decadence" with all their artistic clutter, cultivate an inflated but supposedly disinterested dandyism, and above all strain constantly to out-do one another with witty bon-mots.[16] Most daringly, the book identifies its heroes with a "phase of Harvard life" that carries an unmistakable suggestion of homosexuality. By 1902 such a connection was unavoidable: the Oscar Wilde Trials of 1895 had quite publicly attached sexuality to his name, seven years before* Cult *was published. Johnson's little tale, so seemingly careless and light-hearted, is clearly a brave act.*

## FROM *THE CULT OF THE PURPLE ROSE: A PHASE OF HARVARD LIFE* (1902)

### II. The Cult of the Purple Rose

It was after midnight when DeLancy invited us to his rooms in Holworthy to help him eat a light lunch. He is a charmingly original fellow, and we knew that an hour could not be spent more pleasantly than with him, and we accepted; besides, we were the least bit hungry.

When we had gone upstairs and thrown ourselves with reckless abandon in the easy chairs, DeLancy said something which made us laugh, and told us to make ourselves comfortable and to smoke cigarettes.

He retired to an ante-room to prepare the informal feast, so we thought, and we were particular to talk about everything—except the forthcoming lunch.

He returned shortly, clad—*mirabile dictu*[17]—in a linen suit which was a faint echo of the summer, and would have been decidedly out of place in anyone but DeLancy,—he was nothing if not odd. "What shall I get for you fellows to eat?" he asked with a slightly bored air, which is now quite the thing, for you know a man should always act extremely tired and disgusted when he entertains. The effect is marvelous, inasmuch as his guests seek to entertain him.

"Oh, bring out anything," said Howard; "it is not aesthetic to be particular!" Lucius Howard was a tall fellow who smiled seraphically at times, particularly after he had indulged his fancy in an epigram; at other times he was wont to look as if he might write verses of a somber tone.

He smiled now, and said to a spectacled philosophic fellow, who wasn't so philosophic after all, "Nothing is so expected as expectation!" and then sank among the cushions to think of something better.

Meantime, Denholm and Henderson were quietly waiting for Eddie DeLancy to complete his table setting, which wasn't especially arduous, since six plates and six rather good-sized glasses were already placed upon a dainty oriental tea-table that stood in the centre[18] of the study; in fine, it was a little to the right, so that the light from the single gas burner of an odd-hammered-iron chandelier[19] would be directly above it. Howard had remarked the fact in summing up the appearance of the room: "Nothing is so ideally perfect as irregularity."

Eddie DeLancy belonged to the most original set at Harvard, and his study was one that could have belonged only to a very erudite man. There was a grand piano over against the wall, with Grieg's "Peer Gynt Suite"[20] open on the rack. On top lay Chopin and Mozart and the Harvard Song Book, together with a few pieces in manuscript.

On the wall were pictures hung with incongruity, for beside a large photograph of St. John's Cathedral was a nude from the Salon;[21] and there was a group of college editors hanging between a pen imitation of one of Mr. Aubrey Beardsley's drawings[22] and a picture of Phillips Brooks.[23]

In a cosy nook, made by a fish net and some ribbons, was a small wood carving, and on the mantel stood a statuette of Apollo Belvedere,[24] surrounded by queerly-shaped pipes, daily themes[25] and glasses which alternately held beer and dust.

And on a side table was a silver card receiver loaded with small bits of paper and cards and letters, to say nothing of an inviting box of cigarettes, and there was a prayer book partly hidden by a rumpled copy of the Harvard *Crimson*.[26]

In another part of the room stood a desk, unique in design but clumsy in appearance, littered with books and papers, which nearly hid from view a quaint little inkstand. Before this desk was a low seat fashioned after an organ stool, whose chief virtues are found in its uncomfortable hardness and its usefulness in wearing out one's trousers.

This bench-like stool was wheeled around beside the little tea table, and DeLancy proceeded to carve a chicken for his guests. There were pickles, olives, a chunk of cheese left from the last rarebit, a portion of hard French bread, and a goodly number of full bottles of beer.

"Ah!" said Henderson, in his rich, deep voice, which, being distinctive was therefore original: "It is pleasant to lounge and eat when one is really hungry."

"Oh, how awfully commonplace," put in Denholm, making his first remark for the evening; and Howard added slyly: "Nothing is so beautiful as hunger when one is not famished." He smiled serenely as he took a large mouthful of chicken sandwich, religiously striving to be unconventional.

"Help yourselves to beer, fellow; it is delightfully odd to have to ask you to drink," said DeLancy, with the self-conscious air of genius.

The spectacled-philosophic fellow, who wasn't so philosophic after all, declined chicken but took an olive and a bottle of beer, and then asked with a serio-comic seriousness: "What do you fellows think of 'The Green Carnation?'"[27]

"Oh!" exclaimed every one, anxious to express his opinion, witty or otherwise, before the rest.

"Now, one at a time, fellows," said Hobson, the philosophic, beer-drinking, olive-eating fellow. "You first, Eddie; you are the host."

"Ah-er-oh!" he replied, in an effort to show that he was going to be bright spontaneously. "Ah-er! I think it is a wicked little book." And his intonations were so inimitable that we all thought it very bright.[28]

Then Warren Henderson, he of that musical, deep voice, remarked, with dignity which could not be affected: "I consider it a mass of brilliant sayings which one is sure to tire of; it is painfully artificial."

And Denholm who had time to think up what his criticism would be, followed with: "It is verily the most modern of modern books; so modern, indeed, that its very modernity makes one regret that he is modern."

This effort was loudly applauded, and everybody took more beer, in expectation of Lucius Howard's carefully chosen phrases. "You expect me to make an epigram," said Howard, with that bland smile which never fails to win attention, "but, as I said earlier to-night, nothing is so unexpected as expectation, and I have to report that I felt that it was necessary to my spirit of originality not to read 'The Green Carnation.' Therefore, I do not think about it at all."

Before we could remonstrate with Howard three fellows came in to pay early morning calls—a custom which will have to be given up, I fear, because it is becoming too commonplace.

"Ah!" exclaimed Eddie, addressing one of the new comers, "we are so glad you have come; we have longed for your epigrams and bright things. We have been talking about 'The Green Carnation;' what have you to say about it?"

"Well," said Egbert Barnaby, the one addressed, "let me remove my coat and light a cigarette, then I shall try to be brilliant for you,"—and the other two fellows joined me in being artistically non-committal by saying nothing.

"Oh, how delightful!" said Eddie, his cheeks glowing like a girl's with anticipated joy. "Won't you have some beer? I know it *très bourgeois*, but it's all we have; and it's so original to make the best of what one has, just as if it were one's ideal."

"No, thank you; thank you, no!" and all breathed easier, knowing that the bright things were yet to come.

"Won't drink! How delightfully sacrificing! One should hardly think you would have to stop drink for the sake of Art!" exclaimed Howard, smiling more divinely than before because his eyes now sparkled brightly.

"Now, fellows," said Barnaby, rather deliberately, "you see I have stopped drinking because I am in love. Through this I have made a discovery, namely, that when we so frequently hear that a man is intoxicated because he is in love, it is all wrong. The true solution is, that nothing is more intoxicating than temperance."

"Oh, how very novel!" said Eddie; "your ideas and discoveries are always so refreshing."

"But what do you think of 'The Green Carnation'?" asked Henderson, who had become temporary leader, as Hobson was interested more in his cup than in the rather too philosophic discussion of modern art.

"Well, let me see," he replied. "'The Green Carnation'! Oh, yes; I have read it, and, if I remember rightly, I wrote on the last page:

The Green Carnation—'tis absinthe
    In far more ways than one;
It makes me long for crème de menthe—
    My last debauch is done!"

"Admirable, indeed!" said Henderson, in his deep voice, after the burst of applause.

Howard then blurted out this proposition: "I say, fellows, let us form a new club, to be known as 'The Cult of the Purple Rose.' What do you say?"

Lucian Denholm, the tall, slender man with a pensive face, who was really brilliant and therefore said little, was now the first to speak, because the name had been suggested by his Purple Tea. He was enthusiastic in favor of the scheme, and said he was complimented by the recognition of his efforts to be original. Then he outlined his plan.

"Oh, it will be simply lovely," he said, "and so original! We will all wear purple roses, and write on purple linen,—I might say purple and fine linen,—use three-cent purple stamps instead of the customary twos, and if any of us should ever write on white paper, he must invariably use purple ink.

"Besides, we would attract so much attention with our purple handkerchiefs and hat ribands. It will be so gratifying to hear people remark how hideous they are, and we can be as truly happy as the end and aim of art will allow.

"And to carry it further, we can write purple verses and purple stories and tell purple lies, in lieu of the commonplace white lies. And just as it has been shown how lying is a fine art,[29] so much the more will purple lying be art.

"We may even go so far—and, indeed, I should strongly advise it—that we take every care to decorate our rooms in purple and have purple curtains."

Here Howard sighed, and when he said: "After all there is nothing so purple as green save purple," we knew that he was thinking of his most aesthetically green curtains. Yet he was willing to sacrifice them for the Society and the interest of art.

"In fact, I consider this a most valuable opportunity for us to show our true colors, which may be expressed by the one word—Purple."

"But whom shall we have for officers?" asked Henderson, already converted to the scheme.

The philosophical Hobson stopped drinking beer long enough to observe: "How dreadfully commonplace to have officers; let us all be officers of equal power, taking turn in buying the beer."

This met with the unqualified indorsement of "The Cult of the Purple Rose,"—the latest and most original society at Harvard,—although Denholm looked a trifle sadder than usual, and Henderson remarked how unfortunate that we couldn't have purple beer, and then added that we could drink from purple glasses.

Then Barnaby said, "It is all arranged except the meetings. Let them likewise follow no rule; let them be beautifully irregular. If you fellows see a pale, purple light shining from my windows,—for we all must have purple lamp shades,—why, we'll hold the first meeting tomorrow night."

"What shall the motto of the Cult be?" asked Howard, just before we left, all the beer being consumed, and the reply came back as with one voice "Pale is thy purple light,"—the phrase being lifted bodily from one of Howard's recent poems in the *Advocate*. [...]

## Notes

1 This novel is reprinted in full in Axel Nissen's excellent *Romantic Friendship Reader* (2003). For further discussion, see Douglass Shand-Tucci's *The Crimson Letter* (29–36) and Jonathan Ned Katz's *Love Stories* (141–46).

2 Loring used the full poem "The Volunteer" by Elbridge J. Cutler (1831–70) as the novel's epigraph, then took each stanza to preface four of the book's chapters. The poem follows an ill-fated soldier's career.

3 It is a noteworthy subtext in Loring's novel that the professor is lecturing on the Domestic Arts, of all subjects. Tom himself is similarly feminized: not only his looks are described so, but the fact that he is photographed in drag as "Marton,

the Pride of the Market" (a popular 1846 comic melodrama by J.R. Planché). It is this photograph, mentioned in the above chapter, that Ned will carry to his grave. Further adding to the gender confusion is the nickname of Tom's other friend: the "Blush Rose."

4   At Harvard College during this period, one of the milder punishments was what was called "private admonition," by which a deduction of 32 marks was made from the rank of the offender; it was so called in contradistinction to "public admonition," which added to the deduction a letter sent to the student's parents.

5   This line is only one among many in the novel to suggest an alternative reading of the text.

6   Cereal stores (Latin), i.e., the oyster crackers.

7   The Allison Classical Academy was located in Oconomowoc, Wisconsin, here and elsewhere affectionately referred to as "Coonie."

8   "To get back to all that followed" [somewhat mangled Latin].

9   Sad to say (Latin).

10   Nowhere to be found (Latin).

11   All ears (Latin).

12   In the ancient Greek epic, *The Odyssey*, Telemachus was the son of Odysseus and Penelope; here, refers to a younger person in need of tutoring.

13   Former (Latin).

14   Max Nordau (1849–1923) was a Hungarian social critic whose best-selling book *Degeneration* (1892) was a moralistic attack on so-called degenerate art, attempting to explain all modern art, music, and literature by pointing out the decadent characteristics of the artists involved. He developed a biological explanation for social problems; in a similar vein the medical establishment was also attempting to use science at this time to "explain" homosexuality.

15   Pun on *savoir faire*, the French term for tact; an intuition for appropriate behavior in any situation. In this instance, "savoir taire" means knowing when to keep quiet.

16   Clever sayings or remarks (French).

17   Strange to say (Latin).

18   The British spelling is worth noting in this American document: Johnson is doing his best to emulate Wilde, so British spellings are sprinkled throughout his book.

19   Hand-forged pieces of iron are literally hammered into shape to create a rustic lighting piece. More to the point, Johnson's insistence on the eclectic décor with all its exotica stands here as a homosexual marker. See my discussion on décor and homosexuality in *Dayneford's Library*, 125–26.

20   In 1875 Edvard Grieg (1843–1907) composed incidental music for a production of Henrik Ibsen's play of the same name (1867), which focuses on a character who runs from commitment and who is completely selfish, having little concern for the sacrifices others are forced to make in accommodating him. Johnson may well be making a wry comment here on DeLancy's character.

21  The Salon was nineteenth-century France's state-sponsored exhibition of (usually conservative) paintings.

22  Beardsley (1872–98) was a well-known Decadent artist, and the darling of the aesthetic movement, whose often risqué and daring prints such as *Salome* (after Oscar Wilde's play of the same name) and *Lysistrata* were quite "notorious."

23  Phillips Brooks (1835–93) was a well-known preacher from Boston. Again, the insistence on describing the details of DeLancy's room reflects a tendency to convey otherness—and perhaps sexual orientation—by a description of idiomatic, aesthetic, and nearly baroque décor.

24  This statue (second century AD Roman copy of a fourth century BC Greek original) was one of the most influential ancient statues, exemplifying the androgynous treatment of the male nude. The legends of Apollo included numerous same-sex encounters, and thus the statue was associated with homoerotic desire. The (homosexual) critic Johann Winkelmann (1717–68) had early rhapsodized on its beauty. The statue is also humorously mentioned in this anthology's *Mrs. Dee's Encore* (see below, pp. 00–00).

25  I.e., essays required in English classes.

26  Founded in 1875, the *Crimson* is the oldest continuously published daily college newspaper in the United States.

27  Robert Hichens' satirical novel (1894) lampooned Wilde and the Aesthetic Movement.

28  Cf. Evelyn Waugh's *Brideshead Revisited* (1945), where a similar character affecting studied brilliance is also given a stutter.

29  Oscar Wilde's essay "The Decay of Lying" (1889).

PART FIVE

# THE OSCAR MODEL

*An essentially British creation, Oscar Wilde was arguably the celebrity of the nineteenth century most identified with homosexuality. Years before his trials of 1895, he made a wide-ranging tour of Gilded Age America.[1] An anonymous newspaper reporter covered his stop at snowbound Utica, New York, leaving a fascinating picture of the Wildean persona—one that would arguably come to be identified most closely with homosexuality's public face—that of a somewhat effete, dandified "quipper." Through the writer's cynicism surfaces a bemused respect for Wilde's showmanship, and we are treated to an intriguing picture, down to clothing, manners, and décor, of what would soon be labeled as sexually suspicious.*

# "WILDE IN UTICA: YE LAST SWEET THING IN OSCARS"

[*The Utica Daily Observer*, 7 February 1882]

A GENUINE SENSATION AT THE CITY OPERA HOUSE—WILDE UNFOLDING THE FLAWLESS ESSENCES OF HIS KOSMIC SOUL UNDER THE AUSPICES OF THE HOUSEHOLD ART ROOMS—GETTING DOWN FROM HIS PEDESTAL OF DAFFODILS AND COMING IN CONTACT WITH ONEIDA COUNTY SNOW BANKS AND AN INQUISITIVE "OBSERVER" REPORTER.

Oscar Wilde reached Utica at 5:15 yesterday afternoon and departed at 11:22 to-day. The young poet was expected earlier, but, as Conductor Ferrell remarked: "The glaukous-haired[2] disciple of poesy is nothing if intelligible." Oscar's coming was eagerly anticipated. Public opinion in regard to the young Oxford graduate is so divided that while some insist he is only "utter," many urge that there is a method underlying it all which stamps Wilde as a level-headed money getter. Candidly, he doesn't look like a fellow whose nerves are constantly thrilling like throbbing violins in exquisite pulsation. In his eyes there is nothing of the "lone delight of soft communion with sweet antiphonal souls." Not a bit of it. Wilde came to Utica in a drawing-room car like any one else, and when he shook hands with Commissioner Earll and Architect Cooper, no one about the depot suspected that the young Irishman had a Kosmic soul or that he dealt in mystic symphonies. He did not even flaunt the burnished disk of the sunflower, and as for a lily—it would have been paralyzed by the surrounding snow banks in seventeen seconds. Wilde is a remarkable creation. If he is playing a part in his tour through this country, he is a finished actor. If he is "acting out" himself, he is simply unique. No picture that has yet appeared does him justice. It has been either an extravagant burlesque or a colorless reproduction of his pale, classical features and long hair. Wilde is 26 years of age and six feet two inches in height. He has an interesting face of feminine mould, and when he speaks shows a fine upper row of teeth. His accent and manner is that of a refined cockney. He speaks slowly, with just a suggestion of the Dundreary drawl. His sentences are long but he carries an idea with or behind them. He is perfectly self-possessed and his individuality or egotism is constantly apparent. Speaking to the writer of his experience in this country, last evening, he said:

WILDE'S IMPRESSIONS OF AMERICA.

"Your country is vast. I suppose I have no conception of it as yet but your distances are very remarkable."

"You are simply on the borders of the Continent, Mr. Wilde."

"Y-a-a-s, so I am informed. In our own ugly little Island we cannot appreciate the vastness of America. You call it a country, but I call it a w-o-r-l-d."

"You have spoken every night since you began lecturing, have you not?"

"Ya-a-s, but not always to an audience. It is not my lecturing that tires me. The sensation is so novel I fairly enjoy it. The exactions of traveling are wearisome, and then there have been so many receptions and pleasant little entertainments. America is a constantly growing wonder to me. You are decidedly cosmopolitan. There is a suggestion of all countries about you, and I have yet to meet the Yankee as a distinctive character."

Wilde attracts much attention. He wears an olive-green overcoat, gaily trimmed, a low, wide collar and a necktie of mammoth proportions and gradated colors. As he stepped from the train he placed the fingers of his right hand gracefully to the side of his face and whether this movement was natural or mere affectation will never be known. His dress throughout was "a symphony of color" down to the patent leather shoes with decorated uppers of cream-colored broadcloth. He has the stooping shoulders and the gait of *Bunthorne*,[3] but this, together with his cockneyed accent, is as natural as running water. In full evening dress Wilde is a revelation. He looks younger, more aesthetic and more ethereal. Last night he wore the most pronounced fashionable evening costume ever seen in the Valley of the Mohawk. We shall not attempt to describe it save to remark that Wilde wore it with a naturalness and grace that is inimitable.

THE LECTURE.

The lecture was given under the auspices of the Household Art Rooms. The audience that listened to it was a large and cultivated one. The stage was handsomely set and covering the desk in the centre was a rich drapery embroidered with lilies. The lecturer glided upon the stage with a movement that suggested a change in the dance known as "the German." In a slow, measured monotone he unfolded the text of his discourse. In England, he said, the aim of the new artistic movement was "to search out, in our great, ugly manufacturing cities, those men and women who can work with their hands as well as their minds and hearts. Such as your life is, so is your art sure to be. The spirit of art is one and eternally the same. Byron was a rebel and Shelley a dreamer, but Keats was the forerunner of the pre-Raphaelite school."

Before the lecture began Wilde said to the writer: "There is just one criticism which the American press has passed on me that I do not like. I do not think I deserve it. Here in this account (the reporter handed him a slip from the Albany *Argus*) they say I am not practical. I should like to meet that horrid Albany fellow and I believe I could convince him that I am practical. I want you to listen to what I say about the workman." His allusion to the handicraftsmen was made in these words:

"Great movements must originate with the workmen. I believe in practical art. I believe the musical value of a word is greater than its intellectual value and nowhere is this better exemplified than in that supreme imaginative work of the young American who wrote 'The Raven.' To educate and refine a country you must begin with the masses. There must be stately and simple architecture in your cities and bright and simple dress for men and women. You should have among your people some permanent canon and standard of taste. Creeds and philosophies decay, but beauty is the only thing time cannot harm. We should have in our houses things that gave pleasure to the men who made them."

THE GOOD IN ART.

"The good in art is not what we directly learn from it but what we indirectly become through it. All the arts are fine arts and all the arts are decorative arts. By separating the handicraftsman from the artist you ruin both. Labor without art is merely barbarism. Decoration is the form of expression of the joy the handicraftsman has in his work. Design is the study and result of cumulative habit and observation. I believe in the elevation and education of the poorer classes. I want to see the homes of the humble beautiful. The rich in England have too many beautiful things—more than their share—they might very well be divided."

After the lecture Wilde received an informal reception at the residence of Ex-Mayor Hutchinson. He is more entertaining when met socially than upon the rostrum. He is a young man of ideas, a wide reader and a close observer. He says the assertion that he is not practical is the only distasteful stricture that has been passed upon him in this country.

"But your reception in Music Hall, Boston, by the Harvard boys?"[4]

Wilde smiled. He rarely laughs. It was a smile that displayed to the best advantage that fine row of teeth and flashed the merest suspicion of "the whites of his eyes."

"Ya-a-s, you know, but I enjoyed it—merely a bit of badinage from the college boys. I understood it, for I know how it is myself."

"When do you expect to return to England?"

"Late in April. I shall spend June in Paris and then go to Venice. No, this is not my last visit to America. I want to see your country in the summer and autumn."

A gentleman asked Mr. Wilde to explain the secret of the sunflower and lily craze. The lecturer said: "I regard those flowers as the most perfect models of design—the most naturally adapted for decorate [sic] art—the gaudy, leonine beauty of the one and the precious loveliness of the other giving to the artist his best ideas. Here in Utica you have art rooms. Cultivate them. You have young artists. Cheer them on in their race through the meadows."

A full report of Mr. Wilde's lecture would fill five columns of this paper. We present below a few sentences verbatim, in order to give those readers who did not hear him an idea of his style:

"And so with you; let there be no flower in your meadows that does not wreathe its tendrils around your pillows, no little leaf in your titan forests that does not lend its form to design, no curving spray of wild rose or briar that does not live forever in carven arch or window of marble, no bird in your air that is not giving the iridescent wonder of its color, the exquisite curves of its wings in flight, to make more precious the preciousness of simple adornment; for the voices that have their dwelling in sea and mountain are not the chosen music of liberty only. Other messages are there in the wonder of windswept heights and the majesty of silent deep—messages that, if you will listen to them, will give you the wonder of all new imagination, the treasure of all new beauty. We spend our days, each one of us, in looking for the secret of life. Well, the secret of life is art."

After the reception at Mr. Hutchinson's last evening, Mr. Wilde was entertained at the Utica Club.

This morning, at half-past ten, upon invitation of Messrs. Earll, Cooper and Latimore, Mr. Wilde visited the Household Art Rooms and met a large company of ladies and gentlemen. He wore a light velvet coat and other apparel perfectly harmonized and attuned to said velvet coat. After the members of the company had been introduced the poet inspected the features of the art rooms alternately praising and criticizing what he saw. The tapestry struck his fancy; the bust of Venus he did not like. The embroideries were pronounced superior, "but," (turning to Mr. Cooper) "don't let your young ladies paint landscapes on placques."

After half an hour's chat with the ladies, in which decorative art was discussed in all its length, breadth and border, Mr. Wilde shook hands with some, bowed comprehensively to the rest, donned his olive green overcoat, muffled his throat in a silken scarf of gradated wine color, put on his gloves and was driven to the depot. There he wrote his autograph and assured a friend that he should always remember with pleasure his visit to Utica.

Wilde is a brainy boy. Peculiar, but he makes his peculiarities profitable.

*We know nothing about the true identity of Earl Lind, except what he tells us about himself in his life story,* The Autobiography of an Androgyne *(1918) (see below, 334–38). He felt he was a woman trapped in a man's body (hence the Greek word for man-woman, androgyne). Though he purportedly wrote his book near the turn of the century, he was unable to locate a publisher for his frank "confessions" until the end of World War I, and even then only a medical press would print it. Lind appended the following essay to his own story; it is reprinted here not only for his analysis of Wilde (always in contrast to his own "case study"), but also because it shows that Wilde, who had died nearly two decades earlier, was still studied as a homosexual model by homosexuals themselves.*

# "The Case of Oscar Wilde" (1918)

Oscar Wilde presents a different phase of homosexuality from the author, that is, active pederasty. Apparently his was the active role *in paedicatio*[5] or *inter femora*.[6] According to Frank Harris, Wilde's confidant and the author of his best biography,[7] Wilde thus analyzes his penchant: "What is the food of passion but beauty, beauty alone, beauty always, and in beauty of form and vigor of life there is no comparison (with the female sex).[8] If you loved beauty as intensely as I do, you would feel as I feel. It is beauty which gives me joy, makes me drunk as with wine, blind with insatiable desire." "There are people in the world who cannot understand the deep affection that an artist can feel for a friend with a beautiful personality."

Like the author, Wilde was born and reared in the best environment and enjoyed unexcelled educational advantages. But as a boy and youth, he betrayed no feminine mental traits. Unlike the author, he was not feminesque [sic] physically. Further, while the author during youth and early "manhood" was notably small, Wilde grew to be one of the largest of men, six feet, two inches in height, and of stout build.

Apparently instinct did not become sufficiently powerful to cry for appeasement until he became a student at Oxford. While one of the leaders in scholarship and already a society favorite, it was nevertheless being whispered that he was a pederast. This was due to his openness, he not seeming to care if every one knew of his penchant, and not realizing that he was guilty of anything scandalous.

Having graduated from Oxford with the highest honors, Wilde took up his residence in London. Unlike the author, he was capable *cum femina*,[9] but did not marry until twenty-nine. Two sons resulted. Marriage and fatherhood are the two strongest arguments against him in any judgment on his pederasty.

Hardly another human being has at the age of thirty achieved such fame. In the family of the author, then a boy of ten, and living in a different country and 3,000 miles away, the name "Oscar Wilde" was a household term. Even every child of the village was as familiar with that name as with that of the man next door. This fame resulted from his being the idol of England's aristocracy, the greatest social light of the nineteenth century in any land, one of the most brilliant conversationalists that ever breathed, a poet of high rank, and the foremost English playwright of his generation.

But notwithstanding that during the late eighties and early nineties of the nineteenth century, Wilde was the most widely known and the most talked about man in London, he was so disdainful of the opinion of mankind as to visit regularly—not incognito, but under his own illustrious name—the leading *maison publique*[10] of London which catered exclusively to active pederasts. He here made the acquaintance of adolescents—little better than guttersnipes—some of whom he subsequently entertained in private rooms of London's foremost hostelry. He also had a habit of leaving his meek, long-suffering wife at home with the children, and taking up his residence in a furnished apartment, where he entertained his adolescent friends. Occasional visits would be paid his wife and children. Some of London's leaders of thought, although at the same time "men-about-town," have been known to exclaim at what they witnessed in the city's drinking palaces: "Is this the great Oscar Wilde who sits, chats, and drinks here with ragamuffins whom he has picked up off the street!"

Blackmail was looked upon as an everyday occurrence. As money both came and went easily, he never gave it a second thought.

Gradually stories of his doings spread throughout all grades of London society. The middle and lower classes soon came to hold his name in abomination, but comparatively few of the "upper crust"—with whom he exclusively associated apart from his nights with adolescent menials—held anything against him because of his almost unrivaled talents and delightful personality.

In 1895, at the age of forty-one, Wilde had reached the zenith of earthly glory. But the puritan element had naturally come to hold him in the greatest detestation. He was thoroughly pagan in thought and in his published works. Particularly was he thoroughly saturated with the writings and ideas of the ancient Greeks, with whom pederasty was common and open. Unlike the author, he had had no religious training, and when adult seems always to have turned the cold shoulder on the Church. Some of his writings were positively blasphemous. He would boast also that for him morality was non-existent—only the beautiful. While possibly irresponsible to a considerable degree for his pederasty, he was decidedly to be blamed for flaunting it in the face of everybody. On the whole, he was, because of his exalted position and his writings, the most pernicious influence on the 19th century on British morals. The puritan element were quick to take advantage of his arrest under the charge of being a "corrupter of youth," and jumped into the fray. The slums of London were combed in order to find witnesses.

From Harris's *Oscar Wilde and His Confessions* I quote Wilde's most striking defensive statement at his trial:

> The 'love' that dare not speak its name in this century is such a great affection of an older for a younger man as there was between David and Jonathan, such as Plato made the very base of his philosophy, and such as you find in the sonnets of Michael Angelo and Shakespeare—a deep spiritual affection that is as pure as it is perfect, and dictates great works of art like those of Shakespeare and Michael Angelo and those two letters of mine [evidence against him], such as they are, and which is in this century misunderstood—so misunderstood that, on account of it, I am placed where I am now [in the prisoner's dock]. It is beautiful; it is fine; it is the noblest form of affection. It is intellectual, and it repeatedly exists between an elder and younger man, when the elder man has intellect, and the younger man has all the joy, hope, and glamour of life. That it should be so the world does not understand. It mocks at it and sometimes puts one into the pillory for it.

Subsequently his confidant, Harris, asked in private: "There is another point against you which you have not touched on yet: Gill asked you what you had in common with those serving men and stable boys? You have not explained that."

"Difficult to explain, Frank, isn't it, without the truth?".... "How weary I am of the whole thing, of the same and the struggling and the hatred. To see those people coming into the box one after the other to witness against me makes me sick. ... Oh, it's terrible. I feel inclined to stretch out my hands and cry to them, 'Do what you will with me, in God's name, only do it quickly; cannot you see that I am worn out? If hatred gives you pleasure, indulge it.'"

In other conversations with Harris, Wilde justified his penchant, as narrated in the biography, as follows:

"There is no general rule of health; it is all personal, individual.... I only demand that freedom which I willingly concede to others. No one condemns another for preferring green to gold. Why should any taste be ostracized? Liking and disliking are not under our control. I want to choose the nourishment which suits *my* body and *my* soul."

"Each man ought to do what he likes, to develop as he will.... They punished me because I did not share their tastes. What an absurdity it all was! How dared they punish me for what is good in my eyes? ...."

"What you call vice, Frank, is not vice. ... It has been made a crime in recent times. ... They all damn the sins they have no mind to, and that's their morality. ... Why, even Bentham[11] refused to put what you call a vice in his penal code, and you yourself admitted that it should not be punished as a crime; for it carries no temptation with it. It may be a malady; but, if so, it appears only to attack the highest natures. ... The wit of man can find no argument which justifies its punishment. ... You admit you don't share the prejudice; you don't feel the horror, the instinctive loathing. Why? Because you are educated, Frank, because you know that the passion Socrates felt was not a low passion, because you know that Caesar's weakness, let us say, or the weakness of Michael Angelo, or of Shakespeare, is not despicable. If the desire is not a characteristic of the highest humanity, at least it is consistent with it. ... Suppose I like a food that is poison to other people, and yet quickens me; how dare they punish me for eating of it? ... It is all ignorant prejudice, Frank; the world is slowly growing more tolerant and one day men will be ashamed of their barbarous treatment of me, as they are now ashamed of the torturing of the Middle Ages."

Harris constitutes himself an apologist for his friend. He outlines a conversation in which he defended Wilde during the time of the latter's imprisonment. After demolishing the argument of a leading English journalist that "any one living a clean life is worth more than a writer of love songs or the maker of clever comedies—Mr. John Smith worth more than Shakespeare [who was a rake and very likely a psychical hermaphrodite]," Harris "pointed out that Wilde's offence was pathological and not criminal and would not be punished in a properly constituted state." Harris quoted further:

"You admit that we punish crime to prevent it spreading; wipe this sin off the state book and you would not increase the sinners by one: then why punish them?"

[Another guest of the journalist:] "Oi'd whip such sinners to death, so I would. Hangin's too good for them."

"You only punished lepers in the Middle Ages because you believed that leprosy was catching: this malady is not even catching."

"Faith, Oi'd punish it with extermination." ...

"You are very bitter: I'm not; you see, I have no sexual jealousy to inflame me."

Oscar Wilde deserved his fall—possibly not because he was a pederast, but because he flaunted his pederasty before the world, and because he was otherwise anti-ethical and anti-religious in the highest degree. After two years in prison, he never again set foot in the British Empire. His wife would never again even see him. He lost all ambition to put to use his extraordinary literary talents. For the rest of his life he made his home for the most part in Paris. Apparently he indulged his penchant more than ever. He remarked once that life would not be worth living if desire should die, as compared with the author's heartfelt wish that it might die in himself. He was constantly pursuing adolescents of the laboring class. He was known to call in to dine with him at a high-class restaurant a dirty, unkempt, but Adonis-faced gutter-snipe. He now acquired syphilis. The chase appeared to be the chief aim of his life, although he now distinguished himself also as an extreme gourmand, tippler, and sybarite in general, not to mention his habitually swindling his old friends out of money.

According to general belief, death came in 1900 at the age of forty-six, and was due to a general breakdown occasioned by gluttony, alcoholism, absinthism,[12] and syphilis. But strong reasons existed why he and his confidants should palm off his death upon the world. In 1918 it is rumored that he is still alive, at the age of sixty-four.

Wilde has given evidence of a slight approach toward feminine mentality. (1) He was unequalled in vanity. (2) During his twenties, he wore his hair in tufts several inches long and partially concealing his ears and coat-collar. (3) He was the most extreme esthete (extravagant feeder on beauty wherever it is to be found, like the author) the world has ever seen. Estheticism and homosexuality are often linked together. (4) At thirty-three he became editor of England's leading woman's magazine. (5) Harris speaks of his "extraordinary femininity and gentle weakness of his nature, and instead of condemning him as I have always condemned that form of sexual indulgence, I felt only pity for him and a desire to protect and help him." Harris further expresses Wilde's reaction to the prison atmosphere as essentially that of a "woman."

Wilde's case suggests an hypothesis: Homosexuality is due to innate abnormal participation in the mentality of the opposite sex. Whether an active pederast or a passive invert results, depends on the degree of feminization. If slight, the former results, who is also capable of heterosexual love and coitus—a psychical hermaphrodite, as was Wilde, who however had a far stronger leaning toward the homosexual than toward the heterosexual. If the degree is high—for example, almost entirely feminine psychically and even inducing feminesque anatomy—a passive invert results, as in the case of the author.

September, 1918.

## Notes

1  The Gilded Age is the period from the end of the Civil War (1861–65) to 1900. The term comes from the title of Mark Twain and Charles Dudley Warner's novel (1873), which characterized the era as one of increasing industrialization, and economic and political corruption.

2  Light bluish green or greenish blue (Greek).

3  Reginald Bunthorne was the name of the lily-carrying poet in Gilbert and Sullivan's operetta *Patience* (1881), a lampoon of the aesthetic movement.

4   Only a few days before, on 31 January, Wilde's Boston lecture had been notoriously interrupted by a coterie of Harvard students who had reserved seats together; they arrived late, and ostentatiously paraded to their seats, dressed in imitation of Wilde. Tipped in advance as to their stunt, Wilde himself that night wore conventional evening dress and so turned the tables on his mockers (Ellmann, 182–83).

5   Unnatural vice (Latin). Medical writing resorted to Latin terms to describe sexual activity considered too graphic even for professional readers. Lind's use of Latin mimics the case study style with which he is familiar, and which provides him with an "excuse" to publish his own story.

6   Between the thighs (Latin).

7   *Oscar Wilde, His Life and Confessions* (1916).

8   All brackets in this selection are original to the text.

9   Able to have sex with women (Latin).

10  Public house, inn, hostelry (French).

11  Jeremy Bentham (1748–1832), the founder of British utilitarianism, wrote his *Introduction to the Principles of Morals and Legislation* (1789) suggesting the idea that the greatest happiness of the greatest number should govern our judgment of every institution and action.

12  Absinthe is a strong herbal liqueur made with wormwood, illegal in many countries including the United States.

# PART SIX

# ARCADIA

*A writer of popular fiction, travel books, and poetry, Bayard Taylor frequently touched on homoerotic themes. A recurring subject was the fantasy of a mystical location, an Eden where human beings would be free to express their true feelings toward each other. Taylor found that Greece and the Near East were imaginatively open to a wider interpretation of love than the more puritanical United States. We see in the poetry below how he often encoded homosexuality in his depiction of these cultures. (The Romantic love of the exotic and faraway lands offered similar freedom to Herman Melville and Charles Warren Stoddard; see below, 93–103.)*

*Taylor's 1870 novel* Joseph and His Friend *now seems so direct in its depiction of same-sex love that it is surprising it did not raise more objections, even in an age that idolized romantic friendship.[1] Joseph and Philip will envisage an Arcadian valley where men can be free to express their love for one another—surprisingly this location is in California, rather than the Near East! Though the novel ends with a forced and prosaical marriage, this does not happen before Taylor has broken new ground in the American novel. The preface to this novel is significant: "To those who prefer quiet pictures of life to startling incidents, the attempt to illustrate the development of character to the mysteries of an elaborate plot, and the presentation of men and women in their mixed strength and weakness to the painting of wholly virtuous ideals and wholly evil examples: who are as interested in seeing moral and intellectual forces at work in a simple country community as on a more conspicuous plane of human action: who believe in the truth and tenderness of man's love for man, as of man's love for woman: who recognize the trouble which confused ideas of life and the lack of high and intelligent culture bring upon a great portion of our country population,—to all such, no explanation of this volume is necessary. Others will not read it."*

# FROM *POEMS OF THE ORIENT* (1855)

## To a Persian Boy, in the Bazaar at Smyrna

The gorgeous blossoms of that magic tree
Beneath whose shade I sat a thousand nights,
Breathed from their opening petals all delights
Embalmed in spice of Orient Poesy,
When first, young Persian, I beheld thine eyes,
And felt the wonder of the beauty grow
Within my brain, as some fair planet's glow

Deepens, and fills the summer evening skies.
From under thy dark lashes shone on me
The rich, voluptuous soul of Eastern land,
Impassioned, tender, calm, serenely sad—
Such as immortal Hafiz[2] felt when he
Sang by the fountain-streams of Rocnabad,[3]
Or in the bowers of blissful Samarcand.[4]

## A Paean to the Dawn

I.
The dusky sky fades into blue,
And bluer surges bind us;
The stars are glimmering faint and few,
The night is left behind us!
Turn not where sinks the sullen dark
Before the signs of warning,
But crowd the canvas on our bark
And sail to meet the morning.
Rejoice! Rejoice! The hues that fill
The orient, flush and lighten;
And over the blue Ionian hill
The Dawn begins to brighten!

II.
We leave the Night, that weighed so long
Upon the soul's endeavor,
For Morning, on these hills of Song,
Has made her home forever.
Hark to the sound of trump and lyre,
In the olive groves before us,
And the rhythmic beat, the pulse of fire,
Throb in the full-voiced chorus!
More than Memnonian grandeur speaks
In the triumph of the paean,
And all the glory of the Greeks
Breathes o'er the old Aegean.

III.
Here shall the ancient Dawn return,
That lit the earliest poet,
Whose very ashes in his urn
Would radiate glory through it—

The dawn of Life, when Life was Song,
And Song the life of Nature,
And the Singer stood amid the throng—
A God in every feature!
When Love was free, and free as air
The utterance of Passion,
And the heart in every fold lay bare,
Nor shamed its true expression.

IV.

Then perfect limb and perfect face
Surpassed our best ideal;
Unconscious Nature's law was grace—
The Beautiful was real.
For men acknowledged true desires,
And light as garlands wore them;
They were begot by vigorous sires,
And noble mothers bore them.
O, when the shapes of Art they planned
Were living forms of passion,
Impulse and Deed went hand in hand,
And Life was more than Fashion!

V.

The seeds of Song they scattered first
Flower in all later pages;
Their forms have woke the Artist's thirst
Through the succeeding ages:
But I will seek the fountain-head
Whence flowed their inspiration,
And lead the unshackled life they led,
Accordant with Creation.
The World's false life, that follows still,
Has ceased its chain to tighten,
And over the blue Ionian hill
I see the sunrise brighten!

## L'Envoi

Unto the Desert and the desert steed
Farewell! The journey is completed now:
Struck are the tents of Ishmael's wandering breed,
And I unwind the turban from my brow.

The sun has ceased to shine; the palms that bent,
Inebriate with light, have disappeared;
And naught is left me of the Orient
But the tanned bosom and the unshorn beard.
Yet from that life my blood a glow retains,
As the red sunshine in the ruby glows;
These songs are echoes of its fiercer strains—
Dreams, that recall its passion and repose.
I found, among those Children of the Sun,
The cipher of my nature—the release
Of baffled powers, which else had never won
That free fulfillment, whose reward is peace.
For not to any race or any clime
Is the completed sphere of life revealed;
He who would make his own that round sublime,
Must pitch his tent on many a distant field.
Upon his home a dawning luster beams,
But through the world he walks to open day,
Gathering from every land the prismal gleams,
Which, when united, form the perfect ray.
Go, therefore, Songs!—which in the East were born
And drew your nurture—from your sire's control:
Haply to wander through the West forlorn,
Or find a shelter in some Orient's soul.
And if the temper of our colder sky
Less warmth of passion and of speech demands,
They are the blossoms of my life—and I
Have ripened in the suns of many lands.

# From *The Poet's Journal* (1863)

## On the Headland

I sit on the lonely headland,
Where the sea-gulls come and go:
The sky is gray above me,
And the sea is gray below.
There is no fisherman's pinnace[5]
Homeward or outward bound;
I see no living creature
In the world's deserted round.
I pine for something human,

Man, woman, young or old,—
Something to meet and welcome,
Something to clasp and hold.
I have a mouth for kisses,
But there's no one to give or take,
I have a heart in my bosom
Beating for nobody's sake.
O warmth of love that is wasted!
Is there none to stretch a hand?
No other heart that hungers
In all the living land?
I could fondle the fisherman's baby,
And rock it into rest;
I could take the sunburnt sailor,
Like a brother, to my breast.
I could clasp the hand of any
Outcast of land or sea,
If the guilty palm but answered
The tenderness in me!
The sea might rise and drown me,—
Cliffs fall and crush my head,—
Were there one to love me, living,
Or weep to see me dead!

## FROM *JOSEPH AND HIS FRIEND* (1870)

[...] All at once his eye was attracted by a new face, three or four seats from his own. The stranger had shifted his position, so that he was no longer seen in profile. He was apparently a few years older than Joseph, but still bright with all the charm of early manhood. His fair complexion was bronzed from exposure, and his hands, graceful without being effeminate, were not those of the idle gentleman. His hair, golden in tint, thrust its short locks as it pleased about a smooth, frank forehead; the eyes were dark gray, and the mouth, partly hidden by a mustache, at once firm and full. He was moderately handsome, yet it was not of that which Joseph thought; he felt that there was more of developed character and a richer past history expressed in those features than in any other face there. He felt sure—and smiled at himself, notwithstanding, for the impression—that at least some of his own doubts and difficulties had found their solution in the stranger's nature. The more he studied the face, the more he was conscious of its attraction, and his instinct of reliance, though utterly without grounds, justified itself to his mind in some mysterious way.

It was not long before the unknown felt his gaze, and, turning slowly in his seat, answered it. Joseph dropped his eyes in some confusion, but not until he had caught the full, warm, intense expression of those that met them. He fancied that he read in them, in that momentary flash, what he had never before found in the eyes of strangers,—a simple, human interest, above curiosity and above mistrust. The usual reply to such a gaze is an unconscious defiance: the unknown nature is on its guard: but the look which seems to answer, "We are men, let us know each other!" is, alas! too rare in this world.

While Joseph was fighting the irresistible temptation to look again, there was a sudden thud of the car-wheels. Many of the passengers started from their seats, only to be thrown into them again by a quick succession of violent jolts. Joseph saw the stranger springing towards the bell-rope; then he and all others seemed to be whirling over each other; there was a crash, a horrible grinding and splintering sound, and the end of all was a shock, in which his consciousness left him before he could guess its violence.

After a while, out of some blank, haunted by a single lost, wandering sense of existence, he began to awaken slowly to life. Flames were still dancing in his eyeballs, and waters and whirlwinds roaring in his ears; but it was only a passive sensation, without the will to know more. Then he felt himself partly lifted and his head supported, and presently a soft warmth fell upon the region of his heart. There were noises all about him, but he did not listen to them; his effort to regain his consciousness fixed itself on that point alone, and grew stronger as the warmth calmed the confusion of his nerves.

"Dip this in water!" said a voice, and the hand (as he now knew it to be) was removed from his heart.

Something cold came over his forehead, and at the same time warm drops fell upon his cheek.

"Look out for yourself: your head is cut!" exclaimed another voice.

"Only a scratch. Take the handkerchief out of my pocket and tie it up; but first ask yon gentleman for his flask!"

Joseph opened his eyes, knew the face that bent over his, and then closed them again. Gentle and strong hands raised him, a flask was set to his lips, and he drank mechanically, but a full sense of life followed the draught. He looked wistfully in the stranger's face.

"Wait a moment," said the latter; "I must feel your bones before you try to move. Arms and legs all right,—impossible to tell about the ribs. There! now put your arm around my neck, and lean on me as much as you like, while I lift you."

Joseph did as he was bidden, but he was still weak and giddy, and after a few steps, they both sat down together upon a bank. The splintered car lay near them upside down; the passengers had been extricated from it, and were now busy in aiding the few who were injured. The train had stopped and was waiting on the track above. Some were very pale and grave, feeling that Death had touched without taking them; but the greater part were concerned only about the delay to the train.

"How did it happen?" asked Joseph: "where was I? how did you find me?"

"The usual story,—a broken rail," said the stranger. "I had just caught the rope when the car went over, and was swung off my feet so luckily that I somehow escaped the hardest shock. I don't think I lost my senses for a moment. When we came to the bottom you were lying just before me; I thought you dead until I felt your heart. It is a severe shock, but I hope nothing more."

"But you,—are you not badly hurt?"

The stranger pushed up the handkerchief which was tied around his head, felt his temple, and said: "It must have been one of the splinters; I know nothing about it. But there is no harm in a little blood-letting except"—he added, smiling—"except the spots on your face."

By this time the other injured passengers had been conveyed to the train; the whistle sounded a warning of departure.

"I think we can get up the embankment now," said the stranger. "You must let me take care of you still: I am traveling alone."

When they were seated side by side, and Joseph leaned his head back on the supporting arm, while the train moved away with them, he felt that a new power, a new support, had come to his life. The face upon which he looked was no longer strange; the hand which had rested on his heart was warm with kindred blood. Involuntarily he extended his own; it was taken and held, and the dark-gray, courageous eyes turned to him with a silent assurance which he felt needed no words.

"It is a rough introduction," he then said: "my name is Philip Held. I was on my way to Oakland Station; but if you are going farther—"

"Why, that is my station also!" Joseph exclaimed, giving his name in return.

"Then we should have probably met, sooner or later, in any case. I am bound for the forge and furnace at Coventry, which is for sale. If the company who employ me decide to buy it,—according to the report I shall make,— the works will be placed in my charge."

"It is but six miles from my farm," said Joseph, "and the road up the valley is the most beautiful in our neighborhood. I hope you can make a favorable report."

"It is only too much to my own interest to do so. I have been mining and geologizing in Nevada and the Rocky Mountains for three or four years, and long for a quiet, ordered life. It is a good omen that I have found a neighbor in advance of my settlement. I have often ridden fifty miles to meet a friend who cared for something else than horse-racing or *monte*,[6] and your six miles,—it is but a step!"

"How much you have seen!" said Joseph. "I know very little of the world. It must be easy for you to take your own place in life."

A shade passed over Philip Held's face. "It is only easy to a certain class of men," he replied,—"a class to which I should not care to belong. I begin to think that nothing is very valuable, the right to which a man don't earn,—except human love, and that seems to come by the grace of God."

"I am younger than you are,—not yet twenty-three," Joseph remarked. "You will find that I am very ignorant."

"And I am twenty-eight, and just beginning to get my eyes open, like a nine-days' kitten. If I had been frank enough to confess my ignorance, five years ago, as you do now, it would have been better for me. But don't let us measure ourselves or our experience against each other. That is one good thing we learn in Rocky Mountain life; there is no high or low, knowledge or ignorance, except what applies to the needs of men who come together. So there are needs which most men have, and go all their lives hungering for, because they expect them to be supplied in a particular form. There is something," Philip concluded, "deeper than that in human nature."

Joseph longed to open his heart to this man, every one of whose words struck home to something in himself. But the lassitude which the shock left behind gradually overcame him. He suffered his head to be drawn upon Philip Held's shoulder, and slept until the train reached Oakland Station. When the two got upon the platform, they found Dennis waiting for Joseph, with a light country vehicle. The news of the accident had reached the station, and his dismay was great when he saw the two bloody faces. A physician had already been summoned from the neighboring village, but they had little need of his services. A prescription of quiet and sedatives for Joseph, and a strip of plaster for his companion, were speedily furnished, and they set out together for the Asten place.

It is unnecessary to describe Rachel Miller's agitation when the party arrived; or the parting of the two men who had been so swiftly brought near to each other; or Philip Held's farther journey to the forge that evening. He resisted all entreaty to remain at the farm until morning, on the ground of an appointment made with the present proprietor of the forge. After his departure Joseph was sent to bed, where he remained for a day or two, very sore and a little feverish. He had plenty of time for thought,—not precisely of the kind which his aunt suspected, for out of pure, honest interest in his welfare, she took a step which proved to be of doubtful benefit. If he had not been so innocent,—if he had not been quite as unconscious of his inner nature as he was over-conscious of his external self,—he would have perceived that his thoughts dwelt much more on Philip Held than on Julia Blessing. His mind seemed to run through a swift, involuntary chain of reasoning, to account to himself for his feeling towards her, and her inevitable share in his future; but towards Philip his heart sprang with an instinct beyond his control. It was impossible to imagine that the latter also would not be shot, like a bright thread, through the web of his coming days. […]

# CHARLES WARREN STODDARD (1843–1909)

*Charles Warren Stoddard's exotic tales of the South Pacific,* South-Sea Idyls *(1873), often talk as much about his homosexual life as about palm trees. In an airy, campy style—which could easily be dismissed by chuckling readers as exaggeration—he describes his sexual escapades with willing native men. These escapades are so carefully couched in codes and puns and symbols that most— but not all—critics failed to spot the book's "other" meaning. Although fellow writers like Ambrose Bierce, William Dean Howells, and Bret Harte detected Stoddard's "difference" ("Such a nice girl," Mark Twain called him[7]), his public saw him as a new Melville or Bayard Taylor: a witty adventurer whose sarcasm lent quite a fresh tone to the ever-popular travel narrative. One wonders if these readers ever understood the "difference" in Stoddard's prose.*

## "PEARL HUNTING IN THE POMOTOUS" (1873)

The Great Western ducked in the heavy swell, shipping her regular deck-load of salt-water every six minutes. Now, the Great Western was nothing more nor less than a seventeen-ton schooner, two hours out from Tahiti. She was built like an old shoe, and shoveled in a head-sea as though it was her business.

It was something like sea life, wading along her submerged deck from morning till night, with a piece of raw junk in one hand and a briny biscuit in the other; we never *could* keep a fire in *that* galley, and as for hard tack, the sooner it got soaked through the sooner it was off our minds, for we knew to this complexion it must shortly come.

Two hours out from Tahiti we settled our course, wafting a theatrical kiss or two toward the gloriously green pyramid we were turning our backs on, as it slowly vanished in the blue desert of the sea.

A thousand palm-crowned and foam-girdled reefs spangled the ocean to the north and east of Tahiti. This train of lovely satellites is known as the Dangerous Archipelago, or, more commonly in that latitude, the Pomotou Islands. It's the very hot-bed of cocoanut-oil, pearls, half-famished Kanakas,[8] shells, and shipwrecks. The currents are rapid and variable; the winds short, sharp, and equally unreliable. If you would have adventure, the real article and plenty of it, make your will, bid farewell to home and friends, and embark for the Pomotous. I started on this principle, and repented knee-deep in the deck-breakers, as we butted our way through the billows, bound for one of the Pomotous on a pearl hunt.

Three days I sat in sackcloth and salt water. Three nights I swashed in my greasy bunk, like a solitary sardine in a box with the side knocked out. In my heart of hearts I prayed for deliverance: you see there is no backing out of a schooner, unless you crave death in fifty fathoms of phosphorescent liquor and a grave in a shark's maw. Therefore I prayed for more wind from the right quarter, for a sea like a boundless mill-pond; in short, for speedy deliverance on the easiest terms possible. Notwithstanding my prayers, we continued to bang away at the great waves that crooked their backs under us and hissed frightfully as they enveloped the Great Western with spray until the fourth night out, when the moon gladdened us and promised much while we held our breath in anxiety.

We were looking for land. We'd been looking for three hours, scarcely speaking all that time. It's a serious matter raising a Pomotou by moonlight.

"Land!" squeaked a weak voice about six feet above us. A lank fellow, with his legs corkscrewed around the shrouds, and his long neck stretched to windward, where it veered like a weather-cock in a nor'wester, chuckled as he sang out "Land!" and felt himself a little lower than Christopher Columbus thereafter. "Where away?" bellowed our chunky little captain, as important as if he were commanding a grown-up ship. "Two points on the weather-bow!" piped the lookout, with the voice of one soaring space, but unhappily choked in the last word by a sudden lurch of the schooner that brought him speedily to the deck, where he lost his identity and became a proper noun, second person, singular, for the rest of the cruise.

Now, "two points" is an indefinite term that embraces any obstacle ahead of anything; but the "weather-bow" has been the salvation of many a craft in her distress; so we gave three cheers for the "weather-bow," and proceeded to sweep the horizon with unwinking gaze. We could scarcely tell how near the land might lie; fancied we could already hear the roar of surf-beaten reefs, and every wave that reared before us seemed the rounded outline of an island. Of course we shortened sail, not knowing at what moment we might find ourselves close upon some low sea-garden nestling under the rim of breakers that fenced it in, and being morally averse to running it down without warning.

It was scarcely midnight; the moon was radiant; we were silently watching wrapped in the deep mystery that hung over the weather-bow.

The wind suddenly abated; it was as though it sifted through trees and came to us subdued with a whisper of fluttering leaves and a breath of spice. We knew what it meant, and our hearts leaped within us as over the bow loomed the wave-like outline of shadow that sank not again like the other waves, neither floated off cloud-like, but seemed to be bearing steadily down upon us—a great whale hungry for a modern Jonah.

What a night it was! We heard the howl of waters now; saw the palm-boughs glisten in the moonlight, and the glitter and the flash of foam that fringed the edges of the half-drowned islet.

It looked for all the world like a grove of cocoa-trees that had waded out of sight of land, and didn't know which way to turn next. This was the Ultima Thule of the Great Western's voyage, and she seemed to know it, for she behaved splendidly at last, laying off and on till morning in fine style, evidently as proud as a ship-of-the-line.

I went below and dozed, with the low roar of the reef quite audible: a fellow gets used to such dream-music, and sleeps well to its accompaniment.

At daybreak we began beating up against wind and tide, hoping to work into smooth water by sunrise, which we did easily enough, shaking hands all around over a cup of thick coffee and molasses as three fathoms of chain whizzed overboard after a tough little anchor that buried itself in a dim wilderness of corals and sea-grass.

Then and there I looked about me with delighted eyes. The Great Western rode at anchor in a shallow lake, whose crystal depths seemed never to have been agitated by any harsher breath than at that moment kissed without ruffling its surface. Around us swept an amphitheatre of hills, covered with a dense growth of tropical foliage and cushioned to the hem of the beach with thick sod of exquisite tint and freshness. The narrow rim of beach that sloped suddenly to the tideless margin of the lake was littered with numberless slender canoes drawn out of the water like so many fish, as though they would navigate themselves in their natural element, and they were, therefore, not to be trusted alone too near it. Around the shore, across the hills, and along the higher ridges waved innumerable cocoa-palms, planted like a legion of lances about the encampment of some barbaric prince.

As for the very blue sky and the very white scud that shot across it, they looked windy enough; moreover we could all hear the incoherent booming of the sea upon the reef that encircled our nest. But we forgot the wind and the waves in the inexpressible repose of that armful of tropical seclusion. It was a drop of water in a tuft of moss, on a very big scale; that's just what it was.

In a few moments, as with one impulse, the canoes took to water with a savage or two in each, all gravitating to the schooner, which was for the time being the head-centre of their local commerce; and for an hour or more we did a big business in the exchange of fish-hooks and fresh fruit.

The proportion of canoes at Motu Hilo (Crescent Island) to the natives of said fragment of Eden was as one to several; but the canoeless could not resist the superior attraction of a foreign invader, therefore the rest of the inhabitants went head-first into the lake, and struck out for the middle, where we peacefully swung at anchor. The place was sharky, but a heavy dirk full twenty inches tall was held between the teeth of the swimmers; and if the smoke-colored dorsal of any devil of a shark had dared to cut the placid surface of the water that morning, he would speedily have had more blades in him than a farrier's knife. A few vigorous strokes of the arms and legs in the neighborhood, a fatal lunge or two, a vermilion cloud in a sea churned to a cream, and a dance over the gaping corpse of some monster who has sucked human blood more than once, probably, does the business in that country.

It was a sensation for unaccustomed eyes, that inland sea covered, littered, I might say, with woolly heads, as though a cargo of cocoanuts had been thrown overboard in a stress of weather. They gathered about as thick as flies at a honey-pot, all talking, laughing, and spouting mouthfuls of water into the air like those impossible creatures that do that sort of thing by the half-dozen in all high-toned and classical fountains.

Out of this amphibious mob one gigantic youth, big enough to eat half our ship's crew, threw up an arm like Jove's, clinched the deck-rail with lithe fingers, and took a rest, swinging there with the utmost satisfaction. I asked him aboard, but he scorned to forsake his natural element; water *is* as natural as air to those natives. Probably he would have suffered financially had he attempted boarding us, for his thick black hair was netted with a kind of spacious nest and filled with eggs on sale. It was quite astonishing to see the ease with which he navigated under his heavy deck-load.

This colossal youth having observed that I was an amateur humanitarian, virtue received its instant reward (which it doesn't in all climates), for he at once offered me three of his eggs in a very winning and patronizing manner.

I took the eggs because I like eggs, and then I was anxious to get his head above water if possible; therefore I unhesitatingly took the eggs, offering him in return a fish-hook, a tenpenny nail, and a dilapidated key-ring.

These tempting *curios* he spurned, at the same moment reaching me another handful of eggs. His generosity both pleased and alarmed me. I saw with joy that his chin was quite out of water in consequence of his charity, even when he dropped back into the sea, floating for a few moments so as to let the blood circulate in his arm again; but whether this was his magnanimous gift, or merely a trap to involve me in hopeless debt, I was quite at a loss to know, and I paused with my hands full of eggs, saying to myself, There is an end to fish-hooks in the South Pacific and dilapidated key-rings are not my staple product!

In the midst of my alarm he began making vows of eternal friendship. This was by no means disagreeable to me. He was big enough to whip any two of his fellows, and one likes to be on the best side of the stronger party in a strange land.

I reciprocated!

I leaned over the stern-rail of the Great Western in the attitude of Juliet in the balcony scene, assuring that egg-boy that my heart was his if he was willing to take it at second-hand.

He liked my sentiments, and proposed touching noses at once (a barbarous greeting still observed in the most civilized countries with even greater license, since with Christians it is allowable to touch mouths).

We touched noses, though I was in danger of sliding headlong into the sea.

After this ceremonial he consented to board the Great Western, which having accomplished with my help, he deposited his eggs at my feet, offered me his nose once more, and communicated to me his name, asking in the same breath for mine.

He was known as Hua Manu, or Bird's Egg. Every native in the South Sea gets named by accident. I knew a fellow whose name was "Cock-eye"; he was a standing advertisement of his physical deformity. A fellow that knew me rejoiced in the singular cognomen of "Thrown-from-a-horse." Fortunately he doesn't spell it with so many letters in his tongue. His christening happened in this wise: A bosom friend of his mother was thrown from a horse and killed the day of his birth. Therefore the bereaved mother reared that child, an animated memorial, who in after years clove to me, and was as jolly as though his earthly mission wasn't simply to keep green the memory of his mother's bosom friend sailing through the air with a dislocated neck.

I turned to my new-found friend. "Hua Manu," said I, "for my sake you have made a bird's-nest of your back hair. You have freely given me your young affection and your eggs. Receive the sincere thanks of yours truly, together with these fish-hooks, these tenpenny nails, this key-ring." Hua Manu smiled and accepted, burying the fish-hooks in his matted forelock, and inserting a tenpenny nail and a key-ring in either ear, thereby making himself the envy of the entire population of Motu Hilo, and feeling himself as grand as the best chief in the archipelago.

So we sat together on the deck of the Great Western, quite dry for a wonder, exchanging sheep's-eyes and confidences, mutually happy in each other's society. Meanwhile the captain was arranging his plans for an immediate purchase of such pearls as he might find in possession of the natives, and for a fresh search for pearl oysters at the earliest possible hour. There were no pearls on hand. What are pearls to a man who has as many wives, children, and cocoanuts as he can dispose of? Pearls are small and colorless. Give him a handful of gorgeous glass beads, a stick of sealing-wax, or some spotted beans, and keep your pale sea-tears, milky and frozen and apt to grow sickly yellow and die if they are not cared for.

Motu Hilo is independent. No man has squatted there to levy tax or toll. We were each one of us privileged to hunt for pearls and keep our stores separate. I said to Hua Manu, "Let's invest in a canoe, explore the lagoon for fresh oyster-beds, and fill innumerable cocoanut shells with these little white seeds. It will be both pleasant and profitable, particularly for me." We were scarcely five minutes bargaining for our outfit, and we embarked at once, having agreed to return in a couple of days for news concerning the success of the Great Western and her probable date of sailing.

Seizing a paddle, Hua Manu propelled our canoe with incredible rapidity out of the noisy fleet in the centre of the lake, toward a green point that bounded it, one of the horns of the crescent. He knew a spot where the oyster yawned in profusion, a secret cave for shelter, a forest garden of fruits, a never-failing spring, etc. Thither we would fly and domesticate ourselves. The long, curved point of land soon hid the inner waters from view. We rose and sank on the swell between the great reef and the outer rim of the island, while the sun glowed fiercely overhead and the reef howled in our ears. Still on we skimmed, the water hissing along the smooth sides of the canoe, that trembled at every fierce stroke of Hua Manu's industrious paddle. No chart, no compass, no rudder, no exchange of references, no letter of introduction, yet I trusted that wild Hercules who was hurrying me away, I knew not whither, with an earnestness that forced the sweat from his naked body in living streams.

At last we turned our prow and shot through a low arch in a cliff, so low we both ducked our heads instinctively, letting the vines and parasites trail over our shoulders and down our backs.

It was a dark passage into an inner cave lit from below—a cave filled with an eternal and sunless twilight that was very soothing to our eyes as we came in from the glare of sea and sky.

"Look!" said Hua Manu. Overhead rose a compressed dome of earth, a thick matting of roots, coil within coil. At the side innumerable ledges, shelves, and seams lined with nests, and never a nest without its egg, often two or more together. Below us, in two fathoms of crystal, sunlit and luminous bowers of coral, and many an oyster asleep with its mouth open, and many a prismatic fish poising itself with palpitating gills, and gauzy fins fanning the water incessantly.

"Hua Manu!" I exclaimed in rapture, "permit me to congratulate you. In you I behold a regular South Sea Monte Cristo,[9] and no less magnificent title can do you justice." Thereat Hua Manu laughed immoderately, which laugh having run out we both sat in our canoe and silently sucked eggs for some moments.

A canoe-length from where we floated, a clear rill stole noiselessly from above, mingling its sweet waters with the sea; on the roof of our cavern fruits flourished, and we were wholly satisfied. After such a lunch as ours it behooved us to cease idling and dive for pearls. So Hua Manu knotted his long hair tightly about his forehead, cautiously transferred himself from the canoe to the water, floated a moment, inhaling a wonderfully long breath, and plunged under. How he struggled to get down to the gaping oysters, literally climbing down head first! I saw his dark form wrestling with the elements that strove to force him back to the surface, crowding him out into the air again. He seized one of the shells, but it shut immediately, and he tugged and jerked and wrenched at it like a young demon till it gave way, when he struck out and up for the air. All this seemed an age to me. I took full twenty breaths while he was down. Reaching the canoe, he dropped the great, ugly-looking thing into it, and hung over the out-rigger gasping for breath like a man half hanged. He was pale about the mouth, his eyes were suffused with blood, blood oozed from his ears and nostrils; his limbs, gashed with the sharp corals, bled also. The veins of his forehead looked ready to burst, and as he tightened the cords of hair across them it seemed his only salvation.

I urged him to desist, seeing his condition and fearing a repetition of his first experience; but he would go once more; perhaps there was no pearl in that shell; he wanted to get me a pearl. He sank again and renewed his efforts at the bottom of the sea. I scarcely dared to count the minutes now, nor the bubbles that came up to me like little balloons with a death-message in each. Suppose he were to send his last breath in one of those transparent globes, and I look down and see his body snared in the antlers of coral, stained with his blood? Well, he came up all right, and I postponed the rest of my emotion for a later experience.

Some divers remain three minutes under water, but two or three descents are as many as they can make in a day. The ravages of such a life are something frightful.

No more pearl-hunting after the second dive that day; nor the next, because we went out into the air for a stroll on shore to gather fruit and stretch our legs. There was a high wind and a heavy sea that looked threatening enough, and we were glad to return after an hour's tramp. The next day was darker, and the next after that, when a gale came down upon us that seemed likely to swamp Motu Hilo. A swell rolled over the windward reef and made our quarters in the grotto by no means safe or agreeable. It was advisable for us to think of embarking upon that tempestuous sea, or get brained against the roof of our retreat.

Hua Manu looked troubled, and my heart sank. I wished the pearl oysters at the bottom of the sea, the Great Western back at Tahiti, and I loafing under the green groves of Papeete, never more to be deluded abroad.

I observed no visible changes in the weather after I had been wishing for an hour and a half. The swell rather increased; our frail canoe was tossed from side to side in imminent danger of upsetting.

Now and then a heavy roller entirely filled the mouth of our cavern, quite blinding us with spray; having spent its fury it subsided with a concussion that nearly deafened us, and dragged us with fearful velocity toward the narrow mouth of the cave, where we saved ourselves from being swept into the sea by grasping the roots overhead and within reach.

"Could I swim?" asked Hua Manu. Alas, no! That we must seek new shelter at any risk was but too evident. "Let us go on the next wave," said Hua, as he seized a large shell and began clearing the canoe of the water that had accumulated. Then he bound his long hair in a knot to keep it from his eyes, and gave me some hasty directions as to my deportment in the emergency.

The great wave came. We were again momentarily corked up in an air-tight compartment. I wonder the roof was not burst open with the intense pressure that nearly forced the eyes out of my head and made me faint and giddy. Recovering from the shock, with a cry of warning from Hua, and a prayer scarcely articulated, we shot like a bomb from a mortar into the very teeth of a frightful gale.

Nothing more was said, nothing seen. The air was black with flying spray, the roar of the elements more awful than anything I had ever heard before. Sheets of water swept over us with such velocity that they hummed like circular saws in motion.

We were crouched as low as possible in the canoe, yet now and then one of these, the very *blade* of the wave, struck us on the head or shoulders, cutting us like knives. I could scarcely distinguish Hua's outline, the spray was so dense, and as for him, what could he do? Nothing, indeed, but send up a sort of death-wail, a few notes of which tinkled in my ear from time to time, assuring me how utterly without hope we were.

One of those big rollers must have lifted us clean over the reef, for we crossed it and were blown into the open sea, where the canoe spun for a second in the trough of the waves, and was cut into slivers by an avalanche of water that carried us all down into the depths.

I suppose I filled at once, but came up in spite of it (almost everyone has that privilege), when I was clutched by Hua Manu and made fast to his utilitarian back hair. I had the usual round of experiences allotted to all half-drowned people: a panoramic view of my poor life crammed with sin and sorrow and regret; a complete biography written and read through inside of ten seconds. I was half strangled, call it two-thirds, for that comes nearer the truth; heard the water singing in my ears, which was *not* sweeter than symphonies, nor beguiling, nor in the least agreeable. I deny it! In the face of every corpse that ever was drowned I emphatically deny it!

Hua had nearly stripped me with one or two tugs at my thin clothing, because he didn't think that worth towing off to some other island, and he was willing to float me for a day or two, and run the risk of saving me.

When I began to realize anything, I congratulated myself that the gale was over. The sky was clear, the white caps scarce, but the swell still sufficient to make me dizzy as we climbed one big, green hill, and slid off the top of it into a deep and bubbling abyss.

I found Hua leisurely feeling his way through the water, perfectly self-possessed and apparently unconscious that he had a deck passenger nearly as big as himself. My hands were twisted into his hair in such a way that I could rest my chin upon my arms, and thus easily keep my mouth above water most of the time.

My emotions were peculiar. I wasn't accustomed to traveling in that fashion. I knew it had been done before. Even there I thought with infinite satisfaction of the Hawaiian woman who swam for forty hours in such a sea, with an aged and helpless husband upon her back. Reaching land at last she tenderly drew her burden to shore and found him—dead! The fact is historical, and but one of several equally marvelous.

We floated on and on, cheering each other hour after hour; the wind continuing, the sea falling, and anon night coming like an ill omen—night, that buried us alive in darkness and despair.

I think I must have dozed, or fainted, or died several times during the night, for it began to grow light long before I dared to look for it, and then came sunrise—a sort of intermittent sunrise that gilded Hua's shoulder whenever we got on the top of a high wave, and went out again as soon as we settled into the hollows.

Hua Manu's eyes were much better than mine; he seemed to see with all his five senses, and the five told him that *there was land not far off!* I wouldn't believe him; I think I was excusable for questioning his infallibility then and there. The minute he cried out "Land!" I gave up and went to sleep, or to death, for I thought he was daft, and it was a discouraging business, and I wished I could die for good. Hua Manu, what a good egg you were, though it's the bad that usually keep atop of the water, they tell me!


Hua Manu was right. He walked out of the sea an hour later and stood on a mound of coarse sand in the middle of the ocean, with my miserable, waterlogged body lying in a heap at his feet.

The place was as smooth and shiny and desolate as anybody's bald head. That's a nice spot to be merry in, isn't it? Yet he tried to make me open my eyes and be glad.

He said he knew the Great Western would be coming down that way shortly; she'd pick us off the shoal, and water and feed us.

Perhaps she might! meantime we hungered and thirsted as many a poor castaway had before us. That was a good hour for Christian fortitude: beached in the middle of the ocean; shelterless under a sun that blistered Hua's tough skin; eyes blinded with the glare of sun and sea; the sand glowing like brass and burning into flesh already irritated with salt water; a tongue of leather cleaving to the roof of the mouth, and no food within reach, nor so much as a drop of fresh water for Christ's sake!

Down went my face into the burning sand that made the very air *hop* above it.... Another night, cool and grateful; a bird or two flapped wearily overhead, looking like spirits in the moonlight. Hua scanned earnestly our narrow horizon, noting every inflection in the voices of the wind and waves—voices audible to him, but worse than dumb to me—mocking monotones reiterated through an agonizing eternity.

A wise monitor was Hua Manu, shaming me to silence in our cursed banishment. Toward the morning after our arrival at the shoal, an owl fluttered out of the sky and fell at our feet quite exhausted. It might have been blown from Motu Hilo, and seemed ominous of something, I scarcely knew what. When it had recovered from its fatigue, it sat regarding us curiously. I wanted to wring its short, thick neck, and eat it, feathers and all. Hua objected; there was a superstition that gave that bland bird its life. It might continue to ogle us with one eye as long as it liked. How the lopsided thing smirked! how that stupid owl-face, like a rosette with three buttons in it, haunted me! It was enough to craze anyone; and, having duly cursed him and his race, I went stark mad and hoped I was dying forever....

There are plenty of stars in this narrative. Stars, and plenty of them, cannot account for the oblivious intervals, suspended animation, or whatever it was, that came to my relief from time to time. I cannot account for them myself. Perhaps Hua Manu might; he seemed always awake, always on the lookout, and ever so patient and faithful. A dream came to me after that owl had stared me into stone—a dream of an island in a sea of glass; soft ripples lapping on the silver shores; sweet airs sighing in a starlit grove; someone gathering me in his arms, hugging me close with infinite tenderness; I was consumed with thirst, speechless with hunger; like an infant I lay in the embrace of my deliverer, who moistened my parched lips and burning throat with delicious and copious draughts. It was an elixir of life; I drank health and strength in every drop; sweeter than mother's milk flowed the warm tide unchecked, till I was satisfied and sank into a deep and dreamless sleep....

The Great Western was plunging in her old style, and I swashed in my bunk as of yore. The captain sat by me with a bottle in his hand and anxiety in his countenance.

"Where are we?" I asked.

"Two hours out from Tahiti, inward bound."

"How! What! When!" etc.; and my mind ran up and down the record of the last fortnight, finding many blots and some blanks.

"As soon as I got into my right mind I could hear all about it"; and the captain shook his bottle, and held on to the side of my bunk to save himself from total wreck in the lee-corners of the cabin.

"Why, wasn't I right-minded? I could tell a hawk from a hernshaw; and, speaking of hawks, where was that cursed owl?"

The captain concluded I was bettering, and put the physic into the locker, so as to give his whole attention to keeping right side up. Well, this is how it happened, as I afterward learned: The Great Western suffered somewhat from the gale at Motu Hilo, though she was comparatively sheltered in that inner sea. Having repaired, and given me up as a deserter, she sailed for Tahiti. The first day out, in a light breeze, they all saw a man apparently wading up to his middle in the sea. The fellow hailed the Great Western, but as she could hardly stand up against the rapid current in so light a wind, the captain let her drift past the man in the sea, who suddenly disappeared. A consultation of officers followed. Evidently someone was cast away and ought to be looked after; resolved to beat up to the rock, big turtle, or whatever it might be that kept that fellow afloat, provided the wind freshened sufficiently; wind immediately freshened; Great Western put about and made for the spot where Hua Manu had been seen hailing the schooner. But when that schooner passed he threw himself upon the sand beside me and gave up hoping at last, and was seen no more.

What did he then? I must have asked for drink. He gave it me from an artery in his wrist, severed by the finest teeth you ever saw. That's what saved me. On came the little schooner, beating up against the wind and tide, while I had my lips sealed to that fountain of life.

The skipper kept banging away with an old blunderbuss that had been left over in his bargains with the savages, and one of these explosions caught the ears of Hua. He tore my lips from his wrist, staggered to his feet, and found help close at hand. Too late they gathered us up out of the deep and strove to renew our strength. They transported us to the little cabin of the schooner, Hua Manu, myself, and that mincing owl, and swung off into the old course. Probably the Great Western never did better sailing since she came from the stocks than that hour or two of beating that brought her up to the shoal. She seemed to be emulating it in the home run, for we went bellowing through the sea in a stiff breeze and the usual flood tide on deck.

I lived to tell the tale. I should think it mighty mean of me not to live after such a sacrifice. Hua Manu sank rapidly. I must have nearly drained his veins, but I don't believe he regretted it. The captain said when he was dying, his faithful eyes were fixed on me. Unconsciously I moved a little; he smiled, and the soul went out of him in that smile, perfectly satisfied. At that moment the owl fled from the cabin, passed through the hatchway, and disappeared.

Hua Manu lay on the deck, stretched under a sail, while I heard this. I wondered if a whole cargo of pearls could make me indifferent to his loss. I wondered if there were many truer and braver than he in Christian lands. They call him a heathen. It *was* heathenish to offer up his life vicariously. He might have taken mine so easily, and perhaps have breasted the waves back to his own people, and been fêted and sung of as the hero he truly was.

Well, if he is a heathen, out of my heart I would make a parable, its rubric bright with his sacrificial blood, its theme this glowing text: "Greater love hath no man than this, that a man lay down his life for a friend."

*Born in New York City to a wealthy family, Henry James was a major figure on the American literary scene of his age, the author of many novels, short stories, plays, and criticism of such high quality that he was known as "The Master" by the turn of the century. His talent for creating intricately observed psychological portraits are evident in such works as "Daisy Miller" (1879),* The Portrait of a Lady *(1881), and* The Ambassadors *(1903). In his later years, James assembled the definitive "New York Edition" of his fiction, where he provided detailed prefaces to his works. It is interesting, though, that for this tale he is curiously reticent: "There remains 'The Great Good Place' (1900)—to the spirit of which, however, it strikes me, any gloss or comment would be a tactless challenge. It embodies a calculated effect, and to plunge into it, I find, even for a beguiled glance—a course I indeed recommend—is to have left all else outside. There then my indications must wait." His silence is a challenge—and an invitation—to read this work without his guidance, and in a different light. The "Arcadia" James imagines for himself has no women in it (indeed, the character of Dane seeks to escape them); its reason for existence is the escape from society's demands; its centerpiece is a library; and its mode of entry is the touch of a young acolyte's hand on his knee. Certainly the story can be deconstructed in many ways, but the sense of the true nature of that fraternity of like-minded men grows stronger with each reading.*

# "THE GREAT GOOD PLACE" (1900, REV. 1909)

## I

George Dane had opened his eyes to a bright new day, the face of nature well washed by last night's downpour and shining as with high spirits, good resolutions, lively intentions—the great glare of recommencement in short fixed in his patch of sky. He had sat up late to finish work—arrears overwhelming, then at last had gone to bed with the pile but little reduced. He was now to return to it after the pause of the night; but he could only look at it, for the time, over the bristling hedge of letters planted by the early postman an hour before and already, on the customary table by the chimney-piece, formally rounded and squared by his systematic servant. It was something too merciless, the domestic perfection of Brown. There were newspapers on another table, ranged with the same rigour of custom, newspapers too many—what could any creature want of so much news?—and each with its hand on the neck of the other, so that the row of their bodiless heads was like a series of decapitations. Other journals, other periodicals of every sort, folded and in wrappers, made a huddled mound that had been growing for several days and of which he had been wearily, helplessly aware. There were new books, also in wrappers as well as disenveloped and dropped again—books from publishers, books from authors, books from friends, books from enemies, books from his own bookseller, who took, it sometimes struck him, inconceivable things for granted. He touched nothing, approached nothing, only turned a heavy eye over the work, as it were, of the night—the fact, in his high wide-windowed room, where duty shed its hard light into every corner, of the still unashamed admonitions. It was the old rising tide, and it rose and rose even under a minute's watching. It had been up to his shoulders last night—it was up to his chin now.

Nothing had *gone*, had passed on while he slept—everything had stayed; nothing, that he could yet feel, had died—so naturally, one would have thought; many things on the contrary had been born. To let them alone, these things, the new things, let them utterly alone and see if that, by chance, wouldn't somehow prove the best way to deal with them: this fancy brushed his face for a moment as a possible solution, just giving it, as so often before, a cool wave of air. Then he knew again as well as ever that leaving was difficult, leaving impossible—that the only remedy, the true soft effacing sponge, would be to BE left, to be forgotten. There was no footing on which a man who had ever liked life—liked it at any rate as *he* had—could now escape it. He must reap as he had sown. It was a thing of meshes; he had simply gone to sleep under the net and had simply waked up there. The net was too fine; the cords crossed each other at spots too near together, making at each a little tight hard knot that tired fingers were this morning too limp and too tender to touch. Our poor friend's touched nothing—only stole significantly into his pockets as he wandered over to the window and faintly gasped at the energy of nature. What was most overwhelming was that she herself was so ready. She had soothed him rather, the night before, in the small hours by the lamp. From behind the drawn curtain of his study the rain had been audible and in a manner merciful; washing the window in a steady flood, it had seemed the right thing, the retarding interrupting thing, the thing that, if it would only last, might clear the ground by floating out to a boundless sea the innumerable objects among which his feet stumbled and strayed. He had positively laid down his pen as on a sense of friendly pressure from it. The kind full swish had been on the glass when he turned out his lamp; he had left his phrase unfinished and his papers lying quite as for the flood to bear them away in its rush. But there still on the table were the bare bones of the sentence—and not all of those; the single thing borne away and that he could never recover was the missing half that might have paired with it and begotten a figure.

Yet he could at last only turn back from the window; the world was everywhere, without and within, and the great staring egotism of its health and strength wasn't to be trusted for tact or delicacy. He faced about precisely to meet his servant and the absurd solemnity of two telegrams on a tray. Brown ought to have kicked them into the room—then he himself might have kicked them out.

"And you told me to remind you, sir—"

George Dane was at last angry. "Remind me of nothing!"

"But you insisted, sir, that I was to insist!"

He turned away in despair, using a pathetic quaver at absurd variance with his words: "If you insist, Brown, I'll kill you!" He found himself anew at the window, whence, looking down from his fourth floor, he could see the vast neighbourhood, under the trumpet-blare of the sky, beginning to rush about. There was a silence, but he knew Brown hadn't left him—knew exactly how straight and serious and stupid and faithful he stood there. After a minute he heard him again.

"It's only because, sir, you know, sir, you can't remember—"

At this Dane did flash round; it was more than at such a moment he could bear. "Can't remember, Brown? I can't forget. That's what's the matter with me."

Brown looked at him with the advantage of eighteen years of consistency. "I'm afraid you're not well, sir."

Brown's master thought. "It's a shocking thing to say, but I wish to heaven I weren't! It would be perhaps an excuse."

Brown's blankness spread like the desert. "To put them off?"

"Ah!" The sound was a groan; the plural pronoun, *any* pronoun, so mistimed. "Who is it?"

"Those ladies you spoke of—to luncheon."

"Oh!" The poor man dropped into the nearest chair and stared a while at the carpet. It was very complicated.

"How many will there be, sir?" Brown asked.

"Fifty!"

"Fifty, sir?"

Our friend, from his chair, looked vaguely about; under his hand were the telegrams, still unopened, one of which he now tore asunder. "'Do hope you sweetly won't mind, to-day, 1.30, my bringing poor dear Lady Mullet, who's so awfully bent,'" he read to his companion.

His companion weighed it. "How many does *she* make, sir?"

"Poor dear Lady Mullet? I haven't the least idea."

"Is she—a—deformed, sir?" Brown enquired, as if in this case she might make more.

His master wondered, then saw he figured some personal curvature. "No; she's only bent on coming!" Dane opened the other telegram and again read out: "'So sorry it's at eleventh hour impossible, and count on you here, as very greatest favour, at two sharp instead.'"

"How many does *that* make?" Brown imperturbably continued.

Dane crumpled up the two missives and walked with them to the waste-paper basket, into which he thoughtfully dropped them. "I can't say. You must do it all yourself. I shan't be there."

It was only on this that Brown showed an expression. "You'll go instead—"

"I'll go instead!" Dane raved.

Brown, however, had had occasion to show before that *he* would never desert their post. "Isn't that rather sacrificing the three?" Between respect and reproach he paused.

"*Are* there three?"

"I lay for four in all."

His master had at any rate caught his thought. "Sacrificing the three to the one, you mean? Oh I'm not going to *her!*"

Brown's famous "thoroughness"—his great virtue—had never been so dreadful. "Then where *are* you going?"

Dane sat down to his table and stared at his ragged phrase. "'*There* is a happy land—far far away!'" He chanted it like a sick child and knew that for a minute Brown never moved. During this minute he felt between his shoulders the gimlet of criticism.

"Are you quite sure you're all right?"

"It's my certainty that overwhelms me, Brown. Look about you and judge. Could anything be more 'right,' in the view of the envious world, than everything that surrounds us here: that immense array of letters, notes, circulars; that pile of printers' proofs, magazines and books; these perpetual telegrams, these impending guests, this retarded, unfinished and interminable work? What could a man want more?"

"Do you mean there's too much, sir?"—Brown had sometimes these flashes.

"There's too much. There's too much. But *you* can't help it, Brown."

"No, sir," Brown assented. "Can't *you?*"

"I'm thinking—I must see. There are hours—!" Yes, there were hours, and this was one of them: he jerked himself up for another turn in his labyrinth, but still not touching, not even again meeting, his admonisher's eye. If he was a genius for any one he was a genius for Brown; but it was terrible what that meant, being a genius for Brown. There had been times when he had done full justice to the way it kept him up; now, however, it was almost the worst of the avalanche. "Don't trouble about me," he went on insincerely and looking askance through his window again at the bright and beautiful world. "Perhaps it will rain—that MAY not be over. I do love the rain," he weakly pursued. "Perhaps, better still, it will snow."

Brown now had indeed a perceptible expression, and the expression was of fear. "Snow, sir—the end of May?" Without pressing this point he looked at his watch. "You'll feel better when you've had breakfast."

"I dare say," said Dane, whom breakfast struck in fact as a pleasant alternative to opening letters. "I'll come in immediately."

"But without waiting—?"

"Waiting for what?"

Brown at last, under his apprehension, had his first lapse from logic, which he betrayed by hesitating in the evident hope his companion might by a flash of remembrance relieve him of an invidious duty. But the only flashes now were the good man's own. "You say you can't forget, sir; but you do forget—"

"Is it anything very horrible?" Dane broke in.

Brown hung fire. "Only the gentleman you told me you had asked—"

Dane again took him up; horrible or not it came back—indeed its mere coming back classed it. "To breakfast to-day? It WAS to-day; I see." It came back, yes, came back; the appointment with the young man—he supposed him young—whose letter, the letter about—what was it?—had struck him. "Yes, yes; wait, wait."

"Perhaps he'll do you good, sir," Brown suggested.

"Sure to—sure to. All right!" Whatever he might do he would at least prevent some other doing: that was present to our friend as, on the vibration of the electric bell at the door of the flat, Brown moved away. Two things in the short interval that followed were present to Dane: his having utterly forgotten the connexion, the whence, whither and why of his guest; and his continued disposition not to touch—no, not with the finger. Ah if he might *never* again touch! All the unbroken seals and neglected appeals lay there while, for a pause he couldn't measure, he stood before the chimney-piece with his hands still in his pockets. He heard a brief exchange of words in the hall, but never afterwards recovered the time taken by Brown to reappear, to precede and announce another person—a person whose name somehow failed to reach Dane's ear. Brown went off again to serve breakfast, leaving host and guest confronted. The duration of this first stage also, later on, defied measurement; but that little mattered, for in the train of what happened came promptly the second, the third, the fourth, the rich succession of the others. Yet what happened was but that Dane took his hand from his pocket, held it straight out and felt it taken. Thus indeed, if he had wanted never again to touch, it was already done.

## II

He might have been a week in the place—the scene of his new consciousness—before he spoke at all. The occasion of it then was that one of the quiet figures he had been idly watching drew at last nearer and showed him a face that was the highest expression—to his pleased but as yet slightly confused perception—of the general charm. What *was* the general charm? He couldn't, for that matter, easily have phrased it; it was such an abyss of negatives, such an absence of positives and of everything. The oddity was that after a minute he was struck as by the reflexion of his own very image in this first converser seated with him, on the easy bench, under the high clear portico and above the wide far-reaching garden, where the things that most showed in the greenness were the surface of still water and the white note of old statues. The absence of everything was, in the aspect of the Brother who had thus informally joined him—a man of his own age, tired distinguished modest kind—really, as he could soon see, but the absence of what he didn't want. He didn't want, for the time, anything but just to *be* there, to steep in the bath. He was in the bath yet, the broad deep bath of stillness. They sat in it together now with the water up to their chins. He hadn't had to talk, he hadn't had to think, he had scarce even had to feel. He had been sunk that way before, sunk—when and where?—in another flood; only a flood of rushing waters in which bumping and gasping were all. *This* was a current so slow and so tepid that one floated practically without motion and without chill. The break of silence was not immediate, though Dane seemed indeed to feel it begin before a sound passed. It could pass quite sufficiently without words that he and his mate were Brothers, and what that meant.

He wondered, but with no want of ease—for want of ease was impossible—if his friend found in *him* the same likeness, the proof of peace, the gage of what the place could do. The long afternoon crept to its end; the shadows fell further and the sky glowed deeper; but nothing changed—nothing *could* change—in the element itself. It was a conscious security. It was wonderful! Dane had lived into it, but he was still immensely aware. He would have been sorry to lose that, for just this fact as yet, the blest fact of consciousness, seemed the greatest thing of all. Its only fault was that, being in itself such an occupation, so fine an unrest in the heart of gratitude, the life of the day all went to it. But what even then was the harm? He had come only to come, to take what he found. This was the part where the great cloister, enclosed externally on three sides and probably the largest lightest fairest effect, to his charmed sense, that human hands could ever have expressed in dimensions of length and breadth, opened to the south its splendid fourth quarter, turned to the great view an outer gallery that combined with the rest of the portico to form a high dry loggia, such as he a little pretended to himself he had, in the Italy of old days, seen in old cities, old convents, old villas. This recalled disposition of some great abode of an Order, some mild Monte Cassino,[10] some Grande Chartreuse[11] more accessible, was his main term of comparison; but he knew he had really never anywhere beheld anything at once so calculated and so generous.

Three impressions in particular had been with him all the week, and he could but recognise in silence their happy effect on his nerves. How it was all managed he couldn't have told—he had been content moreover till now with his ignorance of cause and pretext; but whenever he chose to listen with a certain intentness he made out as from a distance the sound of slow sweet bells. How could they be so far and yet so audible? How could they be so near and yet so faint? How above all could they, in such an arrest of life, be, to *time* things, so frequent? The very essence of the bliss of Dane's whole change had been precisely that there was nothing now to time. It was the same with the slow footsteps that, always within earshot to the vague attention, marked the space and the leisure, seemed, in long cool arcades, lightly to fall and perpetually to recede. This was the second impression, and it melted into the third, as, for that matter, every form of softness, in the great good place, was but a further turn, without jerk or gap, of the endless roll of serenity. The quiet footsteps were quiet figures; the quiet figures that, to the eye, kept the picture human and brought its perfection within reach. This perfection, he felt on the bench by his friend, was now more within reach than ever. His friend at last turned to him a look different from the looks of friends in London clubs.

"The thing was to find it out!"

It was extraordinary how this remark fitted into his thought. "Ah wasn't it? And when I think," said Dane, "of all the people who haven't and who never will!" He sighed over these unfortunates with a tenderness that, in its degree, was practically new to him, feeling too how well his companion would know the people he meant. He only meant some, but they were all who'd want it; though of these, no doubt—well, for reasons, for things that, in the world, he had observed—there would never be too many. Not all perhaps who wanted would really find; but none at least would find who didn't really want. And then what the need would have to have been first! What it at first had had to be for himself! He felt afresh, in the light of his companion's face, what it might still be even when deeply satisfied, as well as what communication was established by the mere common knowledge of it.

"Every man must arrive by himself and on his own feet—isn't that so? We're Brothers here for the time, as in a great monastery, and we immediately think of each other and recognise each other as such; but we must have first got here as we can, and we meet after long journeys by complicated ways. Moreover we meet—don't we?—with closed eyes."

"Ah don't speak as if we were dead!" Dane laughed.

"I shan't mind death if it's like this," his friend replied.

It was too obvious, as Dane gazed before him, that one wouldn't; but after a moment he asked with the first articulation as yet of his most elementary wonder: "Where is it?"

"I shouldn't be surprised if it were much nearer than one ever suspected."

"Nearer 'town,' do you mean?"

"Nearer everything—nearer every one."

George Dane thought. "Would it be somewhere for instance down in Surrey?"

His Brother met him on this with a shade of reluctance. "Why should we call it names? It must have a climate, you see."

"Yes," Dane happily mused; "without that—!" All it so securely did have overwhelmed him again, and he couldn't help breaking out: "*What* is it?"

"Oh it's positively a part of our ease and our rest and our change, I think, that we don't at all know and that we may really call it, for that matter, anything in the world we like—the thing for instance we love it most for being."

"I know what *I* call it," said Dane after a moment. Then as his friend listened with interest: "Just simply 'The Great Good Place.'"

"I see—what can you say more? I've put it to myself perhaps a little differently." They sat there as innocently as small boys confiding to each other the names of toy animals. "'The Great Want Met.'"

"Ah yes—that's it!"

"Isn't it enough for us that it's a place carried on for our benefit so admirably that we strain our ears in vain for a creak of the machinery? Isn't it enough for us that it's simply a thorough hit?"

"Ah a hit!" Dane benignantly murmured.

"It does for us what it pretends to do," his companion went on; "the mystery isn't deeper than that. The thing's probably simple enough in fact, and on a thoroughly practical basis; only it has had its origin in a splendid thought, in a real stroke of genius."

"Yes," Dane returned, "in a sense—on somebody or other's part—so exquisitely personal!"

"Precisely—it rests, like all good things, on experience. The 'great want' comes home—that's the great thing it does! On the day it came home to the right mind this dear place was constituted. It always moreover in the long run *has* been met—it always must be. How can it not require to be, more and more, as pressure of every sort grows?"

Dane, with his hands folded in his lap, took in these words of wisdom. "Pressure of every sort *is* growing!" he placidly observed.

"I see well enough what that fact has done to *you*," his Brother declared.

Dane smiled. "I couldn't have borne it longer. I don't know what would have become of me."

"I know what would have become of *me*."

"Well, it's the same thing."

"Yes," said Dane's companion, "it's doubtless the same thing." On which they sat in silence a little, seeming pleasantly to follow, in the view of the green garden, the vague movements of the monster—madness, surrender, collapse—they had escaped. Their bench was like a box at the opera. "And I may perfectly, you know," the Brother pursued, "have seen you before. I may even have known you well. We don't know."

They looked at each other again serenely enough, and at last Dane said: "No, we don't know."

"That's what I meant by our coming with our eyes closed. Yes—there's something out. There's a gap, a link missing, the great hiatus!" the Brother laughed. "It's as simple a story as the old, old rupture—the break that lucky Catholics have always been able to make, that they're still, with their innumerable religious houses, able to make, by going into 'retreat.' I don't speak of the pious exercises—I speak only of the material simplification. I don't speak of the putting off of one's self; I speak only—if one has a self worth sixpence—of the getting it back. The place, the time, the way were, for those of the old persuasion, always there—are indeed practically there for them as much as ever. They can always get off—the blessed houses receive. So it was high time that we—we of the great Protestant peoples, still more, if possible, in the sensitive individual case, overscored and overwhelmed, still more congested with mere quantity and prostituted, through our 'enterprise,' to mere profanity—should learn how to get off, should find somewhere *our* retreat and remedy. There was such a huge chance for it!"

Dane laid his hand on his companion's arm. "It's charming how when we speak for ourselves we speak for each other. That was exactly what I said!" He had fallen to recalling from over the gulf the last occasion.

The Brother, as if it would do them both good, only desired to draw him out. "What you 'said'—?"

"To *him*—that morning." Dane caught a far bell again and heard a slow footstep. A quiet presence passed somewhere—neither of them turned to look. What was little by little more present to him was the perfect taste. It was supreme—it was everywhere. "I just dropped my burden—and he received it."

"And was it very great?"

"Oh such a load!" Dane said with gaiety.

"Trouble, sorrow, doubt?"

"Oh no—worse than that!"

"Worse?"

"'Success'—the vulgarest kind!" He mentioned it now as with amusement.

"Ah I know that too! No one in future, as things are going, will be able to face success."

"Without something of this sort—never. The better it is the worse—the greater the deadlier. But my one pain here," Dane continued, "is in thinking of my poor friend."

"The person to whom you've already alluded?"

He tenderly assented. "My substitute in the world. Such an unutterable benefactor. He turned up that morning when everything had somehow got on my nerves, when the whole great globe indeed, nerves or no nerves, seemed to have appallingly squeezed itself into my study and to be bent on simply swelling there. It wasn't a question of nerves, it was a mere question of the dislodgement and derangement of everything—of a general submersion by our eternal too much. I didn't know *où donner de la tête*[12]—I couldn't have gone a step further."

The intelligence with which the Brother listened kept them as children feeding from the same bowl. "And then you got the tip?"

"I got the tip!" Dane happily sighed.

"Well, we all get it. But I dare say differently."

"Then how did *you*—?"

The Brother hesitated, smiling. "You tell me first."

### III

"Well," said George Dane, "it was a young man I had never seen—a man at any rate much younger than myself—who had written to me and sent me some article, some book. I read the stuff, was much struck with it, told him so and thanked him—on which of course I heard from him again. Ah *that*—!" Dane comically sighed. "He asked me things—his questions were interesting; but to save time and writing I said to him: 'Come to see me—we can talk a little; but all I can give you is half an hour at breakfast.' He arrived to the minute on a day when more than ever in my life before I seemed, as it happened, in the endless press and stress, to have lost possession of my soul and to be surrounded only with the affairs of other people, smothered in mere irrelevant importunity. It made me literally ill—made me feel as I had never felt that should I once really for an hour lose hold of the thing itself, the thing that did matter and that I was trying for, I should never recover it again. The wild waters would close over me and I should drop straight to the dark depths where the vanquished dead lie."

"I follow you every step of your way," said the friendly Brother. "The wild waters, you mean, of our horrible time."

"Of our horrible time precisely. Not of course—as we sometimes dream—of any other."

"Yes, any other's only a dream. We really know none but our own."

"No, thank God—that's enough," Dane contentedly smiled. "Well, my young man turned up, and I hadn't been a minute in his presence before making out that practically it would be in him somehow or other to help me. He came to me with envy, envy extravagant—really passionate. I was, heaven save us, the great 'success' for him; he himself was starved and broken and beaten. How can I say what passed between us?—it was so strange, so swift, so much a matter, from one to the other, of instant perception and agreement. He was so clever and haggard and hungry!"

"Hungry?" the Brother asked.

"I don't mean for bread, though he had none too much, I think, even of that. I mean for—well, what *I* had and what I was a monument of to him as I stood there up to my neck in preposterous evidence. He, poor chap, had been for ten years serenading closed windows and had never yet caused a shutter to show that it stirred. *My* dim blind was the first raised to him an inch; my reading of his book, my impression of it, my note and my invitation, formed literally the only response ever dropped into his dark alley. He saw in my littered room, my shattered day, my bored face and spoiled temper—it's embarrassing, but I must tell you—the very proof of my pudding, the very blaze of my glory. And he saw in my repletion and my 'renown'—deluded innocent!—what he had yearned for in vain."

"What he had yearned for was to *be* you," said the Brother. Then he added: "I see where you're coming out."

"At my saying to him by the end of five minutes: 'My dear fellow, I wish you'd just try it—wish you'd for a while just *be* me!' You go straight to the mark, good Brother, and that was exactly what occurred—extraordinary though it was that we should both have understood. I saw what he could give, and he did too. He saw moreover what I could take; in fact what he saw was wonderful."

"He must be very remarkable!" Dane's converser laughed.

"There's no doubt of it whatever—far more remarkable than I. That's just the reason why what I put to him in joke—with a fantastic desperate irony—became, in his hands, with his vision of his chance, the blessed means and measure of my sitting on this spot in your company. 'Oh if I could just *shift* it all—make it straight over for an hour to other shoulders! If there only *were* a pair!'—that's the way I put it to him. And then at something in his face, 'Would *you*, by a miracle, undertake it?' I asked. I let him know all it meant—how it meant that he should at that very moment step in. It meant that he should finish my work and open my letters and keep my engagements and be subject, for better or worse, to my contacts and complications. It meant that he should live with my life and think with my brain and write with my hand and speak with my voice. It meant above all that I should get off. He accepted with greatness—rose to it like a hero. Only he said: 'What will become of *you?*'"

"There was the rub!" the Brother admitted.

"Ah but only for a minute. He came to my help again," Dane pursued, "when he saw I couldn't quite meet that, could at least only say that I wanted to think, wanted to cease, wanted to do the thing itself—the thing that mattered and that I was trying for, miserable me, and that thing only—and therefore wanted first of all really to *see* it again, planted out, crowded out, frozen out as it now so long had been. 'I know what you want,' he after a moment quietly remarked to me. 'Ah what I want doesn't exist!' 'I know what you want,' he repeated. At that I began to believe him."

"Had you any idea yourself?" the Brother's attention breathed.

"Oh yes," said Dane, "and it was just my idea that made me despair. There it was as sharp as possible in my imagination and my longing—there it was so utterly *not* in the fact. We were sitting together on my sofa as we waited for breakfast. He presently laid his hand on my knee—showed me a face that the sudden great light in it had made, for me, indescribably beautiful. 'It exists—it exists,' he at last said. And so I remember we sat a while and looked at each other, with the final effect of my finding that I absolutely believed him. I remember we weren't at all solemn—we smiled with the joy of discoverers. He was as glad as I—he was tremendously glad. That came out in the whole manner of his reply to the appeal that broke from me: 'Where is it then in God's name? Tell me without delay where it is!'"

The Brother had bent such a sympathy! "He gave you the address?"

"He was thinking it out—feeling for it, catching it. He has a wonderful head of his own and must be making of the whole thing, while we sit here patching and gossiping, something much better than ever *I* did. The mere sight of his face, the sense of his hand on my knee, made me, after a little, feel that he not only knew what I wanted but was getting nearer to it than I could have got in ten years. He suddenly sprang up and went over to my study-table—sat straight down there as if to write me my prescription or my passport. Then it was—at the mere sight of his back, which was turned to me—that I felt the spell work. I simply sat and watched him with the queerest deepest sweetest sense in the world—the sense of an ache that had stopped. All life was lifted; I myself at least was somehow off the ground. He was already where I had been."

"And where were you?" the Brother amusedly asked.

"Just on the sofa always, leaning back on the cushion and feeling a delicious ease. He was already me."

"And who were *you?*" the Brother continued.

"Nobody. That was the fun."

"That *is* the fun," said the Brother with a sigh like soft music.

Dane echoed the sigh, and, as nobody talking with nobody, they sat there together still and watched the sweet wide picture darken into tepid night.

## IV

At the end of three weeks—so far as time was distinct—Dane began to feel there was something he had recovered. It was the thing they never named—partly for want of the need and partly for lack of the word; for what indeed was the description that would cover it all? The only real need was to know it, to see it in silence. Dane had a private practical sign for it, which, however, he had appropriated by theft—"the vision and the faculty divine." That doubtless was a flattering phrase for his idea of his genius; the genius was at all events what he had been in danger of losing and had at last held by a thread that might at any moment have broken. The change was that little by little his hold had grown firmer, so that he drew in the line—more and more each day—with a pull he was delighted to find it would bear. The mere dream-sweetness of the place was superseded; it was more and more a world of reason and order, of sensible visible arrangement. It ceased to be strange—it was high triumphant clearness. He cultivated, however, but vaguely the question of where he was, finding it near enough the mark to be almost sure that if he wasn't in Kent he was then probably in Hampshire. He paid for everything but that—that wasn't one of the items. Payment, he had soon learned, was definite; it consisted of sovereigns and shillings—just like those of the world he had left, only parted with more ecstatically—that he committed, in his room, to a fixed receptacle and that were removed in his absence by one of the unobtrusive effaced agents (shadows projected on the hours like the noiseless march of the sundial) that were always at work. The scene had whole sides that reminded and resembled, and a pleased resigned perception of these things was at once the effect and the cause of its grace.

Dane picked out of his dim past a dozen halting similes. The sacred silent convent was one; another was the bright country-house. He did the place no outrage to liken it to an hotel; he permitted himself on occasion to feel it suggest a club. Such images, however, but flickered and went out—they lasted only long enough to light up the difference. An hotel without noise, a club without newspapers—when he turned his face to what it was "without" the view opened wide. The only approach to a real analogy was in himself and his companions. They were brothers, guests, members; they were even, if one liked—and they didn't in the least mind what they were called—"regular boarders." It wasn't they who made the conditions, it was the conditions that made them. These conditions found themselves accepted, clearly, with an appreciation, with a rapture, it was rather to be called, that proceeded, as the very air that pervaded them and the force that sustained, from their quiet and noble assurance. They combined to form the large simple idea of a general refuge—an image of embracing arms, of liberal accommodation. What was the effect really but the poetisation by perfect taste of a type common enough? There was no daily miracle; the perfect taste, with the aid of space, did the trick. What underlay and overhung it all, better yet, Dane mused, was some original inspiration, but confirmed, unquenched, some happy thought of an individual breast. It had been born somehow and somewhere—it had had to insist on being—the blest conception. The author might remain in the obscure, for that was part of the perfection: personal service so hushed and regulated that you scarce caught it in the act and only knew it by its results. Yet the wise mind was everywhere—the whole thing infallibly centred at the core in a consciousness. And what a consciousness it had been, Dane thought, a consciousness how like his own! The wise mind had felt, the wise mind had suffered; then, for all the worried company of minds, the wise mind had seen a chance. Of the creation thus arrived at you could none the less never have said if it were the last echo of the old or the sharpest note of the modern.

Dane again and again, among the far bells and the soft footfalls, in cool cloister and warm garden, found himself wanting not to know more and yet liking not to know less. It was part of the high style and the grand manner that there was no personal publicity, much less any personal reference. Those things were in the world—in what he had left; there was no vulgarity here of credit or claim or fame. The real exquisite was to be without the complication of an identity, and the greatest boon of all, doubtless, the solid security, the clear confidence one could feel in the keeping of the contract. That was what had been most in the wise mind—the importance of the absolute sense, on the part of its beneficiaries, that what was offered was guaranteed. They had no concern but to pay—the wise mind knew what they paid for. It was present to Dane each hour that he could never be overcharged. Oh the deep deep bath, the soft cool plash in the stillness!—this, time after time, as if under regular treatment, a sublimated German "cure," was the vivid name for his luxury. The inner life woke up again, and it was the inner life, for people of his generation, victims of the modern madness, mere maniacal extension and motion, that was returning health. He had talked of independence and written of it, but what a cold flat word it had been! This was the wordless fact itself—the uncontested possession of the long sweet stupid day. The fragrance of flowers just wandered through the void, and the quiet recurrence of delicate plain fare in a high, clean refectory where the soundless simple service was a triumph of art. That, as he analysed, remained the constant explanation: all the sweetness and serenity were created calculated things. He analysed, however, but in a desultory way and with a positive delight in the residuum of mystery that made for the great agent in the background the innermost shrine of the idol of a temple; there were odd moments for it, mild meditations when, in the broad cloister of peace or some garden-nook where the air was light, a special glimpse of beauty or reminder of felicity seemed, in passing, to hover and linger. In the mere ecstasy of change that had at first possessed him he hadn't discriminated—had only let himself sink, as I have mentioned, down to hushed depths. Then had come the slow soft stages of intelligence and notation, more marked and more fruitful perhaps after that long talk with his mild mate in the twilight, and seeming to wind up the process by putting the key into his hand. This key, pure gold, was simply the cancelled list. Slowly and blissfully he read into the general wealth of his comfort all the particular absences of which it was composed. One by one he touched, as it were, all the things it was such rapture to be without.

It was the paradise of his own room that was most indebted to them—a great square fair chamber, all beautified with omissions, from which, high up, he looked over a long valley to a far horizon, and in which he was vaguely and pleasantly reminded of some old Italian picture, some Carpaccio[13] or some early Tuscan, the representation of a world without newspapers and letters, without telegrams and photographs, without the dreadful fatal too much. There, for a blessing, he *could* read and write; there above all he could do nothing—he could live. And there were all sorts of freedoms—always, for the occasion, the particular right one. He could bring a book from the library— he could bring two, he could bring three. An effect produced by the charming place was that for some reason he never wanted to bring more. The library was a benediction—high and clear and plain like everything else, but with something, in all its arched amplitude, unconfused and brave and gay. He should never forget, he knew, the throb of immediate perception with which he first stood there, a single glance round sufficing so to show him that it would give him what for years he had desired. He had not had detachment, but there was detachment here—the sense of a great silver bowl from which he could ladle up the melted hours. He strolled about from wall to wall, too pleasantly in tune on that occasion to sit down punctually or to choose; only recognising from shelf to shelf every dear old book that he had had to put off or never returned to; every deep distinct voice of another time that in the hubbub of the world, he had had to take for lost and unheard. He came back of course soon, came back every day; enjoyed there, of all the rare strange moments, those that were at once most quickened and most caught— moments in which every apprehension counted double and every act of the mind was a lover's embrace. It was the quarter he perhaps, as the days went on, liked best; though indeed it only shared with the rest of the place, with every aspect to which his face happened to be turned, the power to remind him of the masterly general care.

There were times when he looked up from his book to lose himself in the mere tone of the picture that never failed at any moment or at any angle. The picture was always there, yet was made up of things common enough. It was in the way an open window in a broad recess let in the pleasant morning; in the way the dry air pricked into faint freshness the gilt of old bindings; in the way an empty chair beside a table unlittered showed a volume just laid down; in the way a happy Brother—as detached as one's self and with his innocent back presented—lingered before a shelf with the slow sound of turned pages. It was a part of the whole impression that, by some extraordinary law, one's vision seemed less from the facts than the facts from one's vision; that the elements were determined at the moment by the moment's need or the moment's sympathy. What most prompted this reflexion was the degree in which Dane had after a while a consciousness of company. After that talk with the good Brother on the bench there were other good Brothers in other places—always in cloister or garden some figure that stopped if he himself stopped and with which a greeting became, in the easiest way in the world, a sign of the diffused amenity and the consecrating ignorance. For always, always, in all contacts, was the balm of a happy blank. What he had felt the first time recurred: the friend was always new and yet at the same time—it was amusing, not disturbing—suggested the possibility that he might be but an old one altered. That was only delightful— as positively delightful in the particular, the actual conditions as it might have been the reverse in the conditions abolished. These others, the abolished, came back to Dane at last so easily that he could exactly measure each difference, but with what he had finally been hustled on to hate in them robbed of its terror in consequence of something that had happened. What had happened was that in tranquil walks and talks the deep spell had worked and he had got his soul again. He had drawn in by this time, with his lightened hand, the whole of the long line, and that fact just dangled at the end. He could put his other hand on it, he could unhook it, he was once more in possession. This, as it befell, was exactly what he supposed he must have said to a comrade beside whom, one afternoon in the cloister, he found himself measuring steps.

"Oh it comes—comes of itself, doesn't it, thank goodness?—just by the simple fact of finding room and time!"

The comrade was possibly a novice or in a different stage from his own; there was at any rate a vague envy in the recognition that shone out of the fatigued yet freshened face. "It has come to *you* then?—you've got what you wanted?" That was the gossip and interchange that could pass to and fro. Dane, years before, had gone in for three months of hydropathy,[14] and there was a droll echo, in this scene, of the old questions of the water-cure, the questions asked in the periodical pursuit of the "reaction"—the ailment, the progress of each, the action of the skin and the state of the appetite. Such memories worked in now—all familiar reference, all easy play of mind; and among them our friends, round and round, fraternised ever so softly till, suddenly stopping short, Dane, with a hand on his companion's arm, broke into the happiest laugh he had yet sounded.

V

"Why it's raining!" And he stood and looked at the splash of the shower and the shine of the wet leaves. It was one of the summer sprinkles that bring out sweet smells.

"Yes—but why not?" his mate demanded.

"Well—because it's so charming. It's so exactly right."

"But everything *is*. Isn't that just why we're here?"

"Just exactly," Dane said; "only I've been living in the beguiled supposition that we've somehow or other a climate."

"So have I, so I dare say has every one. Isn't that the blest moral?—that we live in beguiled suppositions. They come so easily here, where nothing contradicts them." The good Brother looked placidly forth—Dane could identify his phase. "A climate doesn't consist in its never raining, does it?"

"No, I dare say not. But somehow the good I've got has been half the great easy absence of all that friction of which the question of weather mostly forms a part—has been indeed largely the great easy perpetual air-bath."

"Ah yes—that's not a delusion; but perhaps the sense comes a little from our breathing an emptier medium. There are fewer things *in* it! Leave people alone, at all events, and the air's what they take to. Into the closed and the stuffy they have to be driven. I've had too—I think we must all have—a fond sense of the south."

"But imagine it," said Dane, laughing, "in the beloved British islands and so near as we are to Bradford!"

His friend was ready enough to imagine. "To Bradford?" he asked, quite unperturbed. "How near?"

Dane's gaiety grew. "Oh it doesn't matter!"

His friend, quite unmystified, accepted it. "There are things to puzzle out—otherwise it would be dull. It seems to me one can puzzle them."

"It's because we're so well disposed," Dane said.

"Precisely—we find good in everything."

"In everything," Dane went on. "The conditions settle that—they determine us."

They resumed their stroll, which evidently represented on the good Brother's part infinite agreement. "Aren't they probably in fact very simple?" he presently enquired. "Isn't simplification the secret?"

"Yes, but applied with a tact!"

"There it is. The thing's so perfect that it's open to as many interpretations as any other great work—a poem of Goethe, a dialogue of Plato, a symphony of Beethoven."

"It simply stands quiet, you mean," said Dane, "and lets us call it names?"

"Yes, but all such loving ones. We're 'staying' with some one—some delicious host or hostess who never shows."

"It's liberty-hall—absolutely," Dane assented.

"Yes—or a convalescent home."

To this, however, Dane demurred. "Ah that, it seems to me, scarcely puts it. You weren't *ill*—were you? I'm very sure *I* really wasn't. I was only, as the world goes, too 'beastly well'!"

The good Brother wondered. "But if we couldn't keep it up—?"

"We couldn't keep it *down*—that was all the matter!"

"I see—I see." The good Brother sighed contentedly; after which he brought out again with kindly humour: "It's a sort of kindergarten!"

"The next thing you'll be saying that we're babes at the breast!"

"Of some great mild invisible mother who stretches away into space and whose lap's the whole valley—?"

"And her bosom"—Dane completed the figure—"the noble eminence of our hill? That will do; anything will do that covers the essential fact."

"And what do you call the essential fact?"

"Why that—as in old days on Swiss lakesides—we're *en pension*."

The good Brother took this gently up. "I remember—I remember: seven francs a day without wine! But alas it's more than seven francs here."

"Yes, it's considerably more," Dane had to confess. "Perhaps it isn't particularly cheap."

"Yet should you call it particularly dear?" his friend after a moment enquired.

George Dane had to think. "How do I know, after all? What practice has one ever had in estimating the inestimable? Particular cheapness certainly isn't the note we feel struck all round; but don't we fall naturally into the view that there *must* be a price to anything so awfully sane?"

The good Brother in his turn reflected. "We fall into the view that it must pay—that it does pay."

"Oh yes; it does pay!" Dane eagerly echoed. "If it didn't it wouldn't last. It has *got* to last of course!" he declared.

"So that we can come back?"

"Yes—think of knowing that we shall be able to!"

They pulled up again at this and, facing each other, thought of it, or at any rate pretended to; for what was really in their eyes was the dread of a loss of the clue. "Oh when we want it again we shall find it," said the good Brother. "If the place really pays it will keep on."

"Yes, that's the beauty; that it isn't, thank goodness, carried on only for love."

"No doubt, no doubt; and yet, thank goodness, there's love in it too." They had lingered as if, in the mild moist air, they were charmed with the patter of the rain and the way the garden drank it. After a little, however, it did look rather as if they were trying to talk each other out of a faint small fear. They saw the increasing rage of life and the recurrent need, and they wondered proportionately whether to return to the front when their hour should sharply strike would be the end of the dream. Was this a threshold perhaps, after all, that could only be crossed one way? They must return to the front sooner or later—that was certain: for each his hour would strike. The flower would have been gathered and the trick played—the sands would in short have run.

There, in its place, *was* life—with all its rage; the vague unrest of the need for action knew it again, the stir of the faculty that had been refreshed and reconsecrated. They seemed each, thus confronted, to close their eyes a moment for dizziness; then they were again at peace and the Brother's confidence rang out. "Oh we shall meet!"

"Here, do you mean?"

"Yes—and I dare say in the world too."

"But we shan't recognise or know," said Dane.

"In the world, do you mean?"

"Neither in the world nor here."

"Not a bit—not the least little bit, you think?"

Dane turned it over. "Well, so is it that it seems to me all best to hang together. But we shall see."

His friend happily concurred. "We shall see." And at this, for farewell, the Brother held out his hand.

"You're going?" Dane asked.

"No, but I thought *you* were."

It was odd, but at this Dane's hour seemed to strike—his consciousness to crystallise. "Well, I am. I've got it. You stay?" he went on.

"A little longer."

Dane hesitated. "You haven't yet got it?"

"Not altogether—but I think it's coming."

"Good!" Dane kept his hand, giving it a final shake, and at that moment the sun glimmered again through the shower, but with the rain still falling on the hither side of it and seeming to patter even more in the brightness. "Hallo—how charming!"

The Brother looked a moment from under the high arch—then again turned his face to our friend. He gave this time his longest happiest sigh. "Oh it's all right!"

But why was it, Dane after a moment found himself wondering, that in the act of separation his own hand was so long retained? Why but through a queer phenomenon of change, on the spot, in his companion's face—change that gave it another, but an increasing and above all a much more familiar identity, an identity not beautiful, but more and more distinct, an identity with that of his servant, with the most conspicuous, the physiognomic seat of the public propriety of Brown? To this anomaly his eyes slowly opened; it was not his good Brother, it was verily Brown who possessed his hand. If his eyes had to open it was because they had been closed and because Brown appeared to think he had better wake up. So much as this Dane took in, but the effect of his taking it was a relapse into darkness, a recontraction of the lids just prolonged enough to give Brown time, on a second thought, to withdraw his touch and move softly away. Dane's next consciousness was that of the desire to make sure he *was* away, and this desire had somehow the result of dissipating the obscurity. The obscurity was completely gone by the time he had made out that the back of a person writing at his study-table was presented to him. He recognised a portion of a figure that he had somewhere described to somebody—the intent shoulders of the unsuccessful young man who had come that bad morning to breakfast. It was strange, he at last mused, but the young man was still there. How long had he stayed—days, weeks, months? He was exactly in the position in which Dane had last seen him. Everything—stranger still—was exactly in that position; everything at least but the light of the window, which came in from another quarter and showed a different hour. It wasn't after breakfast now; it was after—well, what? He suppressed a gasp—it was after everything. And yet—quite literally—there were but two other differences. One of these was that if he was still on the sofa he was now lying down; the other was the patter on the glass that showed him how the rain—the great rain of the night—had come back. It was the rain of the night, yet when had he last heard it? But two minutes before? Then how many were there before the young man at the table, who seemed intensely occupied, found a moment to look round at him and, on meeting his open eyes, get up and draw near?

"You've slept all day," said the young man.

"All day?"

The young man looked at his watch. "From ten to six. You were extraordinarily tired. I just after a bit let you alone, and you were soon off." Yes, that was it; he had been "off"—off, off, off. He began to fit it together: while he had been off the young man had been on. But there were still some few confusions; Dane lay looking up. "Everything's done," the young man continued.

"Everything?"

"Everything."

Dane tried to take it all in, but was embarrassed and could only say weakly and quite apart from the matter: "I've been so happy!"

"So have I," said the young man. He positively looked so; seeing which George Dane wondered afresh, and then in his wonder read it indeed quite as another face, quite, in a puzzling way, as another person's. Every one was a little some one else. While he asked himself who else then the young man was, this benefactor, struck by his appealing stare, broke again into perfect cheer. "It's all right!" That answered Dane's question; the face was the face turned to him by the good Brother there in the portico while they listened together to the rustle of the shower. It was all queer, but all pleasant and all distinct, so distinct that the last words in his ear—the same from both quarters—appeared the effect of a single voice. Dane rose and looked about his room, which seemed disencumbered, different, twice as large. It *was* all right.

## Notes

1  In a letter to J.B. Phillips on 8 February 1871, Taylor said "What you say of 'Joseph' delights me, for you have recognized exactly what I attempted to do,— that is, to throw some indirect light on the great questions which underlie civilized life, and the existence of which is only dimly felt, not intelligently perceived, by most Americans. I allowed the plot to be directed by these *cryptic* forces; hence, a reader who does not feel them will hardly be interested in the

external movement of the story. [...] I will tell you, now, that *I* consider it my best novel, with all its deficiencies. So do a few others; but the blessed half-educated public sees nothing in the book but dullness" (*Life and Letters of Bayard Taylor*, ed. Marie Hansen-Taylor & Horace E. Scudder, Vol. 2, 2nd ed. Boston: Houghton, Mifflin, 1885).

2   The great Sufi poet of Persia (c.1320–c.1388), known for his spiritual writings.

3   Famous stream of Shiráz.

4   City in southern Uzbekistan; Tamerlane's opulent capital in the fourteenth century.

5   A light boat propelled by sails or oars.

6   A gambling card game.

7   Qtd. in Roger Austen's *Genteel Pagan*, 20.

8   Originally, native Hawaiians; but gradually a derogatory term for native South Sea islanders, especially those who were indentured or forced laborers in Australia.

9   Alexander Dumas' 1844 novel *The Count of Monte Cristo* features a hero who discovers hidden wealth on the island of Monte Cristo and assumes the title of count.

10   Monte Cassino is a rocky hill about eighty miles south of Rome, Italy, about 1700 feet in altitude. It is noted as the site where St. Benedict of Norcia established his monastery, the source of the Benedictine Order, around 529 AD.

11   The monastery of the Grand Chartreuse, the mother-house of the Carthusians, lies in a valley of the Alps of Dauphine near Grenoble. Founded originally by St. Bruno in 1084, it has been burnt and rebuilt at least eight times since its founding.

12   "Where the head of it was" [French].

13   Vittore Carpaccio (1472–1526), an Italian painter of the Venetian school.

14   The water-cure, or the treatment of disease by water, used outwardly and inwardly (Greek). This form of hydrotherapy was developed in eighteenth-century England by a doctor named Richard Russell. It generally consisted of bathing in sea water, the drinking of sea water, and activities reminiscent of modern-day spas. It became extremely popular in the nineteenth century where fashionable resorts devoted to the "cure" (such as Brighton) were well-known medical institutions for the upper class.

PART SEVEN

# THE DOMESTIC HOMOSEXUAL

*Born to American parents, Sturgis spent most of his life in England, where he enjoyed close friendships with Henry James and Edith Wharton. His first novel* Tim: A Story of Eton *(1891) depicted a young boy caught in the throes of a schoolboy crush. James's withering criticism of his third novel* Belchamber *caused him to withdraw from writing, although its portrait of Sainty, the model of an effeminate (and, we may infer, homosexual) aristocrat forced into a loveless marriage must have had resonance for knowing readers. The hero is a close portrait of the author himself (see George Santayana's deft biography of Sturgis in this volume, 138–45), and like himself,* Belchamber *is full of a cynical wit that criticizes the aristocracy that Sturgis adored at the same time as he despised aspects of it. In portraying a man trapped by an overbearing mother, wife, and brother, Sainty is a model for what we might term a "domestic homosexual."[1] Sturgis dedicated* Belchamber *to William Haynes Smith, his lifelong companion.*

## FROM *BELCHAMBER* (1905)

### Chapter II

The world is like a huge theatrical company in which half the actors and actresses have been cast for the wrong parts. There are heavy fathers who ought to be playing the lover, and young men on whose downy chins one seems to see the spectre of the grey beard that would be suitable to their natures. Perhaps the hardest case is theirs who by their sex are called upon to "have a swaggering and martial outside," "a gallant curtle-axe upon their thigh," and yet, like Rosalind in her boy's dress, start and turn faint at the sight of blood.[2] The right to be a coward is one of the dearest prerogatives of woman. No man may be one with impunity, and it is precisely the women who are the first to despise him if he be. Those who are born with the gift of personal courage (and they are happily the greater number) have no adequate idea of their blessing. To be in harmony with one's environment, to like the things one ought to like—that surely is the supreme good. If that be so, then few people have come into the arena of life less suitably equipped for the part they had to play than the subject of this history.

Charles Edwin William Augustus Chambers, Marquis and Earl of Belchamber, Viscount Charmington, and Baron St. Edmunds and Chambers, for all his imposing list of names and titles, started in life without that crowning gift—wanting which all effort is paralysed—a good conceit of himself. And in fact, except for the gewgaw of his rank, which sat on him as uneasily as a suit of his ancestral armour, he had not much that would win him consideration from the people among whom his lot was cast. From his father he inherited his feeble constitution, his irresolution and want of moral courage, from his mother her sallow complexion and lack of charm, her reserve and shyness, and the rigid conscience which a long line of Covenanting ancestors[3] had passed down to her, and which in him, who had none of their counterbalancing force of character, tended always to become morbid. In his babyhood he had been called Lord St. Edmunds, as was the custom in the family for the eldest son's eldest son; his father in half derisive affection had abbreviated the title into "Sainty," and Sainty he always continued to be to all who were intimate enough, and to many who were not. He was only three when his father died, and his baby brother, Arthur, was not yet two. Even in those early days the contrast was strongly marked between the brothers. Sainty was a pale, nervous child who cried if spoken to suddenly, while Arthur was as fine a pink and white fat baby as you could see in a picture-book, who crowed and gurgled and clapped his hands and liked his bath and took kindly to his food, so that the nurses adored him. When he had a stomach-ache or was thwarted in his wishes he roared lustily for a minute or two and then returned to his usual placidity, whereas poor Sainty, if anything "put him out," as his nurse would say, whined and fretted, and kept up a little, sad, bleating cry for hours.

He could not remember his father, but with the help of the large coloured portrait in uniform that stood on a gilt easel in the corner of his mother's room he had built up for himself a shadowy heroic figure, strangely unlike poor Charmington, which in his imagination did duty for this departed parent. He never spoke of him to any one but Arthur, but to him he talked with such conviction of "Papa," that the child, not very attentive and perhaps not greatly interested, gathered an impression that the elder boy was drawing on his memory for his facts, and indeed he almost thought so himself, until one day Lady Charmington, hearing some such talk between the two, sharply rebuked poor Sainty for telling falsehoods to his little brother. His earliest impression of his mother was in her black dress with the gleaming white on head and throat and wrists, a dress that lent a dignity to Lady Charmington's somewhat commonplace figure. When she left off her cap, it was of the nature of a blow to him. Though he could not have described his sensations, she seemed somehow discrowned with her sleek, bare head.

Grandpapa's funeral was a different matter from these early fleeting impressions. That he remembered clearly, for he was seven when it happened, and had a little black suit of knickerbockers and black stockings and gloves, and led Arthur by the hand similarly attired. Every incident of that frightening, gloomy, yet strangely fascinating and exciting day, remained engraved in his recollection. He remembered the crowd in the churchyard, the murmur that greeted his own appearance, the staggering of the bearers under that long, heavy burthen, the gloom of the church full of people in black, and the great yawning hole in the chancel pavement. What he did not grasp until very long afterwards, and then only most imperfectly and by degrees, was the difference the event of that day made in his own position; but his mother realised it fully, and indeed it made much more difference to her than to the meek little boy accustomed from earliest infancy to swallow distasteful puddings and nauseous drugs at her command, and anxiously to examine his conscience, if some remnant of the old Adam ever led him to question her decrees. Henceforth Lady Charmington entered into her kingdom, and it must be confessed that on the whole she ruled it well and wisely, and entirely in the interests of her children. Almost the only sensible thing the old lord had ever done was to appoint her and her brother the guardians of his grandchildren, and under the careful management of his daughter-in-law, aided by the wise advice of Lord Corstorphine, the property was nursed through his grandson's long minority back to a tolerably healthy condition.

As to Lady Belchamber, nothing would have bored her more than being cumbered in any way with the guardianship of her grandchildren. She carried off what her daughter-in-law declared to be a most ridiculously disproportionate jointure, and the furniture of her private apartments, in which some valuable china and cabinets, that she had certainly not brought into the family, somehow found themselves included at the time of the move. She even showed a decided inclination to keep the famous emeralds which, as Lady Charmington said, everybody knew were heirlooms; but these she was made to send back by her second husband, the Duke of Sunborough, one of the oldest and most faithful of her admirers, whom she married just a year after her lord's death. On the other hand, she generously abandoned all claim to a damp and mouldy dower-house in which she had a right to reside for life, which, considering that the duke had a palace in London and five country seats, was very handsome of her. Three generations of gambling and extravagance leave their mark on the most imposing fortunes, and if the Belchamber estates did not come to the hammer, it was due to the action of the last person who might have been expected to save them, in marrying a hardheaded Scotswoman and dying before his father. To get the estate into order was Lady Charmington's prime object in life. To this end she inaugurated a rigid system of economy, and made a clean sweep of the heads of almost every department under the old *régime*, toiling early and late to make herself mistress of many details of which she was ignorant; for this, she endured the dislike of the poor, whom she benefited in her own autocratic manner, and much hostile comment from her equals. She was rigidly just, and generous, too, in her own way; only prodigality and waste she would not tolerate, nor look with a lenient eye on the small peculations which those who serve the great come to regard as quite within the pale of honesty.

If the mother spared neither time nor labour that she might be able to hand over his property to her son free of encumbrances when he came of age, she was not less eager and indefatigable in her efforts to fit him for the position she was making for him; and this task she found incomparably the harder of the two. It was not that he was naughty or insubordinate. A meeker, more obedient child did not live. The difficulty was far more intangible; it is easier to drive a slightly pulling horse in crowded thoroughfares than one with so light a mouth that he never will go properly up to his bit; and Lady Charmington had not the blessed gift of light hands in conducting the education of a child, whatever she might have on horseback. As a girl she had ridden a good deal, and even hunted; and though she gave that up after her marriage, she still found it possible to keep a more effectual eye on all corners of the huge estate from her square seat on the back of a substantial cob than from any other coign of vantage. No farmer ever rode more diligently and thoroughly about his fields; and on these excursions it was her pleasure that the boys, and especially Sainty, should accompany her. Arthur had a natural seat, took to horses from the first, and wanted to gallop his pony and make him jump before the family coachman had thought fit to abandon the leading-rein. With poor Sainty it was far otherwise. He rode, as he ate rice pudding, because he was told to; but he was cold for an hour beforehand, and he sat his pony, as his mother remarked, like a sack of potatoes. The smallest thing unseated him; he was always rolling ignominiously off.

On this and similar shortcomings, he received many admonitions from his mother and uncle, from which the chief impression he derived was a rooted belief in the immense superiority of his younger brother. "At the worst there will always be Arthur." When and under what circumstances had he overheard that remark? He never was quite sure that he had not formulated it for himself. Be that as it might, it early became the burthen to which his life set itself. Far from resenting the point of view, he drew from it a certain consolation under his abiding sense of his many imperfections. He was still quite a small boy when he decided that his *rôle* in life would be to die young, and make way for the younger brother who was so eminently fitted for the position that suited himself so ill; and he found a certain gloomy satisfaction in settling the details of pathetic deathbed scenes. I fear an element in these imaginings which was not without attraction for him, was the thought of exhorting Arthur with his latest breath on matters in which his brother's conduct did not always square with his own more evangelical standard, such as a certain looseness of statement, and somewhat lax ideas of property. If Arthur could not find his own cap, or bat, or riding-whip (and his things were generally tossed about the great house wherever he happened to be when he last used them), it was always less trouble to take Sainty's, which were sure to be in the right place, than to go and look for his own. He also on occasion carried the juvenile habit of untruth rather further than mere thoughtlessness warranted; but he told his stories with so open a countenance, and such a fearless gaze, that he was invariably believed, as against poor Sainty, whose knitted brow and downcast eyes, while he sought in his mind for the exact truth, had all the appearance of an effort after invention. "Arthur is very thoughtless and tiresome," Lady Charmington would say, "but there's one comfort about him, I can always depend on his telling me the truth if I ask him. I wish I could say the same for Sainty; I am sometimes afraid he is rather sly. I try not to be hard on him, for he is timid, and I don't want to frighten him into telling untruths; but I do wish he was a little more straightforward, and would look one in the face when he talks."

Many such hints, all showing a like perspicacious insight into the characters of her sons, were given by this conscientious lady to the governess she had engaged to assist her in moulding their dispositions. Alice Meakins was the daughter of the rector of Great Charmington, and had the prime recommendation in her employer's eyes of being her humble slave and completely under her orders. Had she been a little less in awe of Lady Charmington, and less impressed with the enormity of differing from her, she might perhaps have enlightened her on many matters concerning the little boys. Her mild rule, while it galled his more spirited brother, sat very lightly on Sainty, who worshipped the governess as the most talented and accomplished of mortals. "But I like her, I'm fond of her; I don't want to do what she tells me not," he pleaded to the indignant Arthur, as usual incensed by his brother's want of pluck in refusing to join in some plot against the authority of their instructress. "Ho, ho, Miss Moddlecoddle, you can't ride, you've got no seat and no hands; Bell said so. You're jolly bad at games, and you like to sit and suck up to an old governess, and do needlework with her, like a beastly girl. I'm a man, and I shan't do what she tells me. What business has she to order me about? She is only a servant like the others."

Sainty was shocked. "O Arthur! you do say *horrid* things," he said. It was true that he did like sitting with the gentle Meakins, and acquiring the modest arts of which she was the mistress. She had many little manual dexterities such as governesses impart to children, whereby the world is filled with innocent horrors, kettleholders in cross-stitch, penwipers faintly resembling old women with cloth cloaks and petticoats, and little black seeds for faces, and book-markers in the shape of crosses with many steps, plaited of strips of gilt and coloured paper. In all these manufactures Sainty soon became proficient. He also illuminated texts, "Be thou faithful unto death," and "The greatest of these is Charity," which were presented to Lady Charmington on her birthday. On the subject of the texts and the little plaited crosses Lady Charmington had a word to say to Miss Meakins in private, as being rather too papistical in tendency; but she was not displeased with the simple presents, on the whole, until her anxious maternal eye was led to detect the danger that might lurk in cross-stitch by some petulant remarks of Arthur's, who wanted Sainty to come out and play Red Indians in the long shrubbery. "Muvver," he cried, bursting into the boudoir, where his mother was busy with some farm accounts, "isn't Sainty howid? He won't come out, though he's done his lessons, 'cos he will stick in and do beastly woolwork." One of Arthur's many charms was a babyish imperfection of speech. He never could pronounce "th" or "r," even when quite grown up.

"What is it he's doing?" asked Lady Charmington.

"Oh, beastly woolwork; he's got two-fwee fings he's makin', and he likes to sit like a girl, instead of coming out and playing."

A shade of annoyance crossed the mother's face. "I wish you wouldn't use such words as 'beastly,' Arthur," she said severely, but the severity was really addressed to the absent first-born and the effeminacy of his tastes; and the schoolroom was presently visited by the mistress of the house, and Sainty duly turned out to distasteful recreation. When he had gone forth to be scalped by the fraternal savage, his mother turned to the instructress. "I think, Alice," she said, holding up the offending kettleholder, "that it is a pity, on the whole, to teach Sainty to work; he's quite sufficiently effeminate by nature, without having that side of him encouraged. I will speak to him about it. I shall tell him I don't approve of his working; it's not manly." She was surprised, when she carried out this intention, by meeting with passionate tears and protestations.

"O mother, I love my work; it's the only thing I do enjoy, except botany, and reading, and some lessons (not 'rithmetic or spelling); and I have to do so many things I *don't* like, cricket and riding, and—and—all the dreadful things that men and gentlemen have to do," the little boy concluded, quoting a formula frequently used for his encouragement.

Though not habitually distrustful of her own judgment, nothing so confirmed Lady Charmington in a view she adopted as any opposition to it; and the kettleholders became taboo from that day forward. Poor Sainty's confession of dislike for the manlier sports that, as he said, were considered a necessary part of the education of a gentleman, was perhaps the most unfortunate argument he could have chosen, for it naturally convinced his mother that the mischief lay deeper than she supposed, and suggested to her the advisability of transferring the boys from petticoat government altogether; that is, of course, as far as the subordinate powers were concerned. The particular petticoat that typified her own sway remained in undisturbed possession of the throne in all her plans for the future.

"I think the boys are getting too much for poor Miss Meakins," she said to her brother, on his next visit. "She is an excellent girl, though a little inclined to be high church;[4] but they ought to be under a man, I feel sure."

"Don't tell me that Sainty is becoming insubordinate?" said Lord Corstorphine.

"No; but Arthur hasn't the smallest respect for her. With Sainty the danger is of a different kind; he is perhaps too fond of women's society."

"Not a precocious passion for the governess! I can't believe that."

Lady Charmington looked resigned. "I don't deny, Corstorphine," she said, "that you have been a great help to me in the management of my fatherless boys; that is why I am consulting you on the present occasion. But it is no help to be flippant and funny. What I mean is that Sainty is quite sufficiently inclined by nature to be a milksop, without living perpetually with women, and adopting their ways. He likes better than any game to sit indoors with Miss Meakins on fine days, and do woolwork."

"Have him out, Sarah, by all means," returned her brother. "I can't help being a little pleased at his liking reading. A Chambers who occasionally opens a book, and is tolerably well behaved, will be an agreeable variation of the type. But it's bad his not wanting to be out and playing games; it isn't natural."

Lord Corstorphine felt that he was as near normal as it was possible to be, without becoming commonplace, and that those whose tastes differed widely from his own must always be more or less blamably eccentric. Still, his greater commerce with the world had given him a wider toleration than either of his sisters, who had been known to call him a Laodicean,[5] and Sarah once went so far as to draw a parallel between her brother and Gallio.[6] But though she affected to be shocked at the looseness of his views, his known moderation made her lean the more confidently on his judgment. The knowledge that her opinion was backed by one whom the world praised for common-sense gave a pleasing security that her own noble zeal was not hurrying her into extremes. It was invariably she who initiated every change in the education of her sons. But, though it may be doubted how she would have borne opposition from her fellow-guardian, his agreement was always a comfort to her.

So Alice Meakins, with her little crosses and penwipers, returned to the paternal rectory, with the highest testimonials from her dear Lady Charmington, to look out for another situation.

Poor Sainty could not be comforted. To be sure, no one tried much to comfort him. For the first time he felt a rebellious bitterness towards his mother. Though he could imagine nothing so dashing as active disobedience, he cherished a dark determination to be very cold and reserved towards the new tutor, with the natural result that Miss Meakins's successor, a youth fresh from Oxford, and also of the children of the clergy, conceived a great liking for Arthur, and favoured him prodigiously.

This young man, who had been selected mainly for his reputation as a cricketer, left Lady Charmington nothing to desire in the matter of sport, and was quite ready to ride any horse in her limited stable; nor need she feel anxiety as to his holding extreme views in religious matters. It is true he attended family prayers with exemplary punctuality, and accompanied his charges to service twice on Sundays; but she could detect no sign of the interest in matters ecclesiastical which she looked for in a son of the Church, and his waistcoats and riding-boots had a decidedly worldly air.

Under Mr. Kirkpatrick, Sainty early proved the cynical dictum that life were endurable but for its pleasures, the hated pastimes in which his sex and position in life inexorably demanded that he should find enjoyment. He stood like a martyr at the stake, to be bowled at with the Englishman's fetish, that terrible disc of solid leather which he knew he should not hit, but which not infrequently hit him; and he would unhesitatingly have indorsed Mr. Pinchbold's remark that "the horse was a fearful animal." He was so painstaking, however, and anxious to do what was expected of him, that he might possibly have attained in time to some sort of proficiency in these alien arts, had his efforts been greeted with a little more encouragement, and a little less ridicule; but the race is not yet extinct of those who hold that the best way to teach a child to swim is to throw him into the water.

Meanwhile, a new terror arose on Sainty's horizon. When Mr. Kirkpatrick had been at Belchamber eighteen months, he one day intimated to Lady Charmington that he had been offered a mastership in a public school, and could not afford to remain much longer with his pupils. It was therefore suggested that, as they were both presently to go to Eton, a few years at a private school would not be undesirable as a preparation. Even Arthur was a little daunted at the prospect, while rather fascinated by it; but to Sainty it loomed black as the final end of all brightness, closing in the vista of his life and blotting out the sun. It seemed to him that each step in the *via dolorosa*[7] of his existence was fated to be more awful than the last. When his beloved Miss Meakins had been replaced by the hated Kirkpatrick, he thought to have tasted the dregs of bitterness; but now a new prospect had come to make life in the familiar places that he loved with a catlike fidelity appear the one thing desirable, even shadowed by the tutor and his cricketball. I suppose it seemed a hard thing to our first parents when the Serpent was introduced into Eden; but life in Paradise, even with a snake in the garden, was a very different thing from the flaming sword that drove them out into an unknown world of work and briars. Sainty said little to earthly ears, but he prayed nightly with intense fervour that he might die before the day came to go to school, which seemed the only escape to his poor little hunted mind.

But there was another way, which, if he could have foreseen it, would have taxed his courage with a far more genuine fright than that vague abstraction, death, for which we all cry aloud so readily in our youth when things do not go as we wish. Arthur went to school alone when the time arrived, and this was how it came about.

It was a beautiful day at the end of March. Mr. Kirkpatrick was to leave at Easter, and the dreaded exodus was only a month away. It was a late spring, and the snow still lay on the north side of the hedgerows. But it had rained in the night, and there was that indefinable sense of spring in the air that sometimes comes quite suddenly. The primroses were beginning to gem the coppices, the birds to sing late in the long twilights. Daffodils waved in the fields where the young lambs were bleating.

"What are you and the boys going to do this afternoon, Mr. Kirkpatrick?" asked Lady Charmington at lunch.

The tutor looked inquiringly at the boys. "I'll do whatever they wish, Lady Charmington. What should you like?" he asked of Sainty.

"I should like to go to One-tree Wood, and get primroses," Sainty answered, after the usual slight struggle that it always cost him to express a wish or an opinion.

"Get Gwanmuvvers!" burst in Arthur. "Bovver pwimwoses; you don't care about 'em, do you, Mr. Kirkpatrick? I want to wide; Bell says the gwound's in quite good order to-day, after the wain. We've hardly widden at all lately, 'cos it's been so hard."

As usual Arthur had his way, and poor Sainty was condemned to ride. Generally he gained confidence when he had been out a little while, but to-day, somehow, everything went wrong. He began by rolling off at the hall door, because his stirrups were too long, and the pony moved on unexpectedly while they were being taken up. He was much chaffed for this misadventure by his companions, and he did not like chaff. Then the pony was fresh and inclined to shy, after the inaction of the long frost, so that he had a bad time of it altogether; but he managed to stick on somehow until they were on their way home.

They had been round by Little Charmington, and their way lay through one of the high woods. When they came to the gate that led into the park, they found it locked.

"I never knew this gate locked before," said Kirkpatrick, pulling feebly at it with his whip. "I don't suppose either of you have got the key by any chance?"

"Jaggins must have locked it. He's got some young pheasants further up the wood," said Arthur; "he told me so."

"I suppose we must go back," said Kirkpatrick, "but it's an awful long way round. We shall be late for tea, which your mother doesn't like, and you've got some more work to do afterwards. There's a gap in the hedge a little way along here," he added more hopefully. "I suppose you couldn't jump the ditch? It would save us a good two miles, and it's really nothing of a jump."

"Of course we can jump the ditch. Hurray! what fun!" cried Arthur, and without more words he wheeled his pony, put him at the gap, and the next moment was careering about on the turf beyond, in a great state of excitement and jubilation.

"You see, it's quite easy," the tutor said, turning to Sainty, whose pony was already beginning to fidget, excited by the trampling about on snapping twigs and the rush past of the other. Sainty was very white.

"You know I can't jump, Mr. Kirkpatrick," he said, gulping tears. "I'm sure to fall off if I try; I always do."

"Not you," the young man replied encouragingly. "You see your little brother has done it. I should be ashamed to have him ride so much better than me, if I were you." The poor man was rather in a fix, with one pupil already across the obstacle and the other resolutely declining to follow.

"See," he said, "I'll give you a lead. It's as easy as easy; you've only to sit well back, and give him his head." And so saying, he put his horse at the gap, and followed Arthur into the park. "Come on," he called.

"Jump, Sainty, jump," piped Arthur. "I wouldn't be such a funk."

Whether Sainty would ever have found the courage to attempt the jump is doubtful, if the pony at this stage of the proceedings had not decided matters by bolting at the gap. But bothered and bewildered by the tugging of his rider's despairing hands, he swerved just at the jump, and, slipping on the trodden earth where Kirkpatrick's horse had taken off, he came to the ground; then, struggling to his feet, galloped off through the wood by the road they had come.

The young man was horror-stricken when he saw the accident; he was off his horse and by the side of the fallen boy in a second. Sainty was unconscious, that was all he could tell.

"Now, Arthur," he cried to the younger boy, who was beginning to tremble and cry, "this is the moment to show the stuff you're made of. I must stay here with Sainty, but you must get home across the park as hard as you can go, so as to tell your mother what's happened, and save her the shock of seeing Donald come home without his rider. And then send people here to carry Sainty in; he may be more hurt than we think."

Arthur waited for no more, but galloped off in the direction of the house, glad to have something definite to do, instead of staring at poor Sainty.

Lady Charmington had come home sooner than she expected, and was taking off her hat when she saw Arthur come galloping across the park alone. She looked with pride at the boy, thinking how well he sat his pony; and she gave a little sigh at the half-formed thought that just crossed her mind, "What a pity he wasn't the elder!" The next minute her heart stood still; she had caught sight in the far distance of a speck, which as it drew nearer she recognised with sickening terror as Sainty's pony, riderless, and with his saddle turned under his belly. "Not *that* way, my God! I did not mean *that*." Was it possible that God was punishing her for her rebellious thought? could He have thought that she desired the death of her first-born? And she prayed with all the intensity of her soul that whatever had happened her boy might not die. "Maimed, crippled, or an idiot, if so it must be; only let him live." This was the cry of her heart, again and again repeated, as, guided by the child, she stumbled across the park with the men who were to bring him home. Arthur could tell her little, except that Sainty had had a fall and was hurt. Perhaps even then her child was lying dead, while she was wishing in her sinful heart that his brother had his heritage.

But Sainty was not dead, and did not die. The pony had kicked him in its struggles to rise, and he had fainted. There were long nights and days of pain to be borne, and he bore it as nervous people often do, who can stand anything but anticipation.

At first he made sure that the death he had asked for had come to him, and even, one day, when he was a little better, attempted to bring off one of the beautiful scenes with Arthur which he had so often rehearsed. But somehow it was not a great success. Arthur did not do his part at all nicely. He only said, "Oh! bovver, dear old Sainty. You ain't going to die; what's ve good of jawing?" and went off to more congenial pursuits.

Though his life was not in danger, Sainty's injury was a grave one; the hip was broken, and the great London surgeon who was called down did not conceal from Lady Charmington that the boy would probably always be more or less lame.

On one of his visits, Sainty astonished the great man not a little.

"Sir John," he said, "I want you to tell me something. Shall I ever be able to walk and run again?"

The famous surgeon had boys of his own, and his heart smote him at the pathetic question. "Yes, my boy, yes," he said; "certainly to walk. As to running, oh! well, you won't be very good at running, not for some time; we mustn't go too fast, not too fast, you know. Walking comes first; we must get you on your legs first."

"But I shan't ever be able to play games, shall I? not like other boys, I mean."

"Oh! well, never's a long word. I can't say, I'm sure. Not for a long while, I fear. But we never know, we never know—"

"Well, at any rate, I shan't be able to ride, shall I?" persisted the patient.

Poor Sir John hated to extinguish hope; but thus pushed into a corner, he admitted, "Oh! well, ride, you know—I don't know. I doubt if *riding* would be advisable. My poor little man, if you must know, I'm afraid you mustn't count on riding again."

To his surprise, the boy heaved a sigh of unmistakable relief. "Ah! well, that's a comfort, anyhow," he said.

# George Santayana (1863–1952)

*Born in Spain, George Santayana was a poet, novelist, literary critic, and philosopher. As an instructor at Harvard (1889–1912), he helped to introduce the writings of Walt Whitman to his students. His status as a bachelor was frowned upon by the school's administration, however, and in spite of his colleagues' high regard he was not promoted to professor until 1907. Santayana's brief biography of his distant relative Howard Overing Sturgis certainly tells us a great deal about Sturgis (see 127, above), but it is just as revealing about contemporary social attitudes, and more specifically about one homosexual person's view of another. When he revised* Persons and Places *for publication in 1944, Santayana omitted this indelible portrait; it is now restored in the MIT Press edition of his complete works (1986).*

## FROM *PERSONS AND PLACES: FRAGMENTS OF AN AUTOBIOGRAPHY* (1986)

[...] I had been expressly summoned in order that I might make the acquaintance of Howard Sturgis, "Cousin Lucy's" youngest brother, who might well have been her son, being then thirty-three years of age. Howard, too, comes properly under the head of friendship, since I began the next year to make him almost yearly visits, sometimes reduplicated, at his house in Windsor: but since I first saw him in America, and it was my Sturgis connection that established a kind of family intimacy between us, I will say something about him here.

He had come to America for a complete change of scene, hoping it might help to heal the wound that, in his excessively tender heart, had been left by the death of his mother. She had not been, from all I have gathered, at all a remarkable woman, but luxurious and affectionate, surrounded in London by a few rich American friends, especially the daughters of Motley, the historian, who were married to Englishmen, and beyond them, more by hearsay than acquaintance, by the whole British aristocracy. Howard had been her last and permanent baby. The dear child was sensitive and affectionate, with abundant golden hair, large blue eyes, and well-turned chubby arms and legs. Her boudoir became his nursery and his playroom. As if by miracle, for he was wonderfully imitative, he became, save for the accident of sex, which was not yet a serious encumbrance, a perfect young lady of the Victorian type. He acquired a good accent in French, German, and Italian, and instinctively embraced the proper liberal humanitarian principles in politics and history. There was an absolutely right and an absolutely wrong side in every war and every election; only the wicked, selfish, and heartless still prevented the deserving from growing rich, and maintained an absurd and cruel ascendancy of birth, superstition, and military power. These were the sentiments of the Great Merchants, economists, and reformers of the earlier nineteenth century, and Howard would have embraced them in any case because they appealed to his heart, and his feminine nature would never have allowed his intellect, no matter how keen, to do anything but defend his emotions. When women's opinions waver, it means that their hearts are not at rest. Let them once settle their affections and see their interests, and theoretical doubt becomes impossible for them. Howard's affections and interests were inextricably bound up with the liberal epoch; and no evidence would ever have convinced him that this was the only ground for his liberal dogmatism.

This was not all that he imbibed from his mother's circle. He was not only imitative, but he also had a theory that there was nothing women did that a man couldn't do better. Pride therefore seconded inclination in making him vie with the ladies and surpass them. He learned to sew, to embroider, to knit, and to do crochet; these occupations were not only guiltless of any country's blood, but helped to pass away the empty hours. He became wedded to them, and all his life, whether he sat by the fire or in his garden, his work-basket stood by his low chair. His needlework was exquisite, and he not only executed gorgeous embroideries, but designed them, for he was clever also with the pencil. Imitation, or a sort of involuntary caricature, sometimes went further with him. He would emit little frightened cries, if the cab he was in turned too fast round a corner; and in crossing a muddy road he would pick up the edge of his short covert-coat, as the ladies in those days picked up their trailing skirts.

Some of these automatisms were so extreme and so ridiculous that I can't help suspecting that there was something hypnotic or somnambulistic about them. He was too intelligent and too satirical to have done such things if he could have helped it. There may have been some early fixation at work, probably to his mother, of the kind that induces dreams, and develops into grotesque exaggerations and symbolic fancies. He mimicked people, sometimes on purpose, but often involuntarily; and his imagination penetrated their motives and thoughts, as his novels show, not necessarily with truth, but plausibly and with an endless capacity for extensions. He may have been at times the victim of this dramatic fertility in his own person, and found himself playing a part, that the real circumstances did not call for.

He had not yet written his best novels, only an ultrapathetic story about a little boy "Tim"[8] but one morning we found him sitting in the porch outside the living-room, on one of the wicker chairs with red-cotton cushions that adorned it, and that he copied later in the addition made to Queen's Acre; and we found him armed, not with his usual work-basket, but with a red leather writing case, and an absorbed and far-away air. He was writing poetry:

verses about the loss of his mother. We asked him to read them: he would not have brought them down-stairs if he had wished them to bloom and die unseen. He read them very nicely, without self-consciousness or affectation: the sentiment was intimate, but the form restrained and tactful.

Courage and distinction will save a man in almost any predicament; and Howard had been at Eton, where he acquired distinction and showed remarkable courage. Sending him must have been a last desperate measure insisted on by his brothers, to cure him of his girlishness. A cruel remedy, it might seem, as if he had been sent to sea before the mast. Why hadn't his father and mother corrected him sooner? His father's mind had been growing feeble, and his mother probably thought him sweeter as he was. After all, too, they were Bostonians; and would it have been *right* to correct dear little sweet Howard for girlishness, when girlishness wasn't *morally wrong?* Let him go to Eton, properly safeguarded, if his brothers thought it absolutely necessary. And this heroic remedy didn't prove in the least cruel, or in the least efficacious. Young Howard calmly defied all those schoolboys with his feminine habits and arts, which he never dreamt of disguising. He was protected by his wit and intellectual assurance; while his tutor, Mr. Ainger, author of the *Carmen Etonense*, and the two Misses Ainger, adopted him and screened him from the rude mob. Besides, Howard attracted affection, and however astonished one might be at first, or even scornful, one was always won over in the end.

After Eton, Trinity College, Cambridge, was plain sailing, and confirmed his humanitarian principles and aristocratic habits. His studies don't seem to have been serious; but he remembered what he had read of *belles-lettres*, just as ladies do. He had even dipped into Berkeley's philosophy and had laid it aside, not unwisely, as an academic curiosity. To see interesting people, or at least fashionable people, and to hear about them, made his chief entertainment later. Of course he had traveled abroad, and seen everything that everybody should see; he remained old-fashioned, without pre-Raphaelite affectations, in matters of art. His novels were exquisitely felt and observed, full of delicately satirical phrases, and not without an obvious moral aimed against domestic prejudice and social tyranny: but his writing had hardly force enough, either in style or in thought, to leave a lasting impression.

In what he felt to be his homeless plight, he had looked about for a house, and had finally taken a small one, with a nice garden, on the outskirts of Windsor Park. Its name had been Queensmead, but there was a Kingsmead next door, and seeing that the land was little more than an acre—at least the part of it visible from the house—he re-christened it Queen's Acre, familiarly and ironically abbreviated to Quaker. The nearness of Eton, and of the Aingers, had attracted him, for as often happens he retained a much greater affection for his school than for his College or University. In those first years his garden and his table were often enlivened by groups of Eton boys. To some of them he gave pet names, such as The Lion, The Bear, or The Babe;

this last being Willie Haines Smith, a distant cousin of his, who became his adopted younger brother and companion for life.

\*\*\*

In those same months a suggestion that might have enticed me twenty-five years earlier came to me from a different quarter: it was that I should go to live as a paying guest with Howard Sturgis and the Babe. But twenty-five years earlier, Howard was rich and would not have dreamt of making me such a proposal, while I was poor, and could not have accepted it. Now the tables, in some measure, were turned. He was old, desolate, ill, and hard up; and I was a friend of long standing, free, with a comfortable income, and beginning to be esteemed as a writer. Moreover, I had always been on pleasant terms with the Babe, liked him, and didn't despise him for not being intellectual or for letting Howard adopt him and support him. If anything it was the Babe that was making the greater sacrifice; which indeed Howard would not have demanded if his affection had been more heroic and his character less feminine. He could perfectly well have helped the Babe to find some comfortable post and to marry, and not have allowed him to grow old in an ambiguous dependence, and incidently to waste Howard's fortune, not in riotous living, but in foolish speculation. The Babe was certainly a minor personage, and feeble; but he kept his head and his spirits up in a difficult position, and was really the victim of the devotion that Howard insisted on showing him.

It was the Babe, on my last visit to them, who dropped a hint, evidently in consequence of confabulations that they had had together. Why didn't I settle down in England? Didn't I have a thousand pounds a year? No? Not so much? Anyhow, I could contribute a tidy sum, if I lived with friends who already had an establishment, but were suffering from the hard times. It would be so much more comfortable for me than living always in temporary quarters, in foreign countries, entirely alone.

How came Howard, with his knowledge of the world and of all his friends' weaknesses, to entertain such a project? He was living in the past. He saw himself, Queen's Acre, and me as we had been twenty-five years before. He knew how enchanting he and his circle had seemed to me then: a little Russian ballet in real life, great airs, extreme elegance in a diminutive setting, wide margins left on every side for glimpses of high life, of Royalty, of politics, of poetry, of grotesque philosophy and grotesque morals; he himself a figurine, a voluntary caricature, sitting with his golden hair beautifully brushed, his small feet daintily crossed, in the middle of a square carpet on the emerald lawn, with his work-basket and menageries of little dogs about him. His sparkling talk, while he embroidered some large design in gold thread, was alternately tender and merciless, mimicking and ridiculing everyone not present; yet he trembled, like a universal mother, at the mention of any illness, any death, any public disaster. And through all this a drift of charming relatives, guests, and casual visitors, all perfectly at home there, yet all in a holiday mood, acting their various parts appropriately in the comedy, and saying delicate things with a dancing mind.

The happy presence of reason in human life is therefore better exemplified in comedy than in tragedy. In comedy we see no terrible sub-human and super-human fatality to render reason vain. Reason therefore can make its little runs and show its comic contradictions and clever solutions without disturbing the sound vegetative substance and free flowerings of human society. We laugh at our foolish errors, correct them with a word, and know no reason why we shouldn't be happy ever after.

Sparks of this free spirit of comedy flew constantly from Howard in his youth; but soon each spark threatened to be extinguished by a little suppressed gasp of compunction. Ridicule and pity seemed to chase each other in his mind. When pity had the start, ridicule dropped out in despair; but when ridicule came first, as it usually did, pity was sure to overtake and smother it before the finish. Sentimental plays with comic relief do not make good comedy; and that was the trouble with Howard's life. He lacked genuine British stamina to keep him jolly in old age, and religion or genius would have been requisite to stiffen the sentimental side.

A change at Howard's had to come. Long before the war, during my summer visits, I had seen it approach. In 1890, when I first saw him at home, it seemed a bower of roses. Life there was a pantomime in which he played by turns the fairy prince and the disconsolate Pierrot, now full of almost tearful affection, now sitting dressed in sky-blue silk at the head of his sparkling table, surrounded by young dandies and distinguished elderly dames; or when he drove his waggonette and high-stepping pair skillfully and festively, holding high the reins in his white-gloved hands, as if he were dancing a minuet.

Gradually all that gaiety and joyfulness had faded from the scene. First his fancy clothes were discarded: they had lost their freshness and perhaps they had got too tight, for he was no longer very slender. Anyhow masquerades at home were ridiculous and unsuitable. Then he gave up mimicking people, except involuntarily in little touches when he repeated what anyone had said. His imitations had been works of art, taking off not only voice and manner to perfection, but supplying diction and sentiments to suit, and only slightly exaggerated. But mockery, his aging conscience warned him, was unkind; and if he gave up being kind, what would remain of him? The irony of fate would have it that now when he disciplined himself in kindness he was really far less kind than he had been when merry and ready to make fun of everybody; for just as he had loved lame little mongrel dogs for being lame and mongrel, so he had really loved us all in his youth for being absurd and full of little weaknesses; whereas now the merry sentimentalist had become a melancholy one, and sadly censorious. And while the freedom and light faded from his spirit, the sunshine seemed also to fade from his garden and the joyousness from his house.

Anticipations had not been realized. The house had been enlarged, but seemed smaller, the furniture old-fashioned and worn, the once flowering garden grey and bald like our respective heads. The ribaldry had been expunged from conversation, but also the wit, the frankness, the variety. Political intolerance had set in, and a thick mist of sadness. Any straggling guest like myself caused evident disturbance. I knew that some white wine had been ordered expressly on my arrival, so that it might not seem that there was nothing to drink. If I came to live with them I should be an expense, as well as a help: nor could it be an act of kindness on my part in other ways, because our views now clashed not in merriment any longer but in displeasure. People do not grow better when they grow old; they remain the same, but later circumstances cause them to exhibit their character sometimes in a minor key with the soft pedal, so that they seem to us grown sweeter, and sometimes more harshly and disagreeably, when we think them soured or depraved. No: we are no longer charmed by their virtues or interested in their vices.

With the lapse of years Howard and I had begun to see each other in this less favourable light. He thought I was abominably selfish. Certainly, I am profoundly selfish in the sense that I resist human contagion, except provisionally, on the surface, and in matters indifferent to me. For pleasure and conviviality, I like to share the life about me, and have often done it: but never so as, at heart, to surrender my independence. On the other hand, I am not selfish in a competitive way. I don't want to snatch money or position or pleasures from other people, nor do I attempt to dominate them, as an unselfish man would say, for their own good. I sincerely wish them joy in their native ways of living, as if they were wild animals; but I decidedly refuse to hunt with them unless the probable result recommends itself to me independently.

\*\*\*

I happened to be at Queen's Acre in 1914 shortly after the outbreak of war, when Howard was suffering from a cruel sense of the folly of mankind. What could be more senseless than destruction, destruction, destruction? Yet in his intense liberalism he had applauded the destruction of ancient institutions and ways of life, because destruction there had made room for liberty. The destruction of modern works, on the contrary, would make for poverty; and like a true child of the Great Merchants, Howard was convinced that riches exalted worthy people and made them beneficent. Destruction is indeed cruel and odious when it is carried on for its own sake, malignantly or covetously, like the destruction of the monasteries during the Reformation and the Revolution; but if we take a broad cosmic view, destruction is only the shady side of progress. Like natural death it is inevitable; and though we regret it when premature or needlessly painful, there would be as much sentimental folly in disallowing it as in mourning the coming on of night or of autumn. So the war of 1914–18 was intended by the Germans to be, for them and for the future of the world, a step in industrial and political progress; and so too the next war, wickedly destructive and arrogant on both sides, was conceived, first again by the Germans, and then by all the combatants. The Great Merchants' wealth and the whole economic system of which they were the flower, proved in fact less beneficent and much less durable than the *ancien régime*.[9] Howard himself was a pathetic victim of this system; he was generosity and refinement personified; but he couldn't help envying the dying aristocracy that he imitated and denounced; and the necessary soil to sustain his wealth, refinement, and generosity slipped visibly from under his feet.

During that first climacteric war, I heard that Howard had taken lodgings in London in order to do "War Work" by reading, censoring and readdressing German prisoners' correspondence. This was a marked sacrifice of his comfort and leisure; but solitary comfort with moral irritation and loneliness is not happiness; and the change of scene, the dutiful occupation, and the sense of helping to console mothers, sweethearts, and wives, in spite of possible bombs, was surely some compensation. But there was a tragic background to this charitable act. Howard was beginning to suffer from the mortal illness, cancer in the bowels; and though he had been reprieved by one dangerous operation, another was destined to be necessary. Fortune proved faithless to him with a vengeance; but he showed a remarkable fortitude, not stoical but tender. The fountains of pleasure and gaiety, so sparkling in his youth, had run dry. It was not difficult to surrender them, when the affections remained which need never be surrendered.

When months later, in Italy, I saw in *The Times* that Howard was dead, and on writing to the Babe received assurances that Howard had died peacefully, without pain, and nobly resigned, then the whole long and curious chapter of my friendship with him came up before me, much as I have recorded it here; and I was glad that the end, which had to be sad, at least had not been harrowing. If I had jumped at the chance of going to live at Queen's Acre, thinking I had found a home at last, my illusion would have been short-lived, and our brief life in common would not have been happy. Still, when I returned to England, in 1923, I went to see the Babe where he was living with his father near Bath; but it was an unsatisfactory postscript. What a ghastly pleasure this is, to pull the dead out of their graves! My morning tea was served me in a beautiful china cup, one of a familiar set in the old days at Howard's, now apparently the last survivor, glued and riveted together in many places, like a mutilated veteran of the Guard. Was I sorry that Howard was dead? No: but I was glad that he had lived. And here I repeated the experience of my uncle Santiago on the death of his daughter. "I had already lost her," he said, "when she was married." I had already, gradually and insensibly, lost Howard when he began to shed his rare self, with its inimitable honest mixture of effeminacy and courage, sensibility and wit, mockery and devoted love. [...]

## Notes

1  I.e., a homosexual who attempts to define and understand himself within the nexus of family and society rather than outside them, however transgressive his sexuality might be. He might be the father/husband/brother who cannot play the game of marriage but who nonetheless continues the familial ties of a domestic relationship. Sainty, the hero of *Belchamber*, is a domestic homosexual who plays the role assigned to him, however unfit his heart and sexuality might be. For more on this idea, see my study *Dayneford's Library*, 64–79.

2  Rosalind, the central character in Shakespeare's *As You Like It*, spends most of the play disguised as a young man.

3  The Scottish Covenanters were anti-Catholic religious reformers of the seventeenth century who joined together in defiance of the British throne. Under Charles II they endured a reign of terror and were eventually defeated. They suffered much persecution and were known for their aggressive moral purity. This clearly provides a clue to the personality of Lady Charmington.

4  "High Church" (1687) stresses the liturgical, ceremonial, traditional, and Catholic elements in Anglican worship. Lady Charmington, descended from anti-Catholic Covenanters, implies that the governess' religion is too Roman Catholic.

5  A person who is lukewarm or indifferent, especially in matters of religion, as the early Christians of Laodicea were accused of being (Revelation 3: 14–16).

6  Gallio (d. 65 AD?) was the Roman proconsul in Achaea who refused judgment on a question of Jewish religious law when Paul was on trial before him; later he refused to interfere between Sosthenes and his Greek assailants. The image here is of a man who refuses to take sides in an issue.

7  The way of the Cross; i.e., Jesus' path on the road to crucifixion.

8  *Tim: A Story of Eton* (1891), a sympathetic but tragic depiction of a sensitive child in British public school, was the first of Sturgis's three novels. Edward Prime-Stevenson labeled *Tim* "a minute study of psychic Uranianism between two school-lads."

9  "The old regime," i.e., the past, former times (French).

PART EIGHT

HAUNTED

# Henry Blake Fuller (1857–1929)

*We have already seen Fuller's reminiscences in* The Allisonian Classical Academy *(see above, 51–58). He became a professional writer whose novel* The Cliff-Dwellers *(1893) was a realistic examination of people in a Chicago skyscraper. In 1919 he published* Bertram Cope's Year, *a daring study of a homosexual college instructor, but it was not received well by the public and he retreated from any further treatment of the theme. Earlier, however, Fuller had foregrounded homosexuality in* At St. Judas's, *a tragic one-act drama that had been relatively "hidden" in a collection of twelve other plays called* The Puppet-Booth *(1896), enveloped perhaps where it would not be especially noticed, for its subject-matter would have been quite shocking to a world still reeling from the trials of Oscar Wilde (which had taken place the previous year; see xix). It is "closet drama" in more ways than one. Such a play was never intended to be performed on a stage—its effects would have been all but impossible—but rather to be read as a poetic form.*

# *AT ST. JUDAS'S* (1896)

*… al fondo che divora*
*Lucifero con Giuda …*
    *(Inferno, XXXI)*
*… in the abyss which swallows up*
*Judas with Lucifer …*
    (Longfellow's translation)[1]

Persons

THE BRIDEGROOM
THE BEST MAN
THE SACRISTAN

A Procession of priests and acolytes

EIGHT PAINTED WINDOWS

*The sacristy of the church of St. Judas. Time: ten minutes before noon. A pealing of bells is heard.*
    *The sacristy is a great octagonal room of sculptured stone; its groined vaulting is upheld by one central column which is wreathed from base to capital with a band of pale*

*carven flowers, and its eight windows—broad and high, trefoiled and quatrefoiled—
flood both floor and roof with an endless dapple and ripple of variegated light. Under
one of these windows an open door leads into the church. Through this doorway one sees
the chancel banked with flowers; and above the decorous murmur of a thousand tongues
one hears the tones of the organ and the voices of the choir-boys.*

*Present in the sacristy: The BRIDEGROOM and his BEST MAN. Both are in full
uniform; each wears white gloves and carries a sword.*

THE BRIDEGROOM (*gaily*). In ten minutes—ten minutes more!

THE BEST MAN (*with constraint*). In ten minutes—as you say.

THE BRIDEGROOM (*fastening his glove*). Is that a long time, or a short time?
A long time, I think.

THE BEST MAN. A short time. But much may happen within a short time;
much may happen in ten minutes.

THE BRIDEGROOM. How soberly said! Are you as jovial as one's closest
friend should be?

THE BEST MAN. Perhaps not. This day—it means so much for me.

THE BRIDGROOM (*unfastening his glove*). As much as it means for me?

THE BEST MAN. As much, yes. Quite as much. Perhaps more.

THE BRIDEGROOM. Not more. For it means everything in the world for me.

THE BEST MAN. It means everything in the world for *me.*

THE BRIDEGROOM. *Now* that voice vibrates with such a degree of interest
as I have felt this day demanded! *Now* I begin to recognize you!—the first
time for a month.

THE BEST MAN. I am the same. I am unaltered.

THE BRIDEGROOM (*refastening his glove*). No, no; you have never been quite
the same since I told you—since you heard of the great change in store for
me.

THE BEST MAN. How did you tell me? In your sleep—your own pillow close
to mine. I felt myself an eavesdropper; I felt that I had betrayed your confidence.

THE BRIDEGROOM. Not betrayed; only anticipated. You would have known
within a day. You have known everything else. You have shared my
thoughts, my ideas, my secrets, my ambitions. We have eaten together; we
have slept together; we have fought side by side. We are of the same age,
the same height—my eyes have always been able to look level into yours.
We are of the same bulk as well;—who shall say that even at the present
moment I am not wearing your coat and you mine?

THE BEST MAN. That has happened more than once.

THE BRIDEGROOM. You have saved my life; I have saved yours. Have we not
pledged an unbreaking friendship?

THE BEST MAN. We have.

[The FIRST of the EIGHT WINDOWS comes to life; there is a flux of color and of outline among its mullioned lights. Gradually two figures among its ranks of churchly warriors become strangely secularized; they raise their crossed swords on high, while their left hands meet in a clasp of friendship. The colors upon the pavement shift in correspondence, and from the church, or from spaces far above and beyond it, there come the tones of the *Ecce, quam bonum.*[2]]

THE BRIDEGROOM. But for *you* my bones, hacked by African sabers, might now be bleaching upon the desert sands.

THE BEST MAN. But for *you* my own, gnawed by nameless fishes, might now be lying at the bottom of the sea.

THE BRIDEGROOM. Your arm, sweeping through that burning air, saved me for today.

THE BEST MAN. Yours, cleaving through those angry waters, saved me for— for—(*to himself*) for—what?

THE BRIDEGROOM. Yes, you have saved me for today. A moment more, and I shall stand where I have long hoped to stand, and shall take the vow that so long has been ready on my lips. At last all obstacles are brushed aside— at last the way stands clear. Those obstacles—you know my combat with them as well as I myself. At every step, on every hand, this mysterious opposition, this determined and unceasing enmity. From what source could it come? From what motive? What enemy have I? The worst should stay his hand at such a time as this.

THE BEST MAN (*vaguely*). True—true.

THE BRIDEGROOM. I pass over the attempt to embarrass my fortune; and I will say nothing of the efforts made to transfer me to another regiment and to have me sent back to wars. Nor will I dwell upon the conspiracy disclosed by the repeated advice from so many friends to forego this marriage. For few of these advisers were close enough to me to have the right to speak; fewer still had any definite reason to tender; and all were but too plainly moved—some of them unconsciously, perhaps—by one hidden yet dexterous hand. Let all that pass. How did the real attack begin? What was the first thing to be insinuated?

THE BEST MAN (*as before*). Yes, I remember.

[The SECOND of the EIGHT WINDOWS is endowed with a moving consciousness. Ten honorable Knights rise in a semicircle and look down, with an open apprehension in their pure young eyes, upon the pair beneath. An indignant diapason rolls in from the organ, and distant voices are heard to chant the *In quo corriget?*[3]]

THE BRIDEGROOM. A shameful whisper, creeping hither and thither, named me a cheat, a trickster, a gamester. I have played—yes; it is the privilege of my order, of my profession. But I have never played otherwise than honorably.

THE BEST MAN. None otherwise than honorably.

THE BRIDEGROOM. A hundred tongues came to my defense. Only one was silent—yours. I can never thank you enough for that. Your perfect confidence would not deign.…Your certainty of my innocence made it seem.…

THE BEST MAN. Unnecessary to defend.

[The Knights look into one another's eyes and shake their heads and turn away their faces.]

THE BRIDEGROOM. I strangled this slanderous report—though *she* indeed had never doubted me; and I struck down the only man who dared repeat it openly. But what came next? After defending my honor as an officer, I was compelled to defend my honor as a suitor.

[The THIRD WINDOW sets itself in motion. A band of chaste young Damsels brush forward through ranks of tall and rigid lilies and curve their lustrous palms before their ears to hear the coming words of ill-report. Voices (not theirs) intone the words of the *Noli aemulari*.[4]]

THE BRIDEGROOM. A score of lying words placed in an honest hand—a villainous bit of paper brought to the gaze of a pair of trusting eyes. Who could have done it, I ask—and why?

THE BEST MAN. We never learned.

THE BRIDEGROOM. I have indeed lived freely, but who shall say that I have seriously overstepped the bounds?

[The Damsels blush, and stoop to hide their faces among the lilies. But their blushes are repeated upon the pavement.]

THE BEST MAN. No one.

THE BRIDEGROOM. I went to her brother. What I told him satisfied him. But who could have written that letter? And why?

THE BEST MAN. You never learned.

THE BRIDEGROOM. But as bad followed—or worse. What was next attacked? My courage as a soldier. Mine—mine!

[The FOURTH WINDOW. An army with banners. The leaders of the host rest on their swordhilts and gaze downward with satirical and contemptuous smiles. Above the ranks rise flags of scarlet and purple that flaunt in airy derision and dapple the sculptured pillar.]

THE BRIDEGROOM. I demanded a hearing. I combated the unworthy charges sent back across those wastes of sand and of sea. I summoned my witnesses. *You* spoke for me; briefly, quietly, one might almost have said reluctantly.

THE BEST MAN. You were above such accusations.

THE BRIDEGROOM. Your words, added to those of others, sufficed. And that evening Angela kissed me for the untarnished soldier that I was.

THE BEST MAN. Then I said enough. *(To himself.)* Too much, perhaps.

[The leader of the Army lifts a foreshortened sword, and makes a movement as if of warning. But neither of the pair interprets his movement, for neither sees it.]

THE BRIDEGROOM. I came at last, then, to stand forth whole, sound, unscathed. I. But the others?—my bride? Her parents?...

[The FIFTH WINDOW. A rising of the sheeted Dead. The sun, half hidden by a passing cloud, but partly penetrates the dull and spectral panes.]

THE BRIDEGROOM. A rumor ran that my orphaned bride had been born out of wedlock—that no priest had ever blessed the union of.... O, it was foul! I beat at the doors of townhalls; I rained blows upon the portals of parish churches: my Angela should not be thus doubly and disgracefully orphaned. I searched the records, dim and dusty as they were. And I brought the truth triumphantly to light.

[The sun reappears. The Dead throw back their cowls. Their eyes sparkle, their cheeks are flushed with life. They raise their full-fleshed hands in benediction.]

THE BRIDEGROOM. But who could have started that rumor? And why?

THE BEST MAN. Who, indeed? You have never learned.

THE BRIDEGROOM. But even that was not enough. Worse followed—you know what. Word passed that Angela herself.... No, no; I cannot say it. I—I heard that she was false....

[The SIXTH WINDOW. A trio of female figures—Love, Truth and Purity—entwined in one another's arms. Their eyes are startled; their garments quiver and scintillate in reds and ambers and pale greens. Their mouths open, but whether in condemnation or in defense it is too soon to say. From that quarter, or from another, there comes the chant: *Iniquos odio habui.*[5]]

THE BRIDEGROOM.—that she was untrue ... impure....Yes, but the last great lie was faced and routed. Here I await her; one moment more and she will have come. *(Happy tears course iridescently down the cheeks of the three Virgins.)* Hark, hark! I hear even now their carriage-wheels without.

[The SACRISTAN enters.]

THE SACRISTAN. Noon, and past noon. And the bride does not come.
THE BEST MAN. The chimes have long since ceased pealing.
THE SACRISTAN. The whole church questions, and whispers;—do you not hear?
THE BRIDEGROOM. Nothing can prevent that. Let the bells be heard too.

[The SACRISTAN closes the door leading into the church, and retires by means of a second one opposite. Through walls, or doors, or windows are heard the words: *Quare fremuerent gentes?*[6]]

THE BEST MAN. The bells may ring, but they will bring you nothing.
THE BRIDEGROOM. What do you mean, my friend?
THE BEST MAN. She will not come.

[The SEVENTH WINDOW. The Seven Cardinal Virtues; they change, with a slow but relentless movement of color, of outline, of feature, into the Seven Deadly Sins. This transformation, like all the others, passes unheeded.]

THE BEST MAN. She will not come. Have you not heard?
THE BRIDEGROOM. Heard what?
THE BEST MAN. What everyone else has heard; what fills the church with smiles and whispers even now.
THE BRIDGROOM. What have you to tell me?
THE BEST MAN. It is always thus. The most concerned is ever the last to learn.
THE BRIDEGROOM. What have I to learn?
THE BEST MAN. This: that she has sinned.
THE BRIDEGROOM. That should have been said before. Or, better and more truly, not at all.
THE BEST MAN. They say that she has sinned, and sinned—with me.
THE BRIDEGROOM. O, my enemy! unseen, but unrelenting! And what is your response?
THE BEST MAN. Were the other reports true?
THE BRIDGROOM. Not one of them.
THE BEST MAN. Ah.... Perhaps the chimes will begin again. Perhaps the bride will yet appear. Perhaps those whisperings will cease. Do you hear them?
THE BRIDEGROOM. Yes—even through that door.

THE BEST MAN. Do you hear the bells?
THE BRIDEGROOM. No.
THE BEST MAN. Do you hear the bride arriving?
THE BRIDEGROOM. Not yet.
THE BEST MAN. Ah....

[A pause]

THE BRIDEGROOM. Is it true—what you say? Is it true? Is it true?
THE BEST MAN. Why need that matter? It is nothing; let it pass.
THE BRIDEGROOM. Nothing?... Let it pass?...
THE BEST MAN. Yes. *I* am here. And *she* will never be. You may wait, but you
    shall wait in vain. *(He places his hand on the other's shoulder.)* If she were to come,
    I should not let her have you. She shall not have you. Nobody shall have you.
THE BRIDEGROOM. What is your meaning, Oliver?

[The Deadliest of the Seven Sins[7] hides her face; it is too hideous for contemplation.]

THE BEST MAN. I shall not let you go. Our friendship has been too long, too
    close, too intimate. It shall not be destroyed; it shall not be broken. No one
    shall come between us.
THE BRIDEGROOM. Peace, Oliver, in heaven's name!
THE BEST MAN. Why have we lived so long together—why shared each
    other's every thought? To be completely sundered now?—Why did I save
    your life? To have it taken from me thus?—Why did you save mine? That
    you might cast this blight upon it in the end?—She shall not have you! I
    will do everything to prevent it! I *have* done everything to pre—....
THE BRIDEGROOM. Ha! It is *you* who have attacked my honor?
THE BEST MAN. Your honor is secure.
THE BRIDEGROOM. It is *you* who have questioned my courage?
THE BEST MAN. You are brave; I believe that.
THE BRIDEGROOM. It is *you* who have insulted my love?
THE BEST MAN. No one loves you more than I.

[The sculptured wreath entwined round the great central column writhes in
descending spirals, like a vast serpent.]

THE BRIDEGROOM. You are a liar, a traitor, a perjurer, and you shall die.
THE BEST MAN. One of us shall die.
THE BRIDEGROOM. One of us two shall die. It shall be you.
THE BEST MAN. One of us shall die—one of us three. *She* shall die; it is she
    who has come between us.

THE BRIDEGROOM *(drawing his sword)*. You shall die. I shall kill you with my own hands.

[The chimes begin to ring. A sound of rumbling wheels and trampling hoofs is heard outside. A procession of priests and acolytes crosses the sacristy on the way into the church. They pause at the signs of combat.]

THE BRIDEGROOM. Ah! She comes! She believes in me! And so shall all the others! They do, already; I will not believe the throng makes sport of our fair fame. *(To the priests.)* Move on; move on! I will follow you within a moment.

[The procession traverses the sacristy and moves on toward the high altar. THE BRIDEGROOM shuts the door behind it. The BEST MAN, springing forward, thrusts him from it, and then stands staunchly with his own back against its panels.]

THE BEST MAN. You shall not pass. You shall never pass—to her.
THE BRIDEGROOM. Stand aside. Let me through.
THE BEST MAN. I do not mean to fail at the last moment. I shall not allow so many good endeavors to go for naught.
THE BRIDEGROOM. Stand aside. I hate you; I detest you; I despise you; I loathe you.
THE BEST MAN. You hate me? That cannot be!
THE BRIDEGROOM. I hate you with my whole heart. I loathe you with my whole soul.
THE BEST MAN. You loathe me? I, who have done so much....
THE BRIDEGROOM. You are not fit to live. You are not fit to die. But die you shall. I shall not kill you. You shall kill yourself. You shall do it now, and I shall see you do it. You have no other road to redemption.
THE BEST MAN. We have been friends always.... I have loved you all my life.... The thought of *her* made me mad—made me desperate....
THE BRIDEGROOM. Time presses. Use your blade.

[The EIGHTH WINDOW. The Angelic Host trumpeting from the clouds, while Lucifer plunges headlong toward the Pit: the wonder is that he can fall so long, so fast, so far.
   When THE BRIDEGROOM opens the door into the church, THE BRIDE is seen coming up the aisle, while the choirboys and the organ unite in a resounding Gloria. Upon the floor of the sacristy lies the body of a man in a pool of blood. As THE BRIDE and THE BRIDEGROOM meet before the altar rail, the EIGHT WINDOWS, dappling the floor of the sacristy with a thousand varied splotches of color—(but there is one, broader and brighter than them all)—shudder back convulsively to their pristine selves.]

# GERTRUDE ATHERTON (1857–1948)

*Gertrude Atherton was famous for a series of historical novels about her native California (e.g.,* The Californians *[1898] and* The Ancestors *[1907] as well as a fictionalized biography of Alexander Hamilton,* The Conqueror *[1902]); but this little tale of terror shows her at the height of her storytelling powers. The genre of horror stories became increasingly popular in the nineteenth century, when many writers drew upon advancements in the field of "dynamic psychology" (the school of psychology concerned with motivation and/or the structure and functioning of personality) for their stories, with ghosts providing a convenient and fashionable dimension to characters' psyches. Certainly this story—with or without a ghost—is an interesting example, not only for the shock of its ending, but also for what it might be saying "between its lines" about the relationship between the two men. The character of the thirty-two-year-old bachelor Weigall is described as "continental and detached," who finally cannot "face up"—quite literally, as we see!—to his true feelings. The original title of this tale was "The Twins," which further suggests the closeness of the relationship between the hero and his missing friend. Is this, like "Marjorie Daw" (see below, 186–201), another example of what Eve Kosofsky Sedgwick would call "homosexual panic"?[8]*

# "THE STRIDING PLACE" (1896)

Weigall, continental and detached, tired early of grouse-shooting. To stand propped against a sod fence while his host's workmen routed up the birds with long poles and drove them towards the waiting guns, made him feel himself a parody on the ancestors who had roamed the moors and forests of this West Riding of Yorkshire in hot pursuit of game worth the killing. But when in England in August he always accepted whatever proffered for the season, and invited his host to shoot pheasants on his estates in the South. The amusements of life, he argued, should be accepted with the same philosophy as its ills.

It had been a bad day. A heavy rain had made the moor so spongy that it fairly sprang beneath the feet. Whether or not the grouse had haunts of their own, wherein they were immune from rheumatism, the bag had been small. The women, too, were an unusually dull lot, with the exception of a new-minded *débutante* who bothered Weigall at dinner by demanding the verbal restoration of the vague paintings on the vaulted roof above them.

But it was no one of these things that sat on Weigall's mind as, when the other men went up to bed, he let himself out of the castle and sauntered down to the river. His intimate friend, the companion of his boyhood, the chum of his college days, his fellow-traveller in many lands, the man for whom he possessed stronger affection than for all men, had mysteriously disappeared two days ago, and his track might have sprung to the upper air for all trace he had left behind him. He had been a guest on the adjoining estate during the past week, shooting with the fervour of the true sportsman, making love in the intervals to Adeline Cavan, and apparently in the best of spirits. As far as was known, there was nothing to lower his mental mercury, for his rent-roll was a large one, Miss Cavan blushed whenever he looked at her, and, being one of the best shots in England, he was never happier than in August. The suicide theory was preposterous, all agreed, and there was as little reason to believe him murdered. Nevertheless, he had walked out of March Abbey two nights ago without hat or overcoat, and had not been seen since.

The country was being patrolled night and day. A hundred keepers and working men were beating the woods and poking the bogs on the moors, but as yet not so much as a handkerchief had been found.

Weigall did not believe for a moment that Wyatt Gifford was dead, and although it was impossible not to be affected by the general uneasiness, he was disposed to be more angry than frightened. At Cambridge Gifford had been an incorrigible practical joker, and by no means had outgrown the habit; it would be like him to cut across the country in his evening clothes, board a cattle train, and amuse himself touching up the picture of the sensation in West Riding.

However, Weigall's affection for his friend was too deep to companion with tranquility in the present state of doubt, and, instead of going to bed early with the other men, he determined to walk until ready for sleep. He went down to the river and followed the path through the woods. There was no moon, but the stars sprinkled their cold light upon the pretty belt of water flowing placidly past wood and ruin, between green masses of overhanging rocks or sloping banks tangled with tree and shrub, leaping occasionally over stones with the harsh notes of an angry scold, to recover its equanimity the moment the way was clear again.

It was very dark in the depths where Weigall trod. He smiled as he recalled a remark of Gifford's: "An English wood is like a good many other things in life—very promising at a distance, but a hollow mockery when you get within. You see daylight on both sides, and the sun freckles the very bracken. Our woods need the night to make them seem what they ought to be—what they once were, before our ancestors' descendants demanded so much more money, in these so much more various days."

Weigall strolled along, smoking, and thinking of his friend, his pranks—many of which had done more credit to his imagination than this—and recalling conversations that had lasted the night through. Just before the end of the London season they had walked the streets one hot night after a party, discussing the various theories of the soul's destiny. That afternoon they had met at the coffin of a college friend whose mind had been a blank for the past three years. Some months previously they had called at the asylum to see him. His expression had been senile, his face imprinted with the record of debauchery. In death the face was placid, intelligent, without ignoble lineation—the face of the man they had known at college. Weigall and Gifford had had no time to comment there, and the afternoon and evening were full; but, coming forth from the house of festivity together, they had reverted almost at once to the topic.

"I cherish the theory," Gifford had said, "that the soul sometimes lingers in the body after death. During madness, of course, it is an impotent prisoner, albeit a conscious one. Fancy its agony, and its horror! What more natural than that, when the life-spark goes out, the tortured soul should take possession of the vacant skull and triumph once more for a few hours while old friends look their last? It has had time to repent while compelled to crouch and behold the result of its work, and it has shrived itself into a state of comparative purity. If I had my way, I should stay inside my bones until the coffin had gone into its niche, that I might obviate for my poor old comrade the tragic impersonality of death. And I should like to see justice done to it, as it were—to see it lowered among its ancestors with the ceremony and solemnity that are its due. I am afraid that if I dissevered myself too quickly, I should yield to curiosity and hasten to investigate the mysteries of space."

"You believe in the soul as an independent entity, then—that it and the vital principle are not one and the same?"

"Absolutely. The body and soul are twins, life comrades—sometimes friends, sometimes enemies, but always loyal in the last instance. Some day, when I am tired of the world, I shall go to India and become a mahatma, solely for the pleasure of receiving proof during life of this independent relationship."

"Suppose you were not sealed up properly, and returned after one of your astral flights to find your earthly part unfit for habitation? It is an experiment I don't think I should care to try, unless even juggling with soul and flesh had palled."

"That would not be an uninteresting predicament. I should rather enjoy experimenting with broken machinery."

The high wild roar of water smote suddenly on Weigall's ear and checked his memories. He left the wood and walked out on the huge slippery stones which nearly close the River Wharfe at this point, and watched the waters boil down into the narrow pass with their furious untiring energy. The black quiet of the woods rose high on either side. The stars seemed colder and whiter just above. On either hand the perspective of the river might have run into a rayless cavern. There was no lonelier spot in England, nor one which had the right to claim so many ghosts, if ghosts there were.

Weigall was not a coward, but he recalled uncomfortably the tales of those that had been done to death in the Strid.[9] Wordsworth's Boy of Egremond had been disposed of by the practical Whitaker; but countless others, more venturesome than wise, had gone down into that narrow boiling course, never to appear in the still pool a few yards beyond. Below the great rocks which form the walls of the Strid was believed to be a natural vault, on to whose shelves the dead were drawn. The spot had an ugly fascination. Weigall stood, visioning skeletons, uncoffined and green, the home of the eyeless things which had devoured all that had covered and filled that rattling symbol of man's mortality; then fell to wondering if any one had attempted to leap the Strid of late. It was covered with slime; he had never seen it look so treacherous.

He shuddered and turned away, impelled, despite his manhood, to flee the spot. As he did so, something tossing in the foam below the fall—something as white, yet independent of it—caught his eye and arrested his step. Then he saw that it was describing a contrary motion to the rushing water—an upward backward motion. Weigall stood rigid, breathless; he fancied he heard the crackling of his hair. Was that a hand? It thrust itself still higher above the boiling foam, turned sidewise, and four frantic fingers were distinctly visible against the black rock beyond.

Weigall's superstitious terror left him. A man was there, struggling to free himself from the suction beneath the Strid, swept down, doubtless, but a moment before his arrival, perhaps as he stood with his back to the current.

He stepped as close to the edge as he dared. The hand doubled as if in imprecation, shaking savagely in the face of that force which leaves its creatures to immutable law; then spread wide again, clutching, expanding, crying for help as audibly as the human voice.

Weigall dashed to the nearest tree, dragged and twisted off a branch with his strong arms, and returned as swiftly to the Strid. The hand was in the same place, still gesticulating as wildly; the body was undoubtedly caught in the rocks below, perhaps already half-way along one of those hideous shelves. Weigall let himself down upon a lower rock, braced his shoulder against the mass beside him, then, leaning out over the water, thrust the branch into the hand. The fingers clutched it convulsively. Weigall tugged powerfully, his own feet dragged perilously near the edge. For a moment he produced no impression, then an arm shot above the waters.

The blood sprang to Weigall's head; he was choked with the impression that the Strid had him in her roaring hold, and he saw nothing. Then the mist cleared. The hand and arm were nearer, although the rest of the body was still concealed by the foam. Weigall peered out with distended eyes. The meager light revealed in the cuffs links of a peculiar device. The fingers clutching the branch were as familiar.

Weigall forgot the slippery stones, the terrible death if he stepped too far.

He pulled with passionate will and muscle. Memories flung themselves into the hot light of his brain, trooping rapidly upon each other's heels, as in the thought of the drowning. Most of the pleasures of his life, good and bad, were identified in some way with this friend. Scenes of college days, of travel, where they had deliberately sought adventure and stood between one another and death upon more occasions than one, of hours of delightful companionship among the treasures of art, and others in the pursuit of pleasure, flashed like the changing particles of a kaleidoscope. Weigall had loved several women; but he would have flouted in these moments the thought that he had ever loved any woman as he loved Wyatt Gifford. There were so many charming women in the world, and in the thirty-two years of his life he had never known another man to whom he had cared to give his intimate friendship.

He threw himself on his face. His wrists were cracking, the skin was torn from his hands. The fingers still gripped the stick. There was life in them yet.

Suddenly something gave way. The hand swung about, tearing the branch from Weigall's grasp. The body had been liberated and flung outward, though still submerged by the foam and spray.

Weigall scrambled to his feet and sprang along the rocks, knowing that the danger from suction was over and that Gifford must be carried straight to the quiet pool. Gifford was a fish in the water and could live under it longer than most men. If he survived this, it would not be the first time that his pluck and science had saved him from drowning.

Weigall reached the pool. A man in his evening clothes floated on it, his face turned towards a projecting rock over which his arm had fallen, upholding the body. The hand that had held the branch hung limply over the rock, its white reflection visible in the black water. Weigall plunged into the shallow pool, lifted Gifford in his arms and returned to the bank. He laid the body down and threw off his coat that he might be the freer to practise the methods of resuscitation. He was glad of the moment's respite. The valiant life in the man might have been exhausted in that last struggle. He had not dared to look at his face, to put his ear to the heart. The hesitation lasted but a moment. There was no time to lose.

He turned to his prostrate friend. As he did so, something strange and disagreeable smote his senses. For a half-moment he did not appreciate its nature. Then his teeth clacked together, his feet, his outstretched arms pointed towards the woods. But he sprang to the side of the man and bent down and peered into his face. There was no face.

# GEORGE SYLVESTER VIERECK (1884–1962)

*Much loved and much hated during his lifetime but little-known today, Viereck was a poet, novelist, and active Socialist. Viereck drew Teddy Roosevelt's admiration—but later his animosity—for staunchly supporting Germany throughout World War I. Viereck was highly sexually charged, and spent his life unashamedly exploring as many sides of his libido as he could. A great admirer of Oscar Wilde, he defended him throughout his career, and modeled several works after Wilde's. He supported Dr. Magnus Hirschfeld and his controversial Sex Institute in a little book co-authored with Havelock Ellis,* Plain Talks with Husbands and Wives *(1927) for the medical establishment. His 1907 homoerotic novel (and later a stage play, now lost)* The House of the Vampire *portrayed the sinister hold of an older man on a series of younger acolytes. It is, however, in his two collections of poetry that Viereck's "Greek" side boldly surfaces alongside more conventional love poetry.*

## FROM *NINEVEH AND OTHER POEMS* (1908)

## Mr. W.H.

*"To Mr. W.H., the onlie begetter of these ensuing sonnets."*
*—Inscription to Shakespeare's Sonnets*

I sometimes dream and dreaming long
For thee, strange boy whose golden head
With blossoms of unending song
   Was garlanded.

Sad, surely, and contemptuous
And smiling thou beheld'st the game
Of life, as once Antinous[10]
   His splendid shame.

A softer light was in thine eyes
Than any that the moonbeam paints,
Or in some dead queen's hair that lies
   Or blessed saint's.

And yet, perchance thou hadst no art,
Nor depth, nor subtlety,—a boy
To whom a poet's singing heart
   Was but a toy.

## For Antinous in his Old Age

Snow's in thy hair and wrinkles on thy brow,
   The years have strewn the ashes on thy face;
   Of all things wretched, wanting most in grace,
Of all things sad, the saddest thing art thou.
Now has thy boyish smile become a leer,
   Thy lips are swollen and thy vision blinks,
   And in thy heart, more ancient than the Sphinx,
Abide alone the memory and the tear.

O lovely lad reborn in many a land,
   Of Shakespeare loved and Michelangelo![11]
Not thine this age's crown of sorrow, and
   Thou shouldst have died these many years ago,
     Not grown into a spectre of the past,
     To be a thing of horror at the last.

## Friendship

Lo, in my hour of need I called on thee,
   Asking thy friendship's none too heavy toll;
   Comrades were we when I was glad and whole,
And yet thou cam'st not, and at last I see
Twain are the ways of friendship, and there be
   One that laughs with us o'er the fragrant bowl,
   And one that wanders with the troubled soul
In the great silence of Gethsemane.

I can forgive, and while glad days abound
   Thou shalt be with me; but when Autumn flings
The rose-leaf and the wine-cup to the ground,
     Then would I call upon the heart that hears
     With intimate love the depth of human things,
     The eye that knows the sanctity of tears.

## Hadrian

How pale, how wan, my Caesar, is thy smile,
   Grey with the ashes of the heart's desire.
   Shall not thy slave with sweet pleasaunce beguile
The hosts of care that to thy hurt conspire?

Shall shimmering silks before thy throne be spread
   From the far sands where patient camels plod?
   Or black-robed seers draw nigh, who long have read
   The secret lines that cross the face of God?

Shall steaming blood thine anguish drive away,
   When in the arena's madness and its din
   Huge bright-eyed tigers crouch upon the prey,
   Or groan beneath the poisoned javelin?

Nay, wilt thou scourge the arrogant sea with chains,
   And make thy footstool of an ocean's might?
   Lo, at thy nod the storm-tossed ship regains
   The friendly shore, or sinks from human sight.

Wilt thou, perfumed and burning as the fire,
   The grape's red blood from jeweled chalice drain?
   Till drunken gladness to the gods aspire,
   Shall vine-wreathed Bacchus revel with his train?

Far kingdoms send unto thy regal seat
   The fairest maids with lucent step and glance,
   That at thy bidding shall with naked feet
   Swing in the maze of bacchanalian dance!

Or, shall the slave-boy from the Lydian land
   With sound of lute-string charm thine ear, and thou
   The minstrel raising, feel a lily hand
   Soft as the snow upon thine aching brow?

But the pale Caesar sadly smiled and drear,
   "Enough," he said, and yet again: "Enough,
   The purple fades, the laurel soon grows sere,
   Death lays his finger on the lips of love.

"Thy words, O slave, ring hollow as the tomb;
   Like evil damps, thine incense too shall pass,
   One thing alone escapes the general doom:
   Love's haloed image in art's magic glass!

"Wounds past all cure are burning in my breast,
   Beauty's last kiss on lips that perish thus,
   Bring, that at last my weary heart find rest,
   The marble statue of Antinous.

"I care not now for any earthly toy,
  Life's zenith lies behind me many a mile....
  White lotus-blossoms bury all my joy,
  And all my realm and all my self the Nile.

"His face was heavenly transport to mine eyes,
  Sweet was his breath, as scented winds that blow
  O'er fields of purple hyacinths and rise
  In the glad May-time from the floral snow.

"Approach in silence; holy is the ground
  Where beauty's feet have trod the desolate earth.
  Bow to the slave that freed my soul, and bound
  My love with loving to his greater worth.

"Thoughout all time shall sound his far laudations,
  From sea to land and on from land to sea,
  I, even I, imperial lord of nations,
  Before this shrine in worship bend the knee,

"Antinous, thy beauty is not dead—
  Thou liv'st in realms of marble and of song!"
  And wearily the pallid Caesar's head
  Sank on his breast. Then silence deep and long.

But where to Beauty sacrifice is given
  We too shall kneel to worship and adore,
  Whether its star resplendent rose in heaven
  From Grecian hill or Galilean shore.


# FROM *THE CANDLE AND THE FLAME* (1912)

## A Ballad of Montmartre

Within the graveyard of Montmartre
  Where wreath on wreath is piled,
Where Paris huddles to her breast
  Her genius like a child,
The ghost of Heinrich Heine met
  The ghost of Oscar Wilde.[12]

The wind was howling desolate,
  The moon's dead face shone bright;

The ghost of Henrich Heine hailed
   The sad wraith with delight:
"Is it the slow worm's slimy touch
   That makes you walk the night?

"Or rankles still the bitter jibe
   Of fool and Pharisee,
When angels wept that England's law
   Had nailed you to the Tree,
When from her brow she tore the rose
   Of golden minstrelsy?"

Then spake the ghost of Oscar Wilde
   While shrill the night hawk cried:
"Sweet singer of the race that bare
   Him of the Wounded Side,
(I loved them not on earth, but men
   Change somehow, having died).

"In Père La Chaise my head is laid,
   My coffin-bed is cool,
The mound above my grave defies
   The scorn of knave and fool,
But may God's mercy save me from
   The Psychopathic School![13]

"Tight though I draw my cerecloth, still
   I hear the din thereof
When with sharp knife and argument
   They pierce my soul above,
Because I drew from Shakespeare's heart
   The secret of his love....[14]

"Cite not Krafft-Ebing,[15] nor his host
   Of lepers in my aid,
I was sufficient as God's flowers
   And everything He made;
Yea, with the harvest of my song
   I face Him unafraid.

"The fruit of Life and Death is His;
   He shapes both core and rind..."
Cracked seemed and thin the golden voice,

(The worm to none is kind),
While through the graveyard of Montmartre
    Despairing howled the wind.

## A Ballad of King David[16]

As David with Bath-Sheba lay,
    Both drunk with kisses long denied,
The King, with quaking lips and gray,
    Beheld a spectre at his side
That said no word nor went away.

Then to his leman spake the King,
The ghostly presence challenging:
    "Bath-Sheba, erst Uriah's wife,
    Thy lips are as the Cup of Life
That holds the purplest wine of God,
Too sweet for any underling."

"Yet," spake Bath-Sheba, sad of mien,
"Why from thy visage went the sheen
As though thy troubled eye had seen
    A shadow, like a dead man's curse,
Rise threatening from the mound terrene?"

"'Twas but the falling dusk, that fills
The palace with phantastic ills.
    Uriah sleeps in alien sands
Soundly. 'Tis not his ghost that stands,
Living or dead, or anything
'Twixt the King's pleasure and the King."

Bath-Sheba's glad heart rose, then fell:
"Where is it that thy fancies dwell?
Is there some maid in Israel
    Broad-hipped, with blue eyes like the sea,
Whose mouth is like a honey-cell,
    And sweeter than the mouth of me?"

"The pressure of thy lips on mine
Is exquisite like snow-cooled wine.
Over the wasteness of my life
    Thy love is risen like a sun:

All other loves that once seemed sweet
  Are seized by black oblivion."

Again upon the shadow-thing
He gazed in silence, questioning.
And lo! With quaint familiar ring
A spectral voice addressed the King:
  "O David, David, Judah's swan!
Why unto me dost thou this thing?"
    "Who are thou?"
      "I am Jonathan,
  My heart is like a wounded fawn.

"When Saul's fierce anger, like a bull,
Rose, by the Evil One made blind,
My love to thee was wonderful,
  Passing the love of womankind.
Hast thou forgotten everything
My heart aches in remembering?
Is such the harvest of our spring
Of war and love and lute-playing?

"Oh, why, such transient love to win
Bring on thy soul this heavy sin?
  Ah, happy they who die in grace,
    Ere time can mar their lovely face,
And their young hearts grow hard within!
  Yeah, happy they who die as I,
    And as thine unborn child shall die.
Already at the palace gate
Stands Nathan with the word of fate!"

Was it a ghost's voice or the wind?
  For still Bath-Sheba, unaware,
Smiled. But King David ill in mind
  Scarce deemed her Beauty half so fair:
"Stale is the wine this evening,
  And sick with roses is the air!"
  He tore the garland from his hair,
  And left Bath-Sheba lying there
Perturbed, and vaguely wondering....

## The Ballad of the Golden Boy
*For Leonard Abbott*[17]

Da Vinci's brow in curious lines
    Of contemplation deep was knit.[18]
    Fair dreams before his eyes alit
Like water when the moonlight shines,
    Or amber bees that come and flit:
    How to make rare and exquisite
A pageant for the Florentines.

He beckoned to his page, a lad
    Whose lips were like two crimson spots,
    Eyes had he like forget-me-nots.
Yet all his boyhood sweet and glad
In frock of homely-spun was clad.

And of his multi-colored whims
    The strangest thus the master told:
    "Child, I shall crown thy head with gold,
And stain with gold thy lovely limbs.
    For once in this sad age uncouth
    The bloom of boyhood and of youth
Shall be with splendour aureoled."

The boy's heart leaped in one great bound.
    "Thy gracious will," said he, "be done!"
And ere the lad was disengowned
    The eager painter had begun
To clothe his hair with glory round
    And make his visage like the sun.

Then, seven stars upon his breast,
    And in his hands a floral horn,
Like a young king or like a guest
    From heaven, riding on the morn,
    Splendid and nude, the boy was borne
In triumph on the pageant's crest.

Like the sea surging on the beach,
    Reverberant murmurs rise to greet
    The masqueraders on the street.
But what is this? A learned leech

Hatless, disheveled, runs to meet
The train. White terror halts his speech.

"Poor lad, my lad, for Heaven's pity,"
    Shakes on the air a father's cry,
    "Strip from thy flesh this gilded lie,
Else, for the pleasure of the city,
    A self-slain Midas, thou must die!"

And terror smote the revelry.
    The master's features white and sad
Twitched, yet no single word spake he,
    But full and straight rose up the lad,
Upon his lips curled wistfully
    The smile that Mona Lisa had.

"Good Sir," said he, "what mortal power
    In all the dark-winged years and fleet,
Could me, a lowly lad, endower
    With any boon more great, more sweet,
Than to have felt one epic hour
    A city's homage at my feet?

"By the slow tooth of time uneaten,
    And all the foul things that destroy,
From Life's mad game I rise unbeaten,
    Drenched with the wine of youth and joy,
    Great Leonardo's Golden Boy.[19]

"Let this be told in song and story,
    Until the eyes of the world grow dim,
Till the sun's rays are wan, and hoary
    The ringlets of the cherubim,
That in my boyhood's glow and glory
    I died for Florence and for him.

"And when the damp and dreary mould
Full soon my little limbs shall hold,
    Let Leonardo's finger write
Upon my grave, in letters bold:
*'His life was as a splash of gold*
    *Against the plumage of the night.'"*
Thus spake the lad; and onward rolled
    The world's great pageant fierce and bright.

## 2 Samuel I 26[20]
*To T.E.H.*[21]

God's iron finger wrote the law
   Upon an adamantine scroll
That thrilled my life with tender awe
   When first I met you soul to soul.

Thence springs the great flame heaven-lit,
   Predestined when the world began,
Whereby my heart to yours is knit
   As David's was to Jonathan.

## Children of Lilith[22]
*To François Villon*[23]

Now tell me, Villon, where is he,
   Young Sporus, lord of Nero's lyre,
Who marked with languid ecstasy
   The seven hills grow red with fire?
And he whose madness choked the hall
   With roses and made night of day?
Rome's rulers for an interval,
   Its boyish Caesars, where are they?

Where is that city by the Nile,
   Reared by an emperor's bronze distress
When the enamoured crocodile
   Clawed the Bithynian's loveliness?
The argent pool whose listening trees
   Heard Echo's voice die far away?
Narcissus, Hylas, Charmides,
   O brother Villon, where are they?

Say where the Young Disciple roved
   When the Messiah's blood was spilt?
None knows: for he whom Jesus loved
   Was not the rock on which He built.
And tell me where is Gaveston,
   The second Edward's dear dismay?
And Shakespeare's love, and Jonathan,
   O brother Villon, where are they?

Made—for what end?—by God's great hand,
　Frail enigmatic shapes, they dwell
In some phantastic borderland,
　But on the hitherside of hell!
Children of Lilith, each a sprite,
　Yet wrought like us of Adam's clay,
And when they haunt us in the night
　What, brother Villon, shall we say?

## The Master Key
*To William Shakespeare*[24]

Two loves have I, both children of delight:
　One is a youth, like Eros' self, to whom
　My heart unfolds, as lotus blossoms bloom
When her mysterious service chants the Night;
And one is like a poppy burning bright.
　Her strong black tresses bind the hands of doom,
　She is a wraith from some imperial tomb,
Of love enhungered, in the grave's despite.

Lord, though thou be, O Shakespeare, of all rhyme,
　Life is more strong than any song of thine.
　　For thou wast thrall to circumstance, and Care
With rankling poison marred thy singing time:
　From hell's own lees I still crush goodly wine,
　　And like a Greek, and smiling, flout despair!

## Notes

1　Fuller's epigraph comes from Dante's *Divine Comedy* (1308–21), where the traitor Judas is depicted as punished at the deepest level of Hell.

2　Fuller employs five motets, all based on various Psalms, to add a quasi-religious fervor to his drama. This first is from Psalm 132: "Behold, how good and how pleasing it is for brothers to dwell in unity."

3　Psalm 188, verse 9: "How shall a young man keep his life pure?"

4　Psalm 36: "Be not angry because of evil-doers, nor envious of those who work iniquity."

5　Psalm 118, verse 113: "I hate half-hearted men, and I love thy law."

6　Psalm 2: "Why do the nations rage and the people devise vain things?"

7　Pride, according to Dante, which he locates in the last two circles of Hell in *The Divine Comedy*.

8　I.e., the feeling that a heterosexual man might face when he feels he is tempted to engage in a homosexual act; the acute and severe attack of anxiety based on unconscious conflicts involving gender identity. Sedgwick popularized the term in her seminal study *Between Men* (1985), where she describes homosexual panic as a male's fear of his own potential for homosexual desire, or the psychological state of a male "who not only is persecuted by, but considers himself transparent to and often under the compulsion of, another male" (9).

9   "This striding-place is called the 'Strid,'
  A name which it took of yore;
  A thousand years hath it borne the name,
  And it shall a thousand more." [Atherton's note.]
  Though Atherton quotes Wordsworth correctly, she gets the title wrong. The verse is from his poem "The Force of Prayer; or, The Founding of Bolton Priory" (1815), where a boy dies in a torrent after failing to leap over a two-meter river crossing. "The Boy of Egremond" (1819) was the title of a poem by Samuel Rogers, also about an ugly death by drowning.

10   The Roman emperor Hadrian (76–138 AD) had in his entourage a handsome boy named Antinous, who drowned in the Nile while still a young man, sending the emperor into unending grief.

11   Both Shakespeare and Michelangelo were examples to Viereck of artists who had been in love with younger men.

12   Oscar Wilde (1854–1900) and Heinrich Heine (1797–1856), the great German poet, are both buried in Père Lachaise cemetery in Montmartre.

13   Viereck sarcastically refers to the medical establishment which had pathologized homosexuality in the late nineteenth century.

14   Wilde's essay "To Mr. W.H." (1889) examines the feelings of Shakespeare for an unnamed young man, the subject of a lengthy sonnet sequence.

15   Richard von Krafft-Ebing (1840–1902) wrote *Psychopathia Sexualis* (1886), a famous study of sexual perversity.

16   King David, married to Bathsheba, recalls his friendship for the dead Jonathan (1 Samuel 20), the son of Saul. After Jonathan's death, David says "I am distressed for thee, my brother Jonathan: very pleasant hast thou been unto me: thy love to me was wonderful, passing the love of women" (2 Samuel 1:26).

17   Leonard Dalton Abbott (1878-1953) was the editor of *Current Literature* and a notable anarchist.

18   In 1476 Leonardo da Vinci was accused of sodomy with one of his apprentices.

19   This sentiment echoes the chief conceit of Viereck's hero Oscar Wilde's creation, *The Picture of Dorian Gray* (1890).

20   This Biblical verse reads, "I am distressed for thee, my brother Jonathan: very pleasant hast thou been unto me: thy love to me was wonderful, passing the love of women."

21   "T.E.H." has not been identified. But in the Marginalia to *The Candle and the Flame* Viereck annotated the poem by fancifully asserting that "Friendships, like love, are predetermined. There must be some physiological and spiritual law of

affection that can be expressed—and perhaps will be some day—in an algebraic equation."

22  According to Hebrew legend, Lilith was Adam's first wife: because she was made from the same dust as Adam she proved strong-willed and asserted her equality to Adam. She was replaced by Eve who, created from Adam's rib, proved more subservient.

23  "Où sont les neiges d'antan?" ("Where are the snows of yesteryear?") asked François Villon (1431–63?) in "Ballade des dames du temps jadis" ("Ballad of Women of Times Gone By") (c.1460), a famous poem cataloguing the loves of his past and asking where they've gone. In like manner, Viereck asks what have become of all the homosexual lovers of famous men in history, i.e., Nero and his page Sporus, Edward II of England and Lord Gaveston, et al. The inclusion of Jesus and St. John in this list would shock devout Christians, as Viereck well knew.

24  Viereck saw himself, like Shakespeare in the sonnets, torn between heterosexuality and homosexuality.

PART NINE

PURLOINED POPULAR FICTION

# BRET HARTE (1836–1902)

*With the publication of "The Luck of Roaring Camp" (1868), "The Outcasts of Poker Flat" (1869), and "Tennessee's Partner" (1869) in the periodical* The Overland Monthly, *Bret Harte's fame as a local colorist of frontier California began. Capitalizing on his early experiences in the mines and ranches of the West Coast, where he even rode shotgun on stagecoaches (in the Old West, an armed guard rode next to the driver and carried a shotgun for defense against robbers, wild animals, and Indians). Harte fictionalized "The Wild West" in his popular stories. The tales' settings were invariably the rough camps and towns which featured characters of every stripe, most of them misfits who had fled the East for the possibilities that the gold rush symbolized. Such all-male enclaves as he describes provide a perfect homosocial setting for romantic friendships between men, as several of his stories, such as "Uncle Jim and Uncle Billy" (1897) and "Tennessee's Partner" reveal. Humorous as well as touching, the classic tale below of unexpected love between men has as its center a unique representation of the Damon-and-Pythias[1] story which becomes all the more effective for taking place—as always with Harte—among the rough society of "Poker Flat."*

# "TENNESSEE'S PARTNER" (1869)

I do not think that we ever knew his real name. Our ignorance of it certainly never gave us any social inconvenience, for at Sandy Bar in 1854 most men were christened anew. Sometimes these appellatives were derived from some distinctiveness of dress, as in the case of "Dungaree Jack"; or from some peculiarity of habit, as shown in "Saleratus Bill," so called from an undue proportion of that chemical in his daily bread; or from some unlucky slip, as exhibited in "The Iron Pirate," a mild, inoffensive man, who earned that baleful title by his unfortunate mispronunciation of the term "iron pyrites." Perhaps this may have been the beginning of a rude heraldry; but I am constrained to think that it was because a man's real name in that day rested solely upon his own unsupported statement. "Call yourself Clifford, do you?" said Boston, addressing a timid newcomer with infinite scorn; "hell is full of such Cliffords!" He then introduced the unfortunate man, whose name happened to be really Clifford, as "Jaybird Charley"—an unhallowed inspiration of the moment that clung to him ever after.

But to return to Tennessee's Partner, whom we never knew by any other than this relative title. That he had ever existed as a separate and distinct individuality we only learned later. It seems that in 1853 he left Poker Flat to go to San Francisco, ostensibly to procure a wife. He never got any farther than

Stockton. At that place he was attracted by a young person who waited upon the table at the hotel where he took his meals. One morning he said something to her which caused her to smile not unkindly, somewhat coquettishly to break a plate of toast over his upturned, serious, simple face, and to retreat to the kitchen. He followed her and emerged a few moments later, covered with more toast and victory. That day week they were married by a Justice of the Peace and returned to Poker Flat. I am aware that something more might be made of this episode, but I prefer to tell it as it was current at Sandy Bar— in the gulches and bar-rooms—where all sentiment was modified by a strong sense of humor.

Of their married felicity but little is known, perhaps for the reason that Tennessee, then living with his partner, one day took occasion to say something to the bride on his own account, at which, it is said, she smiled not unkindly and chastely retreated—this time as far as Marysville, where Tennessee followed her, and where they went to housekeeping without the aid of a Justice of the Peace. Tennessee's Partner took the loss of his wife simply and seriously, as was his fashion. But to everybody's surprise, when Tennessee one day returned from Marysville, without his partner's wife—she having smiled and retreated with somebody else—Tennessee's Partner was the first man to shake his hand and greet him with affection. The boys who had gathered in the cañon[2] to see the shooting were naturally indignant. Their indignation might have found vent in sarcasm, but for a certain look in Tennessee's Partner's eye that indicated a lack of humorous appreciation. In fact, he was a grave man, with a steady application to practical detail which was unpleasant in a difficulty.

Meanwhile a popular feeling against Tennessee had grown up on the Bar. He was known to be a gambler; he was suspected to be a thief. In these suspicions Tennessee's Partner was equally compromised; his continued intimacy with Tennessee after the affair above quoted could only be accounted for on the hypothesis of a copartnership of crime. At last Tennessee's guilt became flagrant. One day he overtook a stranger on his way to Red Dog. The stranger afterwards related that Tennessee beguiled the time with interesting anecdote and reminiscence, but illogically concluded the interview in the following words: "And now, young man, I'll trouble you for your knife, your pistols, and your money. You see, your wrappings might get you into trouble at Red Dog, and your money's a temptation to the evilly disposed. I think you said your address was San Francisco. I shall endeavor to call." It may be stated here that Tennessee had a fine flow of humor, which no business preoccupation could wholly subdue.

This exploit was his last. Red Dog and Sandy Bar made common cause against the highwayman. Tennessee was hunted in very much the same fashion as his prototype, the grizzly. As the toils closed around him he made a desperate dash through the Bar, emptying his revolver at the crowd before the

Arcade Saloon, and so on up Grizzly Cañon; but at its farther extremity he was stopped by a small man on a grey horse. The men looked at each other a moment in silence. Both were fearless, both self-possessed and independent, and both types of a civilization that in the seventeenth century would have been called heroic, but in the nineteenth simply "reckless." "What have you got there?—I call," said Tennessee quietly. "Two bowers and an ace," said the stranger, as quietly, showing two revolvers and a bowie-knife. "That takes me," returned Tennessee; and with this gambler's epigram, he threw away his useless pistol and rode back with his captor.

It was a warm night. The cool breeze which usually sprang up with the going down of the sun behind the *chaparral*-crested[3] mountain was that evening withheld from Sandy Bar. The little cañon was stifling with heated resinous odors, and the decaying driftwood on the Bar sent forth faint, sickening exhalations. The feverishness of day and its fierce passions still filled the camp. Lights moved restlessly along the bank of the river, striking no answering reflection from its tawny current. Against the blackness of the pines the windows of the old loft above the express-office stood out staringly bright; and through their curtainless panes the loungers below could see the forms of those who were even then deciding the fate of Tennessee. And above all this, etched on the dark firmament, rose the Sierra, remote and passionless, crowned with remoter passionless stars.

The trial of Tennessee was conducted as fairly as was consistent with a judge and jury who felt themselves to some extent obliged to justify, in their verdict, the previous irregularities of arrest and indictment. The law of Sandy Bar was implacable, but not vengeful. The excitement and personal feeling of the chase were over; with Tennessee safe in their hands they were ready to listen patiently to any defense, which they were already satisfied was insufficient. There being no doubt in their own minds, they were willing to give the prisoner the benefit of any that might exist. Secure in the hypothesis that he ought to be hanged on general principles, they indulged him with more latitude of defence than his reckless hardihood seemed to ask. The Judge appeared to be more anxious than the prisoner, who, otherwise unconcerned, evidently took a grim pleasure in the responsibility he had created. "I don't take any hand in this yer game," had been his invariable but good-humoured reply to all questions. The Judge—who was also his captor—for a moment vaguely regretted that he had not shot him "on sight" that morning, but presently dismissed this human weakness as unworthy of the judicial mind. Nevertheless, when there was a tap at the door, and it was said that Tennessee's Partner was there on behalf of the prisoner, he was admitted at once without question. Perhaps the younger members of the jury, to whom the proceedings were becoming irksomely thoughtful, hailed him as a relief.

For he was not, certainly, an imposing figure. Short and stout, with a square face, sunburned into a preternatural redness, clad in a loose duck "jumper" and trousers streaked and splashed with red soil, his aspect in any circumstances would have been quaint, and was now even ridiculous. As he stooped to deposit at his feet a heavy carpet-bag he was carrying, it became obvious, from partially developed legends and inscriptions, that the material with which his trousers had been patched had been originally intended for a less ambitious covering. Yet he advanced with great gravity, and after having shaken the hand of each person in the room with labored cordiality, he wiped his serious perplexed face on a red bandanna handkerchief, a shade lighter than his complexion, laid his powerful hand upon the table to steady himself, and thus addressed the Judge:—

"I was passin' by," he began, by way of apology, "and I thought I'd just step in and see how things was gittin' on with Tennessee thar—my pardner. It's a hot night. I disremember any sich weather before on the Bar."

He paused a moment, but nobody volunteering any other meteorological recollection, he again had recourse to his pocket-handkerchief, and for some moments mopped his face diligently.

"Have you anything to say in behalf of the prisoner?" said the Judge finally.

"Thet's it," said Tennessee's Partner, in a tone of relief. "I come yar as Tennessee's pardner—knowing him nigh on four year, off and on, wet and dry, in luck and out o'luck. His ways ain't allers my ways, but thar ain't any p'ints in that young man, thar ain't any liveliness as he's been up to, as I don't know. And you sez to me, sez you—confidential-like, and between man and man— sez you, 'Do you know anything in his behalf?' and I sez to you, sez I—confidential-like, as between man and man—'What should a man know of his pardner?'"

"Is this all you have to say?" asked the Judge impatiently, feeling, perhaps, that a dangerous sympathy of humor was beginning to humanize the Court.

"Thet's so," continued Tennessee's Partner. "It ain't for me to say anything agin' him. And now, what's the case? Here's Tennessee wants money, wants it bad, and doesn't like to ask it of his old pardner. Well, what does Tennessee do? He lays for a stranger and he fetches that stranger; and you lays for *him*, and you fetches *him*;—and the honors is easy. And I put it to you, bein' a far-minded man, and to you, gentlemen all, as far-minded men, ef this isn't so."

"Prisoner," said the Judge, interrupting, "have you any questions to ask this man?"

"No! no!" continued Tennessee's Partner hastily. "I play this yer hand alone. To come down to the bed-rock, it's just this: Tennessee, thar, has played it pretty rough and expensive-like on a stranger, and on this yer camp. And now, what's the fair thing? Some would say more; some would say less. Here's seventeen hundred dollars in coarse gold and a watch—it's about all my pile—and call it square!" And before a hand could be raised to prevent him, he had emptied the contents of the carpet-bag upon the table.

For a moment his life was in jeopardy. One or two men sprang to their feet, several hands groped for hidden weapons, and a suggestion to "throw him from the window" was only overridden by a gesture from the Judge. Tennessee laughed. And apparently oblivious of the excitement, Tennessee's Partner improved the opportunity to mop his face again with his handkerchief.

When order was restored, and the man was made to understand, by the use of forcible figures and rhetoric, that Tennessee's offence could not be condoned by money, his face took a more serious and sanguinary hue, and those who were nearest to him noticed that his rough hand trembled slightly on the table. He hesitated a moment as he slowly returned the gold to the carpet-bag, as if he had not yet entirely caught the elevated sense of justice which swayed the tribunal, and was perplexed with the belief that he had not offered enough. Then he turned to the Judge, and saying, "This yer is a lone hand, played alone, and without my pardner," he bowed to the jury, and was about to withdraw, when the Judge called him back. "If you have anything to say to Tennessee, you had better say it now." For the first time that evening the eyes of the prisoner and his strange advocate met. Tennessee smiled, showed his white teeth, and, saying, "Euchred, old man!" held out his hand. Tennessee's Partner took it in his own, and saying, "I just dropped in as I was passin' to see how things was gittin' on," let the hand passively fall, and adding that "it was a warm night," again mopped his face with his handkerchief, and without another word withdrew.

The two men never again met each other alive. For the unparalleled insult of a bribe offered to Judge Lynch—who, whether bigoted, weak, or narrow, was at least incorruptible—firmly fixed in the mind of that mythical personage any wavering determination of Tennessee's fate; and at the break of day he was marched, closely guarded, to meet it at the top of Marley's Hill.

How he met it, how cool he was, how he refused to say anything, how perfect were the arrangements of the committee, were all duly reported, with the addition of a warning moral and example to all future evil-doers, in the *Red Dog Clarion* by its editor, who was present, and to whose vigorous English I cheerfully refer the reader. But the beauty of that midsummer morning, the blessed amity of earth and air and sky, the awakened life of the free woods and hills, the joyous renewal and promise of Nature, and above all, the infinite serenity that thrilled through each, were not reported, as not being a part of the social lesson. And yet, when the weak and foolish deed was done, and a life, with its possibilities and responsibilities, had passed out of the misshapen thing that dangled between earth and sky, the birds sang, the flowers bloomed, the sun shone, as cheerily as before; and possibly the *Red Dog Clarion* was right.

Tennessee's Partner was not in the group that surrounded the ominous tree. But as they turned to disperse, attention was drawn to the singular appearance of a motionless donkey-cart halted at the side of the road. As they approached they at once recognized the venerable "Jenny" and the two-wheeled cart as the property of Tennessee's Partner, used by him in carrying dirt from his claim;[4] and a few paces distant the owner of the equipage himself, sitting under a buckeye-tree, wiping the perspiration from his glowing face. In answer to an inquiry, he said he had come for the body of the "diseased," "if it was all the same to the committee." He didn't wish to "hurry anything"; he could "wait." He was not working that day; and when the gentlemen were done with the "diseased," he would take him. "Ef thar is any present," he added, in his simple, serious way, "as would care to jine in the fun'l, they kin come." Perhaps it was from a sense of humor, which I have already intimated was a feature of Sandy Bar—perhaps it was from something even better than that, but two-thirds of the loungers accepted the invitation at once.

It was noon when the body of Tennessee was delivered into the hands of his partner. As the cart drew up to the fatal tree, we noticed that it contained a rough oblong box—apparently made from a section of sluicing—and half filled with bark and the tassels of pine. The cart was further decorated with slips of willow, and made fragrant with buckeye-blossoms. When the body was deposited in the box, Tennessee's Partner drew over it a piece of tarred canvas, and gravely mounting the narrow seat in front, with his feet upon the shafts, urged the little donkey forward. The equipage moved slowly on, at that decorous pace which was habitual with "Jenny" even under less solemn circumstances. The men—half curiously, half jestingly, but all good-humouredly—strolled along beside the cart, some in advance, some a little in the rear of the homely catafalque.[5] Whether from the narrowing of the road, or some present sense of decorum, as the cart passed on the company fell to the rear in couples, keeping step, and otherwise assuming the external show of a formal procession. Jack Folinsbee, who had at the outset played a funeral march in dumb-show upon an imaginary trombone, desisted, from a lack of sympathy and appreciation—not having, perhaps, your true humorist's capacity to be content with the enjoyment of his own fun.

The way led through Grizzly Cañon, by this time clothed in funeral drapery and shadows. The redwoods, burying their moccasined feet in the red soil, stood in Indian file along the track, trailing an uncouth benediction from their bending boughs upon the passing bier. A hare, surprised into helpless inactivity, sat upright and pulsating in the ferns by the roadside as the *cortège* went by. Squirrels hastened to gain a secure outlook from higher boughs; and the blue-jays, spreading their wings, fluttered before them like outriders, until the outskirts of Sandy Bar were reached, and the solitary cabin of Tennessee's Partner.

Viewed under more favorable circumstances, it would not have been a cheerful place. The unpicturesque site, the rude and unlovely outlines, the unsavory details, which distinguish the nest-building of the California miner, were all here with the dreariness of decay superadded. A few paces from the cabin there was a rough enclosure, which, in the brief days of Tennessee's Partner's matrimonial felicity, had been used as a garden, but was now overgrown with fern. As we approached it, we were surprised to find that what we had taken for a recent attempt at cultivation was the broken soil about an open grave.

The cart was halted before the enclosure, and rejecting the offers of assistance with the same air of simple self-reliance he had displayed throughout, Tennessee's Partner lifted the rough coffin on his back, and deposited it unaided within the shallow grave. He then nailed down the board which served as a lid, and, mounting the little mound of earth beside it, took off his hat, and slowly mopped his face with his handkerchief. This the crowd felt was a preliminary to speech, and they disposed themselves variously on stumps and boulders, and sat expectant.

"When a man," began Tennessee's Partner slowly, "has been running free all day, what's the natural thing for him to do? Why, to come home! And if he ain't in a condition to go home, what can his best friend do? Why, bring him home! And here's Tennessee has been running free, and we brings him home from his wandering." He paused, and picked up a fragment of quartz, rubbed it thoughtfully on his sleeve, and went on: "It ain't the first time that I've packed him on my back, as you see'd me now. It ain't the first time that I brought him to this yer cabin when he couldn't help himself; it ain't the first time that I and 'Jinny' have waited for him on yon hill, and picked him up and so fetched him home, when he couldn't speak and didn't know me. And now that it's the last time, why—" he paused and rubbed the quartz gently on his sleeve—"you see, it's sort of rough on his pardner. And now, gentlemen," he added abruptly, picking up his long-handled shovel, "the fun'l's over; and my thanks, and Tennessee's thanks, to you for your trouble."

Resisting any proffers of assistance, he began to fill in the grave, turning his back upon the crowd, that after a few moments' hesitation gradually withdrew. As they crossed the little ridge that hid Sandy Bar from view, some, looking back, thought they could see Tennessee's Partner, his work done, sitting upon the grave, his shovel between his knees, and his face buried in his red bandanna handkerchief. But it was argued by others that you couldn't tell his face from his handkerchief at that distance, and this point remained undecided.

In the reaction that followed the feverish excitement of that day, Tennessee's Partner was not forgotten. A secret investigation had cleared him of any complicity in Tennessee's guilt, and left only a suspicion of his general sanity. Sandy Bar made a point of calling on him and proffering various uncouth but well-meant kindnesses. But from that day his rude health and great strength seemed visibly to decline; and when the rainy season fairly set in, and the tiny grass-blades were beginning to peep from the rocky mound above Tennessee's grave, he took to his bed.

One night, when the pines beside the cabin were swaying in the storm and trailing their slender fingers over the roof, and the roar and rush of the swollen river were heard below, Tennessee's Partner lifted his head from the pillow, saying, "It is time to go for Tennessee; I must put 'Jinny' in the cart"; and would have risen from his bed but for the restraint of his attendant. Struggling, he still pursued his singular fancy: "There, now, steady, 'Jinny,'—steady, old girl. How dark it is! Look out for the ruts—and look out for him, too, old gal. Sometimes, you know, when he's blind drunk, he drops down right in the trail. Keep on straight up to the pine on the top of the hill. Thar! I told you so!—thar he is—coming this way, too—all by himself, sober, and his face a-shining. Tennessee! Pardner!"

And so they met.

[In the poem that follows, Harte explores a similar situation to the story above. His tendency to understatement in depicting close feelings between men finds touching expression in this short but effective dramatic monologue.]

# "Jim" (1870)

Say there! P'r'aps
  Some of you chaps
    Might know Jim Wild?
Well,—no offence:
Thar ain't no sense
    In gittin' riled!

Jim was my chum
  Up on the Bar:
That's why I come
  Down from up yar,
Lookin' for Jim.
Thank ye, sir! *You*
Ain't of that crew,—
    Best if you are!

Money?—Not much:
  That ain't my kind:
I ain't no such.
    Rum?—I don't mind,
Seein' it's you.

Well, this yer Jim,
Did you know him?—
Jess 'bout your size;
Same kind of eyes?—
Well, that is strange:
  Why, it's two year
  Since he came here,
Sick, for a change.
Well, here's to us:
  Eh?
The h— you say!
  Dead?—
That little cuss?

What makes you star,—
You over thar?
Can't a man drop
's glass in yer shop
But you must rar'?
  It wouldn't take
  D—— much to break
You and your bar.

  Dead!
Poor—little—Jim!
—Why, thar was me,
Jones, and Bob Lee,
Harry and Ben,—
No-account men:
Then to take *him!*

Well, thar—Good by,—
No more, sir,—I—
  Eh?
What's that you say?—
Why, dern it!—sho!—
No? Yes! By Jo!
  Sold!
Sold! Why, you limb,
You ornery,
  Derned old
Long-legged Jim!

# THOMAS BAILEY ALDRICH (1836–1907)

*Thomas Bailey Aldrich's most successful book was a novel titled* The Story of a Bad Boy *(1870), which offered an amusing and realistic portrayal of American boyhood, drawing upon his own experiences growing up in Portsmouth, New Hampshire. Mark Twain found it impressive enough to claim that this book had provided him inspiration for his own classic portrayal of an American boy,* Tom Sawyer. *Aldrich went on to a successful career as an author of fiction and poetry, full of kindly realism and reticent humor. Nowhere is his humor more in evidence than in his epistolary tale "Marjorie Daw," however, which appeared in a collection of short stories in 1873. The ending of the story provokes real laughter in the reader, but after the initial amusement fades, there is a temptation to read the story again—to see what indeed it might be really saying about the true nature of Jack and Ned's friendship.*

## "MARJORIE DAW" (1873)

### I

Dr. Dillon to Edward Delaney, Esq., at the Pines. Near Rye, N.H.
August 8, 187-.

My Dear Sir: I am happy to assure you that your anxiety is without reason. Flemming will be confined to the sofa for three or four weeks, and will have to be careful at first how he uses his leg. A fracture of this kind is always a tedious affair. Fortunately the bone was very skillfully set by the surgeon who chanced to be in the drugstore where Flemming was brought after his fall, and I apprehend no permanent inconvenience from the accident. Flemming is doing perfectly well physically; but I must confess that the irritable and morbid state of mind into which he has fallen causes me a great deal of uneasiness. He is the last man in the world who ought to break his leg. You know how impetuous our friend is ordinarily, what a soul of restlessness and energy, never content unless he is rushing at some object, like a sportive bull at a red shawl; but amiable withal. He is no longer amiable. His temper has become something frightful. Miss Fanny Flemming came up from Newport, where the family are staying for the summer, to nurse him; but he packed her off the next morning in tears. He has a complete set of Balzac's works, twenty-seven volumes, piled up near his sofa, to throw at Watkins whenever that exemplary serving-man appears with his meals. Yesterday I very innocently brought Flemming a small basket of lemons. You know it was a strip of lemon-peel on the curbstone that caused our friend's mischance. Well, he no sooner set is eyes upon those lemons than he fell into such a rage as I cannot adequately describe. This is only one of his moods, and the least distressing. At other times he sits with bowed head regarding his splintered limb, silent, sullen, despairing. When this fit is on him—and it sometimes lasts all day—nothing can distract his melancholy. He refuses to eat, does not even read the newspapers; books, except as projectiles for Watkins, have no charms for him. His state is truly pitiable.

Now, if he were a poor man, with a family depending on his daily labor, this irritability and despondency would be natural enough. But in a young fellow of twenty-four, with plenty of money and seemingly not a care in the world, the thing is monstrous. If he continues to give way to his vagaries in this manner, he will end by bringing on an inflammation of the fibula. It was the fibula he broke. I am at my wits' end to know what to prescribe for him. I have anesthetics and lotions, to make people sleep and to soothe pain; but I've no medicine that will make a man have a little common-sense. That is beyond my skill, but maybe it is not beyond yours. You are Flemming's intimate friend, his *fidus Achates*.[6] Write to him, write to him frequently, distract his mind, cheer him up, and prevent him from becoming a confirmed case of melancholia. Perhaps he has some important plans disarranged by his present confinement. If he has you will know, and will know how to advise him judiciously. I trust your father finds the change beneficial? I am, my dear sir, with great respect, etc.

## II

Edward Delaney to John Flemming, West 38th Street, new York.
August 9, ——.

My Dear Jack: I had a line from Dillon this morning, and was rejoiced to learn that your hurt is not so bad as reported. Like a certain personage, you are not so black and blue as you are painted. Dillon will put you on your pins again in two to three weeks, if you will only have patience and follow his counsels. Did you get my note of last Wednesday? I was greatly troubled when I heard of the accident.

I can imagine how tranquil and saintly you are with your leg in a trough! It is deuced awkward, to be sure, just as we had promised ourselves a glorious month together at the sea-side; but we must make the best of it. It is unfortunate, too, that my father's health renders it impossible for me to leave him. I think he has much improved; the sea air is his native element; but he still needs my arm to lean upon in his walks, and requires some one more careful than a servant to look after him. I cannot come to you, dear Jack, but I have hours of unemployed time on hand, and I will write you a whole post-office full of letters, if that will divert you. Heaven knows, I haven't anything to write about. It isn't as if we were living at one of the beach houses; then I could do you some character studies, and fill your imagination with groups of sea-goddesses, with their (or somebody else's) raven and blonde manes hanging down their shoulders. You should have Aphrodite in morning wrapper, in evening costume, and in her prettiest bathing suit. But we are far from all that here. We have rooms in a farm-house, on a cross-road, two miles from the hotels, and lead the quietest of lives.

I wish I were a novelist. This old house, with its sanded floors and high wainscots, and its narrow windows looking out upon a cluster of pines that turn themselves into aeolian harps every time the wind blows, would be the place in which to write a summer romance. It should be a story with the odors of the forest and the breath of the sea in it. It should be a novel like one of that Russian fellow's—what's his name?—Tourguenieff, Turguenef, Turgenif, Toorguniff, Turgenjew—nobody knows how to spell him. Yet I wonder if even a Liza or an Alexandra Paulovna[7] could stir the heart of a man who has constant twinges in his leg. I wonder if one of our own Yankee girls of the best type, haughty and *spirituelle*, would be of any comfort to you in your present deplorable condition. If I thought so, I would hasten down to the Surf House and catch one for you; or, better still, I would find you one over the way.

Picture to yourself a large white house just across the road, nearly opposite our cottage. It is not a house, but a mansion, built, perhaps, in the colonial period, with rambling extensions, and gambrel roof, and a wide piazza on three sides—a self-possessed, high-bred piece of architecture, with its nose in the air. It stands back from the road, and has an obsequious retinue of fringed elms and oaks and weeping willows. Sometimes in the morning, and oftener in the afternoon, when the sun has withdrawn from that part of the mansions, a young woman appears on the piazza with some mysterious Penelope web of embroidery[8] in her hand, or a book. There is a hammock over there—of pineapple fiber, it looks from here. A hammock is very becoming when one is eighteen, and has golden hair, and dark eyes, and an emerald-colored illusion dress looped up after the fashion of a Dresden china shepherdess, and is *chaussée*[9] like a belle of the time of Louis Quatorze. All this splendor goes into that hammock, and sways there like a pond-lily in the golden afternoon. The window of my bedroom looks down on that piazza—and so do I.

But enough of the nonsense, which ill becomes a sedate young attorney taking his vacation with an invalid father. Drop me a line, dear Jack, and tell me how you really are. State your case. Write me a long, quiet letter. If you are violent or abusive, I'll take the law to you.

### III

John Flemming to Edward Delaney.
August 11, ——.

Your letter, dear Ned, was a godsend. Fancy what a fix I am in—I, who never had a day's sickness since I was born. My left leg weighs three tons. It is embalmed in spices and smothered in layers of fine linen, like a mummy. I can't move. I haven't moved for five thousand years. I'm of the time of Pharaoh.

I lie from morning till night on a lounge, staring into the hot street. Everybody is out of town enjoying himself. The brown-stone-front houses across the street resemble a row of particularly ugly coffins set up on end. A green mould is settling on the names of the deceased, carved on the silver doorplates. Sardonic spiders have sewed up the key-holes. All is silence and dust and desolation.—I interrupt this a moment, to take a shy at Watkins with the second volume of *César Birotteau.*[10] Missed him! I think I could bring him down with a copy of Sainte-Beuve[11] or the *Dictionnaire Universel*, if I had it. These small Balzac books somehow do not quite fit my hand; but I shall fetch him yet.[12] I've an idea that Watkins is tapping the old gentleman's Chateau Yquem.[13] Duplicate key of the wine-cellar. Hibernian swarries[14] in the front basement. Young Cheops up stairs, snug in his cerements.[15] Watkins glides into my chamber, with that colorless, hypocritical face of his drawn out long like an accordion; but I know he grins all the way down stairs, and is glad I have broken my leg. Was not my evil star in the very zenith when I ran up to town to attend that dinner at Delmonico's? I didn't come up altogether for that. It was partly to buy Frank Livingstone's roan mare Margot. And now I shall not be able to sit in the saddle these two months. I'll send the mare down to you at The Pines,—is that the name of the place?

Old Dillon fancies that I have something on my mind. He drives me wild with lemons. Lemons for a mind diseased! Nonsense. I am only as restless as the devil under this confinement,—a thing I'm not used to. Take a man who has never had so much as a headache or a toothache in his life, strap one of his legs in a section of water-spout, keep him in a room in the city for weeks, with the hot weather turned on, and then expect him to smile and purr and be happy! It is preposterous. I can't be cheerful or calm.

Your letter is the first consoling thing I have had since my disaster, ten days ago. It really cheered me up for half an hour. Send me a screed, Ned, as often as you can, if you love me. Anything will do. Write me more about that little girl in the hammock. That was very pretty, all that about the Dresden china shepherdess and the pond-lily; the imagery a little mixed, perhaps, but very pretty. I didn't suppose you had so much sentimental furniture in your upper story. It shows how one may be familiar for years with the reception-room of his neighbor, and never suspect what is directly under his mansard. I supposed your loft stuffed with dry legal parchments, mortgages, and affidavits; you take down a package of manuscript, and lo! there are lyrics and sonnets and canzonettas. You really have a graphic descriptive touch, Edward Delaney, and I suspect you of anonymous love-tales in the magazines.

I shall be a bear until I hear from you again. Tell me all about your pretty *inconnue*[16] across the road. What is her name? Who is she? Who's her father? Where's her mother? Who's her lover? You cannot imagine how this will occupy me. The more trifling, the better. My imprisonment has weakened me intellectually to such a degree that I find your epistolary gifts quite considerable. I am passing into my second childhood. In a week or two I shall take to India rubber rings and prongs of coral. A silver cup, with an appropriate inscription, would be a delicate attention on your part. In the meantime, write!

## IV

Edward Delaney to John Flemming.
August 12, ———.

The sick pasha[17] shall be amused. *Bismillah!*[18] he wills it so. If the story-teller becomes prolix and tedious—the bow-string and the sack, and two Nubians to drop him into the Piscataqua![19] But truly, Jack, I have a hard task. There is literally nothing here,—except the little girl over the way. She is swinging in the hammock at this moment. It is to me compensation for many of the ills of life to see her now and then put out a small kid boot, which fits like a glove, and set herself going. Who is she, and what is her name? Her name is Daw. Only daughter of Mr. Richard W. Daw, ex-colonel and banker. Mother dead. One brother at Harvard, elder brother killed at the battle of Fair Oaks, ten years ago. Old, rich family, the Daws. This is the homestead, where father and daughter pass eight months of the twelve; the rest of the year in Baltimore and Washington. The New England winter too many for the old gentleman. The daughter is called Marjorie,—Marjorie Daw. Sounds odd at first, doesn't it? But after you say it over to yourself half a dozen times, you like it. There's a pleasing quaintness to it, something prim and violet-like. Must be a nice sort of girl to be called Marjorie Daw.

I had mine host of The Pines in the witness-box last night, and drew the foregoing testimony from him. He has charge of Mr. Daw's vegetable-garden, and has known the family these thirty years. Of course I shall make the acquaintance of my neighbors before many days. It will be next to impossible for me not to meet Mr. Daw or Miss Daw in some of my walks. The young lady has a favorite path to the sea-beach. I shall intercept her some morning, and touch my hat to her. Then the princess will bend her fair head to me with courteous surprise not unmixed with haughtiness. Will snub me, in fact. All this for thy sake, O Pasha of the Snapt Axle-tree! ... How oddly things fall out! Ten minutes ago I was called down to the parlor,—you know the kind of parlors in farm-houses on the coast, a sort of amphibious parlor, with sea-shells on the mantel-piece and spruce branches in the chimney-place,—where I found my father and Mr. Daw doing the antique polite to each other. He had come to pay his respects to his new neighbors. Mr. Daw is a tall, slim gentleman of about fifty-five, with a florid face and snow-white mustache and side-whiskers. Looks like Mr. Dombey, or as Mr. Dombey would have looked if he had served a few years in the British Army. Mr. Daw was a colonel in the late war, commanding the regiment in which his son was a lieutenant. Plucky old boy, backbone of New Hampshire granite. Before taking his leave, the colonel delivered himself of an invitation as if he were issuing a general order. Miss Daw has a few friends coming, at 4 p.m., to play croquet on the lawn (parade-ground) and have tea (cold rations) on the piazza. Will we honor them with our company? (or be sent to the guard-house.) My father declines on the plea of ill-health. My father's son bows with as much suavity as he knows, and accepts.

In my next I shall have something to tell you. I shall have seen the little beauty face to face. I have a presentiment, Jack, that this Daw is a *rara avis!*[20] Keep up your spirits, my boy, until I write you another letter—and send me along word how's your leg.

## V

Edward Delaney to John Flemming.
August 13, ——.

The party, my dear Jack, was as dreary as possible. A lieutenant of the navy, the rector of the Episcopal Church at Stillwater, and a society swell from Nahant. The lieutenant looked as if he had swallowed a couple of his buttons, and found the bullion rather indigestible; the rector was a pensive youth, of the daffydowndilly sort; and the swell from Nahant was a very weak tidal wave indeed. The women were much better, as they always are; the two Miss Kingsburys of Philadelphia, staying at the Seashell House, two bright and engaging girls. But Marjorie Daw!

The company broke up soon after tea, and I remained to smoke a cigar with the colonel on the piazza. It was like seeing a picture, to see Miss Marjorie hovering around the old soldier, and doing a hundred gracious little things for him. She brought the cigars and lighted the tapers with her own delicate fingers, in the most enchanting fashion. As we sat there, she came and went in the summer twilight, and seemed, with her white dress and pale gold hair, like some lovely phantom that had sprung into existence out of the smokewreaths. If she had melted into air, like the statue of Galatea[21] in the play, I should have been more sorry than surprised.

It was easy to perceive that the old colonel worshipped her and she him. I think the relation between an elderly father and a daughter just blooming into womanhood the most beautiful possible. There is in it a subtle sentiment that cannot exist in the case of mother and daughter, or that of son and mother. But this is getting into deep water.

I sat with the Daws until half past ten, and saw the moon rise on the sea. The ocean, that had stretched motionless and black against the horizon, was changed by magic into a broken field of glittering ice, interspersed with marvelous silvery fjords. In the far distance the Isle of Shoals loomed up like a group of huge bergs drifting down on us. The Polar Regions in a June thaw! It was exceedingly fine. What did we talk about? We talked about the weather—and *you!* The weather has been disagreeable for several days past,—and so have you. I glided from one topic to the other very naturally. I told my friends of your accident; how it had frustrated all our summer plans, and what our plans were. I played quite a spirited solo on the fibula. Then I described you; or, rather, I didn't. I spoke of your amiability, of your patience under this severe affliction; of your touching gratitude when Dillon brings you little presents of fruit; of your tenderness to your sister Fanny, whom you would not allow to stay in town to nurse you, and how you heroically sent her back to Newport, preferring to remain alone with Mary, the cook, and your man Watkins, to whom, by the way, you were devotedly attached. If you had been there, Jack, you wouldn't have known yourself. I should have excelled as a criminal lawyer, if I had not turned my attention to a different branch of jurisprudence.

Miss Marjorie asked all manner of leading questions concerning you. It did not occur to me then, but it struck me forcibly afterwards, that she evinced a singular interest in the conversation. When I got back to my room, I recalled how eagerly she leaned forward, with her full, snowy throat in strong moonlight, listening to what I said. Positively, I think I made her like you!

Miss Daw is a girl whom you would like immensely, I can tell you that. A beauty without affectation, a high and tender nature,—if one can read the soul in the face. And the old colonel is a noble character, too.

I am glad that the Daws are such pleasant people. The Pines is an isolated spot, and my resources are few. I fear I should have found life here somewhat monotonous before long, with no other society than that of my excellent sire. It is true, I might have made a target of the defenseless invalid; but I haven't a taste for artillery, *moi.*

VI

John Flemming to Edward Delaney.
August 17, ——.

For a man who hasn't a taste for artillery, it occurs to me, my friend, you are keeping up a pretty lively fire on my inner works. But go on. Cynicism is a small brass field-piece that eventually bursts and kills the artilleryman.

You may abuse me as much as you like, and I'll not complain; for I don't know what I should do without your letters. They are curing me. I haven't hurled anything at Watkins since last Sunday, partly because I have grown more amiable under your teaching, and partly because Watkins captured my ammunition one night, and carried it off to the library. He is rapidly losing the habit he had acquired of dodging whenever I rub my ear, or make any slight motion with my right arm. He is still suggestive of the wine-cellar, however. You may break, you may shatter Watkins, if you will, but the scent of the Roederer[22] will hang round him still.

Ned, that Miss Daw must be a charming person. I should certainly like her. I like her already. When you spoke in your first letter of seeing a young girl swinging in a hammock under your chamber window, I was somehow strangely drawn to her. I cannot account for it in the least. What you have subsequently written of Miss Daw has strengthened the impression. You seem to be describing a woman I have known in some previous state of existence, or dreamed of in this. Upon my word, if you were to send me her photograph, I believe I should recognize her at a glance. Her manner, that listening attitude, her traits of character, as you indicate them, the light hair and the dark eyes,—they are all familiar things to me. Asked a lot of questions, did she? Curious about me? That is strange.

You would laugh in your sleeve, you wretched old cynic, if you knew how I lie awake nights, with my gas turned down to a star, thinking of The Pines and the house across the road. How cool it must be down there! I long for the salt smell in the air. I picture the colonel smoking his cheroot[23] on the piazza. I send you and Miss Daw off on afternoon rambles along the beach. Sometimes I let you stroll with her under the elms in the moonlight, for you are great friends by this time, I take it, and see each other every day. I know your ways and your manners! Then I fall into a truculent mood, and would like to destroy somebody. Have you noticed anything in the shape of a lover hanging around the colonel Lares and Penates?[24] Does that lieutenant of the horse-marines or that young Stillwater parson visit the house much? Not that I am pining for news of them, but any gossip of the kind would be in order. I wonder, Ned, you don't fall in love with Miss Daw. I am ripe to do it myself. Speaking of photographs, couldn't you manage to slip one of her *cartes-de-visite*[25] from her album—she must have an album, you know—and send it to me? I will return it before it could be missed. That's a good fellow! Did the mare arrive safe and sound? It will be a capital animal this autumn for Central Park.

Oh—my leg? I forgot about my leg. It's better.

## VII

Edward Delaney to John Flemming.
August 20, ——.

You are correct in your surmises. I am on the most friendly terms with our neighbors. The colonel and my father smoke their afternoon cigar together in our sitting-room or on the piazza opposite, and I pass an hour or two of the day or the evening with the daughter. I am more and more struck by the beauty, modesty, and intelligence of Miss Daw.

You asked me why I do not fall in love with her. I will be frank, Jack; I have thought of that. She is young, rich, accomplished, uniting in herself more attractions, mental and personal, than I can recall in any girl of my acquaintance; but she lacks the something that would be necessary to inspire in me that kind of interest. Possessing this unknown quality, a woman neither beautiful nor wealthy nor very young could bring me to her feet. But not Miss Daw. If we were shipwrecked together on an uninhabited island—let me suggest a tropical island, for it costs no more to be picturesque—I would build her a bamboo hut, I would fetch her bread-fruit and cocoanuts, I would fry yams for her, I would lure the ingenuous turtle and make her nourishing soups, but I wouldn't make love to her—not under eighteen months. I would like to have her for a sister, that I might shield her and counsel her, and spend half my income on old threadlace and camel's-hair shawls. (We are off the island now.) If such were not my feeling, there would still be an obstacle to my loving Miss Daw. A greater misfortune could scarcely befall me than to love her. Flemming, I am about to make a revelation that will astonish you. I may be all wrong in my premises and consequently in my conclusions; but you shall judge.

That night when I returned to my room after the croquet party at the Daws', and was thinking over the trivial events of the evening, I was suddenly impressed by the air of eager attention with which Miss Daw had followed my account of your accident. I think I mentioned this to you. Well, the next morning, as I went to mail my letter, I overtook Miss Daw on the road to Rye, where the post-office is, and accompanied her thither and back, an hour's walk. The conversation again turned to you, and again I remarked that inexplicable look of interest which had lighted up her face the previous evening. Since then, I have seen Miss Daw perhaps ten times, perhaps oftener, and on each occasion I found that when I was not speaking of you, or your sister, or some person or place associated with you, I was not holding her attention. She would be absent-minded, her eyes would wander away from me to the sea, or to some distant object in the landscape; her fingers would play with the leaves of a book in a way that convinced me she was not listening. At these moments if I abruptly changed the theme,—I did it several times as an experiment,—and dropped some remark about my friend Flemming, then the somber blue eyes would come back to me instantly.

Now, is not this the oddest thing in the world? No, not the oddest. The effect which you tell me was produced on you by my casual mention of an unknown girl swinging in a hammock is certainly as strange. You can conjecture how that passage in your letter of Friday startled me. Is it possible, then, that two people who have never met, and who are hundreds of miles apart, can exert a magnetic influence on each other? I have read of such psychological phenomena, but never credited them. I leave the solution of the problem to you. As for myself, all other things being favorable, it would be impossible for me to fall in love with a woman who listens to me only when I am talking of my friend!

I am not aware that any one is paying marked attention to my fair neighbor. The lieutenant of the navy—he is stationed at Rivermouth—sometimes drops in of an evening, and sometimes the rector from Stillwater; the lieutenant the oftener. He was there last night. I should not be surprised if he had an eye to the heiress; but he is not formidable. Mistress Daw carries a neat little spear of irony, and the honest lieutenant seems to have a particular facility for impaling himself on the point of it. He is not dangerous, I should say; though I have known a woman to satirize a man for years, and marry him after all. Decidedly, the lowly rector is not dangerous; yet, again, who has not seen Cloth of Frieze[26] victorious in the lists where Cloth of Gold went down?

As to the photograph. There is an exquisite ivory-type of Marjorie, in passe-partout, on the drawing room mantel-piece. It would be missed at once if taken. I would do anything reasonable for you, Jack; but I've no burning desire to be hauled up before the local justice of the peace, on a charge of petty larceny.

P.S.—Enclosed is a spray of mignonette,[27] which I advise you to treat tenderly. Yes, we talked of you again last night, as usual. It is becoming a little dreary for me.

## VIII

Edward Delaney to John Flemming.
August 22, ——.

Your letter in reply to my last has occupied my thoughts all the morning. I do not know what to think. Do you mean to say that you are seriously half in love with a woman whom you have never seen,—with a shadow, a chimera? for what else can Miss Daw be to you? I do not understand it at all. I understand neither you nor her. You are a couple of ethereal beings moving in finer air than I can breathe with my commonplace lungs. Such delicacy of sentiment is something that I admire without comprehending. I am bewildered. I am of the earth earthy, and I find myself in the incongruous position of having to do with mere souls, with natures so finely tempered that I run some risk of shattering them in my awkwardness. I am as Caliban among the spirits![28]

Reflecting on your letter, I am not sure that it is wise in me to continue this correspondence. But no, Jack; I do wrong to doubt the good sense that forms the basis of your character. You are deeply interested in Miss Daw; you feel that she is a person whom you may perhaps greatly admire when you know her: at the same time you bear in mind that the chances are ten to five that, when you do come to know her, she will fall far short of your ideal, and you will not care for her in the least. Look at it in this sensible light, and I will hold back nothing from you.

Yesterday afternoon my father and myself rode over to Rivermouth with the Daws. A heavy rain in the morning had cooled the atmosphere and laid the dust. To Rivermouth is a drive of eight miles, along a winding road lined all the way with wild barberry bushes. I never saw anything more brilliant than these bushes, the green of the foliage and the faint blush of the berries intensified by the rain. The colonel drove, with my father in front, Miss Daw and I on the back seat. I resolved that for the first five miles your name should not pass my lips. I was amused by the artful attempts she made, at the start, to break through my reticence. Then a silence fell upon her; and then she became suddenly gay. That keenness which I enjoyed so much when it was exercised on the lieutenant was not so satisfactory directed against myself. Miss Daw has great sweetness of disposition, but she can be disagreeable. She is like the young lady in the rhyme, with the curl on her forehead,

"When she is good,
She is very, very good,
And when she is bad, she is horrid!"

I kept to my resolution, however; but on the return home I relented, and talked of your mare! Miss Daw is going to try a side-saddle on Margot some morning. The animal is a trifle too light for my weight. By the bye, I nearly forgot to say that Miss Daw sat for a picture yesterday to a Rivermouth artist. If the negative turns out well, I am to have a copy. So our ends will be accomplished without crime. I wish, though, I could send you the ivorytype in the drawing-room; it is cleverly colored, and would give you an idea of her hair and eyes, which of course the other will not.

No, Jack, the spray of mignonette did not come from me. A man of twenty-eight doesn't enclose flowers in his letters—to another man. But don't attach too much significance to the circumstance. She gives sprays of mignonette to the rector, sprays to the lieutenant. She has even given a rose from her bosom to your slave. It is her jocund nature to scatter flowers, like Spring.

If my letters sometimes read disjointedly, you must understand that I never finish one at a sitting, but write at intervals, when the mood is on me.

The mood is not on me now.

## IX

Edward Delaney to John Flemming.
August 23, ——.

I have just returned from the strangest interview with Marjorie. She has all but confessed to me her interest in you. But with what modesty and digni-ty! Her words elude my pen as I attempt to put them on paper; and, indeed, it was not so much what she said as her manner; and that I cannot reproduce. Perhaps it was of a piece with the strangeness of this whole busi-ness, that she should tacitly acknowledge to a third party the love she feels for a man she has never beheld! But I have lost, through your aid, the fac-ulty of being surprised. I accept things as people do in dreams. Now that I am again in my room, it all appears like an illusion—the black masses of Rembrandtish[29] shadow under the trees, the fireflies whirling in Pyrrhic dances among the shrubbery, the sea over there, Marjorie sitting on the hammock!

It is past midnight, and I am too sleepy to write more.

Thursday Morning.

My father has suddenly taken it into his head to spend a few days at the Shoals. In the meanwhile you will not hear from me. I see Marjorie walking in the garden with the colonel. I wish I could speak to her alone, but shall probably not have an opportunity before we leave.

## X

Edward Delaney to John Flemming.
August 28, ——.

You were passing into your second childhood, were you? Your intellect was so reduced that my epistolary gifts seemed quite considerable to you, did they? I rise superior to the sarcasm in your favor of the 11th instant, when I notice that five days' silence on my part is sufficient to throw you into the depths of despondency.

We returned only this morning from Appledore, that enchanted island,—at four dollars per day. I find on my desk three letters from you! Evidently there is no lingering doubt in your mind as to the pleasure I derive from your correspondence. These letters are undated, but in what I take to be the latest are two passages that require my consideration. You will pardon my candor, dear Flemming, but the conviction forces itself upon me that as your leg grows stronger your head becomes weaker. You ask my advice on a certain point. I will give it. In my opinion you could do nothing more unwise than to address a note to Miss Daw, thanking her for the flower. It would, I am sure, offend her delicacy beyond pardon. She knows you only through me; you are to her an abstraction, a figure in a dream,—a dream from which the faintest shock would awaken her. Of course, if you enclose a note to me and insist on its delivery, I shall deliver it; but I advise you not to do so.

You say you are able, with the aid of a cane, to walk about your chamber, and that you purpose to come to The Pines the instant Dillon thinks you strong enough to stand the journey. Again I advise you not to. Do you not see that, every hour you remain away, Marjorie's glamour deepens, and your influence over her increases? You will ruin everything by precipitancy. Wait until you are entirely recovered; in any case, do not come without giving me warning. I fear the effect of your abrupt advent here—under the circumstances.

Miss Daw was evidently glad to see us back again, and gave me both hands in the frankest way. She stopped at the door a moment this afternoon in the carriage; she had been over to Rivermouth for her pictures. Unluckily the photographer had spilt some acid on the plate, and she was obliged to give him another sitting. I have an intuition that something is troubling Marjorie. She had an abstracted air not usual with her. However, it may be only my fancy.... I end this, leaving several things unsaid, to accompany my father on one of those long walks which are now his chief medicine,—and mine!

## XI

Edward Delaney to John Flemming.
August 29, ——.

I write in great haste to tell you what has taken place here since my letter of last night. I am in the utmost perplexity. Only one thing is plain,—*you* must not dream of coming to The Pines. Marjorie has told her father everything! I saw her for a few minutes, an hour ago, in the garden; and, as near as I could gather from her confused statement, the facts are these: Lieutenant Bradly—that's the naval officer stationed at Rivermouth—has been paying court to Miss Daw for some time past, but not so much to her liking as to that of the colonel, who it seems is an old friend of the young gentleman's father. Yesterday (I knew she was in some trouble when she drove up to our gate) the colonel spoke to Marjorie of Bradly,—urged his suit, I infer. Marjorie expressed her dislike for the lieutenant with characteristic frankness, and finally confessed to her father—well, I really do not know what she confessed. It must have been the vaguest of confessions, and must have sufficiently puzzled the colonel. At any rate, it exasperated him. I suppose I am implicated in the matter, and that the colonel feels bitterly towards me. I do not see why: I have carried no messages between you and Miss Daw; I have behaved with the greatest discretion. I can find no flaw anywhere in my proceeding. I do not see that anybody has done anything,—except the colonel himself.

It is probable, nevertheless, that the friendly relations between the two houses will be broken off. "A plague o' both your houses," say you.[30] I will keep you informed, as well as I can, of what occurs over the way. We shall remain here until the second week in September. Stay where you are, or, at all events, do not dream of joining me. ... Colonel Daw is sitting on the piazza looking rather wicked. I have not seen Marjorie since I parted with her in the garden.

### XII

Edward Delaney to Thomas Dillon, M.D., Madison Square, New York.
August 30, ——.

My Dear Doctor: If you have any influence over Flemming, I beg of you to exert it to prevent his coming to this place at present. There are circumstances, which I will explain to you before long, that make it of the first importance that he should not come into this neighborhood. His appearance here, I speak advisedly, would be disastrous to him. In urging him to remain in New York, or to go to some inland resort, you will be doing him and me a real service. Of course you will not mention my name in this connection. You know me well enough, my dear doctor, to be assured that, in begging your secret cooperation, I have reasons that will meet your entire approval when they are made plain to you. We shall return to town on the 15th of next month, and my first duty will be to present myself at your hospitable door and satisfy your curiosity, if I have excited it. My father, I am glad to state, has so greatly improved that he can no longer be regarded as an invalid. With great esteem, I am, etc., etc.

## XIII

Edward Delaney to John Flemming.
August 31, ——.

Your letter, announcing your mad determination to come here, has just reached me. I beseech you to reflect a moment. The step would be fatal to your interests and hers. You would furnish just cause for irritation to R.W.D.; and, though he loves Marjorie devotedly, he is capable of going to any lengths if opposed. You would not like, I am convinced, to be the means of causing him to treat her with severity. That would be the result of your presence at The Pines at this juncture. I am annoyed to be obliged to point out these things to you. We are on very delicate ground, Jack; the situation is critical, and the slightest mistake in a move would cost us the game. If you consider it worth the winning, be patient. Trust a little to my sagacity. Wait and see what happens. Moreover, I understand from Dillon that you are in no condition to take so long a journey. He thinks the air of the coast would be the worst thing possible for you; that you ought to go inland, if anywhere. Be advised by me. Be advised by Dillon.

## XIV

Telegrams.
September 1, ——.

1.—To Edward Delaney.
Letter received. Dillon be hanged. I think I ought to be on the ground.
J.F.

2.—To John Flemming.
Stay where you are. You would only complicate matters. Do not move until you hear from me.
E.D.

3.—To Edward Delaney.
My being at The Pines could be kept secret. I must see her.
J.F.

4.—To John Flemming.
Do not think of it. It would be useless. R.W.D. has locked M. in her room. You would not be able to effect an interview.
E.D.

5.—To Edward Delaney.

Locked her in her room. Good God. That settles the question. I shall leave by the twelve-fifteen express.

J.F.

## XV

THE ARRIVAL.

On the second day of September, 187-, as the down express due at 3.40 left the station at Hampton, a young man, leaning on the shoulder of a servant, whom he addressed as Watkins, stepped from the platform into a hack, and requested to be driven to "The Pines." On arriving at the gate of a modest farm-house, a few miles from the station, the young man descended with difficulty from the carriage, and, casting a hasty glance across the road, seemed much impressed by some peculiarity in the landscape. Again leaning on the shoulder of the person Watkins, he walked to the door of the farm-house and inquired for Mr. Edward Delaney. He was informed by the aged man who answered his knock, that Mr. Edward Delaney had gone to Boston the day before, but that Mr. Jonas Delaney was within. This information did not appear satisfactory to the stranger, who inquired if Mr. Edward Delaney had left any message for Mr. John Flemming. There *was* a letter for Mr. Flemming if he were that person. After a brief absence the aged man reappeared with a letter.

## XVI

Edward Delaney to John Flemming.

September 1, ——.

I am horror-stricken at what I have done! When I began this correspondence I had no other purpose than to relieve the tedium of your sick-chamber. Dillon told me to cheer you up. I tried to. I thought that you entered into the spirit of the thing. I had no idea, until within a few days, that you were taking matters *au sérieux*.[31]

What can I say? I am in sackcloth and ashes. I am a pariah, a dog of an outcast. I tried to make a little romance to interest you, something soothing and idyllic, and, by Jove! I have done it only too well! My father doesn't know a word of this, so don't jar the old gentleman any more than you can help. I fly from the wrath to come—when you arrive! For oh, dear Jack, there isn't any piazza, there isn't any hammock,—there isn't any Marjorie Daw!

*"In certain sketches of the late H.C. Bunner something of the uranian strain occasionally echoes," wrote Edward Prime-Stevenson in 1908.[32] A highly prolific writer of poetry and sentimentally humorous pieces for popular magazines, as well as the editor of the satirical periodical* Puck, *Bunner seems to have enjoyed several romantic friendships during his life. In a letter to Walter Learned[33] in 1884 he wrote: "The prospect of Hutton's marriage makes me rather blue. This sounds queer, and I don't know that I can quite explain it even to you; for you have never, I think, had the sort of intimacy that I have had with H.—the regular bachelors' friendship. You married too young to fall into it. It is a sort of tramps' comradeship. The two know the common perils of their state; they understand one another's weaknesses without the need of confidences.... One 'looks after' the other." In this story, first published in* Scribner's, *Bunner does indeed suggest the love and devotion of one man for another that was able to pass muster for a general readership. But surely the character of Uncle David—with his exotic "aroma" suggesting a difference more than just smell—must have reached out to another set of knowing readers.*

# "OUR AROMATIC UNCLE" (1895)

It is always with a feeling of personal tenderness and regret that I recall his story, although it began long before I was born, and must have ended shortly after that important date, and although I myself never laid eyes on the personage of whom my wife and I always speak as "The Aromatic Uncle."

The story begins so long ago, indeed, that I can tell it only as a tradition of my wife's family. It goes back to the days when Boston was so frankly provincial a town that one of its leading citizens, a man of eminent position and ancient family, remarked to a young kinsman whom he was entertaining at his hospitable board, by way of pleasing and profitable discourse: "Nephew, it may interest you to know that it is Mr. Everett who has the *other* hind-quarter of this lamb." This simple tale I will vouch for, for I got it from the lips of the nephew, who has been my uncle for so many years that I know him to be a trustworthy authority.

In those days which seem so far away—and yet the space between them and us is spanned by a lifetime of three-score years and ten—life was simpler in all its details; yet such towns as Boston, already old, had well-established local customs which varied not at all from year to year; many of which lingered in later phases of urban growth. In Boston, or at least in that part of Boston where my wife's family dwelt, it was the invariable custom for the head of the family to go to market in the early morning with his wife's list of the day's needs. When the list was filled, the articles were placed in a basket; and the baskets thus filled were systematically deposited by the market-boys at the back door of the house to which they were consigned. Then the house-keeper came to the back-door at her convenience, and took the basket in. Exposed as this position must have been, such a thing as a theft of the day's edibles was unknown, and the first authentic account of any illegitimate handling of the baskets brings me to the introduction of my wife's uncle.

It was on a summer morning, as far as I can find out, that a little butcher-boy—a very little butcher-boy to be driving so big a cart—stopped in the rear of two houses that stood close together in a suburban street. One of these houses belonged to my wife's father, who was, from all I can gather, a very pompous, severe, and generally objectionable old gentleman; a judge, and a very considerable dignitary, who apparently devoted all his leisure to making life miserable for his family.

The other was owned by a comparatively poor and unimportant man, who did a shipping business in a small way. He had bought it during a period of temporary affluence, and it hung on his hands like a white elephant. He could not sell it, and it was turning his hair gray to pay the taxes on it. On this particular morning he had got up at four o'clock to go down to the wharves to see if a certain ship in which he was interested had arrived. It was due and overdue, and its arrival would settle the question of his domestic comfort for the whole year; for if it failed to appear, or came home with an empty bottom, his fate would be hard indeed; but if it brought him money or marketable goods from its long Oriental trip, he might take heart of grace and look forward to better times.

When the butcher's boy stopped at the house of my wife's father, he set down at the back-door a basket containing fish, a big joint of roast beef, and a generous load of fruit and vegetables, including some fine fat oranges. At the other door he left a rather unpromising-looking lump of steak and a half-peck of potatoes, not of the first quality. When he had deposited these two burdens he ran back and started his cart up the road.

But he looked back as he did so, and he saw a sight familiar to him, and saw the commission of a deed entirely unfamiliar. A handsome young boy of about his own age stepped out of the back-door of my wife's father's house and looked carelessly around him. He was one of the boys who compel the admiration of all other boys—strong, sturdy, and a trifle arrogant.

He had long ago compelled the admiration of the little butcher-boy. They had been playmates together at the public school, and although the judge's son looked down from an infinite height upon his poor little comrade, the butcher-boy worshipped him with the deepest and most fervent adoration. He had for him the admiring reverence which the boy who can't lick anybody has for the boy who can lick everybody. He was a superior being, a pattern, a model; an ideal never to be achieved, but perhaps in a crude, humble way to be imitated. And there is no hero-worship in the world like a boy's worship of a boy-hero.

The sight of this fortunate and adorable youth was familiar enough to the butcher-boy, but the thing he did startled and shocked that poor little work-ingman almost as much as if his idol had committed a capital crime right before his very eyes. For the judge's son suddenly let a look into his face that meant mischief, glanced around him to see whether anybody was observing him or not, and, failing to notice the butcher-boy, quickly and dexterously changed the two baskets. Then he went back into the house and shut the door on himself.

The butcher-boy reined up his horse and jumped from his cart. His first impulse, of course, was to undo the shocking iniquity which the object of his admiration had committed. But before he had walked back a dozen yards, it struck him that he was taking a great liberty in spoiling the other boy's joke. It was wrong, of course, he knew it; but was it for him to rebuke the wrong-doing of such an exalted personage? If the judge's son came out again, he would see that his joke had miscarried, and then he would be displeased. And to the butcher-boy it did not seem right in the nature of things that any-thing should displease the judge's son. Three times he went hesitatingly backward and forward, trying to make up his mind, and then he made it up. The king could do no wrong. Of course he himself was doing wrong in not putting the baskets back where they belonged; but then, he reflected, he took that sin on his own humble conscience, and in some measure took it off the conscience of the judge's son—if, indeed, it troubled that lightsome con-science at all. And, of course, too, he knew that, being an apprentice, he would be whipped for it when the substitution was discovered. But he didn't mind being whipped for the boy he worshipped. So he drove out along the road; and the wife of the poor shipping-merchant, coming to the back-door, and finding the basket full of good things, and noticing especially the beau-tiful China oranges, naturally concluded that her husband's ship had come in, and that he had provided his family with a rare treat. And the judge, when he came home to dinner, and Mrs. Judge introduced him to the rump-steak and potatoes—but I do not wish to make this story any more pathetic than is necessary.

A few months after this episode, perhaps indirectly in consequence of it—I have never been able to find out exactly—the judge's son, my wife's uncle, ran away to sea, and for many years his recklessness, his strength, and his good looks were only traditions in the family, but traditions which he him-self kept alive by remembrances than which none could have been more effective.

At first he wrote but seldom, later on more regularly, but his letters—I have seen many of them—were the most un-communicative documents that I ever saw in my life. His wanderings took him to many strange places on the other side of the globe, but he never wrote of what he saw or did. His family gleaned from them that his health was good, that the weather was such-and-such, and that he wished to have his love, duty, and respects conveyed to his various relatives. In fact, the first positive bit of personal intelligence that they received from him was five years after his departure, when he wrote them from a Chinese port on letter-paper whose heading showed that he was a member of a commercial firm. The letter itself made no mention of the fact. As the years passed on, however, the letters came more regularly and they told less about the weather, and were slightly—very slightly—more expressive of a kind regard for his relatives. But at the best they were cramped by the formality of his day and generation, and we of today would have called them cold and perfunctory.

But the practical assurances that he gave of his undiminished—nay, his steadily increasing—affection for the people at home, were of a most satisfying character, for they were convincing proof not only of his love but of his material prosperity. Almost from his first time of writing he began to send gifts to all the members of the family. At first these were mere trifles, little curios of travel such as he was able to purchase out of a seaman's scanty wages; but as the years went on they grew richer and richer, till the munificence of the runaway son became the pride of the whole family.

The old house that had been in the suburbs of Boston was fairly in the heart of the city when I first made its acquaintance, and one of the famous houses of the town. And it was no wonder it was famous, for such a collection of Oriental furniture, bric-a-brac, and objects of art never was seen outside of a museum. There were ebony cabinets, book-cases, tables, and couches wonderfully carved and inlaid with mother-of-pearl. There were beautiful things in bronze and jade and ivory. There were all sorts of strange rugs and curtains and portières.[34] As to the china-ware and the vases, no house was ever so stocked; and as for such trifles as shawls and fans and silk handkerchiefs, why such things were sent not singly but by dozens.

No one could forget his first entrance into that house. The great drawing-room was darkened by heavy curtains, and at first you had only a dim vision of the strange and graceful shapes of its curious furnishing. But you could not but be instantly conscious of the delicate perfume that pervaded the apartment, and, for the matter of that, the whole house. It was a combination of all the delightful Eastern smells—not sandal-wood only, nor teak, nor couscous, but all these odors and a hundred others blent in one. Yet it was not heavy nor overpowering, but delightfully faint and sweet, diffused through those ample rooms. There was good reason, indeed, for the children of the generation to which my wife belonged to speak of the generous relative whom they had never seen as "Our Aromatic Uncle." There were other uncles, and I have no doubt they gave presents freely, for it was a wealthy and free-handed family; but there was no other uncle who sent such a delicate and delightful reminder with every gift, to breathe a soft memory of him by day and by night.

I did my courting in the sweet atmosphere of that house, and although I had no earthly desire to live in Boston I could not help missing that strangely blended odor when my wife and I moved into an old house in an old part of New York, whose former owners had no connections in the Eastern trade. It was a charming and home-like old house; but at first, although my wife had brought some belongings from her father's house, we missed the pleasant flavor of our aromatic uncle, for he was now my uncle as well as my wife's. I say at first, for we did not miss it long. Uncle David—that was his name—not only continued to send his fragrant gifts to my wife at Christmas and upon her birthday, but he actually adopted me too, and sent me Chinese cabinets and Chinese gods in various minerals and metals, and many articles designed for a smoker's use, which no smoker would ever want to touch with a ten-foot pole. But I cared very little about the utility of these presents, for it was not many years before, among them all, they set up that exquisite perfume in the house, which we had learned to associate with our aromatic uncle.

"Foo-choo-li, CHINA,
January—, 18—.
"DEAR NEPHEW AND NIECE: The Present is to inform you that I have this day shipped to your address, per Steamer Ocean Queen, one marble and ebony Table, six assorted gods, and a blue Dinner set; also that I purpose leaving this Country for a visit to the Land of my Nativity on the 6th of March next, and will, if same is satisfactory to you, take up my Abode temporarily in your Household. Should same not be satisfactory, please cable at my charge. Messrs. Smithson & Smithson, my Customs Brokers, will attend to all charges on the goods, and will deliver them at your readiness. The health of this place is better than customary by reason of the cool weather, which Health I am as usual enjoying. Trusting that you both are at present in the possession of the same Blessing, and will so continue, I remain, dear nephew and niece,
"Your affectionate
"UNCLE."

This was, I believe, by four dozen words—those which he used to inform us of his intention of visiting America—the longest letter that Uncle David had ever written to any member of his family. It also conveyed more information about himself than he had ever given since the day he ran away to sea. Of course we cabled the old gentleman that we should be delighted to see him.

And, late that Spring, at some date at which he could not possibly have been expected to arrive, he turned up at our house.

Of course we had talked a great deal about him, and wondered what manner of man we should find him. Between us, my wife and I had got an idea of his personal appearance which I despair of conveying in words. Vaguely, I should say that we had pictured him as something mid-way between an abnormally tall Chinese mandarin and a benevolent Quaker. What we found, when we got home and were told that our uncle from India was awaiting us, was a shrunken and bent old gentleman, dressed very cleanly and neatly in black broadcloth, with a limp, many-pleated shirt-front of old-fashioned style, and a plain black cravat. If he had worn an old-time stock we could have forgiven him the rest of the disappointment he cost us; but we had to admit to ourselves that he had the most absolutely commonplace appearance of all our acquaintance. In fact, we soon discovered that, except for a taciturnity the like of which we had never encountered, our aromatic uncle had positively not one picturesque characteristic about him. Even his aroma was a disappointment. He had it, but it was of patchouly[35] or some other cheap perfume of the sort, wherewith he scented his handkerchief, which was not even a bandanna, but a plain decent white one of the unnecessarily large sort which clergymen and old gentlemen affect.

But, even if we could not get one single romantic association to cluster about him, we very soon got to like the old gentleman. It is true that at our first meeting, after saying "How d'ye do, how d'ye do," to me, and receiving in impassive placidity the kiss which my wife gave him, he relapsed into dead silence, and continued to smoke a clay pipe with a long stem and a short bowl. This instrument he filled and refilled every few minutes, and it seemed to be his only employment. We plied him with questions, of course, but to these he responded with a wonderful brevity. In the course of an hour's conversation we got from him that he had had a pleasant voyage, that it was not a long voyage, that it was not a short voyage, that it was about the usual voyage, that he had not been sea-sick, that he was glad to be back, and that he was not surprised to find the country very much changed. This last piece of information was repeated in the form of a simple "No," given in reply to the direct question; and although it was given politely, and evidently without the least unamiable intent, it made us both feel very cheap. After all, it *was* absurd to ask a man if he were surprised to find the country changed after fifty or sixty years of absence. Unless he was an idiot, and unable to read at that, he must have expected something of the sort.

But we grew to like him. He was thoroughly kind and inoffensive in every way. He was entirely willing to be talked to, but he did not care to talk. If it was absolutely necessary, he *could* talk, and when he did talk he always made me think of the "French-English Dictionary for the Pocket," compiled by the ingenious Mr. John Bellows; for nobody except that extraordinary Englishman could condense a greater amount of information into a smaller number of words. During the time of his stay with us I think I learned more about China than any other man in the United States knew, and I do not believe that the aggregate of his utterances in the course of that six months could have amounted to one hour's continuous talk. Don't ask me for the information. I had no sort of use for it, and I forgot it as soon as I could. I like Chinese bric-a-brac, but my interest in China ends there.

Yet it was not long before Uncle David slid into his own place in the family circle. We soon found that he did not expect us to entertain him. He wanted only to sit quiet and smoke his pipe, to take his two daily walks by himself, and to read the daily paper one afternoon and Macaulay's "History of England"[36] the next. He was never tired of sitting and gazing amiably but silently at my wife; and, to head the list of his good points, he would hold the baby by the hour, and for some mysterious reason that baby, who required the exhibition of seventeen toys in a minute to be reasonably quiet in the arms of anybody else, would sit placidly in Uncle David's lap, teething away steadily on the old gentleman's watch-chain, as quiet and as solemn and as aged in appearance as anyone of the assorted gods of porcelain and jade and ivory which our aromatic uncle had sent us.

The old house in Boston was a thing of the past. My wife's parents had been dead for some years, and no one remained of her immediate family except a certain Aunt Lucretia, who had lived with them until shortly before our marriage, when the breaking up of the family sent her West to find a home with a distant relative in California. We asked Uncle Davy if he had stopped to see Aunt Lucretia as he came through California. He said he had not. We asked him if he wanted to have Aunt Lucretia invited on to pass a visit during his stay with us. He answered that he did not. This did not surprise us at all. You might think that a brother might long to see a sister from whom he had been separated nearly all of a long lifetime but then you might never have met Aunt Lucretia. My wife made the offer only from a sense of duty; and only after a contest with me which lasted three days and nights. Nothing but loss of sleep during an exceptionally busy time at my office induced me to consent to her project of inviting Aunt Lucretia. When Uncle David put his veto upon the proposition I felt that he might have taken back all his rare and costly gifts, and I could still have loved him.

But Aunt Lucretia came, all the same. My wife is afflicted with a New England conscience, originally of a most uncomfortable character. It has been much modified and ameliorated, until it is now considerably less like a case of moral hives; but some wretched lingering remnant of the original article induced her to write to Aunt Lucretia that Uncle David was staying with us, and of course Aunt Lucretia came without invitation and without warning, dropping in on us with ruthless unexpectedness.

You may not think, from what I have said, that Aunt Lucretia's visit was a pleasant event. But it was, in some respects; for it was not only the shortest visit she ever paid us, but it was the last with which she ever honored us.

She arrived one morning shortly after breakfast, just as we were preparing to go out for a drive. She would not have been Aunt Lucretia if she had not upset somebody's calculations at every turn of her existence. We welcomed her with as much hypocrisy as we could summon to our aid on short notice, and she was not more than usually offensive, although she certainly did herself full justice in telling us what she thought of us for not inviting her as soon as we even heard of Uncle David's intention to return to his native land. She said she ought to have been the first to embrace her beloved brother—to whom I don't believe she had given one thought in more years than I have yet seen.

Uncle David was dressing for his drive. His long residence in tropical countries had rendered him sensitive to the cold, and although it was a fine, clear September day, with the thermometer at about sixty, he was industriously building himself up with a series of overcoats. On a really snappy day I have known him to get into six of these garments; and, when he entered the room on this occasion I think he had on five, at least. My wife had heard his familiar foot on the stairs, and Aunt Lucretia had risen up and braced herself for an outburst of emotional affection. I could see that it was going to be such a greeting as is given only once in two or three centuries, and then on the stage. I felt sure it would end in a swoon, and I was looking around for a sofa-pillow for the old lady to fall upon, for from what I knew of Aunt Lucretia I did not believe she had ever swooned enough to be able to go through the performance without danger to her aged person.

But I need not have troubled myself. Uncle David toddled into the room, gazed at Aunt Lucretia without a sign of recognition in his features, and toddled out into the hall, where he got his hat and gloves, and went out to the front lawn, where he always paced up and down for a few minutes before taking a drive, in order to stimulate his circulation. This was a surprise, but Aunt Lucretia's behavior was a greater surprise. The moment she set eyes on Uncle David the theatrical fervor went out of her entire system, literally in one instant; and an absolutely natural, unaffected astonishment displayed itself in her expressive and strongly marked features. For almost a minute, until the sound of Uncle David's footsteps had died away, she stood absolutely rigid; while my wife and I gazed at her spell-bound.

Then Aunt Lucretia pointed one long bony finger at me, and hissed out, with true feminine disregard of grammar:

"That ain't *him!*"


"David," said Aunt Lucretia, impressively, "had only one arm. He lost the other in Madagascar."

I was too dumfounded to take in the situation. I remember thinking, in a vague sort of way, that Madagascar was a curious sort of place to go to for the purpose of losing an arm; but I did not apprehend the full significance of this disclosure until I heard my wife's distressed protestations that Aunt Lucretia must be mistaken; that there must be some horrible mistake somewhere.

But Aunt Lucretia was not mistaken, and there was no mistake anywhere. The arm had been lost, and lost in Madagascar, and she could give the date of the occurrence, and the circumstances attendant. Moreover, she produced her evidence on the spot. It was an old daguerreotype,[37] taken in Calcutta a year or two after the Madagascar episode. She had it in her handbag, and she opened it with fingers trembling with rage and excitement. It showed two men standing side by side near one of those three-foot Ionic pillars that were an indispensable adjunct of photography in its early stages. One of the men was large, broad-shouldered, and handsome—unmistakably a handsome edition of Aunt Lucretia. His empty left sleeve was pinned across his breast. The other man was, making allowance for the difference in years, no less unmistakably the Uncle David who was at that moment walking to and fro under our windows. For one instant my wife's face lighted up.

"Why, Aunt Lucretia," she cried, "there he is! That's Uncle David, dear Uncle David."

"There he is not," replied Aunt Lucretia. "That's his business partner— some common person that he picked up on the ship he first sailed in—and, upon my word, I do believe it's that wretched creature outside. And I'll Uncle David him."

She marched out like a grenadier going to battle, and we followed her meekly. There was, unfortunately, no room for doubt in the case. It only needed a glance to see that the man with one arm was a member of my wife's family, and that the man by his side, our Uncle David, bore no resemblance to him in stature or features.

Out on the lawn Aunt Lucretia sailed into the dear old gentleman in the five overcoats with a volley of vituperation. He did not interrupt her, but stood patiently to the end, listening, with his hands behind his back; and when, with her last gasp of available breath, Aunt Lucretia demanded: "Who—who—who are you, you wretch?" he responded, calmly and respectfully, "I'm Tommy Biggs, Miss Lucretia."

But just here my wife threw herself on his neck and hugged him, and cried:

"You're my own dear Uncle David, *anyway!*"

It was a fortunate, a gloriously fortunate inspiration. Aunt Lucretia drew herself up in speechless scorn, stretched forth her bony finger, tried to say something and failed, and then she and her handbag went out of my gates, never to come in again.

When she had gone; our aromatic uncle—for we shall always continue to think of him in that light, or rather in that odor—looked thoughtfully after her till she disappeared, and then made one of the few remarks I ever knew him to volunteer.

"Ain't changed a mite in forty-seven years."

Up to this time I had been in a dazed condition of mind. As I have said, my wife's family was extinct save for herself and Aunt Lucretia, and she remembered so little of her parents, and she looked, herself, so little like Aunt Lucretia, that it was small wonder that neither of us remarked Uncle David's unlikeness to the family type. We knew that he did not resemble the ideal we had formed of him; and that had been the only consideration we had given to his looks. Now, it took only a moment of reflection to recall the fact that all the members of the family had been tall and shapely, and that even between the ugly ones, like Aunt Lucretia, and the pretty ones, like my wife, there was a certain resemblance. Perhaps it was only the nose—the nose is the brand in most families, I believe—but whatever it was, I had only to see my wife and Aunt Lucretia together to realize that the man who had passed himself off as our Uncle David had not one feature in common with either of them—nor with the one-armed man in the daguerreotype. I was thinking of this, and looking at my wife's troubled face, when our aromatic uncle touched me on the arm.

"I'll explain," he said, "to you. *You* tell *her.*"

We dismissed the carriage, went into the house, and sat down. The old gentleman was perfectly cool and collected, but he lit his clay pipe, and reflected for a good five minutes before he opened his mouth. Then he began:

"Finest man in the world, sir. Finest *boy* in the world. Never anything like him. But, peculiarities. Had 'em. Peculiarities. Wouldn't write home. Wouldn't—" here he hesitated—"send things home. I had to do it. Did it for him. Didn't want his folks to know. Other peculiarities. Never had any money. Other peculiarities. Drank. Other peculiarities. Ladies. Finest man in the world, all the same. Nobody like him. Kept him right with his folks for thirty-one years. Then died. Fever. Canton. Never been myself since. Kept right on writing, all the same. Also—" here he hesitated again—"sending things. Why? Don't know. Been a fool all my life. Never could do anything but make money. No family, no friends. Only him. Ran away to sea to look after him. Did look after him. Thought maybe your wife would be some like him. Barring peculiarities, she is. Getting old. Came here for company. Meant no harm. Didn't calculate on Miss Lucretia."

Here he paused and smoked reflectively for a minute or two.

"Hot in the collar—Miss Lucretia. Haughty. Like him, some. Just like she was forty-seven years ago. Slapped my face one day when I was delivering meat because my jumper wasn't clean. Ain't changed a mite."

This was the first condensed statement of the case of our aromatic uncle. It was only in reply to patient, and, I hope, loving, gentle, and considerate questioning that the whole story came out—at once pitiful and noble—of the poor little butcher-boy who ran away to sea to be body-guard, servant, and friend to the splendid, showy, selfish youth whom he worshipped; whose heartlessness he cloaked for many a long year, who lived upon his bounty, and who died in his arms, nursed with a tenderness surpassing that of a brother. And as far as I could find out, ingratitude and contempt had been his only reward.

I need not tell you that when I repeated all this to my wife, she ran to the old gentleman's room and told him all the things that I should not have known how to say—that we cared for him; that we wanted him to stay with us; that he was far, far more our uncle than the brilliant, unprincipled scape-grace who had died years before, dead for almost a lifetime to the family who idolized him; and that we wanted him to stay with us as long as kind heaven would let him. But it was of no use. A change had come over our aromatic uncle which we could both of us see, but could not understand. The duplicity of which he had been guilty weighed on his spirit. The next day he went out for his usual walk, and he never came back. We used every means of search and inquiry, but we never heard from him until we got this letter from Foo-choo-li:[38]

"DEAR NEPHEW AND NIECE: The present is to inform you that I am enjoying the Health that might be expected of my Age, and in my condition of Body, which is to say Bad. I ship you by today's steamer, Pacific Monarch, four dozen jars of ginger, and two dozen ditto preserved oranges, to which I would have added some other Comfits, which I purposed offering for your acceptance, if it were not that my Physician has forbidden me to leave my Bed. In case of Fatal Results from this trying Condition, my Will, duly attested, and made in your favor, will be placed in your hands by Messrs. Smithson & Smithson, my Customs Brokers, who will also pay all charges on goods sent. The Health of this place being unfavorably affected by the Weather, you are unlikely to hear more from,

"Dear Nephew and Niece,
   "Your affectionate
      "UNCLE."

And we never did hear more—except for his will—from Our Aromatic Uncle; but our whole house still smells of his love.

# EDWARD PRIME-STEVENSON (1858–1942)

*Prime-Stevenson enjoyed a successful literary career in the 1890s as a writer of poetry, fiction, and music criticism for such popular magazines as* Harper's *and* The Independent, *among others.* Mrs. Dee's Encore, *which was serialized in* Harper's Bazar, *reveals some insights into Prime-Stevenson's life. In the middle of an otherwise melodramatic story he provides a comical glimpse into "homosexual" life, in the form of a bachelor dinner whose appearance is only tangentially related to the plot (Prime-Stevenson, a music critic of some renown in the New York literary scene, would have been familiar with such gatherings). To those "in the know," his portraits of several of the men must have been recognizable, their talk about things Greek a coded reference, the suggestive description of décor and clothing, and quasi-parodic depiction of hypnotism (then often used as a tool to "cure" homosexuality) must have seemed surprisingly direct. Like his contemporary, the successful commercial artist J.C. Leyendecker (the creator of the Arrow Collar Man[39]), Prime-Stevenson often injected gay sensibility into a popular forum. How much of this was visible to its original general audience is still debatable, though we know from Prime-Stevenson's writings (particularly in* The Intersexes *[1908, see above, 3–6]) that homosexual men were often quite aware of such subtexts.*

# FROM *MRS. DEE'S ENCORE* (1896)

## Chapter IV

"—WE ARE ALL MORE OR LESS MAD, YOU KNOW...."
The burdens of Mary Dee and of young Gilbert Rood charged Sylvester's heart heavier and heavier at intervals all the next day. But it was at intervals; for he had much on his hands, and they had no right to be put, even as to a finger-tip, into this sentimental pie that he had discovered a-baking and burning. As it happened, too, he was spared the meeting with Mary Dee that he feared he could not face, however brief, without leading her to divine his discreditable robbery of her secret, along with his intense interest in it. The afternoon brought pupils in their usual quick succession, and his cozy parlor was full of songs and study.

Just after Sard had thrown himself down, in unusual nervous weariness, the last pupil gone, he remembered an invitation several days accepted. Half provoked, he hastily changed his clothes. The invitation was from an artist not far away, with whom he had something like an intimacy.

"Come to dinner at 6.30," it said. "Fail not. I am going to have Mareptos.

There will be only six or seven of us. I expect that it will be interesting. Van."

"Mareptos?" questioned Sylvester, as he ran over the note again. "Who is, what is, Mareptos? A new game? Or a disease?" He could not recall where he had read the name, which nevertheless struck him as not unfamiliar.

"Ah, I have it!" he exclaimed. "Mareptos is the mesmerist, the mind-reader, hypnotist, or whatever they call it now. Van Zile sent me the London *Telegraph* with that article last summer. I wonder when the man came over? I haven't seen the interviews' industry in print yet."

Even if Sylvester had read more carefully in the bewildering chaos of an American newspaper he would have found only a very brief paragraph or two on Mr. Theron Casimir Mareptos. Mr. Mareptos was visiting America incognito, much out of health, and at present wholly unprofessionally. "The nervous demands of his last 'season' in Paris and London" (so noted one curt notice) "had made travel and a complete rest desirable. Mr. Mareptos would give no exhibitions until, at the earliest, the autumn."

Mr. Theron Casimir Mareptos, it may as well be mentioned here, was given out to be (what two-thirds of his name suggested) a Greek. Perhaps, incidentally, he was as Greek as his surname, and his nose so indicated, not to speak of his published bits of autobiography and his allusions to his early home in Athens. But he spoke several languages quite as well as his supposed native one. Every now and then somebody who ought to know insisted that he spoke them better. He had Jewish traits of person and feature, and, like many gifted sons of Israel, he was very much a wanderer in the interests of the occult— and of his pocket. He lived much in London. It is only justice to say that report insisted that the accomplishments of Mr. Mareptos as what he called a "mind-influencer" were so out of the common that he should be admitted a genuine mystery. If at all a humbug, certain of his feats defied analysis of that ready assumption.

Van Zile's studio presented a cheerful aspect when Sylvester entered it that evening. His round-faced, lively host, a picture of comfortable and busy bachelorhood, came hospitably to meet him in the anteroom, and drew Sard into the spacious quarters beyond. It was a good-sized studio, and space was not its only luxury. Van Zile was not constrained to limit his expenditures for greenish-yellow Gobelins, silky rugs devoid of mineral and all other colors, and carved furniture. His workshop looked properly picturesque, though without eye-tiring litter. In the middle of the room extended now a big table, laid, and shining with its white cloth and silver, and graced by a twisted vase full of *cattleya*.[40] Seated here and there, waiting for Sard (as the delayed last guest) and the host's signal to the caterer, were chatting several men.

All of them were known to Sylvester by evenings of the same hospitality. Sylvester shook hands with Udall Forde, the architect; with Breezer, the marine painter; with Lucius Haight, the musical editor of a daily journal; with

Lancaster, the literary reviewer on the same staff. As the centre of their civilities, Van Zile led Sylvester toward a gentleman seated with his back to them as they approached. He turned, and immediately it was obvious that only names, at most, were needed in the introduction. Sylvester and Mr. Theron Casimir Mareptos smiled and shook hands in welcome recognition.

"Of all the men in the world—the rest of the company excepted, of course," remarked Mr. Mareptos, cordially, in a *trainant*[41] voice less Grecian than English-Hebrew—"Of all the men in the world, I am most charmed to have the honor of meeting Mr. Sard—again."

"Again!" said Van Zile. "You don't mean to say that you and Sard—Mr. Sard and you—have ever met until this moment?"

"We most certainly have happened to do so," answered Sylvester.

"And Mr. Sard will assent to my saying that *I* remember the meeting most particularly," added Mareptos, in his dulcet tone.

"You have been ill in your hotel almost ever since you landed last Saturday," quoth Van Zile.

"Nevertheless, the strange, the romantic meeting has occurred. Mr. Sard has given me the privilege of joining him and all of you to-night—I think I may say. For your friend, my dear Van Zile, has saved my life."

"Saved your life!" laughed Van Zile. "Here have we mystery, gentlemen! Pray did it occur in this world, or in another and better—or worse—one, Mareptos? Mr. Sard has not been abroad since the last Bayreuth saturnalia."[42]

"And yet it was across the water that I met Mr. Sard, my dear Mr. Van Zile."

"Don't tell them the facts, Mr. Mareptos," laughed Sylvester. "Already it would disappoint their expectations."

"But we shall insist," remonstrated Udall Forde, holding out a protesting hand. "You have roused the tiger of curiosity."

"Let us have every bit of the supernatural in it, at least," begged Lancaster.

"None but the curious deserve the rare," said Haight.

"Well, the fact is—" began Sylvester.

Mr. Mareptos held up a monitory finger and smiled. "I beg your pardon, Mr. Sard," he interpolated; "but just one moment, please." Then to the others. "Gentlemen, if you will be so *very* amiable as to excuse Mr. Sard and me from this little narrative until after dinner, I think it can then be made more interesting. Indeed, I shall be happy to save Mr. Sard trouble by my share in the telling." And Mr. Mareptos looked inquiringly from one of the group to another with the expression of a rather old but affectionate lad, arguing tentatively for a half-crown.

There was a prompt acceptance. "After dinner it shall be," assented Van Zile. Van Zile suspected that Mr. Mareptos knew what he was about now—as always.

"More and more mysterious," said Breezer. "But make the tale long and strong, to compensate us for the delay."

"Put them next to one another at table, Van Zile," suggested Forde; "then they can cook up the dish and spice it high."

"I wish that I could conceal my stenographer," said Lancaster.

"Ladies are not admitted, Lancaster, *in diesen heil'gen Hallen*."[43]

"Except Van Zile's models, Mr. Sard."

"And models of discretion," Van Zile added, "such as I know Lancaster's young lady surely to be."

"Such another pearl the dark unfathomed caves of typewriting do not bear," remarked Lancaster. "By-the-bye, Breezer, what's become of the corner of 'Fingal's Cave at Sunset' that the plastering fell down on?"

"Mended, concealed, adorned, my good sir!" replied Breezer. "I shall ask my gentleman a hundred dollars more for reparation. Besides that, I am commissioned to paint a sunrise for him—without regard to either variety or expense of colors."

The conversation became desultory again during the dinner-waiting. Sylvester found it a good opportunity to study Mr. Mareptos externally.

The mind-influencer, mesmerist, hypnotist, or whatsoever was the most approved name for his calling, appeared now no more mysterious, not a whit more unconventional, than he had seemed among the passengers on the Brooklyn ferry-boat. He was of modest stature, gracefully built, and possessed remarkably neat hands and feet. His clothes were of a superlatively good fit. His face was gravely pleasant—pale, with a lack of color that did not seem normal to the smooth olive skin, and the features of it were harmonious if not wholly Hellenic. Its fine oval was luminous with the singularly intense concentrated gaze from a pair of the darkest blue eyes that Sylvester had ever remarked. In observing their changeful depths, "All such queer gentlemen have singular eyes, they say," thought Sard, "but really the most noticeable thing about this man's pair is that they suggest male sapphires. Mr. Mareptos, you are probably too busy to be a lady-killer, but your capital for it is obvious." Mr. Mareptos also had extremely even and white little teeth, that nearly always showed themselves in his slow smile at the end of a sentence. Altogether the mesmerist was distinctly good-looking, unobtrusive, gentlemanlike, and but slightly—Oriental. He could talk with ease and ample information on all sorts of topics, it appeared, from old china[44] to Continental politics, in English, seldom at loss for exactly the right phrase, and wholly idiomatic. To his profession he did not refer. He was a practiced listener, though Sylvester noticed that, more skillfully than anybody whom he ever had met, Mareptos concealed the bad habit of quietly observing other people while he talked.

A very sociable and merry little dinner it proved to be. Just before they sat down Sylvester found a chance to speak to his host a private word.

"Is your friend likely to give us a bit of a professional exposition before the evening is over? I suppose that we oughtn't to expect it; and you can't even intimate that it would please us vastly."

"No. I haven't spoken of it. But Mareptos has."

"Ah! so much the better."

"You see, he will very likely make some few public appearances in town next fall, before he sails—doctors or no doctors. Lancaster is here. I have given Lancaster a strong character for influence with the general press. Really, he *can* serve Mareptos a good deal. Mareptos was so civil to me in London last November that I want him to be successful in individualizing himself here. I think we shall see something characteristic later in the night. He's not one of your no-song, no-supper gentlemen, though—as you see."

At the table Sylvester and Mr. Mareptos did not have the privileges of neighborhood that Udall Forde had suggested. The guest of honor sat between his host and Lancaster. There was no exclusiveness in the conversation, and it ranged and changed gaily and cleverly. As the tongues grew freer and the spirits higher, Van Zile's face beamed with quiet satisfaction. Mr. Mareptos told excellent stories—none of them with "mind-influencing" as a theme. In this little company of hard workers nobody took much wine. Sylvester observed that Mr. Mareptos allowed his final glass to stand almost untouched, as the barrier to others. He also found Mr. Mareptos's eyes—those strangely beautiful eyes, so limpid and keen—resting on his own; and seldom without a special and friendly quickening of their brightness. There was nothing psychologically disturbing about the encounter.

As departed what slight formality had hung in the air before dinner owing to unequal acquaintanceship in the group, and with the coffee and smoking, began to spring out allusions to the occult profession of Mr. Mareptos.

"I understand that you have not found it a wholly healthful one," remarked Lancaster, "however easily you utilize it."

"Less so than would be convenient for me, Mr. Lancaster. But no profession is healthful in which we allow ourselves, little by little, to overwork. A railway porter or a mind-influencer—it is quite one as to that result."

"Mr. Mareptos," spoke Breezer, "suppose that during one of your ordinary exhibitions—you call them exhibitions, don't you?—or for two or three of them, you happen to have a good many difficult subjects: you call them 'subjects,' don't you? You know what I mean—the intractable, unsusceptible sort of article, such as I have seen worked over by gentlemen in your line, with whom it is hard to do one's self justice. Now, aside from any annoyance at such a chance, is not that an experience nervously very tiring?"

Mr. Mareptos laughed gently. "I do not somehow recall any experience of that description. No, I think not."

"Really? Then you are fortunate, it seems to me," replied Mr. Breezer, slightly and unnecessarily elevating his eyebrows. "I thought that such situations bothered all mesmerists. There is Binssen, the Norwegian hypnotist—you know of him, I dare say?"

"I know of Mr. Binssen."

"Why, even Binssen and Leon Walter, the Englishman—they confess to meeting subjects so troublesome as to spoil the interest of an evening now and then. Is that really so novel?"

"Perhaps not so with the gentlemen whom you name," answered Mr. Mareptos, sweetly. "I am only drawing on my own experience, you see. And the, the processes of mind-influencing which I have found practicable are not the same, I dare say, with the—the mesmerism of those gentlemen."

"Mr. Breezer inquires because he is a bad 'subject' himself," remarked Van Zile. "Your last test was with Binssen, too, that evening in the Oscarhof."

"True," returned Breezer, with satisfaction; "and I have had good cause to think as much after trying to be sport for the Philistines through more than the potent Mr. Binssen! Mr. Mareptos," he went on, complacently, "I wish, while we are on the topic, you'd define for me the difference between plain old-fashioned mesmerism and these new-fangled systems of some such faculty—this hypnotism, mind-influencing, body-influencing, and so on. Is it true that there is not any difference? Is it true that the doctors would not recognize the intruder into their field without a new name, and so a new name was coined out of the first Greek dictionary at hand?"

Breezer did not mean it; it was a mannerism, for the age and self-assertiveness. There was an implication of saying to his interlocutor, "Now, my good little sir, I'm charmed to meet you, since I'm asked; but you *are* a humbug, aren't you?"

"I'm afraid you don't know that I happen to be a doctor myself, Mr. Breezer," replied Mr. Mareptos. "Generally I do not write after my name, especially in advertisements of my exhibitions, the title M.D. Vienna kindly gave it to me. But I practice still—in connection with several alienistic establishments in England and Paris—and privately, now and then.[45] I dare not discuss so delicate a secret as medical terminology with a layman, you see! Indeed, I can only congratulate myself and confreres[46] in the study of the mind that we do not find all the world as redoubtable as Mr. Breezer. So should we be but laughing-stocks, surely!"

"Instead of making such sad laughing-stocks of other folks, eh? Well, I have one satisfaction: I may paint badly sometimes, but I have never talked baby-talk, nor waltzed with a bolster in a lady's mackintosh, to entertain a select or other audience. And I don't propose to have my dignity and intellect so upset, unless it will sell my worst seascape!"

"Surely worth your best price, Mr. Breezer," Mareptos said, bowing. Then with saccharine leisureliness of tone he continued, addressing Lancaster: "You were referring to the healthfulness of my profession, sir. I presume you had in mind that fatigue which comes from displays before spectators—exhibitions that can indeed be considered much like ordinary mesmerism, and especially if complicated with unmanageable subjects like Mr. Breezer here? I have found the application of—of the force under various private and responsible circumstances much more wearisome. It is such work that has spoiled this year for me—alas!"

"You mean in the continued hypnotic treatment of mental diseases?"

"Precisely."

"Such as—"

Sylvester's listening now was nothing if not careful.

"Such as many—of a sad and confidential nature.[47] It is sometimes hard to characterize them clearly. Hysteria, acute or latent excitability, depression, kleptomania, for example—these phenomena all come nowadays directly into the province of the true medical mind-influencer; or, they should come. They are exciting to him, I can assert, especially as he struggles toward success with them. That he can succeed so frequently is, in my opinion, the only excuse for my profession."

"Why are you so restrictive?" asked Forde.

"Because without such useful and curative effects I do not think that man should stir up a dangerous curiosity, a vulgar interest in his fellow-men as to the very secret of life—thought, and much thought and action affected by thought. Everything, gentlemen, that can be made of real good to us—of a very good—excuses itself. What can accomplish no visible and direct good, what goes only triflingly toward that point, never to reach it—why, it were better laid aside."

"You stifle research," remarked Haight.

"No. I would stifle the influence of the quack; I would put out of his touch fire that should not be played with. Science can be a crime—can it not?— when it is wholly inexact—used as one might use a ball of dynamite taken for tinder. I speak as I feel in the matter of all this mental research—seriously."

It cannot be stated here whether much of the foregoing was to be read in one of Mr. Mareptos's printed essays or not. There were such essays, and the question is open. That he took himself seriously was plain, and perhaps excusable.

"To change the topic," presently said Mareptos, lightly, "and to save myself from the charge of talking as if I were haranguing Parliament, would not this be a good moment for the telling of the promised story of how and where Mr. Sard and I met so particularly?—of how he saved my life, as I have said. Will that be acceptable as a diversion?"

The suggestion was caught at warmly. Sylvester thought that Mr. Mareptos was making more of such a trifle than was necessary or fair.

"I am at the orders of Mr. Mareptos," he said. "Which of us is to do the telling? You or I?"

"Neither I nor you, Mr. Sard. I partially promised to save you any exertion, and I shall be saved it, I assure you, as well. Mr. Breezer is going to do the telling."

"I?" exclaimed Breezer. "When I know nothing about it! How can I?"

"Easily, my dear sir, easily. As you will see. For you are a little mistaken, I imagine. You must know it before you narrate it; and I predict that you can narrate it in a faithful way that none of us can surpass. You will not disoblige us all by declining, at least, to try?"

Breezer, a strongly built man of thirty, with the red hair supposed to betoken inflammatoriness of temper, frowned at this pleasantry that gathered about him so suddenly.

"I don't understand you. I have no more idea of this ridiculous little joke between you and Mr. Sard than I have of who will be the next President of France."

"But that is true—that is undoubtedly wholly true, my dear sir," replied Mr. Mareptos, with honeyed affirmation. "But, Mr. Breezer, I am convinced that *you* could tell us this story better than any man here—that is to say, with a little preparatory help."

"Oh," said Breezer, with something like a sneer, "you mean that I might with the help coming from you? Really? Try to afford me it, Mr. Mareptos! I shall be charmed; I shall be like wax in your hands."

"Thanks. I *will* try," Mareptos returned. Leaning across the table (for Breezer sat directly *vis-à-vis*[48]), he went on: "Only I don't care about your being wax. You might melt, and I be a homicide. Will you, first of all, undertake to do a very simple bit of mental arithmetic with me?" He fixed his calm, strange look on Breezer's irritated countenance. "Suppose we count alternately, slowly, the numbers from one to, say, twenty-five, you and I, you looking me steadily in the eyes while we do so?"

"As you please," answered Breezer. "Are you ready? I am." He did not turn his glance from the face of Mr. Mareptos, as if all at once embarrassed as well as scornful. "One," he began.

"Two," Mareptos returned.

Van Zile, Sard, and the rest were staring in silence. They realized what was going forward, and were not a little admiring and amused at the dexterity and the defiance that had led up to the scene. Mr. Mareptos evidently proposed to gratify their curiosity to the full by it.

Mr. Mareptos leaned further forward across the table. Hardly a muscle of his face moved. A slight contraction of the lines of the mouth was discernible. Sylvester could perceive absolutely nothing in the gaze, which Breezer steadfastly returned, except concentration and perhaps a dilation of those dark pupils. Breezer did not count to "nine." Had he forgotten that odd number? His position was that of an unfortunate undergoing photography. Silent, his look appearing not to take in either his opponent, or the table before him, or the wall behind him, or anything in that room—he was as if paralyzed. He was no paler, but rather of a deeper color than usual. Then, suddenly, a gray white succeeded uniformly all over his face, and even his hands. Mareptos was silent too, after twice slowly and softly repeating "eight."

The Greek leaned back in his seat, but without withdrawing his eyes from the painter.

"I am sure that you do not object to telling that story now, eh? Say 'No,' please."

"No, please," replied Breezer, with exactness.

Mareptos walked around the table to his side. "Kindly rise, then. So! You will go out to the middle of the room there, where we can hear the better."

Breezer pushed back his chair.

"Wait. Sit down again. You must clear your voice." He made a sign to the servant. A plate of raw oysters reserved from the dinner's earliest stage was handed to him. Mareptos deposited the oysters before Breezer, who had resumed his eating. The attention was breathless.

"There are some oranges—oranges. Oranges are good for your throat. You like oranges?"

"Yes," replied the painter, speaking as one preoccupied.

"Say, 'Yes—I like them very little, I don't thank you madam, or George Washington, because the angle of twenty-two thousand five hundred and sixty starved by thirteen thousand and one must be painted magenta, with ecclesiastical intoning of the apogee and a nimbus obedient to a compound fracture.'" Mareptos spoke rapidly.

"Yes—I like them very little, I don't thank you—" Breezer began promptly, continuing the rest of the gibberish as glibly as it had been prescribed him.

"Now eat your oranges; but salt them first. Salt is a great thing on oranges. Here is the salt. Come, a good quantity."

He set a bowl of powdered sugar at Breezer's hand. In horrified awe the party watched the redoubtably bad "subject" cover the oysters heavily with sugar. There are few more nauseous combinations even in Chinese gastronomy. And at a dinner's end!

"Eat them."

Breezer swallowed one with infantile relish.

"Very—very nice, isn't it? Eat another."

Breezer ate another. "They are so—*so* good," he said softly.

"Of course they are. Good oranges are always good, you see. Eat another." It vanished. Those who sat nearby Breezer were rather relieved (of most untimely apprehensions) when Mareptos set aside the plate from his victim. "Enough," he said; "you must not make yourself ill. Please get up."

With a silly satisfaction on his pale lips, up rose Breezer. Mareptos took him by the hand and conducted him toward the model's platform across the room. As they approached it Mareptos took up a stout stool and set it in the middle of the platform, like a model's throne.

"Take off your coat."

The coat was taken off. Mareptos passed it to Sard. "Now your waistcoat—now your cravat and collar."

Breezer divested himself of these articles and dropped them on the rug.

"Take off your shirt."

Van Zile, and more than Van Zile, thought that the performance and Breezer's docility were approaching a degree that was—more spectacular than necessary. If Mr. Mareptos proposed to undress the helpless painter to the bare, and to send him home in indecorous coolness! Before they had decided that they were being too whimsically entertained, the clean shirt was also at Breezer's feet. Mareptos looked up and down the studio. He stepped to a corner and took down an embroidered orange silk stuff. It was a cope.[49] That Breezer was accustomed to wearing blue silk under-vests and a scarlet flannel chin protector had just been made a historically accurate discovery.

"Put this on."

The cope was slowly slipped over Breezer's shoulder. Gayety was of the essence of his costume.

"It is raining!" exclaimed the Greek. "Do you see the rain, Mr. Breezer? Why, you are wet already."

"I am wet—already," replied Breezer. Then pathetically, "What *shall* I do?"

"Oh, keep yourself dry, of course, dear sir! First, roll up your trousers as high as you can. So! And now let us see more of that pretty blue silk stuff. Get up on this big stone. The water is running all around your feet. Too bad! That's right—don't move from the stone." Breezer stood, looking excessively troubled, on the stool.

"Put this on your head," resumed the Greek—"and now hold my umbrella over your head."

Another instant, and a tableau at which the very waiters were peering in disrespectful mirth was complete. The man idly standing on the stool, as his perch of deliverance from a freshet—arrayed gorgeously in the ancient orange cope, his black trouser tucked to mid-leg—"that pretty blue silk stuff" heightening the color contrasts—a hat too large for his head tilted back on it—a soft long broom, long used on Van Zile's polished floors, extended straight up toward the ceiling—the marine painter now presented a spirited and irresistibly ludicrous spectacle. And he was not the less ludicrous because he smiled round with the constancy of a Malvolio,[50] in relief at being protected from unkindly weather.

Van Zile's discomfort had become extreme. He knew Breezer's weaknesses, and, besides, this was taking advantage of a fellow-guest in his house and home quite outrageously. He controlled his laughter; for shake with mirth he did, with all the rest. But no, this must stop. Haight and Forde, however, advanced counter-proof that Breezer would have no right to be annoyed. ... Perhaps, after the exhibition should end, the painter would not know just what it had entailed on him.

"And then, Van Zile, look here," whispered Forde; "he's always so confounded cocky! So sure of himself! And you heard what he said to Mr. Mareptos? It was a challenge. He deserves what he gets."

Mr. Mareptos had not been called upon to consider these queries. He drew nearer to his victim now, and himself mounted a chair close beside the stool for Breezer's placid occupancy. He took Breezer's hand. "Look at me!" he said.

Breezer obediently permitted his head to be turned about, much as one turns a wig-maker's revolving dummy; nor had his countenance much more expression. Mareptos held up his half-closed fists before Breezer's eyes, in the way in which the connoisseur is apt to do before a painting—in wishing to be observed as observing. "Look through these opera-glasses. Tell me what you see."

As Breezer leaned his head a little forward, and peered with some signs of interest, Mr. Mareptos gradually raised and opened his hands. Soon they were flat against Breezer's eyes, and to all purposes that gentleman was gazing into complete darkness. Van Zile, Lancaster, Sard, and the others were now completely bewildered as to what might or might not be forth-coming. Each realized that what had preceded was relatively a trivial programme of mesmeric incidents, in prologue to finer matter.

"What do you see?"

In a low voice, at first hesitating and with the sentences broken, but presently quite assured and matter of fact, Breezer began:

"I see—water—a river. I see a river. Boats—yes, boats on it—boats on the water. Steamboats. Ferry-boats. The city—I see the bridge."

"What bridge?"

"The East River Bridge, of course."

"Yes," said Mareptos, approvingly, at the same time wholly withdrawing from Breezer, and so leaving him staring blankly over into the dim corner of the studio, which he saw not. Next he quickly and lightly left the chair. He stood on the floor, facing Breezer.

"You need not cross that bridge. Where did you say you were?"

"On the boat—the ferry-boat."

"What time is it, please?"

Breezer consulted an imaginary watch. "Ten minutes before twelve."

After that, either in direct reply to set questions, or in unprompted paragraphs of description, he told the promised story.

"There are only a few people. The boat is named the *Fulton*. I am on the deck. We are going into the slip. There is Mr. Mareptos. There is Mr. Sylvester Sard. Mr. Mareptos is just in front of Mr. Sard. He is on the plank. Ha! Look out there! That *was* close! That was a very close escape!" Breezer had thrown his head back. In his observation of what he saw, by some extraordinary process of transfusion of recollection, he had nearly dropped the tall broom. "Why, Mr. Mareptos, you would have gone off that plank, surely you would, if

Mr. Sard hadn't caught hold of you! Good luck! Oh, that piece of yellow stuff was the trouble, was it? Orange-peel, of course. You were a good deal shaken up. Mr. Sard is explaining to the deck-hand. Now I see Mr. Mareptos and Mr. Sard talking in the ferry-house. People are standing by. The woman has a red dress, and no bonnet—she is an Italian. The mail-wagon is the last one coming out. 'If all the fools were shut up except the fools who throw orange-peel about, there would be a small census, almost everywhere.'" (This last observation seemed to be quoted.) "Mr. Sard is going out of the gate with Mr. Mareptos.—'It is the green car.' 'The conductor will probably know.' 'I am sorry that I am not certain about it.' 'An hour, I expect.'" Again quotations apparently.

Mr. Mareptos motioned to the astonished audience to sit again about the table, from which they had risen, one by one. They understood the signal, and slipped into their seats. They were in a state of respectful consternation. There was no humbug and no explanation in this sort of thing.

Mareptos put his hands gently on Breezer's face once more, and smoothed his forehead, and closed his eyes with a disagreeable hint at closing a pair of dead ones. Then Breezer allowed himself to be helped down from the stool and awkwardly to be seated upon it. He still upheld the broom. The long cope swept the floor behind, the hat declined more rakishly.

"Now, Mr. Breezer, you must come back from Brooklyn and the ferry-boat—by the bridge, say? Yes, by the bridge. You are to go to Mr. George Van Zile's studio, to dine and to meet Mr. Mareptos. Indeed, you must hurry. You will be late. Quick—hurry, I say!"

Breezer started up and made a wild plunge. The wary Mareptos caught him firmly, and between a quick shake that was given him and the abrupt grasp, and Mr. Mareptos's sharp "Come, wake up! Wake up!" he woke. Mr. Mareptos slipped down from the platform in a twinkling.

Yes, Breezer "awoke," with a wild, uncanny expression of returned intelligence and self-consciousness.

"Ha—ah!" he ejaculated, his arm falling, the broom dropping with a smart rap on his back.

When a gentleman who thinks extremely well of himself discovers that instead of occupying his chair at a friend's table, enjoying the amenities of conversation, he is squatted on a wooden stool—directed thither by some cause unknown—and that at the same time he has become divested of most of his clothing, for which no dignified garments of ordinary sort are doing duty—such a gentleman may be excused for seeming not only amazed, but ruffled. Nor were the cheerful haw-haws and ho-hos, and other salutes of a reassuring and hilarious kind that met his ears, calculated to soothe Mr. Breezer. For a moment his face was more complicated than his most elaborate study of a ground-swell. It is with reluctance that record is made of his uttering a well-known and profane phrase of three short monosyllables; not as a question, which, in form, it is.

A fresh outbreak of laughter met it.

"'Come down, oh, maid, from yonder mountain height!'" said Lancaster.

"Got back in good order, old man?" asked Haight. "How's Brooklyn?"

Van Zile, anxious to conclude the whole episode, was already acting as Breezer's valet, and soothing his guest's annoyance.

"Sure, 'tis the Apolly Belvy himself!" called Forde.[51]

"Do you think that this dinner was meant as a Greek wrestling match or a Bowery banquet?" demanded Lancaster. "And where *did* you get—"

"That hat?" ejaculated Breezer, hurling it savagely at the ceiling, with an outcry of concern from his host. "The dev—"

"Calmness, calmness, my dear Breezer," Lancaster said, clapping him on the shoulder. "You still live, even if you *have* been butchered to make a Roman holiday."

"Breezer, Breezer. Godlet of the Winds! How could you go for to do it?"

Breezer's face cleared. he saw that the more pleasantly he accepted pleasantry, the better his taste.

"I see!" he remarked, dryly, stepping to the floor, and making an ironical bow to Mr. Mareptos, who was standing, in modest unconcern, behind the table. "I am beaten, Mr. Mareptos. I acknowledge it without reserve. And now will you, or somebody, or all of you, kindly inform me what I have been doing and saying, and for how long?"

Van Zile was relieved that this *réveil*[52] was over. Naturally the entire group undertook the explanation. In course of its vivacity nobody was much surprised to find that Breezer had absolutely no remembrance of a sensation, a delusion, an act, a word, that had been expressed during that ten or fifteen minutes of subjection to "mind-informing." The story of the scene on the ferry-boat was repeated. He was amazed. He accepted the facts of his performance, however, and with few words, and buttoning his shirt collar, allowed Van Zile to carry him off to the next room to arrange his dishevelment.

Everybody was in a ferment of compliment to Mr. Mareptos. "Simply beyond belief," "Knocks out the Magic Mirror of Ink," "Never saw anything so completely supernatural," and so on.

"By such a standard you will stir up all the town's ears if you give public séances," declared Lancaster; "I shall buy myself a two-pronged coral and an ape's left eye!"[53]

Mareptos sat complacently during these compliments, as if accustomed to their sort. He smiled his fine smile; "he was happy to have succeeded so with the subject," and the like. Sylvester, characteristically, said less to him than any of the rest. In the first place, he was really awed by such an unpleasant show of the irresistible "influence." But more particularly, as the reader may suppose, ever since Mr. Mareptos had spoken so authoritatively of the practical uses of mind-influencing, of hypnotism in mental diseases, in questionable conditions of the nervous system, ever since he had alluded to himself as familiarly expert in their treatment, Sylvester had been seized with rash thoughts, and by a rasher wish. He was not projecting it. He could not! But he was resolved to have more conversation with Mr. Mareptos on that same topic of this "practical" work of his art, or gift, before this affable "doctor," who didn't use his title, went to St. Augustine. [...]

# JACK LONDON (1876–1916)

*Though he was "homosocial" to the extreme, preferring the company of men to women, no one would accuse Jack London (to his face) of being homosexual. His hyper-masculine drive approached the levels of his successor Ernest Hemingway (similarly, few would accuse Hemingway of homosexual feelings—to his face). Author of more than fifty books, London, born in San Francisco, explored the Klondike and the South Seas, turning his experiences into adventure stories which examined the fringes of civilization, much like his contemporary Bret Harte. He constantly tested himself in a male world, whether on a dogsled or onboard a tramp steamer. This story, typical of his man-vs.-nature tales, carries, however, the additional weight of strong feelings between the two male heroes, the nature of which remain unacknowledged. "The Malemute Kid" is one of those men whose deepest feelings must be hidden from the eyes of men, though not the eyes of Nature.*[54]

## "THE WHITE SILENCE" (1899)

"Carmen won't last more than a couple of days." Mason spat out a chunk of ice and surveyed the poor animal ruefully, then put her foot in his mouth and proceeded to bite out the ice which clustered cruelly between the toes.

"I never saw a dog with a highfalutin' name that ever was worth a rap," he said, as he concluded his task and shoved her aside. "they just fade away and die under the responsibility. Did ye ever see one go wrong with a sensible name like Cassiar, Siwash, or Husky? No, sir! Take a look at Shookum here, he's—"

Snap! The lean brute flashed up, the white teeth just missing Mason's throat.

"Ye will, will ye?" A shrewd clout behind the ear with the butt of the dog-whip stretched the animal in the snow, quivering softly, a yellow slaver dripping from its fangs.

"As I was saying, just look at Shookum, here—he's got the spirit. Bet ye he eats Carmen before the week's out."

"I'll bank another proposition against that," replied Malemute Kid, reversing the frozen bread placed before the fire to thaw. "We'll eat Shookum before the trip is over. What d'ye say, Ruth?"

The Indian woman settled the coffee with a piece of ice, glanced from Malemute Kid to her husband, then at the dogs, but vouchsafed no reply. It was such a palpable truism that none was necessary. Two hundred miles of unbroken trail in prospect, with a scant six days' grub for themselves and

227

none for the dogs, could admit no other alternative. The two men and the woman grouped about the fire and began their meager meal. The dogs lay in their harnesses, for it was a midday half, and watched each mouthful enviously.

"No more lunches after to-day," said Malemute Kid. "And we've got to keep a close eye on the dogs,—they're getting vicious. They'd just as soon pull a fellow down as not, if they get a chance."

"And I was president of an Epworth[55] once, and taught in the Sunday school." Having irrelevantly delivered himself of this, Mason fell into a dreamy contemplation of his steaming moccasins, but was aroused by Ruth filling his cup. "Thank God, we've got slathers of tea! I've seen it growing, down in Tennessee. What wouldn't I give for a hot corn pone just now! Never mind, Ruth; you won't starve much longer, nor wear moccasins either."

The woman threw off her gloom at this, and in her eyes welled up a great love for her white lord,—the first white man she had ever seen,—the first man whom she had known to treat a woman as something better than a mere animal or beast of burden.

"Yes, Ruth," continued her husband, having recourse to the macaronic[56] jargon in which it was alone possible for them to understand each other; "wait till we clean up and pull for the Outside. We'll take the White Man's canoe and go to the Salt Water. Yes, bad water, rough water,—great mountains dance up and down all the time. And so big, so far, so far away,—you travel ten sleep, twenty sleep, forty sleep" (he graphically enumerated the days on his fingers), "all the time water, bad water. Then you come to great village, plenty people, just the same mosquitoes next summer. Wigwams oh, so high,—ten, twenty pines. Hi-yu skookum!"

He paused impotently, cast an appealing glance at Malemute Kid, then laboriously placed the twenty pines, end on end, by sign language. Malemute Kid smiled with cheery cynicism; but Ruth's eyes were wide with wonder, and with pleasure; for she half believed he was joking, and such condescension pleased her poor woman's heart.

"And then you step into a—a box, and pouf! Up you go." He tossed his empty cup in the air by way of illustration, and as he deftly caught it, cried: "And biff! Down you come. Oh, great medicine-men! You go Fort Yukon, I go Arctic City,—twenty-five sleep,—big string, all the time,—I catch him string,—I say, 'Hello, Ruth! How are ye?'—and you say, 'Is that my good husband?'—and I say 'Yes,'—and you say, 'No can bake good bread, no more soda,'—and then I say, 'Look in cache, under flour; good-by.' You look and catch plenty soda. All the time you Fort Yukon, me Arctic City. Hi-yu medicine-man!"

Ruth smiled so ingenuously at the fairy story, that both men burst into laughter. A row among the dogs cut short the wonders of the Outside, and by the time the snarling combatants were separated, she had lashed the sleds and all was ready for the trail.

"Mush! Baldy! Hi! Mush on!" Mason worked his whip smartly, and as the dogs whined low in the traces, broke out the sled with the gee-pole. Ruth followed with the second team, leaving Malemute Kid, who had helped her start, to bring up the rear. Strong man, brute that he was, capable of felling an ox at a blow, he could not bear to beat the poor animals, but humored them as a dog-driver rarely does,—nay, almost wept with them in their misery.

"Come, mush on there, you poor sore-footed brutes!" he murmured, after several ineffectual attempts to start the load. But his patience was at last rewarded, and though whimpering with pain, they hastened to join their fellows.

No more conversation; the toil of the trail will not permit such extravagance. And of all deadening labors, that of the Northland trail is the worst. Happy is the man who can weather a day's travel at the price of silence, and that on a beaten track.

And of all heart-breaking labors, that of breaking trail is the worst. At every step the great webbed shoe sinks till the snow is level with the knee. Then up, straight up, the deviation of a fraction of an inch being a certain precursor of disaster, the snowshoe must be lifted till the surface is cleared; then forward, down, and the other foot is raised perpendicularly for the matter of half a yard. He who tries this for the first time, if haply he avoids bringing his shoes in dangerous propinquity and measures not his length on the treacherous footing, will give up exhausted at the end of a hundred yards; he who can keep out of the way of the dogs for a whole day may well crawl into his sleeping-bag with a clear conscience and a pride which passeth all understanding; and he who travels twenty sleeps on the Long Trail is a man whom the gods may envy.

The afternoon wore on, and with the awe, born of the White Silence, the voiceless travelers bent to their work. Nature has many tricks wherewith she convinces man of his finity,—the ceaseless flow of the tides, the fury of the storm, the shock of the earthquake, the long roll of heaven's artillery,—but the most tremendous, the most stupefying of all, is the passive phase of the White Silence. All movement ceases, the sky clears, the heavens are as brass; the slightest whisper seems sacrilege, and man becomes timid, affrighted at the sound of his own voice. Sole speck of life journeying across the ghostly wastes of a dead world, he trembles at his audacity, realizes that his is a maggot's life, nothing more. Strange thoughts arise unsummoned, and the mystery of all things strives for utterance. And the fear of death, of God, of the universe, comes over him,—the hope of the Resurrection and the Life, the yearning for immortality, the vain striving of the imprisoned essence,—it is then, if ever, man walks alone with God.

So wore the day away. The river took a great bend, and Mason headed his team for the cut-off across the narrow neck of land. But the dogs balked at the high bank. Again and again, though Ruth and Malemute Kid were shoving on the sled, they slipped back. Then came the concerted effort. The miserable creatures, weak from hunger, exerted their last strength. Up—up—the sled poised on the top of the bank; but the leader swung the string of dogs behind him to the right, fouling Mason's snowshoes. The result was grievous. Mason was whipped off his feet; one of the dogs fell in the traces; and the sled toppled back, dragging everything to the bottom again.

Slash! the whip fell among the dogs savagely, especially upon the one which had fallen.

"Don't, Mason," entreated Malemute Kid; "the poor devil's on its last legs. Wait and we'll put my team on."

Mason deliberately withheld the whip till the last word had fallen, then out flashed the long lash, completely curling about the offending creature's body. Carmen—for it was Carmen—cowered in the snow, cried piteously, then rolled over on her side.

It was a tragic moment, a pitiful incident of the trail,—a dying dog, two comrades in anger. Ruth glanced solicitously from man to man. But Malemute Kid restrained himself, though there was a world of reproach in his eyes, and bending over the dog, cut the traces. No word was spoken. The teams were double-spanned and the difficulty overcome; the sleds were under way again, the dying dog dragging herself along in the rear. As long as an animal can travel, it is not shot, and this last chance is accorded it,—the crawling into camp, if it can, in the hope of a moose being killed.

Already penitent for his angry action, but too stubborn to make amends, Mason toiled on at the head of the cavalcade, little dreaming that danger hovered in the air. The timber clustered thick in the sheltered bottom, and through this they threaded their way. Fifty feet or more from the trail towered a lofty pine. For generations it had stood there, and for generations destiny had had this one end in view,—perhaps the same had been decreed of Mason.

He stooped to fasten the loosened thong of his moccasin. The sleds came to a half and the dogs lay down in the snow without a whimper. The stillness was weird; not a breath rustled the frost-encrusted forest; the cold and silence of outer space had chilled the heart and smote the trembling lips of nature. A sigh pulsed through the air,—they did not seem to actually hear it, but rather felt it, like the premonition of movement in a motionless void. Then the great tree, burdened with its weight of years and snow, played its last part in the tragedy of life. He heard the warning crash and attempted to spring up, but almost erect, caught the blow squarely on the shoulder.

The sudden danger, the quick death,—how often had Malemute Kid faced it! The pine needles were still quivering as he gave his commands and sprang into action. Nor did the Indian girl faint or raise her voice in idle wailing, as might many of her white sisters. At his order, she threw her weight on the end of a quickly extemporized handspike, easing the pressure and listening to her husband's groans, while Malemute Kid attacked the tree with his axe. The steel rang merrily as it bit into the frozen trunk, each stroke being accompanied by a forced, audible respiration, the "Huh!" "Huh!" of the woodsman.

At last the Kid laid the pitiable thing that was once a man in the snow. But worse than his comrade's pain was the dumb anguish in the woman's face, the blended look of hopeful, hopeless query. Little was said; those of the Northland are early taught the futility of words and the inestimable value of deeds. With the temperature at sixty-five below zero, a man cannot lie many minutes in the snow and live. So the sled-lashings were cut, and the sufferer, rolled in furs, laid on a couch of boughs. Before him roared a fire, built of the very wood which wrought the mishap. Behind and partially over him was stretched the primitive fly,—a piece of canvas, which caught the radiating heat and threw it back and down upon him,—a trick which men may know who study physics at the fount.

And men who have shared their bed with death know when the call is sounded. Mason was terribly crushed. The most cursory examination revealed it. His right arm, leg, and back, were broken; his limbs were paralyzed from the hips; and the likelihood of internal injuries was large. An occasional moan was his only sign of life.

No hope; nothing to be done. The pitiless night crept slowly by,—Ruth's portion, the despairing stoicism of her race, and Malemute Kid adding new lines to his face of bronze. In fact, Mason suffered least of all, for he spent his time in Eastern Tennessee, in the Great Smoky Mountains, living over the scenes of his childhood. And most pathetic was the melody of his long-forgotten Southern vernacular, as he raved of swimming-holes and coon-hunts and watermelon raids. It was as Greek to Ruth, but the Kid understood and felt,—felt as only one can feel who has been shut out for years from all that civilization means.

Morning brought consciousness to the stricken man, and Malemute Kid bent closer to catch his whispers.

"You remember when we foregathered on the Tanana, four years come next ice-run? I didn't care so much for her then. It was more like she was pretty, and there was a smack of excitement about it, I think. But d'ye know, I've come to think a heap of her. She's been a good wife to me, always at my shoulder in the pinch. And when it comes to trading, you know there isn't her equal. D'ye recollect the time she shot the Moosehorn Rapids to pull you and me off that rock, the bullets whipping the water like hailstones?—and the time of the famine at Nuklukyeto?—or when she raced the ice-run to bring the news? Yes, she's been a good wife to me, better 'n that other one. Didn't know I'd been there? Never told you, eh? Well, I tried it once, down in the States. That's why I'm here. Been raised together, too. I came away to give her a chance for divorce. She got it.

"But that's got nothing to do with Ruth. I had thought of cleaning up and pulling for the Outside next year,—her and I,—but it's too late. Don't send her back to her people, Kid. It's beastly hard for a woman to go back. Think of it!—nearly four years on our bacon and beans and flour and dried fruit, and then to go back to her fish and caribou. It's not good for her to have tried our ways, to come to know they're better 'n her people's, and then return to them. Take care of her, Kid,—why don't you,—but no, you always fought shy of them,—and you never told me why you came to this country. Be kind to her, and send her back to the States as soon as you can. But fix it so as she can come back,—liable to get homesick, you know.

"And the youngster—it's drawn us closer, Kid. I only hope it is a boy. Think of it!—flesh of my flesh, Kid. He mustn't stop in this country. And if it's a girl, why she can't. Sell my furs; they'll fetch at least five thousand, and I've got as much more with the company. And handle my interests with yours. I think that bench claim will show up. See that he gets a good schooling; and Kid, above all, don't let him come back. This country was not made for white men.

"I'm a gone man, Kid. Three or four sleeps at the best. You've got to go on. You must go on! Remember, it's my wife, it's my boy,—O God! I hope it's a boy! You can't stay by me,—and I charge you, a dying man, to pull on."

"Give me three days," pleaded Malemute Kid. "You may change for the better; something may turn up."

"No."

"Just three days."

"You must pull on."

"Two days."

"It's my wife and my boy, Kid. You would not ask it."

"One day."

"No, no! I charge—"

"Only one day. We can shave it through on the grub, and I might knock over a moose."

"No,—all right; one day, but not a minute more. And Kid, don't—don't leave me to face it alone. Just a shot, one pull on the trigger. You understand. Think of it! Think of it! Flesh of my flesh, and I'll never live to see him!

"Send Ruth here. I want to say good-by and tell her that she must think of the boy and not wait till I'm dead. She might refuse to go with you if I didn't. Good-by, old man; good-by.

"Kid! I say—a—sink a hole above the pup, next to the slide. I panned out forty cents on my shovel there.

"And Kid!" he stooped lower to catch the last faint words, the dying man's surrender of his pride. "I'm sorry—for—you know—Carmen."

Leaving the girl crying softly over her man, Malemute Kid slipped into his *parka* and snowshoes, tucked his rifle under his arm, and crept away into the forest. He was no tyro[57] in the stern sorrows of the Northland, but never had he faced so stiff a problem as this. In the abstract, it was a plain, mathematical proposition,—three possible lives as against one doomed one. But now he hesitated. For five years, shoulder to shoulder, on the rivers and trails, in the camps and mines, facing death by field and flood and famine, had they knitted the bonds of their comradeship. So close was the tie, that he had often been conscious of a vague jealousy of Ruth, from the first time she had come between. And now it must be severed by his own hand.

Though he prayed for a moose, just one moose, all game seemed to have deserted the land, and nightfall found the exhausted man crawling into camp, light-handed, heavy-hearted. An uproar from the dogs and shrill cries from Ruth hastened him.

Bursting into the camp, he saw the girl in the midst of the snarling pack, laying about her with an axe. The dogs had broken the iron rule of their masters and were rushing the grub. He joined the issue with his rifle reversed, and the hoary game of natural selection was played out with all the ruthlessness of its primeval environment. Rifle and axe went up and down, hit or missed with monotonous regularity; lithe bodies flashed, with wild eyes and dripping fangs; and man and beast fought for supremacy to the bitterest conclusion. Then the beaten brutes crept to the edge of the firelight, licking their wounds, voicing their misery to the stars.

The whole stock of dried salmon had been devoured, and perhaps five pounds of flour remained to tide them over two hundred miles of wilderness. Ruth returned to her husband, while Malemute Kid cut up the warm body of one of the dogs, the skull of which had been crushed by the axe. Every portion was carefully put away, save the hide and offal, which were cast to his fellows of the moment before.

Morning brought fresh trouble. The animals were turning on each other. Carmen, who still clung to her slender thread of life, was downed by the pack. The lash fell among them unheeded. They cringed and cried under the blows, but refused to scatter till the last wretched bit had disappeared— bones, hide, hair, everything.

Malemute Kid went about his work, listening to Mason, who was back in Tennessee, delivering tangled discourses and wild exhortations to his brethren of other days.

Taking advantage of neighboring pines, he worked rapidly, and Ruth watched him make a cache similar to those sometimes used by hunters to preserve their meat from the wolverines and dogs. One after the other, he bent the tops of two small pines toward each other and nearly to the ground, making them fast with thongs of moosehide. Then he beat the dogs into submission and harnessed them to two of the sleds, loading the same with everything but the furs which enveloped Mason. These he wrapped and lashed tightly about him, fastening either end of the robes to the bent pines. A single stroke of his hunting-knife would release them and send the body high in the air.

Ruth had received her husband's last wishes and made no struggle. Poor girl, she had learned the lesson of obedience well. From a child, she had bowed, and seen all women bow, to the lords of creation, and it did not seem in the nature of things for woman to resist. The Kid permitted her one outburst of grief, as she kissed her husband,—her own people had no such custom,—then led her to the foremost sled and helped her into her snowshoes. Blindly, instinctively, she took the gee-pole and whip, and "mushed" the dogs out on the trail. Then he returned to Mason, who had fallen into a coma; and long after she was out of sight, crouched by the fire, waiting, hoping, praying for his comrade to die.

It is not pleasant to be alone with painful thoughts in the White Silence. The silence of gloom is merciful, shrouding one as with protection and breathing a thousand intangible sympathies; but the bright White Silence, clear and cold, under steely skies, is pitiless.

An hour passed,—two hours,—but the man would not die. At high noon, the sun, without raising its rim above the southern horizon, threw a suggestion of fire athwart the heavens, then quickly drew it back. Malemute Kid roused and dragged himself to his comrade's side. He cast one glance about him. The White Silence seemed to sneer, and a great fear came upon him. There was a sharp report; Mason swung into his aerial sepulcher; and Malemute Kid lashed the dogs into a wild gallop as he fled across the snow.

# JAMES WELDON JOHNSON (1871–1938)

*Born in Jacksonville, Florida, James Weldon Johnson was a teacher, lawyer, poet, songwriter, and civil rights activist during a long and illustrious career, which included being president of the National Association for the Advancement of Colored People. Although the first explicitly homosexual story written by an African-American author is generally considered to be "Smoke, Lilies, and Jade" by Bruce Nugent (1925), Anne Herrmann in her book* Queering the Moderns *(2000) devotes a chapter to this moving passage from Johnson's much earlier novel. The book's hero, a black musician,*[58] *is taken through Europe by a kindly millionaire patron who—in true Horatio Alger fashion—sets him on his life's course. The nature of the understated feelings between the two men carries a complex of emotions, and the present-day reader may detect homoerotic overtones in the older-younger men's attachment.*

## FROM *THE AUTOBIOGRAPHY OF AN EX-COLORED MAN* (1912)

[...] I now lost interest in our trip. I thought, here I am a man, no longer a boy, and what am I doing but wasting my time and abusing my talent. What use am I making of my gifts? What future have I before me following my present course? These thoughts made me feel remorseful, and put me in a fever to get to work, to begin to do something. Of course I know now that I was not wasting time; that there was nothing I could have done at that age which would have benefited me more than going to Europe as I did. The desire to begin work grew stronger each day. I could think of nothing else. I made up my mind to go back into the very heart of the South, to live among the people, and drink in my inspiration first-hand. I gloated over the immense amount of material I had to work with, not only modern ragtime, but also the old slave songs,—material which no one had yet touched.

The more decided and anxious I became to return to the United States, the more I dreaded the ordeal of breaking with my "millionaire." Between this peculiar man and me there had grown a very strong bond of affection, backed up by a debt which each owed to the other. He had taken me from a terrible life in New York and by giving me the opportunity of traveling and of coming in contact with the people with whom he associated, had made me a polished man of the world. On the other hand, I was his chief means of disposing of the thing which seemed to sum up all in life that he dreaded—Time. As I remember him now, I can see that time was what he was always endeavoring to escape, to bridge over, to blot out; and it is not strange that some years later he did escape it forever, by leaping into eternity.

For some weeks I waited for just the right moment in which to tell my patron of my decision. Those weeks were a trying time to me. I felt that I was playing the part of a traitor to my best friend. At length, one day, he said to me, "Well, get ready for a long trip; we are going to Egypt, and then to Japan." The temptation was for an instant almost overwhelming, but I summoned determination enough to say, "I don't think I want to go." "What!" he exclaimed, "you want to go back to your dear Paris? You still think that the only spot on earth? Wait until you see Cairo and Tokyo, you may change your mind." "No," I stammered, "it is not because I want to go back to Paris. I want to go back to the United States." He wished to know my reason, and I told him, as best I could, my dreams, my ambition, and my decision. While I was talking he watched me with a curious, almost cynical, smile growing on his lips. When I had finished he put his hand on my shoulder.—This was the first physical expression of tender regard he had ever shown me—and looking at me in a big-brotherly way, said, "My boy, you are by blood, by appearance, by education and by tastes, a white man. Now why do you want to throw your life away amidst the poverty and ignorance, in the hopeless struggle of the black people of the United States? Then look at the terrible handicap you are placing on yourself by going home and working as a Negro composer; you can never be able to get the hearing for your work which it might deserve. I doubt that even a white musician of recognized ability could succeed there by working on the theory that American music should be based on Negro themes. Music is a universal art; anybody's music belongs to everybody; you can't limit it to race or country. Now, if you want to become a composer, why not stay right here in Europe? I will put you under the best teachers on the continent. Then if you want to write music on Negro themes, why, go ahead and do it."

We talked for some time on music and the race question. On the latter subject I had never before heard him express any opinion. Between him and me no suggestion of racial differences had ever come up. I found that he was a man entirely free from prejudice, but he recognized that prejudice was a big stubborn entity which had to be taken into account. He went on to say, "This idea you have of making a Negro out of yourself is nothing more than a sentiment; and you do not realize the fearful import of what you intend to do. What kind of a Negro would you make now, especially in the South? If you had remained there, or perhaps even in your club in New York, you might have succeeded very well; but now you would be miserable. I can imagine no more dissatisfied human being than an educated, cultured and refined colored man in the United States. I have given more study to the race question in the United States than you may suppose, and I sympathize with the Negroes there; but what's the use? I can't right their wrongs, and neither can you; they must do that themselves. They are unfortunate in having wrongs to right, and you would be foolish to unnecessarily take their wrongs on your shoulders. Perhaps some day, through study and observation, you will come to see that evil is a force and, like the physical and chemical forces, we cannot annihilate it; we may only change its form. We light upon one evil and hit it with all the might of our civilization, but only succeed in scattering it into a dozen of other forms. We hit slavery through a great civil war. Did we destroy it? No, we only changed it into hatred between sections of the country: in the South, into political corruption and chicanery, the degradation of the blacks through peonage, unjust laws, unfair and cruel treatment; and the degradation of the whites by their resorting to these practices; the paralyzation of the public conscience, and the ever overhanging dread of what the future may bring. Modern civilization hit ignorance of the masses through the means of popular education. What has it done but turn ignorance into anarchy, socialism, strikes, hatred between poor and rich, and universal discontent. In like manner, modern philanthropy hit at suffering and disease through asylums and hospitals; it prolongs the sufferers' lives, it is true; but is, at the same time, sending down strains of insanity and weakness into future generations. My philosophy of life is this: make yourself as happy as possible, and try to make those happy whose lives come into touch with yours; but to attempt to right the wrongs and ease the sufferings of the world in general, is a waste of effort. You had just as well try to bale the Atlantic by pouring the water into the Pacific."

This tremendous flow of serious talk from a man I was accustomed to see either gay or taciturn so surprised and overwhelmed me that I could not frame a reply. He left me thinking over what he had said. Whatever was the soundness of his logic or the moral tone of his philosophy, his argument greatly impressed me. I could see, in spite of the absolute selfishness upon which it was based, that there was reason and common sense in it. I began to analyze my own motives, and found that they, too, were very largely mixed with selfishness. Was it more a desire to help those I considered my people or more a desire to distinguish myself, which was leading me back to the United States? That is a question I have never definitely answered.

For several weeks longer I was in a troubled state of mind. Added to the fact that I was loath to leave my good friend, was the weight of the question he had aroused in my mind, whether I was not making a fatal mistake. I suffered more than one sleepless night during that time. Finally, I settled the question on purely selfish grounds, in accordance with my "millionaire's" philosophy. I argued that music offered me a better future than anything else I had any knowledge of, and, in opposition to my friend's opinion, that I should have greater chances of attracting attention as a colored composer than as a white one. But I must own that I also felt stirred by an unselfish desire to voice all the joys and sorrows, the hopes and ambitions, of the American Negro, in classic musical form.

When my mind was fully made up I told my friend. He asked me when I intended to start. I replied that I would do so at once. He then asked me how much money I had. I told him that I had saved several hundred dollars out of sums he had given me. He gave me a check for $500, told me to write to him care of his Paris bankers if I ever needed his help, wished me good luck, and bade me good-by. All this he did almost coldly; and I often wondered whether he was in a hurry to get rid of what he considered a fool, or whether he was striving to hide deeper feelings of sorrow.

And so I separated from the man who was, all in all, the best friend I ever had, except my mother, the man who exerted the greatest influence ever brought into my life, except that exerted by my mother. My affection for him was so strong, my recollections of him are so distinct; he was such a peculiar and striking character, that I could easily fill several chapters with reminiscences of him; but for fear of tiring the reader I shall go on with my narration.

I decided to go to Liverpool and take ship for Boston. I still had an uneasy feeling about returning to New York; and in a few days I found myself aboard ship headed for home. [...]

*The melodrama in many of Edward Prime-Stevenson's tales may seem over-wrought to modern readers but they are typical of their time (Louisa May Alcott, for example, also wrote various lurid potboilers). At the turn of the century, grand gestures and outsized emotions were standard in plays and operas. Recall that Prime-Stevenson was a music critic and it is no surprise that the plot of this story would make a good libretto. Magnus Hirschfeld's* Jahrbuch für sexuelle Zwis-chenstufen[59] *called this story "A deep Uranian tale of the passionate affection between two musicians, both Urnings, under the spell of which the younger man willingly sacrifices his own reputation for the other, as well as forgiving a terrible infidelity."* [60]

## *"AQUAE MULTAE NON—"* (1913)

### I

"Blessed San Petronio!" exclaimed Father Sebastiano, looking down amiably at the crowd of lively saunterers and merrymakers about the booths in the piazza. "Blessed San Petronio! But it is good surely to see folks enjoy them-selves in a worldly way—when they can honor religion by it!"

It was the day of the very-elect saint named by Father Sebastiano.[61] It was occurring in Bologna in 1682. The world had not mixed piety and pleasure, aristocratic or vulgar, quite as far as somehow we find the process perfected in our time. But it had made very comfortable advances. Leaning both elbows upon the window-sill, the monastery's organist surveyed and approved. The sun was flaring down the west. The last of the daylight's distractions were at their height. The final frolicking, promenading and visiting would be forth-coming, after evening should really begin. Garlands and streamers flaunted in the ruddy glow. Thousands of small lights would be set atwinkling, along with the bonfires presently. Blessed Saint Petronio, indeed!

"Yes, it is an excellent thing that saints and saints-days were invented, I think," continued Father Sebastiano to himself, a little slyly. "If I were the Holy Father, I think I would squeeze even a few more into the calendar—if one could. A handsome collection this morning! It will more than settle those refectory-accounts that the visit of his Eminence made so large. There! That reminds me: I wonder whether Madriale has copied all the mass Monsignore was so obliging as to lend to my library? Aha! I wager that Madriale is the only person in this city who is busy at work on this holiday! By San Petronio! Does not life seem long enough to that young man? He never gives himself one afternoon's rest from our eternal music!"

Apparently life did not indeed seem so long to the subject of Father Sebastiano's query. Up on the fourth floor of a huge dwelling, just around the corner of the monastery, at that moment was seated before a harpsichord "that young man" in question: Felice Madriale. Insofar as writing music was work to him, Felice really had been working all that holiday long, contentedly and diligently. Indeed he had hardly moved from his chair since morning. What little transcribing he had left to do—he was copying, though not copying the mass that Monsignore had lent to Father Sebastiano—he wished quite done before that day's light failed. Felice did not lift his head from his pages. The notes were jotted down swiftly, precisely, according to a rough draft before him. The pages glided from the hand to the floor, with wonderful speed. Felice's blue eyes were full of a strange light. Now and then his parted lips hummed a phrase. Madriale's blond hair (a Saxon trait derived from a Saxon mother) was thrown back in waves almost luminous, from his fair forehead. He might have been studied, in these moments of preoccupation, for a fanciful picture of some young evangelist of music—one whose revelation outsped his eager hand. But it would never have occurred to Madriale to be vain of his beauty any more than to feel vanity in his talents. He would probably have declined posing for a musical celestial, and would have doubted the worth of the materials for even a worldly picture to be composed out of his charming personality—with the dash of sun on the wall beside him, tinting the white sheets of his manuscript, the warm old red-tiled floor, the brass and oak of the carved chest beside him. But such a picture would have sold.

All at once Madriale gave a sigh of relief, drew some double measure with a dash and dropped his pen. He had finished a motet[62]—the longest bit of work from his own head that he had found leisure yet to put on paper.

From without came the distant murmur of the holiday-making city, up, up to the cool, remote room. Madriale laid his head against the tall chair. Little waves of vague melody still surged through his brain.

Young Madriale was not of Bologna. An orphan, educated in music through the charity of a relative now dead, he had turned his back on the South to earn his living elsewhere. Arrived, in Bologna, chiefly after tedious wanderings, Father Sebastiano had found work to keep Felice busy ever since Easter. In the same tall house he had come into on arriving, he had abided, in much satisfaction. It was a singularly quiet existence. Felice delighted in it. He had his work, his thoughts, his art, his acquaintanceships with the old priests in San Liberato, San Petronio and other convents; and a very few lay-acquaintances. His task was ever a companion. More than these Madriale had with him—by happiest fortune, as he daily thought—the fellow-lodger he would choose out of all the world! That companion was his best and oldest friend—Ilario Pretola. Having occupation and Ilario, really the world could not present much else of great consideration to Madriale! For Felice was one of the men born to passional friendship, as other men are born lovers of other sorts. The type has not ceased to exist with Felice, any more than it began with him. Only the world of men of our epoch affects to have neither time nor heart nor respect nor even sense for it—at least not in frank expression.[63]

The door was flung open. A man strolled from the dark little passage into the golden room, whistling a lively air. The reposeful genre-picture was disturbed.

"Upon my word! Still hard at it!" was Ilario Pretola's reproving greeting. The speaker's voice was singularly beautiful; but it often reproved and mocked many beautiful things. Somehow, Felice never particularly remarked that fact. "The idea of a well young man sitting and scratching, scratching, this whole livelong holiday! *Che diamine!* [64] It is a sin, the sin irreligion, my dear boy! You will work yourself into the gate of paradise—or the other place—before they want you there, unless you learn to be lazy. Work! Oh, I fear, I detest work!"

"But I have done no copying today," replied Madriale, amiably.

"In the name of all the blessed, what then has so absorbed you?" demanded Ilario laughing. "I try to stir you up after breakfast. But no, you will have no procession! Pretty girls may go to the devil, for all you care! I come after you at noon, and it is—'My dear Ilario, amuse yourself as you will, but do leave me in peace!' So I leave you in peace. Now I return, and there you sit, with the ink scarcely dry upon your pen, I see. And you are not starving! Come now! For what are you killing yourself, and driving me out of doors, to be gay alone by myself?"

Ilario looked down into Felice's face with a serio-comic frown. Himself had watched processions, had chaffed many fair damsels of Bologna, had eaten and drunk and danced to his heart's content. It was now time for some dullness and irritation. He sat down on the stone window-ledge, waiting his friend's reply.

"It means that I have been keeping a very little secret from you," responded Madriale smiling.

"Which you do not intend to keep any longer," Pretola interrupted. "You choose wisely, my little one! Therefore acquaint me with the weighty secret, as soon as possible."

Felice was two-and-twenty. Ilario was nearly thirty. But Felice had always been "my little one" to the other.

"First of all then, in leisure moments that work has vouchsafed me, I have composed—this." He lifted the manuscript and laid it on the harpsichord.

"What is it?"

"A motet. Completed, every measure of it."

"A motet? So you have been really making music, not copying it only?" replied Ilario. "And you do not think you have wasted your time into the bargain! Let us hope not! That is your motet, is it? For how many voices?"

"That is it. I have finished the copy just this instant. You or I will have small chance of hearing it very speedily; so pray cast an eye over it. It is in rather more the new style—many of our worthy patrons here in Bologna will have no good opinion of such writing, you may be sure. They will think it quite too free."

With a fine air of kindly superiority and interest, Ilario came to the harpsichord. Madriale watched his coming with a mounting color and brightening eye. When Ilario stood beside him, turning over the neat pages with more attentive consideration than his ironical words had betokened, Felice drew his friend's hand in his own and held it. It was easy to see how extremely fond he was of Pretola—easy to guess that whatever that dark-eyed, bronze-skinned Ilario did seemed good in Madriale's eyes; and Ilario beautiful in the doing thereof. Since they had come together as school-lads it had been so. It would always be so, one would say. In this friendship, Ilario ruled. For Felice was among those whose natures are fed with a deeper joy in the regard they feel than that by which they excite.

"Notes enough, my most talented Felice—O Felice sempre felicissimo!"[65] observed Ilario, drawing away his hand in turning over the sheets. "But are your notes music? Not always. Let us look further into your inspiration, my dear Felice."

Therewith Ilario sat down. His attention became more and more uninterruptedly fixed. His bowed head, as he turned the leaves toward the paling light, concealed the keen absorption possessing him. Felice walked around and about him or looked out of the window. Almost in silence, Pretola read on and on. But he read with an expression gathering in his fine features which a kindly physiognomist would not have liked.[66] For it was—jealousy!

Jealous of Madriale? He had not been anything less than that for a long time now. For months there had not been a day, perhaps, when Ilario had not felt a pang of it. Even a good friend may be jealous—though a great soul and a great love will cast jealousy out. Ilario was not really a bad fellow, and he was fond of Felice. But he had not banished that serpent! How often it had bitten at his heart when musicians had said that he, Ilario Pretola, was not without ability as a composer; but that the blond lad, so much with him, seemed to be a sort of genius, especially in "this quite new style" of writing for the church. More than once, in class and in contest, some indiscreet teacher or *dilettante*[67] had poisoned Ilario's mind for hours and days, with comparisons. "Pretola," said old Nardi, after some months with them both, of hard work, "Pretola, my lad, you soon will possess all counterpoint at your finger-ends—but your friend upstairs ought to lend you some of his ideas. You have too few; he has almost too many." One night, the great Alessandro Scarlatti,[68] on his way back to Naples, had happened to listen to a noble Benedictus[69] by Felice, at a *serenata musicale*,[70] given by a Bolognese gentleman. "You are a wonderful young man," said Scarlatti cordially to Felice, pressing his hand heartily, "I shall keep my ears open to *your* doings henceforth! I do not altogether like some of your ideas—they are in a style new to me—somewhat. But you seem to have genius, young sir! I, Alessandro Scarlatti, *I* tell you so!"

Ilario Pretola standing over in a dark corner of the great room, watching, listening enviously, suddenly had drawn back deeper behind a pillar, finding his teeth set and his eyes glittering and his breast hot, at the glorious Neapolitan's words. "Genius? Felice? Always his 'genius'! So he has in him then what I have not!" That thought was growing like the turn of a knife in a stab!

This evening, with a vigilant mind set upon those pages, Ilario surely needed more affection and self-control than ever. For he saw there, really and with his own eyes, just that wonderful, priceless, curious something that he had not—genius; expressed in a measure so astonishing and so prodigal that Ilario was almost confounded. "This is not merely a motet! It is a miracle!" he exclaimed under his breath. "It surpasses Palestrina!" "*Aquae multae non potuerunt extinguere charitatem, nec fluminae obruunt illam*" ("Many waters shall not quench love, neither can the floods drown it") ran the text. Madriale had given those stiff old Vulgate verses a setting that made them sound more of heaven than earth! They were married to a series of limpid and ineffable harmonies, each so delicately exquisite as foil and partner to its fellow—each succession of crescendi and decrescendi,[71] with voice melting into voice through such surpassing taste, ingenuity and loveliness, that when we study such matters in our epoch we feel that their secret died with their day, died with the like of Felice Madriale. As Ilario studied that score, a fabric of such perfectly blended beauty, originality and strength, as he heard it singing itself in his brain, Pretola could well exclaim to himself that there had been nothing quite like it in Italy yet! Only a man sure to rise could have written it. Indeed, with it written, he *must* rise!

"Ebbene, caro mio Ilario?"[72] asked Felice. He had not been watching Ilario. The sunset, now deepening in final colors, had held his attention. Could angelic choirs express in long chromic accords those mystic expanses of orange, carmines and purple-browns? "What do you think of it?"

"I think that you have spent a hard holiday," Ilario replied sweetly, with outward vivacity and inward bitterness of spirit! "A hard holiday, my Felice!—to make many a fair breve[73] and semibreve. The diligent shall prosper, that we know! And your music is very pretty, very pretty. I would I could write such! What will you do with it?"

Felice laughed. He took for twice or thrice its value his friend's doubtful praise. Ilario was pleased with his music; that was enough for Madriale.

"Oh, I shall let it lie in my desk until I can have charge of a good choir to sing it," he replied. "There is no chance of listening to it in Bologna—at present. My new style, as some of you call it, frightens even Father Sebastiano."

"I believe it," returned Pretola, as he handed back the manuscript. Felice laid it away. What Ilario heard, as Felice dropped it into the chest, was a voice from somewhere—not from Heaven, for it was the voice of a devil. The voice said "The man who shall give that piece of music-writing to the world as his, he need not think of a long struggle to make himself famous! All the music-world will soon be at his feet."

*That* was what Felice was shutting up in his old chest? That! Ilario started up. He began walking up and down the room.

He slipped his hand into his pocket. It rustled a letter, lying there since yesterday. The writer was his uncle, a cardinal, no less indeed than the great Cardinal Marucci, of Rome. He was educating Ilario. He wrote: "If you can come here at once, nephew, and with a few ideas in your scores better than what I have heard of yours, come. The musical directorship of the Sistina will be vacant soon. I will undertake to install you. But remember—you must make some impression here. Get to work at once."

A cold tremor, then a heat, pervaded Pretola's body. He thought of his uncle (some vouched for a nearer relationship) the potent, art-loving Cardinal. He saw in his mind a crowded chapel—the Holy Father, ever a connaisseur—the appreciative, subservient papal court—the music-loving capital. He thought of Madriale's objectless, time-wasting talent as to that motet! Oh, irony of circumstances! Oh, unkind accord between opportunity and inability!

Most of this time Felice's eyes were fixed on his friend. How beautiful was Ilario when he was held by a deep thought! How fine his features, how lofty his carriage, what a noble air! A man was blessed to possess his friendship; especially as he, Felice Madriale, was yet only a poor copyist but Pretola a learned music-student, noted in Bologna—with money and grand connections.

"Come my Ilario," he said cheerfully, "do not stalk about so! Cease your meditations on the faults in my motet. I will have my walk with you, instead of in the procession, or with a rattle-tongued lass." He rubbed his blue eyes and stretched himself heartily. He put his arm into Pretola's. "Let us be off whither you will!" he said coaxingly.

Ilario drew himself away. "No my dear boy! I have supped—and I have a headache. Besides, I promised to meet the Signor Conte, my patron, for awhile this evening. I forgot it. You must walk without me, for once. I will come in by and by, to drink a glass with you."

Thereupon Ilario slipped out of the room quickly.

So Madriale spent most of that evening at his writing-table; poring over the scores he was proud to possess, pottering among his papers, scrutinizing again the harmonies in the motet. Once, lifting up his voice, he sang softly the highest voice in a madrigal, through. What a tenor it was!—so resonant and pure, and so naturally controlled by the singer! The convent clock struck nine. Just then, Ilario came in again.

Ilario had gone out not a little saturnine. He came back with nerves at a different tension. He had met, as agreed, the Signor Conte R., and had learned something curiously opportune. The Conte R. had suddenly decided to send his secretary, and a confidential servant of his household, from Bologna, at early daylight, on state business, to Rome. But there chanced to be a little matter, not politics at all, that Signor Conte did not care to put into the hands of his secretary, nor of any member of the family, though he was very anxious to have the affair at once attended to, in Rome by some capable emissary. The Conte R. had put the topic before Ilario Pretola. "Would Sign-or Pretola care to undertake the errand, leaving Bologna that evening with the secretary, but on a pretext?" And so on. Ilario, after the interview with the Signor Conte, had taken a lonely walk, quite by himself, busied with certain exciting—and evil—considerations.

"Come, my San Giovanni!" he cried now, as he shut the door behind him, "I have returned as I promised. No more singing nor music-thinking! The holiday is not yet over."

The two friends sat down. Ilario produced a dusty bottle, holding it high over his head.

"In all your life you have tasted nothing better than that!" he declared. "It is from the cellar of my patron."

And so it was. But the physician of the diplomatist had procured it for Ilario, and it had not come from the physician's hands quite as it had come from Count R.'s bin. Felice drank. Ilario seemed in great spirits. He talked incessantly and animatedly. He told Felice a score of stories of the day's scenes. He sang bits of sparkling ditties. He mimicked incomparably a quar-rel he had seen between two tipsy monks.

"Ilario, Ilario, how droll you are!" laughed Felice, "I wonder that you do not find me dull! You who have such spirits!" But presently Felice felt himself growing sleepy. Ilario's voice began to reach his ears from a point yards away—as if across the room. Ilario's brilliant dark eyes, Ilario's carmine lips, smilingly showing the white teeth behind, began blending, in a curious, kalei-doscope effect beyond the table. Soon Felice did not answer. Ilario's ques-tions, Ilario's voice became a mere murmur that soothed, wordlessly.

Felice's head fell gently forward. Pretola rose and guided his victim, half-carrying Felice to a couch, a few paces behind. Madriale fell back upon it, now sleeping unwakeably. The physician's Arabian powder had done its work admirably. For a moment Pretola feared an overdoing. He listened. No, Felice slept calmly, his young heart beat with regularity and firmness.

Ilario loosened Madriale's clothing, partially undressing him, that his repose should be easier. The breathing of the young composer was the only sound in the room as Ilario opened the chest. He withdrew the manuscript of the motet, along with a dozen other scores, some complete, some incom-plete. He must take everything, or better to take nothing!

Holding the manuscripts in his hands, Ilario paused, breathless now, in the center of the long dim room. He looked over at Felice, stretched unmoving on the low couch. Only Felice's hand—the fine, long-fingered hand that had penned the motet—extended along the couch into the candle-shine, a hand white and tranquil as marble. The rest of Felice's slender young figure lay in deep shadow.

Somehow Ilario could not look away from the sleeper at once. Farewell, Felice! Alas! That was the end of the friendship, of course. Well, they had been coming to it for some time. It was a pity, surely! Ilario lamented the situation, yes! But what was a friendship when one's whole earthly future was at stake? Farewell, Felice! He was certainly fond of him, was Ilario. A good, amiable fellow Felice always had been—gentle, romantic, affectionate … well, one could say he was almost over-warm toward his friends, rather too demonstratively sentimental. It was a pity, this coming to a fork in the road of intimacy. An unpleasing choice to make! But it was a moment in which he, Ilario Pretola, must look to his practical interests bravely. So farewell, Felice! He would half-forgive Ilario, in time; perhaps half-forget him. For this subtraction, a forced loan of a professional kind, why, it meant little in such a career as lay ahead of Madriale.

Pretola left the room. He went to his own chamber not far off, in another street. He packed his effects quickly. The owner of the rooms made no difficulty of the sudden departure—whither Ilario did not say. Before midnight came a servant of the Conte R. He conveyed away some boxes quickly. Ilario followed, to the Palazzo R.

By the time the sun was rising, Ilario and the secretary of his wealthy patron were traveling southward, with much expedition.

Meantime, Felice slept on, dreamlessly, in the tall house in Bologna.

## II

Some twenty hours later, Felice sighed, stirred, opened his eyes, was awake at last. There was still golden sunset in the room. Felice rubbed his eyelids. What did that mean? Was it dawn? Impossible from that quarter! Had he dreamed of the supper in Ilario's company? And of growing drowsy before the supper ended? How clouded was his head! Yet he had drunk no great quantity of that strange fine wine.

"It is impossible that I have slept a whole night and nearly all of a day, too!" he exclaimed, starting up. "Those few glasses! … When and how could Ilario have left me? Ah, I see, I have been ill! Giddiness, faintness must have seized me. But the like of it I have never known before! I dare swear kind Ilario has been tending me all day. God be praised for my recovery!"

He blessed himself, and after waiting for Ilario's appearance some moments, he dressed, and went to seek his friend. His head still was disturbed, his footing was unsteady.

The wife of his host met him in the hallway. "I am glad to see you better," she said. "I have taken care that you were not disturbed."

"Better. Who told you that I was ill? I have not been really ill."

"Signor Pretola said that you had a bad headache. You were to be let alone—I have kept two or three visitors away. He was sorry to leave you so. You have slept all day."

"All day? I don't understand."

Felice stood there, bewildered, incredulous.

But in the next hour, he was an hundred-fold more troubled. Everything spoke of Ilario's departure to somewhere—for good. There was no letter, no clue. Hurt and alarmed, Felice speculated, wondering if it were a joke. No, no: Ilario seldom joked. Joke or anything else, alas! Felice must wait to have the mystery unraveled by Ilario. He went shyly to the Palazzo R. "The Signor Conte is traveling."—"Where? To return when? And Signor Pretola?"—"We know nothing." Felice set himself to copying. Then came discovery of the abstraction of his manuscript compositions and sketches, including that newest and choicest darling, the motet "*Aquae multae non.*" He had not many places to search, but he ransacked, in greater astonishment than ever. "Ah," he exclaimed, sinking down by the table, "—what a night, what a day! Ilario has been summoned, I know not where. While I slept, some robber has come hither and taken all my papers, Ilario's letter with them! Yes, it is the work of a robber, seeking I know not what from poor me! Oh, most unlucky, perplexed Felice! Behold enough of one day's mysteries for me!"

There was a knock at his door. "What cheer with my golden-penned son of art today?" asked the round, comfortable voice of Father Sebastiano. "You are better?" But Sebastiano checked his greeting. "The saints keep us!" he ejaculated. "What has happened to you? Your dragon of a porteress said you must not be disturbed. But really, my lad! You are haggard and disheveled as some of our great folk, after a ball. Are you feverish?"

Father Sebastiano hearkened in silence to Madriale's answer. For some time, the priest had shrewdly suspected that there existed evil traits in Pretola, quite invisible to Felice. The priest felt a certain conceit now as to his vague diagnosis. Felice made an end. He looked at Padre Sebastiano with wild eyes.

"It is an enigma!" Felice exclaimed despairingly. "What can have happened to Ilario?"

"Nothing has happened to Pretola. There is no enigma. Look here, my little innocent! Your fine friend and your fine music have left you *together*. Do you not see?"

"Together? No, I do not understand."

Father Sebastiano went on, without picking nice phrases. "He is a false hound—a vile thief! I have doubted his affection for you—often, my Felice! He has been horribly jealous of you, devilishly jealous, for heaven knows how much time! I suspect that just yesterday he had a chance to leave Bologna for—who knows where? So he stole your music, all your compositions!—

taking precious good care not to forget that glorious *"Aquae multae non"* that I was looking at with you, on Sunday! Yes, my boy, he has stolen it, that he may produce it—and anything else he has filched of yours!—somewhere and sometime, as of his own composing! My dear Felice, your Ilario Pretola is simply the greatest knave in Italy!"

Most unhappy Felice! A long time it was before the truth really took hold upon his soul. When it did, he was stunned. Stunned he remained; no longer arguing with angry Father Sebastiano. Every defense was overthrown under the reasoning of the priest, a worldly-wise as well as heavenly-wise man.

Father Sebastiano got up, to amble back to his convent. "The blessed saints keep you, my son! Almost I am ashamed of my dear San Petronio; he has neglected you badly. You have had a very cruel opening of those child-eyes of yours. Remember that nobody should trust most where he loves most. If that fellow Pretola had been a woman, you couldn't have adored him more! Well, I'll see you tomorrow. Meantime, not a word to anyone—eh?—of this business. It will be better not. Not a word! I know why. Wait. You shall see!"

Father Sebastiano gone, Felice threw himself down upon the couch—that accomplice-couch! which knew so much—all! So violent a passion! It could have wrung one's heart to behold a young spirit suffering so miserably. Anger and disillusionment for himself, and storm of grief and shame for the friend he had believed he knew so clearly! It desolated in a whirlwind the garden of his young soul. Every leaf and flower seemed stripped away. Therewith mounted, too, the virility of the young man's nature in indignation against so contemptible a wrong-doer and wrong-doing; against that calculated theft of his music; above all against the kidnapping of what he might call his fairest child of genius—the motet *"Aquae multae non."* And Ilario had chosen the very hour of its completion for his rascality! On it Ilario might even be planning to build his artistic fortunes! If so, *"Aquae multae non"* would grow old under a false parentage, during how long a time! Or forever so! O, base subterfuge!

But still, under all the sense of wrong, was this deepest, cruelest, most bewildering realization—that he had loved a shadow! For this having happened today, when had there ever been any Ilario? In that hour had the devil made Felice the companion of a changeling? No! There had never been any Ilario friend, loved far more than wife or mistress, dwelt-with and clasped daily to his heart of heart had been only a demon, a mere creation of affection and credulity! Alone in the world Felice felt himself now; long having been alone, yet not knowing his desolate plight till now. Ah, Ilario seemed to vanish farther from actuality—recognition—each instant! Ilario was a shade, a myth, an error of heart, dissolving into chaos and murk, with an ironical, flashing smile on its lips, in perpetual farewell and disillusionment.

"But it shall not be perpetual!" cried Felice upspringing and darting forth his arm. "For, *this* man I have never known! *This* Ilario I have a right to follow, to denounce—to hate! I will pursue him to my last hour and to the world's end. He shall surrender his theft amid the hissing Italy! O, thou vile, false counterfeit of my friend Ilario! My vengeance shall entrap you! The man that I loved is dead and buried. He lived—perhaps—sometime. But now he is dead. So then thou who art but devil in his likeness, woe to thee!"

Next morning Felice Madriale looked like a different young man. In one night, his face had taken on a stern look, foreign to it two or three days earlier—the look of a man brooding a bitter purpose. He spent some days still, trying to discover whither Pretola had gone. All copying lay neglected. The lonely room was deserted. His search was useless. Most successfully had Count R. and Ilario covered distances and traces.

Toward the third afternoon's end Father Sebastiano sent for Felice. "You have discovered nothing? Of course not! You say he missed taking the first draft of that motet, after all? The rough draft that I saw a week ago—luckily— as did also Brother Paolo. Excellent oversight! You must manage to overtake him!—to confound the fellow. *That* you owe to your own future, and to your art, my son! Perhaps I can help you. Listen. Our Superior dispatches me at once on some commissions, to certain southern houses of our order—to quite a dozen different cities, I believe. Now, I have asked leave to take a young layman, as my companion and secretary. Will you go with me? That first step is better than any other."

Felice bowed his head quickly. "I will go. Surely!"

Felice packed, stored, locked. The pair quitted Bologna in four-and-twenty hours. Neither Madriale nor the priest talked much. Father Sebastiano was already troubled at the alteration in the young man's aspect and demeanor. Felice journeyed on, hour by hour, frowning, absorbed in his own reflections.

"He is no longer the same boy," the priest said to himself. "The honey in him is turned to gall! All he thinks of now is finding Pretola, reclaiming those manuscripts! Above all that divine '*Aquae multae non*'! I don't blame him." But Father Sebastiano was wrong.

For, it was not of the robbery Felice thought, league by league and day by day, so much as of the robber! His anger was deepened. Pipe, song or organ-tone fell on ears suddenly deaf. He shunned the sound of music. And if Father Sebastiano had guessed just what vengeance for a lost friend Felice so brooded, he would have been more frightened than he was now, in speculating the outcome of that expedition after some lost music.

Faenza—Firenze—Lucca—Siena—the needs of Father Sebastiano's commission carried them through the pleasant country, from one town to another. They made cunning inquiries as to musical doings and musical patrons, ecclesiastical or lay, wheresoever they went. They learned what they could of any recently-arrived strangers, who followed the art. The priest assisted Felice with all the resources of a discreet and respected ecclesiastic. But they could not trace the recreant Ilario anywhere.

Madriale's search might well be indeed a wearisome matter. The little embassy of Count R. was only one small group among many quitting Bologna on the morning of Ilario's flight. Count R. had taken a specially vague route for Rome. Each halt was invariably at some rural estate of the Count, or of a relative. Hence while Father Sebastiano and Felice were in Siena, Pretola had entered the Eternal City, had discharged satisfactorily Count R.'s secret commission, had enjoyed a most satisfactory audience with Cardinal Marucci; and already was receiving high encouragement for obtaining a post in intrigue among a dozen competitors.

"Have you any news?" asked Felice of the priest one night, at cliff-bound Orvieto, where they were to remain some days. Father Sebastiano had been visiting the bishop.

"None. In God's time, my son! Patience!"

Father Sebastiano by this time heartily repented, more than now, that he had brought Madriale along with him at all. The only consequence the old priest had had in mind was a just exposure—restitution. Alas, he was realizing daily that not merely such punishment did this silent, brooding, transformed Felice Madriale meditate. The countenance of Felice had grown like a marble mask of Vengeance. Father Sebastiano shrank from encountering those eyes. Felice never named Pretola. Sometimes, as a thought crossed the young man's face, it assumed a terribly suggestive expression.

Father Sebastiano was glad when they reached Viterbo; a commission of length was to be fulfilled there. "If Pretola has gone very far southward, then I will no longer help Felice to dog him thus—to his hiding-place," said Padre Sebastiano to himself. "I do not care to have any more of a hand in their meeting than I have had so far! No, not even if it were for fifty motets, all fit for the ears of the Madonna! No, no! Felice must go on his way alone, if I cannot persuade him to return presently to Bologna with me; or to take some post or other down in these parts. He can write better music than those stolen matters. He can afford to forgive that rogue. I must try to manage him."

But lo, at Viterbo came a letter! Father Sebastiano must needs go on—to Rome! In secret dismay, Father Sebastiano told Felice.

"I decided, long ago, not to return northward until I had been to Rome," the young man answered. "We do not part, Father. Rome is a likely place to find sinners as well as saints." And Felice smiled—hatefully.

That night, once more said the priest to himself, in fear, "Yes, yes, I did wrong in bringing him! I see it now. Murder is in that young man's heart! If they meet, two souls may be lost! He thinks now only of revenge upon an Ilario who has taken the place of one he loved and believed in. He will kill Pretola."

Not many days later they reached Rome. Father Sebastiano, at his first interview with his host, a canon of note, heard a carelessly-given bit of news that sent swift blood through his timorous heart. He avoided Felice that night, much perplexed.

But Felice met him, laughing softly and wildly. He looked up at the priest: "He is here! At Cardinal Marucci's. I have found him!" he exclaimed.

The nervous father looked out of the window. "You have not … met?" he faltered. "Be calm, Felice! For I see death in your eyes! Remember, he was your friend …"

"We have not met. But we shall meet, very soon. He has been named for a great musical post here. I thought that the Cardinal had bidden him go about his business; there was no love between them last year, no! And listen—he has been chosen because of a wonderful piece of music, one most particular piece! It won in the competition. It is a motet, '*Aquae multae non potuerunt.*' Think of that! My motet! The Holy Father and all the city have been mad over it! Mad! It is so new—in so beautiful a style, they say."

Felice clenched his hands and stared at Father Sebastiano, yet as if he did not see him with those wide-opened eyes.

"But I have him! Tonight there is a concert in the Holy Father's presence. *His* motet, as they call it, will be sung! Am I not lucky? I have invitations for you and myself."

Father Sebastiano looked piteously at him. "Felice—" he began. The young man did not hear. "Felice," he repeated, rising and laying his unsteady hand on the other's shoulder, "we will not go there, my son. You must not. You know why not."

Felice shook off the hand. "What else is my errand here? Oh, do not fear for him! I swear to you that I despise him too utterly now to hurt a hair of his head! But I shall certainly confront him and expose him, even had he a dozen Cardinal Maruccis at his back!"

"It is no time or place for it, Felice! It will be scandalous! Before such company—the Holy Father—"

"It is exactly the best time for it! Father, you promised to support me, you who saw my work often before it was finished. You cannot refuse! You must go with me tonight. You must. How can you shrink from a just man's act because it must have its course among rich churchmen and strangers?—even before the pope—or twenty popes?"

Father Sebastiano flushed. He was silent for a moment. Then: "So be it," he said resolutely. "It is not the stir of exposure that I fear. I will go with you. When you speak, I will say my say, even before the Holy Father. But Felice— one moment! There, give me your dagger, my son. Wear no arms upon you tonight. And promise me to be calm."

"I will be very calm!" said Madriale ironically, "as calm as a living man before a corpse."

### III

Madriale and the priest made their way betimes to the Palazzo B., well-used to such entertainments. Its owner was a famous patron of arts.

Madriale seemed quiet. They had discussed and decided upon a plan of action when the moment should be most auspicious and public.

The hall was very full already. They distinguished Cardinal Marucci and many other eminent dignitaries of the papal court. There would be a great concourse—fashionables of the city included. Father Sebastiano and Felice were seated modestly, by an attentive acquaintance, in a cool and acceptable spot, a loggia opening beside them. A long terrace descended into a corner of the moon-lighted gardens. The priest tried to divert his excitement by overlooking the brilliant scene. Felice kept his eyes on the door by which the guests of honor were entering. A small choir took its place. But no Ilario Pretola appeared. Presently the Holy Father was welcomed. He reached his seat. There seemed to be some delay. No sign of Pretola in audience or among the musicians! Felice's brow contracted in suspense. The first part of the concert began; and proceeded through several numbers. Other matters—also the new motet by Signor Pretola, his famous "*Aquae multae non potuerunt*" were to follow an intermission, so it was stated. "Signor Pretola could not possibly be present till within an hour's time," and the performance of the great novelty was emphatically one of compliment to the composer's visit to Rome.

This explanation was not clear, but it sufficed. The truth was that Pretola was not far off; but he knew how to stimulate interest in himself and in his share of the programme.

Felice slipped out upon the loggia, during the intermission. His head throbbed. His eyes were dazzled, he was hot and cold by turns. There were but a few dozen steps from the loggia to the turf; he descended them. Air, and a moment's stillness!—he must have them! Father Sebastiano, busy conversing, did not notice the escape.

In the garden all was cool and peaceful, save for sounds of the company in the concert-hall. Felice walked on beyond the nearer shrubbery. He passed the marble oval of a fountain, trickling its silvered water over a glittering Leda with her swan.[74] Felice stood still. How tranquil was the night! And he so agitated!

Around the path came a figure. Ilario Pretola appeared, coming hastily toward a private entrance to the concert-saloon. Ilario looked up. He saw Madriale upright beyond the water, and knew him. Felice stepped forward.

In the small open space, graveled and enclosed with shrubs the two faced each other.

"Ah! It is you Felice!" ejaculated Pretola. Ilario did not say it in any tone of terror, but more in startled, friendly salutation. Ilario's self-control was due to an expectation, day and night—eating, walking, talking, thinking all these weeks—of a sudden meeting. "You—in Rome, Felice! Since when, my dear fellow?"

"You know for what I am here!" responded Felice sharply, icily.

"Possibly," Pretola replied, still with outward composure. "But stand back an instant. Be plain, if you will, that I may be sure that I know."

"Either you will enter yonder room with me," Madriale went on, leaning forward and fixing his eyes on the immobile man before, "either you will enter yonder room—at my side confess to your patron and all the company the base thievery that you have committed—declare who is the author of that motet—my own, my darling labor that they will sing presently in *your* honor, or else—"

"Or else, Felice?" repeated Pretola with perfect guard over himself. "Or else? What is the 'else'?"

"Else as living man you shall not pass me."

Pretola smiled calmly. "An instant to consider, Felice," he answered, looking directly into Madriale's face; still not balking at that name of friendship's long usage. Felice had given a nervous twitch of his lips as he caught name and glance. Pretola continued, "The situation is startling, I confess. But I do not argue what has brought it to us, what has made it justice. For it is just!"

There was a step again on the path—this time behind Madriale. Across the fountain stood a third party to the interview—a servant of Prince C., one well-known to Ilario. Ilario took no advantage of the interruption. He called out:

"Davidde, tell my uncle and the Abbate Leo I am coming. I have a moment's important business here—with a friend. An old friend." He uttered that last word firmly. The domestic withdrew quickly.

"Felice," said Pretola slowly, as the steps died away again, "you ask me to choose in a hard matter. Of course, I—I have no defense. None! I took your music. I stole it from you—especially the '*Aquae multae non*' that has won me my new post, won such a night of honor—of shameful, villainous honor—as this was like to be. But," Ilario went on, speaking clearly, slowly, in a voice that in the past had possessed such a caress, such a charm for Felice Madriale's ears, that it had thrilled his inmost heart at Pretola's will, "but I fancied—I fancy still—that I needed it more than you. For, Felice, I could never, never write one such work as your worst! You can write fifty, as good or better than your best of today. It is not in me—alas, never!—to invent as you! I am nothing save an echo of others, an empty vessel, music-machine, not composer!"

Madriale struggled with a spell that had begun to close upon him, stifling consciousness that his hour of fierce and just reckoning was here. O incantation, O sorcery, devil, or what was it!—that lay in those accents of Ilario? That came in each glance from his eyes, even in the pallid moonlight!

But Felice rallied himself fiercely. "No more!" he whispered hoarsely. He caught at the handle of that second knife he had not given to the prudent priest. "I am desperate! I shall kill you! I shall kill you! Devil, I shall kill you, if only because you look like a demon-friend I once was bound to, to whom I gave heart, soul and body, my Ilario Pretola!"

Madriale stepped forward. Ilario did not move. At that instant there rose, from the concert-hall behind them, the sound of voices. The music in which they blended swelled up with an ineffable purity and sweetness. It was the motet! Out upon the calm night, in the solemn gardens, swelled the words, "*Aquae multae non potuerunt—extinguere charitatem—charitatem...—chari-ta-tem.*"[75]

By an error of the chamberlain, or by a misunderstanding of the Abbate Leo, in charge of the entertainment, it had been understood that the composer was already of the august company, but desired to hearken from an inconspicuous place. The little band of choristers lifted up their voices confidently, transportingly—"*Aquae multae non potuerunt non potuerunt extinguere charitatem—charitatem—!*"

Ah, that word! Containing all, excluding all!

Without, in the garden, the composer and his false friend stood silent, by mutual assent, listening, gazing at each other. It was Felice's first hearing of his motet, by any embodied choir. Its effect upon him now was to astonish, to entrance him. Had *he* written that thing? The fiercely human situation of this moment, the bitter, shameful under-story of its presentation here, as the work of another man, all *that* had grown dim, in listening to such beauty, hitherto unrealized. Felice stood like a statue. A great change stole over his face. Months of storm and embittered brooding were effaced, as if by magic. Loud and clear soared the complex, exquisite harmonies. The moonlight cast an unclouded radiance on the face of the Felice Madriale of old; the joyous, serene child of the heavenly art, the lover of one friend. The stars seemed to shine with a strange luster, as if their radiance accompanied some steadfast symphony, evolved in the eternal courses of the spheres!

Pretola also waited. Motionless, he kept his eyes fixed on Felice—his arms folded. In Ilario, too, a kind of psychic revolution was in surge. His selfish madness, his audacity, even his desire for honor among men—they had fled. What was the whole world worth when abstract Beauty spoke? A sense of unworth, of nothingness, of shame deepened!

On and on went the singers, to the close of the work. As they reached it, a low applause swelled into a loud acclaim. And what happened in the garden to those two?

Remember that Felice Madriale was no ideal of resolute and heroic human nature. Few artist-spirits are such. Felice raised his eyes to the night-sky an instant and sighed, as one might sigh awakening from a dream. Once more regarding Pretola before him there, meeting his glance: "Ah, God!" he cried, "ah, good God! It is too much! It is you—you! No shade, no devil!—just you! I can do nothing against *you*! I would not, no, not for my life!—my salvation!

I have loved you always, I must love you till I die, in spite of a million motets—a million cruel wounds." He cast the knife into the fountain. Rushing forward, he threw himself upon Ilario's neck. "Let us forget all, all! Anything, everything, except that we are here, together again! And as for that which tempted you, let it be that not I wrote it nor you, but some angel of Up-yonder! Or if I did commit it to paper, as a thing of so many notes, shall I, who am a part of you, I a part of whose self you are, balk at my best to do you a little honor when I can?"

That was a long embrace in which the two stood there. Ilario was weeping as one from whom indeed an evil spirit had gone out. Neither friend was able to utter another word. None were needed. A new era of their friendship had begun; and it was one destined to perfect in both all that could mean human unity.

Father Sebastiano suffered torments that half-hour. He could hardly contain his uneasiness when Felice failed to return to his seat after the intermission. The evening's errand and plans were brought to naught! And where was Felice? Had he met and throttled Ilario? When however the two young men came into the room, Father Sebastiano could scarcely believe them to be themselves. There was something transfiguring in their faces as they advanced. The priest marveled that others did not remark it. But none seemed to do so save himself. Nor did another soul in the splendid circle that night, that lauded Pretola (Felice Madriale stood by, beaming with pleasure) suspect the authorship of the motet "*Aquae multae non potuerunt*," nor was ever divulged its real origin. You will find the motet printed in the scarce old folio of Ilario Emanuele Pretola's works, published in 1690, at Rome.

Perhaps, after all, Felice spoke truth. Possibly no mortal man may call himself other than a sort of stenographer, a mouth-piece, of any such noble music. Father Sebastiano said as much to himself a few days later, as he was traveling north from Rome, alone, bound for Bologna; leaving the two friends in Rome. There they dwelt happily long years, Madriale soon as a great figure in his art, and Pretola at least a conspicuous one—albeit people sometimes said that "Pretola himself did not compose his best compositions."

"I shall never let out that queer secret of theirs," mused the priest. "And really to love much, and to forgive much—*ebbene*[76]—it makes the world as melodious as when all the morning-stars sang together their motets and madrigals for joy!"

## Notes

1   According to Greek legend, Pythias was condemned to death for plotting against Dionysius I of Syracuse. He was given leave to arrange his affairs after his loyal friend Damon pledged to give his life if Pythias failed to return. When Pythias returned just in time to save his friend, Dionysius was so impressed that he

released them both. Their names became emblematic of true friendship, and by the nineteenth century they often signified even more, to some readers.

2   I.e., canyon.

3   Covered by a dense thicket of shrubs and small trees (Spanish).

4   Something claimed in a formal or legal manner; here, a tract of public land staked out by a miner or homesteader.

5   A decorated platform on which a coffin rests in state during a funeral.

6   Literally, faithful Achates (Latin); in Greek and Roman mythology, the faithful companion of Aeneas in Virgil's *Aeneid*. The term was much in use in the nineteenth century; it was often a coded term for something more than a faithful friend.

7   A vital, idealistic, and attractive character in Ivan Turgenev's novel *Rudin* (1856).

8   Penelope, the faithful wife of Ulysses in *The Odyssey*, announced that she would remarry only after the completion of a funeral robe she was weaving. During the day she worked, but at night she unraveled what she had done. Penelope's web is a proverbial expression for a task that is perpetually worked at but never completed.

9   Outfitted (French).

10   A novel by Honoré de Balzac (1838).

11   French critic (1804–69).

12   Aldrich is making fun of the size of the French-language books and dictionary that Flemming has to hand to amuse himself with. It clearly is more amusing to throw a volume at the butler rather than read it.

13   Fine French wine.

14   Irish (Hibernian) "swarries" (Anglicized form of the French word "soirées," or parties). Flemming means a drunken orgy.

15   I.e., the Pharaoh is wrapped tight in his mummy-cloths. Flemming means that he is wrapped up in his bed-linens while his servant is down cellar drinking.

16   Unknown woman (French).

17   Minor Turkish or north African potentate.

18   In the name of Allah! (Arabic).

19   Nubians are dark-skinned north Africans, here seen as slaves doing the pasha's bidding. The Piscataqua is a river in New Hampshire where Flemming lives.

20   Literally, a rare bird (Latin); i.e., something wonderful.

21   In Greek mythology, a statue of a beautiful woman carved by Pygmalion was brought to life by Aphrodite in answer to the sculptor's prayers.

22   An elegant French champagne.

23   Cigar with both ends cut flat.

24   In ancient Rome, "Lares" and "Penates" were household gods (Latin).

25   Calling cards, occasionally with a photograph of the subject, as here (French).

26   Rough homespun woolen cloth.

27   Any of several Mediterranean plants of the genus *Reseda*, widely cultivated for its terminal, dense, spike-like clusters of very fragrant but inconspicuous greenish flowers.

28  Caliban is the ugly misshapen spirit in Shakespeare's *Tempest*.

29  Rembrandt van Rijn (1606–69), Dutch painter, was a master of light and shade.

30  Quote from Shakespeare's *Romeo and Juliet* (III.i.94) where Mercutio curses the warring Montague–Capulet families, who have caused his death. Here Ned refers to John's probable response to any family dispute that would stand in his way of reaching Marjorie Daw.

31  So seriously (French). Is there an implication here that Flemming was "onto" Delaney all along?

32  *Intersexes*, 383.

33  Walter Learned (1847–1915), minor American poet.

34  Elegant tapestries or draperies used as wall hangings (French).

35  Perennial herb whose fragrant oil, first brought from India by the British East India Company, was used in making perfume.

36  Classic work of British history, published 1848–61.

37  Early photograph made on a silver-coated metallic plate, named for its inventor Louis Daguerre (1787–1851).

38  City in China.

39  J.C. Leyendecker (1874–1951), a successful commercial artist of his day, created the iconic image of the Arrow Collar Man, a figure whose handsome, athletic, self-confident appearance was used to sell detachable shirt collars. The ad campaign worked so well that it continued from 1905 until about 1930. Leyendecker was homosexual and his artwork held popular appeal while providing a special attraction to a homosexual audience.

40  The appearance of an exotic orchid is one of several clues to the sexuality of the host.

41  Languid, drawling (French).

42  Bayreuth in Germany was and still is the home of the Wagner Opera House, famous for its annual presentation of his operas.

43  Within these hallowed halls (German). This is a direct quote from Sarastro's second aria in Mozart's opera *The Magic Flute* (1791), referring to a sacred Brotherhood based on the Masons.

44  Mareptos' interest in dishes, usually seen as a feminine pursuit, labels him sexually "suspicious," though how many readers might see this is debatable.

45  Prime-Stevenson here draws on his own knowledge of doctors who employed hypnotism as one of their tools to "cure" homosexuality. The title character in E.M. Forster's novel *Maurice* (1913–14) undergoes hypnosis at the hands of an American psychiatrist in an attempt to rid himself of homosexual feelings. See also Havelock Ellis, *Sexual Inversion*, 3rd ed., 328ff.

46  Colleagues, members of a fraternity or profession (French).

47  Prime-Stevenson elaborates more fully on the subject of psychiatry and homosexuality in his novel *Imre: A Memorandum* (1906; see my 2003 edition of this text, published by Broadview Press) and his study *The Intersexes* (1908).

48  Opposite, face-to-face (French).

49  A long ecclesiastical vestment worn over the alb or surplice.

50  A toadying courtier in Shakespeare's *Twelfth Night* who is tricked into dressing foolishly, under the mistaken belief it will impress the lady Olivia.

51  The Apollo Belvedere, a famous nude statue from antiquity, and as we have seen in *The Cult of the Purple Rose* (see above, 62–66), one much admired by nineteenth-century homosexuals in particular.

52  Awakening, disillusionment (French).

53  Objects used to ward off evil. Cf. Edith Wharton's poem "Margaret of Cortona" (1901): "...that two-pronged coral/The others covet 'gainst the evil eye."

54  I am indebted to Charles N. Watson, Jr., for suggesting the inclusion of this story. See his Introduction to *The Son of the Wolf: Tales of the Far North* (New York: Oxford UP, 1996), xix–xxi.

55  A Methodist religious society.

56  Of or involving a mixture of two or more languages.

57  A beginner in learning something; an apprentice.

58  The hero of *The Autobiography of an Ex-Colored Man* is the son of a slave mother and a white father. He vacillates between black and white societies until he witnesses the lynching of a black man. In shame, the "ex-colored man" renounces both races, furious that American whites would commit such a crime, but equally angry that blacks could endure such a thing to happen.

59  A German physician and sexologist, Hirschfeld (1868–1935) founded and edited the *Jahrbuch* (*Yearbook of Sexual Intermediaries*) which during its existence (1899–1923) devoted itself to the scientific explication of homosexuality and to the political struggle for homosexual rights.

60  Vol. III (1901), 515–16. The text of this story is taken from Prime-Stevenson's 1913 collection *Her Enemy, Some Friends—and Other Personages*, although according to the book's introduction, it may have been published earlier in a popular magazine.

61  St. Sebastian, a Roman soldier who had been martyred for his faith by being shot with arrows and was usually portrayed as such with naked torso, had, by the end of the nineteenth century, become associated with homosexuality in art and literature, and the name alone often served as a marker for the "knowing reader."

62  A vocal composition in polyphonic style, often based on Biblical texts and intended for use in a church service.

63  The cult of romantic friendship was still very much alive in the nineteenth century, in spite of Prime-Stevenson's comment here; but clearly he refers to that era's condemnation of homosexuality.

64  What the dickens! (Italian).

65  Always most happy (Italian).

66  Physiognomy, the art of judging human character and mental qualities by facial features, was popular in the nineteenth century.

67  Here, a lover of the arts (though often in a superficial way).

68  A highly respected Italian composer of the baroque era (1659–1725).

69  One of the parts of the Roman mass, often set to music.

70  An evening of musical entertainment (Italian).

71  Sections of music gradually growing louder and softer (Italian).

72  Well, my dear Ilario? (Italian).

73  In music, the longest modern note, equivalent to two semibreves or whole notes.

74  According to Greek myth, Leda the Queen of Sparta was seduced by the god Zeus while he was masquerading as a swan, thereby becoming the mother of Helen of Troy and the twins Castor and Pollux.

75  Many waters cannot—quench love—love ... love. (Latin).

76  Well (Italian).

PART TEN

OF HEARTS THROWN OPEN

# Fitz-Greene Halleck (1790–1867)

*Halleck was one of America's early poets. Although today he is not well-known, his writings provide us with early references to same-sex affection. He had written with Rodman Drake (a young writer who died at 25)* The Croaker Papers *(1819), a series of satirical and humorous verses, and this romantic friendship's abrupt end was the genesis of a series of poems mourning Drake's death, an event he never got over.*[1]

## From "The Lamentation of David over Saul and Jonathan"

[Paraphrased from 2 Sam. I.1–19, etc.][2]

[…]
My fainting spirit is opprest!
Corroding anguish fills my breast.
And is my loved companion gone
And left me friendless and alone?
Alas! pale Death has aimed his blow,
And laid the youthful warrior low;
But long within my mind shall dwell
The memory of our last farewell;
And long his name shall be revered,
By former kindnesses endeared.
Yes! gallant youth, my spirits feel
A wound that time can never heal.
A mutual flame our bosoms fired,
A mutual love our breasts inspired,
Our pleasures and our cares the same;
We felt sweet friendship's hallowed flame,
Purer than that which warms our hearts
When pierced by the fatal darts
   That flash from beauty's eye.
Affection twined our souls around,
And virtuous love our union bound
   With every sacred tie.
The warlike weapons are no more,
The din of battle now is o'er;
No longer on our peaceful shore

Its dreadful sound I hear.
How are the mighty fallen low!
Oh raise the bitter plaint of woe,
And bid the tear of anguish flow
    Around the warrior's bier.

## To ****3

The world is bright before thee,
    Its summer flowers are thine,
Its calm blue sky is o'er thee,
    Thy bosom Pleasure's shrine;
And thine the sunbeam given
    To Nature's morning hour,
Pure, warm, as when from heaven
    It burst on Eden's bower.

There is a song of sorrow,
    The death-dirge of the gay,
That tells, ere dawn of morrow,
    These charms may melt away,
That sun's bright beam be shaded,
    That sky be blue no more,
The summer flowers be faded,
    And youth's warm promise o'er.

Believe it not—though lonely
    Thy evening home may be;
Though Beauty's bark can only
    Float on a summer sea;
Though Time thy bloom is stealing,
    There's still beyond his art
The wild-flower wreath of feeling,
    The sunbeam of the heart.

## On the Death of Joseph Rodman Drake, Of New York, Sept., 1820

"The good die first,
And they, whose hearts are dry as summer dust,
Burn to the socket."
    —Wordsworth

Green be the turf above thee,
    Friend of my better days!

None knew thee but to love thee,
  Nor named thee but to praise.

Tears fell, when thou wert dying,
  From eyes unused to weep,
And long where thou art lying,
  Will tears the cold turf steep.

When hearts, whose truth was proven,
  Like thine, are laid in earth,
There should a wreath be woven
  To tell the world their worth;

And I, who woke each morrow
  To clasp thy hand in mine,
Who shared thy joy and sorrow,
  Whose weal and wo were thine;

It should be mine to braid it
  Around thy faded brow,
But I've in vain essayed it,
  And feel I cannot now.

While memory bids me weep thee,
  Nor thoughts nor words are free,
The grief is fixed too deeply
  That mourns a man like thee.

## The Song of the Unmarried
[also called "Song, By Miss ****"
  Air: "To ladies' eyes a round, boy."
    —Moore]

The winds of March are humming
  Their parting song, their parting song,
And summer skies are coming,
  And days grow long, and days grow long.
I watch, but not in gladness,
  Our garden-tree, our garden-tree;
It buds, in sober sadness,
  Too soon for me, too soon for me.
    My second winter's over,
      Alas! and I, alas! and I

Have no accepted lover:
  Don't ask me why, don't ask me why.

'Tis not asleep or idle
  That Love has been, that Love has been,
For many a happy bridal
  The year has seen, the year has seen;
I've done a bridemaid's duty,
  At three or four, at three or four;
My best bouquet had beauty,
  Its donor more, its donor more.
    My second winter's over,
      Alas! and I, alas! and I
    Have no accepted lover:
      Don't ask me why, don't ask me why.

His flowers my bosom shaded
  One sunny day, one sunny day;
The next they fled and faded,
  Beau and bouquet, beau and bouquet.
In vain, at ball and parties,
  I've thrown my net, I've thrown my net;
This waltzing, watching heart is
  Unchosen yet, unchosen yet.
    My second winter's over,
      Alas! and I, alas! and I
    Have no accepted lover:
      Don't ask me why, don't ask me why.

They tell me there's no hurry
  For Hymen's ring, for Hymen's ring;[4]
And I'm too young to marry:
  'Tis no such thing, 'tis no such thing.
The next spring-tides will dash on
  My eighteenth year, my eighteenth year;
It puts me in a passion,
  Oh, dear, oh dear! oh dear, oh dear!
    My second winter's over,
      Alas! and I, alas! and I
    Have no accepted lover:
      Don't ask me why, don't ask me why.

# JAMES WHITCOMB RILEY (1849–1916)

*Riley was known as the very popular "Hoosier Poet" of Indiana, whose use of dialect made him a sentimental favorite of his day. Although we are given to understand that the relationship between the two men in the following poem is father–son, there is something about the "father's" intense fixation on young Jim that makes us wonder whether this a subterfuge to disguise different feelings that otherwise would find no acceptable trope of explanation.*

## "GOOD-BYE, JIM" (1893)

Old man never had much to say—
   'Ceptin' to Jim,—
And Jim was the wildest boy he had
   And the old man jes' wrapped up in him!

Never heerd him speak but once
Er twice in my life,—and first time was
When the army broke out, and Jim he went,
The old man backin' him, fer three months;

And all 'at I heerd the old man say
Was, jes' as we turned to start away,—
   "Well, good-bye, Jim:
   Take keer of yourse'f!"

'Peared-like, he was more satisfied
   Jes' *lookin'* at Jim
And likin' him all to hisse'f-like, see?—
   'Cause he was jes' wrapped up in him!

And over and over I mind the day
The old man come and stood round in the way
While we was drillin', a-watchin' Jim—

And down at the depot a-heerin' him say,
   "Well, good-bye, Jim:
   Take keer of yourse'f!"

Never was nothin' about the *farm*
   Disting'ished Jim;
Neighbors all ust to wonder why
   The old man 'peared wrapped up in him:

But when Cap. Biggler he writ back
'At Jim was the bravest boy we had
In the whole dern rigiment, white er black
And his fightin' good as his farmin' bad—

'At he had led, with a bullet clean
Bored through his thigh, and carried the flag
Through the bloodiest battle you ever seen,—

The old man wound up a letter to him
'At Cap. read to us, 'at said: "Tell Jim
   Good-bye,
   And take keer of hisse'f."

Jim come home jes' long enough
   To take the whim
'At he'd like to go back in the calvery—
   And the old man jes' wrapped up in him!

Jim 'lowed 'at he'd had sich luck afore,
Guessed he'd tackle her three years more.
And the old man give him a colt he'd raised,
And follered him over to Camp Ben Wade,

And laid around fer a week er so,
Watchin' Jim on dress-parade—
Tel finally he rid away,

And last he heerd was the old man say,—
   "Well, good-bye, Jim:
   Take keer of yourse'f!"

Tuk the papers, the old man did,
   A-watchin' fer Jim—
Fully believin' he'd make his mark
   *Some* way—jes' wrapped up in him!—

And many a time the word 'u'd come
'At stirred him up like the tap of a drum—
At Petersburg, fer instance, where
Jim rid right into their cannons there,

And *tuk* 'em, and p'inted 'em t'other way,
And socked it home to the boys in gray,
As they scooted fer timber, and on and on—

Jim a lieutenant and one arm gone,
And the old man's words in his mind all day,—
   "Well, good-bye, Jim:
   Take keer of yourse'f!"

Think of a private, now, perhaps,
   We'll say like Jim,
'At's clumb clean up to the shoulder-straps—
   And the old man jes' wrapped up in him!

Think of him—with the war plum' through,
And the glorious old Red-White-and-Blue
A-laughin' the news down over Jim,
And the old man, bendin' over him—

The surgeon turnin' away with tears
'At hadn't leaked fer years and years,
As the hand of the dyin' boy clung to
His father's, the old voice in his ears,—

"Well, good-bye, Jim:
Take keer of yourse'f!"

# BLISS CARMAN (1861–1929) AND RICHARD HOVEY (1864–1900)

*Bliss Carman, tall and blond, paired well with fellow-poet Richard Hovey, swarthy and muscular, and between them they produced a best-selling little book of poetry that reflected their youth and Wildean ardor—as well as the influence of their Harvard professor George Santayana. The book was so successful that they published several sequels:* More Songs from Vagabondia *(1896) and* Last Songs from Vagabondia *(1900). Though born in New Brunswick, Carman moved to the United States in 1890 where he enjoyed a successful literary career following the publication of his first collection of nature poems,* Low Tide on the Grand Pré *(1893). Hovey, born in Illinois, was a journalist whose promise was cut short by his death at 34. The call to "Bohemia,"[5] to throw off the chains of society's restraints for the open road of freedom, lends an unmistakable appeal to more "alert" readers.*

## FROM *SONGS FROM VAGABONDIA* (1894)

### Vagabondia

Off with the fetters
That chafe and restrain!
Off with the chain!
Here Art and Letters,
Music and wine,
And Myrtle and Wanda,
The winsome witches,
Blithely combine.
Here are true riches,
Here is Golconda,
Here are the Indies,
Here we are free—
Free as the wind is,
Free as the sea,
Free!

### Houp-la!

What have we
To do with the way

270

Of the Pharisee?
We go or we stay
At our own sweet will;
We think as we say,
And we say or keep still
At our own sweet will,
At our own sweet will.

Here we are free
To be good or bad,
Sane or mad,
Merry or grim
As the mood may be,—
Free as the whim
Of a spook on a spree,—
Free to be oddities,
Not mere commodities,
Stupid and salable,
Wholly available,
Ranged upon shelves;
Each with his puny form
In the same uniform,
Cramped and disabled;
We are not labelled,
We are ourselves.

Here is the real,
Here the ideal;
Laughable hardship
Met and forgot,
Glory of bardship—
World's bloom and world's blot;
The shock and the jostle,
The mock and the push,
But hearts like the throstle
A-joy in the bush;
Wits that would merrily
Laugh away wrong,
Throats that would verily
Melt Hell in Song.

What though the dimes be
Elusive as rhymes be,

And Bessie, with finger
Uplifted, is warning
That breakfast next morning
(A subject she's scorning)
Is mighty uncertain!
What care we? Linger
A moment to kiss—
No time's amiss
To a vagabond's ardor—
Then finish the larder
And pull down the curtain.

Unless ere the kiss come,
Black Richard or Bliss come,
Or Tom with a flagon,
Or Karl with a jag on—
Then up and after
The joy of the night
With the hounds of laughter
To follow the flight
Of the fox-foot hours
That double and run
Through brakes and bowers
Of folly and fun.

With the comrade heart
For a moment's play,
And the comrade heart
For a heavier day,
And the comrade heart
Forever and aye.

For the joy of wine
Is not for long;
And the joy of song
Is a dream of shine;
But the comrade heart
Shall outlast art
And a woman's love
The fame thereof.
But wine for a sign
Of the love we bring!
And song for an oath

That Love is king!
And both, and both
For his worshipping!

Then up and away
Till the break of day,
With a heart that's merry
And a Tom-and-Jerry,
And a derry-down-derry—
What's that you say,
You highly respectable
Buyers and sellers?
We should be decenter?
Not as we please inter
Custom, frugality,
Use and morality
In the delectable
Depths of wine-cellars?

Midnights of revel,
And noondays of song!
Is it so wrong?
Go to the Devil!

I tell you that we,
While you are smirking
And lying and shirking
Life's duty of duties,
Honest sincerity,
We are in verity
Free!
Free to rejoice
In blisses and beauties!
Free as the voice
Of the wind as it passes!
Free as the bird
In the weft of the grasses!
Free as the word
Of the sun to the sea—
Free!

## The Buccaneers

Oh, not for us the easy mirth
Of men that never roam!
The crackling of the narrow hearth,
The cabined joys of home!
Keep your tame, regulated glee,
O pale protected State!
Our dwelling-place is on the sea,
Our joy the joy of Fate!

No long caresses give us ease,
No lazy languors warm;
We seize our mates as the sea-gulls seize,
And leave them to the storm.
But in the bridal halls of gloom
The couch is stern and strait;
For us the marriage rite of Doom,
The nuptial joy of Fate.

Wine for the weaklings of the town,
Their lucky toasts to drain!
Our skoal for them whose star goes down,
Our drink the drink of men!
No Bacchic ivy for our brows!
Like Vikings, we await
The grim, ungarlanded carouse
We keep to-night with Fate.

Ho, gamesters of the pampered court!
What stakes are those at strife?
Your thousands are but paltry sport
To them that play for life.
You risk doubloons, and hold your breath,
Win groats, and wax elate;
But we throw loaded dice with Death,
And call the turn on Fate.

The kings of earth are crowned with care,
Their poets wail and sigh;
Our music is to do and dare,
Our empire is to die.

Against the storm we fling our glee
And shout, till Time abate
The exultation of the sea,
The fearful joy of Fate.

*Born into a wealthy family in Massachusetts, Warren became a prominent art collector specializing in Greek antiquities. Today he is remembered for commissioning Rodin's sculpture* The Kiss; *he was unhappy with the finished product, however, and he stored it in his coach house for the rest of his life. Under the pseudonym "Arthur Lyon Raile" he wrote* The Defence of Uranian Love *(1928) as well as many poems dealing with homosexual themes.*

## FROM *ITAMOS* (1903)

### Wandering in a Wilderness

Wandering in a wilderness
Peopled by terrors of excess,
Scared at my sins, and powerless
Better to live, so weak I seem
I scarce have strength enough to dream;
Unless, in some strange frenzy brought
From realms where passion shadows thought,
Such visions dream I as may waft
The devils who inflame the daft.

### Amor Amicitia[6]

I
'Tis over, then, my Paradise!
  'Twas gold to me: to you 'twas dross.
I welcome at whatever price
  Your gain, my loss.

II
If I were used to pray, there should
  Be wrestling for you day and night.
Now I stand guard, to watch your good,
  To keep you right.

III
And, though 'tis hard to fail of love,
  Yet first to your own self be true.

I prize what you can be above
   My love for you.


IV
Thus twice hath friendship barred the way
   To what I hoped for most of all;
But what is love, if it obey
   Not friendship's call?


## Lad's Love

Down to the deep
   Of sorrowing hope from which thy life arose,
Sink back, my soul, in sleep,
   That youthful dreams may echo round its close;

Or deeper still,
   Even to the fountain of thy youthful dream,
Whence the live blood's deaf will
   Gave forth the end, and loosed the fatal stream.

'Twas justice blind.
   We feel in youth what we confirm in age.
The blood informs the mind,
   And claims its due in midmost pupilage.

Jeer at his word,
   The stammering symbol of a faith unknown;
Show where the lad has erred;
   The truth springs upward from his love alone.

Its test the man,
   Who, when his fiat hath broke through the creed,
As his who loveth can,
   Becomes himself the holy book to read.

Though less my pride,
   A little I knew unwitting, and my friends
That little truth denied,
   As love diverted to ignoble ends—

Love precious now,
  The bloom of boyhood and the flush of Spring.
O gentle, flowery bough,
  I hang thee on my lintel wondering.

## The Loss

Ah, could I bind him to my soul,
If I could have his being whole,
  I should not fear; I should not tire
    With pent desire.

Ah, if his arms the welcome gave,
The welcome which I miss, and crave,
  I should not find my suffering less
    Than happiness.

For his the manhood that I chose,
A darkness dearer than the rose,
  And his it is to understand
    The love I planned.

His is the knowledge of desert,
The power to heal, the power to hurt,
  The power to loose, the power to bind
    A kindred mind.

I fly to him, and find him cold,
For "he is young, and I am old";
  I come in love, and meet a rough
    And hard rebuff.

How shall I prise the gates apart,
And, gaining entrance to his heart,
  Cry from the strong-girt citadel
    That all is well!

I wait: 'tis his to draw the bars;
I wait beneath unclouded stars.
  The stars are faithful, and they know
    That I am so.

## Εἰς Ἔρωτα Οὐράνιον[7]

Thou art my lord, and all my life shall lie
A tangle round thy tombstone, if thou die;
Thou art my hope, and, if thou diest not,
Thy life is bedded in a tomb forgot.
I from thy being have sucked in my strength;
Thou from my dying shalt arise at length.
Thou of all lovers art the living head;
I shall be one of many lovers dead.
But the great fire of thine altar flames
Only with kindling-wood of perished names.
The living worshipper atremble harks
To heart-strings breaking in each crack of sparks;
Hears, 'neath the singing of thy servant's choir,
The ancient unison of lost desire.
I among these, and thou among us all,
Each mantle-fold rewoven of a pall:
Though above all, majestical and sane,
A maddened mortal's life in every vein:
Thou beyond life, a life beyond all death,
Each day of thine, a dying lover's breath:
We scattered in the fields where no man stays,
And thou enshrined in all men's works and ways.
Ah, if thou live, what many lives have lost
Their all to nourish thine eternal ghost!
Ah, if thou die, we shall have given our best
To throb in one pulsation of thy breast!
Then from our souls this one petition take:
Have mercy on our brethren for our sake.
Scourge them in justice, lest their love abate;
But grant to them the guerdon[8] of our fate.
Guard them for us, our weanlings, unreproved;
And let them love in peace, because we loved.
Let this our sacrifice be strong to save,
And our right hand be mighty from the grave.


## Ἀφέλεια[9]
To a Greek Athlete

Lead me beyond the earth, and strip me bare
In vacant places of the air;

The coils that cumber, and the belts that bind
Unloosen from the mind;
For ere I pass, my soul would be,
O loved Hellenic athlete, like to thee.

And I am famished for the nobler food;
Unto more hardy brotherhood
I yearn, enriched and laden with the past;
I tire to find at last
The nakedness of nature strong
To do what little is remembered long.
Yet not as one who scorns the burden of state
That early age unto the late
Bequeathed, the trappings of more splendid days
That dazzle and amaze;
Not as the poor and tame new land
That hath no ancientry to understand;

For where o'er all our dying and undone
There riseth still the eastern sun,
And, lightening the eyelids manifold
That open on things of old,
There falleth streaming still the same
Memory, and man is conscious of his fame,

We bear a load of majesty; our feet
Kings in the toiling pathway meet;
And when the royal treasure handed down,
Scepter, and orb, and crown,
Heavily weights each new-born head,
And all are standard-bearers to the dead,

We learn the blessing, and shall ne'er forget
What once we were, and are not yet;
And poverty scales downward from our eyes,
And man is man's disguise,
And, passing by a ruined wall,
The ages challenge us, and warriors call.

Not this, time's legacy, and life's increase,
The common boast, for me shall cease,
But all my own that limes the upward flight,
Possessions hampering might,

The balms of comfort, if I bleed,
And heavenly strength brought down to daily need.

For simpler is the way unto the lord,
Nor lovelier for his wealthier hoard
The man that might have traveled straight and far,
Risen as a sea-washed star,
And taken as of right the place
Magnificence concedes to human grace.

No raiment but obscures the perfect man;
Unhidden forms Olympian;
And still, beyond the pageantry of awe,
There standeth nature's law
Fearless, nor feared by him whose hope
In beauty finds immeasurable scope.

And haply in the end the ages turn
Backward again, and homeward yearn,
And casting all their luxuries aside,
Burden, and pomp, and pride,
Shall liken life once more to thee
Whose only blessedness is victory.

Let be. At least from hence, my soul, unfold
(To light that all on earth behold,
To properties no lordships may confine)
Thyself, undowered and fine.
Clothe thee but in thy naked worth
And pass, a man and blessed, o'er the earth.


## Boyhood and Manhood

*Thy boyhood (far more precious than thou art)*
*Left unto thee one holy charge, his heart.*

Yet had I hoped to unloose
The bands of effort. Boyhood slings awide
His arrows feathered with "whate'er betide";
But manhood, like a noose,
Catches us at the opening of the breath
With "Only this, or only that—and death";—

Catches the man grown faint,
And fain to take indulgence of the boy,
Whose gentle arms were open with more joy
To sinner than to saint;
And unforeknowing set my soul apart
Warden and reliquary of his heart.

He cried for comfort; I,
Bidden and begged to serve him, am I nought?
Was heaven so far from service in his thought?
He cried. But others cry,
Or manlier snap the bond and break away.
Was my whole lifetime forfeit to his day?

Ah, but I cannot doubt.
Idler than idle to dispute the end.
When was I ever faithless to a friend?
Faithful, the game is out.
He did not come to put my soul in pain.
I gave it him. I give it him again.

## If You Were Dead

If you were dead, my life would be more free
Why, then, should you not leave me?[10]
I only know that, if you went from me
'T would grieve me.

For somehow parting is far worse than death,
And in my life I show it,
Who daily give you half of every breath,
And know it.

Perhaps, if you were wedded, I should try
To serve you as a brother;
But you would never be the same, and I
Were other.

Yet were your happiness the marriage vow
I never should deter you;
But, strong to live by dying then as now
Prefer you.

Your death alone, then, leaves me free and fit
For all my labour yonder,
You think. I know it by your forehead knit
To ponder.

O foolish one! for fancy life unrolled
Before me alone and master,
Would other death (nor lover's death) not hold
Me faster?

Other and never better. So I pray
That not to your undoing
I woo you, and forefend a wedding-day
By wooing.

If this is wrong, believe that for the worth
Of love you need not mind me;
For I have won the earth and left the earth
Behind me.

# GEORGE EDWARD WOODBERRY (1855–1930)

*Woodberry was a scholar at Columbia University whose work as a poet was noted by Edward Prime-Stevenson in* The Intersexes *as revealing a homoerotic strain. (Letters possessed by Harvard's Houghton Library reveal that Prime-Stevenson had sought out Woodberry's counsel in the early 1890s, when he was distraught about the break-up of his romantic friendship with Woodberry's student, Harry Harkness Flagler.*[11]*) In particular, Woodberry's lengthy threnody*[12] *"The North Shore Watch" (1883) lamenting the death of a young friend recalls Shelley's "Adonais" (1821) and Tennyson's* In Memoriam *(1850). Though happily married, he was open enough to attract the confidences of such writers as Prime-Stevenson and George Sylvester Viereck,*[13] *and occasionally—in echoes of A.E. Housman—betrays in his poetry feelings that sensitive readers might recognize as homosexual.*

## FROM *SELECTED POEMS* (1913)

### Comrades

Where are the friends that I knew in my Maying,
  In the days of my youth, in the first of my roaming?
We were dear; we were leal;[14] oh, far we went straying;
  Now never a heart to my heart comes homing!—
Where is he now, the dark boy slender
  Who taught me bare-back, stirrup and reins?
I loved him; he loved me; my beautiful, tender
  Tamer of horses on grass-grown plains.

Where is he now whose eyes swam brighter,
  Softer than love, in his turbulent charms;
Who taught me to strike, and to fall, dear fighter,
  And gathered me up in his boyhood arms;
Taught me the rifle, and with me went riding,
  Supplied my limbs to the horseman's war;
Where is he now, for whom my heart's biding,
  Biding, biding—but he rides far?

O love that passes the love of woman!
  Who that hath felt it shall ever forget,
When the breath of life with a throb turns human,

And a lad's heart is to a lad's heart set?
Ever, forever, lover and rover,
  They shall cling, nor each from other shall part
Till the reign of the stars in the heavens be over,
  And life is dust in each faithful heart!

They are dead, the American grasses under;
  There is no one now who presses my side;
By the African chotts[15] I am riding asunder,
  And with great joy ride I the last great ride.
I am fey; I am fain of sudden dying;
  Thousands of miles there is no one near;
And my heart—all the night it is crying, crying
  In the bosoms of dead lads darling-dear.[16]

Hearts of my music—them dark earth covers;
  Comrades to die, and to die for, were they;
In the width of the world there were no such rovers—
  Back to back, breast to breast, it was ours to stay;
And the highest on earth was the vow that we cherished,
  To spur forth from the crowd and come back never more,
And to ride in the track of great souls perished
  Till the nests of the lark shall roof us o'er.

Yet lingers a horseman on Altai highlands,[17]
  Who hath joy of me, riding the Tartar glissade;
And one, far faring o'er orient islands
  Whose blood yet glints with my blade's accolade;
North, west, east, I fling you my last hallooing,
  Last love to the breasts where my own has bled;
Through the reach of the desert my soul leaps pursuing
  My star where it rises a Star of the Dead.

## Flower of Etna

Boy on the almond bough,
  Clinging against the wind,
A-sway from foot to brow,
  With the emerald sea behind;
The illimitable blue,
The lone tree, and you!

Aloft gleams Etna's snow
  In the bright weather;
The green surf boils below,
  Vast crests together;
On the high hillside we
Plunder the blowing tree.

Boy of the mountain-cave
  Beside the flower-hung pool;
What snowy torrents lave
  The bather beautiful!
And the waters drip all over
The sun glistening on their lover.

O blithest in the tavern,
  Dark head above the wine;
Blooms in the dingy cavern
  A creature of the vine;
Vine-bloom upon his glowing cheeks,
And from soft eyes the vine-light speaks.

He sports; what youthful blisses
  Of trifles there befell!
Magic the poet misses
  The Bacchic boy could spell;
He stuck red cherries in his ears—
He smiled—and slew three thousand years.

Once in the lone wood
  Beyond the long red clover—
Sombre, in solitude,
  The gray rock hung far over;
The parting bushes prest
Their young leaves to his breast.

Dear heart! How had he learned
  The world's magnetic soul?
Sudden on me he turned,
  While the rose twilight stole
Over shy features bright,
A face all love and light.

Fond boy, art cannot limn thee,
  Bud of the white dawn's hour;
And language doth but dim thee,
  Youth's violet, Etna's flower;
But I will bear thy face with me
As far as shines eternity.

## The Sicilian

His golden face, *un tipo*,[18]
  Was minted like a coin;
On the reverse *un toro*—[19]
  So stood his neck and loin.
The bull of Agrigentum[20]
  A thousand years had ploughed
The furrow of his fathers—
  Per Baccho![21] He was proud!

To the beautiful old ages
  His line ran straight and true;
His blood coursed like the clover-tops
  Beneath his cheeks' bronze hue;
And all his skin was polished brown,
  And muscled hard with toil;
And when he turned his back, *Ecco!*[22]
  A classic of the soil.

*Part of the Harvard coterie that included his close friends George Cabot Lodge and William Vaughn Moody (see below, 290–93), Joe Stickney (who later adopted the name "Trumbull") impressed his mentor and friend George Santayana. Santayana wrote of him that he was "too literary and ladylike for Harvard."[23] Caught up in all things Greek and Roman (e.g., his doctoral thesis for the Sorbonne on Greek poetry, "Sonnets from Greece" [1903], and "In Ampezzo" [1898]), Stickney produced an impressive body of poetry (1894–1904) before dying of a brain tumor at the age of thirty.*

## Sonnet I

My friend, who in this March unkind, uncouth,
Biding the full-blown Summer and the skies
That change not, stayest unmoved and true and wise
That in thy love thou lovest not me but Truth,
What should we fear that Age corrode with ruth
Our loves, who love the thing that never dies,
Building us archways unto Paradise
Of all that greets the soul's all-flowering youth?
So is it, that often parted, rarely met,
And never blessed with gifts of genial Time
Wherein might grow the seed we have but sown,
Our hearts remember tho' our minds forget
How on from year to year and clime to clime
Stretches the love that makes of all but one.
(1894)

## Lucretius[24]
*Sperata Voluptas Suavis Amicitiae*[25]

Slow Spring that, slipping thro' the silver light,
Like some young wanderer now returnest home
After strange years,
How like to me! to mine thy timorous plight!
Who quietly near my friendship's altar come
Where yet no God appears.

By many a deed I sought to win his love,
Made him a wreath of all my songs and hours,—
Most vain, most fair!
Now fall about the shroud my years have wove;
My evening drops her large, slow purple flowers
Thro' gardens of gold air.

To him this verse, to him this crown of leaves,
My supreme piety shall I commend:
This is my last,
Wreathed of what Youth endows and Age bereaves,
Bound by the fingers of a lover and friend,
Green with the vital past.

We sunder, he my Truth, I the desire.
I spread my wooing fingers, I would earn
His least address.
But parcels of the heaven-dispersèd fire,
Sky-severed exiles, we divinely learn
To suffer loneliness.

My life was little in joy, little in pain;
Mine were the wise denials, with none coped
To win the sky;
And when I surely saw my love was vain—
The joy of his sweet friendship I had hoped—
I stilled. Now let me die,—

Now that the endless wind is growing warm,
Richer the star, and flowers on many a slope
Undo their sheath;
O let us yield to life's divinest charm
That lured us thro' the blasted field of hope,
Let us return to death.
(1895)

## George Cabot Lodge (1873–1909)

*Born into a wealthy and distinguished Boston Brahmin family, "Bay" Lodge was a remarkably handsome and gifted man who attracted the admiration of several writers as diverse as Charles Warren Stoddard and Theodore Roosevelt. He also seems to have been the epicenter of several romantic friendships. His looks, his affability and talent, and his early death kept his poetry and verse-dramas visible through the 1920s. Though perhaps not homosexual himself, he certainly surrounded himself with men who were, and seemed quite comfortable in homosocial groups.*

## From *Poems and Dramas* (1911)

### To W.W.[26]

I toss upon thy grave,
(After Thy life resumed, after the pause, the backward glance
   of Death;
Hence, hence the vistas on, the march continued,
In larger spheres, new lives in paths untrodden,
On! till the circle rounded, ever the journey on!)
Upon Thy grave,—the vital sod how thrilled as from Thy limbs
   and breast transpired,
Rises the springs sweet utterance of flowers,—
I toss this sheaf of song, these scattered leaves of love!
For thee, Thy Soul and Body spent for me,
—And now still living, now in love, transmitting still Thy
   Soul, Thy Flesh to me, to all!—
These variant phrases of the long-immortal chant
I toss upon Thy grave!

### Life, XI: Tuckanuck, 5[27]

We loved too perfectly for praise
   The spread of noon's sun-startled sea,
   We loved the large tranquility
Of flowing distances and days.
In calm, dark sunsets or the blaze
   Of moonlit waves, the ecstasy

And spacious thought of liberty
Thrilled us in deep and silent ways.
We loved too much for song or speech
   The stars' exalted loneliness,
   And in the tacit tenderness
Of hearts thrown open each to each
   We found the perfect peace that brings
   A foretaste of eternal things.

## Life, XIV: Tuckanuck, 8

How often in the tranquil evenings,
   There by the kindled sea's immense unrest,
   Has love, like music in the human breast,
   Thrilled us with incommunicable things!
How often, as we watched the sea-birds' wings
   Flash in the sunset on their homeward quest,
   Have life's large secrets, by the soul confessed,
   Taught us the pride and peace that freedom brings!
How often have we felt the calm of thought
   Quell the storm-shaken waters of the soul,
   Till, land-locked by the cliffs of Time, they caught
The silent gleam of Truth's unchanging stars,
   And felt the universal ocean roll,
   Muffled and vast, on Life's dissolving bars!

## Death, XXVI[28]

It is not that we loved him, as in sooth
   Beyond all words we loved and love him still;
   It is not that he seemed so to fulfil
   Ineffably the very spirit of Truth;
It is not, day by day, in the uncouth
   Brutality of death, his calm control,
   Courage and tenderness of heart and soul;
   It is not pity even of his mere youth;—
God knows these were alone sufficient cause!
   Yet it is not for all these things that we
   Now keep sure faith with things transcendent, true
And untransmissible:—it is because,
   Even in the presence of the Mystery,
   He knew!—it is because we knew he knew!

# Moriturus
[Trumbull Stickney, died October 11, 1904]

"He sought, believed, dared, found and bore away
  "The light: the deed, the deathless deed was done!
  "What mattered it that then Deukalion[29]
  "Was filled with wrath, resentment and dismay?
"What tho' God's bird, relentless, day by day,
  "Tore his immortal heart, and God's high sun
  "Blistered his eyes?—the man endured and won!"
He said—and smiled in his tremendous way.
And then I knew how fiercely and alone
  The Titan had withstood resistless things
  And let the soul's accomplishment atone;
Had climbed blind pathways thro' the strangling night
  And with the courage of his sufferings
  Had seized and kept, for life and death, the Light!

He felt the blind lost loneliness increase
  As life compelled him to the final test.
  He said: "The refuge of defeat is rest;
  "A soul's dishonor is the price of peace.
"From star to star the flight shall never cease;
  "The truth, perforce, is long and last and best;
  "Thro' life and death with bruised, defenceless breast
  "We seek the sunrise of the soul's release."
And so he lived and almost died and died.
  The night, the silence and the solitude
  Left him magnificent and unsubdued;
And we who kept the vigil by his side
  Saw, when at last the Door was opened wide,
  Clear in his eyes the Dawn his soul pursued.

"At least," he said, "we spent with Socrates
  "Some memorable days, and in our youth
  "Were curious and respectful of the Truth,
  "Thrilled by perfections and discoveries.
"And with the everlasting mysteries
  "We were irreverent and unsatisfied,—
  "And so we are!" he said. And when he died
  His eyes were deep with strange immensities.

And all his words came back to me again
  Like stars after a storm. I saw the light
  And trembled, for I knew the man had won
In solitude and darkness and great pain;—
  But when he leaped headlong into the Night
  He met the dawn of an eternal Sun!

*A major figure on the American cultural scene, Santayana published widely throughout a long career. Although he is remembered today chiefly for his influence on American philosophy (his five-volume* The Life of Reason *[1905–06] only one of many works espousing a life of naturalism and pragmatism), he was a cultural and literary critic whose single novel* The Last Puritan *(1935) enjoyed great popular success. He claimed that he did not understand his sexual preference until much later in life, but the beautiful sonnet sequence below, dedicated to Warwick Potter (a friend who had died in an 1893 boating accident), suggests early same-sex attraction. The homoerotic undertone is strongly reminiscent of Tennyson's* In Memoriam *(1850).*

## To W.P.
(1896)

I

Calm was the sea to which your course you kept,
Oh, how much calmer than all southern seas!
Many your nameless mates, whom the keen breeze
Wafted from mothers that of old have wept.
All souls of children taken as they slept
Are your companions, partners of your ease,
And the green souls of all these autumn trees
Are with you through the silent spaces swept.
Your virgin body gave its gentle breath
Untainted to the gods. Why should we grieve,
But that we merit not your holy death?
We shall not loiter long, your friends and I;
Living you made it goodlier to live,
Dead you will make it easier to die.

II

With you a part of me hath passed away;
For in the peopled forest of my mind
A tree made leafless by this wintry wind
Shall never don again its green array.
Chapel and fireside, country road and bay,
Have something of their friendliness resigned;
Another, if I would, I could not find,
And I am grown much older in a day.

But yet I treasure in my memory
Your gift of charity, your mellow ease,
And the dear honour of your amity;
For these once mine, my life is rich with these.
And I scarce know which part may greater be,—
What I keep of you, or you rob of me.

III
Your bark lies anchored in the peaceful bight[30]
Until a kinder wind unfurl her sail;
Your docile spirit, wingèd by this gale,
Hath at the dawning fled into the light.
And I half know why heaven deemed it right
Your youth, and this my joy in youth, should fail;
God hath them still, for ever they avail,
Eternity hath borrowed that delight.
For long ago I taught my thoughts to run
Where all the great things live that lived of yore,
And in eternal quiet float and soar;
There all my loves are gathered into one,
Where change is not, nor parting any more,
Nor revolution of the moon and sun.

IV
In my deep heart these chimes would still have rung
To toll your passing, had you not been dead;
For time a sadder mask than death may spread
Over the face that ever should be young.
The bough that falls with all its trophies hung
Falls not too soon, but lays its flower-crowned head
Most royal in the dust, with no leaf shed
Unhallowed or unchiselled or unsung.
And though the after world will never hear
The happy name of one so gently true,
Nor chronicles write large this fatal year,
Yet we who loved you, though we be but few,
Keep you in whatsoe'er is good, and rear
In our weak virtues monuments to you.

## Notes

1   For more on Halleck's obsession with Drake, as well as a discussion of his homo-
    sexuality, see John W.M. Hallock's insightful cultural biography *The American*

*Byron: Homosexuality and the Fall of Fitz-Greene Halleck* (Madison: U of Wisconsin P, 2000).

2  This passage tells of King David receiving the news of Saul and his son Jonathan's deaths. David and Jonathan were emblematic of friendship between two men, "above the love of women," and such references throughout nineteenth-century American literature were often markers for same-sex affection. This excerpt is from Halleck's *Juvenalia*, where there is another poem on the same Biblical story; and certainly demonstrates his early interest in the subject.

3  Though the gender of the subject, as in "The Song of the Unmarried," is a woman, John W.M. Hallock presents a compelling argument that Halleck is referring to himself in these two poems (see Hallock 84–85, 125–126).

4  In Greek mythology, Hymen is the god of marriage.

5  "Bohemia" and "Vagabondia" were terms that suggested throwing off societal restrictions, presumably sexual "fetters" as well. See Shand-Tucci's *The Crimson Letter*, p. 88, for further discussion; see also Francis Millet's letters in this collection, addressed from "Where Bohemia Was" (363–71).

6  Love-Friendship (Latin).

7  "To Uranian Love" (Greek).

8  Reward, recompense.

9  Simplicity; innocence (Greek).

10  This poem is probably presciently addressed to Warren's longtime companion John Marshall who did indeed leave him in 1907 to marry Warren's cousin.

11  For more see Edward Prime-Stevenson's *Imre: A Memorandum*, ed. James Gifford, pp. 152–59.

12  Poem or song of mourning.

13  See Viereck's letter to Woodberry, p. 375, below.

14  Loyal, true (Scotch).

15  The plateau region of the Atlas Mountains of Northern Algeria.

16  Cf. *A Shropshire Lad* (1896) by A.E. Housman.

17  A mountain range in central Asia.

18  A type, i.e., classic (Italian).

19  A bull (Italian).

20  In ancient Greece, Phalaris (570–554 BC), Tyrant of Agrigentum in Sicily, had a bull cast entirely of bronze as an execution device. A victim was shut up in the bull and a fire set under it, causing the victim to be roasted to death.

21  By Bacchus! (Italian). Bacchus was the Roman god of wine and intoxication.

22  Behold! (Italian).

23  *The Middle Span*, vol. 2 of *Persons and Places* (New York: Scribner, 1945), 103.

24  The Roman Epicurean philosopher Lucretius (c.99–55 BC) often displays a fear of emotional involvement. In the philosophical treatise *On the Nature of Things* Lucretius warns against the wounding shafts of Venus whether they proceed from a woman or from "a boy with womanish limbs." He urges the afflicted man to plunge into promiscuity as a remedy for love.

25 *On the Nature of Things*, I.140–41: "the hoped-for pleasure of [your] sweet friendship." This poem roughly paraphrases Lucretius in describing a lover's rejection.

26 Lodge was an ardent admirer of Walt Whitman, and tried, with uneven success, to copy his poetic style. Indeed, he uses many Whitmanian "variant phrases," cribbed from titles such as "A Backward Glance O'er Travel'd Roads" (1888), "Democratic Vistas" (1871), and "In Paths Untrodden" from *Calamus* (1860).

27 William Sturgis Bigelow (1850–1926), Lodge's father's close friend, with his erudition and interest in Buddhism and Eastern philosophy, exerted a profound effect on young Lodge. Bigelow owned a summer retreat on a private island, Tuckernuck, and Lodge spent many summers in bachelor Bigelow's male-only conclave (as did Charles Warren Stoddard). For more see John W. Crowley's "Eden off Nantucket: W.S. Bigelow and 'Tuckanuck.'" Suffering from heart problems, Lodge died here in the summer of 1909, after an apparent attack of food (bacterial) poisoning.

28 The sudden death in 1904 of his close Harvard friend Trumbull Stickney from a brain tumor brought Lodge to near-collapse. In *The Great Adventure* (1905), Lodge dedicated his "Death" sonnet cycle to Stickney.

29 Deukalion was the son of Prometheus who according to legend was the lone survivor when Zeus destroyed the first race of men. Saved in an ark from a great flood, the second race of humans descended from him.

30 I.e., your boat is safe in the shoreline's bend.

# PART ELEVEN

# DOCTORS, CASE STUDIES, AND EROTOPATHS

# James Mills Peirce (1834–1906)

*Perhaps the first cogent defense of homosexuality by an American was the excerpt by "Professor X" in Havelock Ellis and John Addington Symonds' 1897 pioneering study* Sexual Inversion, *a book which argued that homosexuality was inborn, in contrast to contemporary notions that it was immoral and corrupt behavior. The volume contained many case histories (including Symonds' own) whose names were necessarily withheld. Jonathan Ned Katz convincingly argues that "Prof. X" was James Mills Peirce, a distinguished professor of mathematics at Harvard.[1] Ellis attests at the end of the excerpt: "I present this statement of Prof. X.'s as representing the furthest point to which the defence of sexual inversion has gone, or, indeed, could go, unless anyone were bold enough to assert that homosexuality is the only normal impulse, and heterosexual love a perversion."*

## From *Sexual Inversion* "Letter from 'Professor X'" (1897)

I have considered and enquired into this question for many years; and it has long been my settled conviction that no breach of morality is involved in homosexual love; that, like every other passion, it tends, when duly understood and controlled by spiritual feeling, to the physical and moral health of the individual and the race, and that it is only its brutal perversions which are immoral. I have known many persons more or less the subjects of this passion, and I have found them a particularly high-minded, upright, refined, and (I must add) pure-minded class of men. In view of what everybody knows of the vile influence on society of the intersexual passion, as it actually exists in the world, making men and women sensual, low-minded, false, every way unprincipled and grossly selfish, and this especially in those nations which self-righteously reject homosexual love, it seems a travesty of morality to invest the one with divine attributes and denounce the other as infamous and unnatural. There is an error in the view that feminine love is that which is directed to a man, and masculine love that which is directed to a woman. That doctrine involves a begging of the whole question. It is a fatal concession to vulgar prejudice, and a contradiction to all you have so firmly adduced from Greek manners, and, indeed, I may say, to all the natural evolution of our race. Passion is in itself a blind thing. It is a furious pushing out, not with calculation or comprehension of its object, but to anything which strikes the imagination as fitted to its need. It is not characterised or differentiated by the nature of its object, but by its own nature. Its instinct is to a certain form of action or submission. But how that instinct is determined is largely accidental. Sexual passion is drawn by certain qualities which appeal to it. It may see them, or think that it sees them, in a man or a woman. But it is in either case the same person. The controlling influence is a certain spiritual attraction, and that may lie in either. The two directions are equally natural to unperverted man, and the abnormal form of love is that which has lost the power of excitability in either the one or the other of these directions. It is unisexual love (a love for one sexuality) which is a perversion. The normal men love both.

It is true enough that in primitive society all passion must have been wholly or mainly animal, and spiritual progress must have been conditioned on subduing it. But there is no reason why this subjugation should have consisted in extirpating, or trying to extirpate, one of the two main forms of sexual passion, and cultivating the other. The actual reasons were, I take it, two: (1) to reserve all sexual energy for the increase of the race; (2) to get the utmost merely fleshly pleasure out of the exercise of passion. Whether either of these reasons adds to the spiritual elevation of love may be doubted. Certainly not the second, which is now the moving influence in the matter. It is true enough that all passion needs to be unceasingly watched, because the worst evils for mankind lie hidden in its undisciplined indulgence. But this is quite as true of intersexual as of homosexual love. I clearly believe that the Greek morality on this subject was far higher than ours, and truer to the spiritual nature of man; that our civilisation suffers for want of the pure and noble sentiment which they thought so useful to the state; and that we ought to think and speak of homosexual love, not as "inverted" or "abnormal," as a sort of colourblindness of the genital sense, as a lamentable mark of inferior development, or as an unhappy fault, a "masculine body with a feminine soul," but as being in itself a natural, pure and sound passion, as worthy of the reverence of all fine natures as the honourable devotion of husband and wife, or the ardour of bride and groom.

# CLAUDE HARTLAND (PSEUDONYM) (1871–?)

*Published in St. Louis "for the consideration of the Medical Fraternity" in 1901, Hartland's book is perhaps the earliest American autobiography by an open homosexual. While his pseudonym remains appropriately symbolic (i.e., "clawed heart-land" with its multiple meanings of wounded emotions and dysfunctional Heartland/America—from the central United States where Hartland was from) we still do not know Hartland's true identity. We do, however, know one of the physicians who "treated" him. Dr. Charles H. Hughes, a distinguished alienist[2] of his day, wrote in his essay "The Gentleman Degenerate" that the "autobiographic reflections of a sexual pervert, with reverse sexual instinct feelings and impulses, are given place here, as contributing to complete the portraiture of the homosexual form of hereditary perversion and also to call attention to the often revealed psychic accompaniment of morbid egoism and craving for sympathy. Such of this class who have come under my observation and care as patients, have been inclined to write up their cases, without suggestion to that effect and without urging. The morbid egoism to disclose the self-feeling is like that of Claud [sic] Hartland, another patient of the editor's, whose book was excluded from the mails."[3] Written in the style of the case study demanded by the medical press who was publishing him, Hartland's words slyly undercut its inability to circumscribe his experience, and he subverts the form into a (sym)pathetic plea for understanding.*

# FROM *THE STORY OF A LIFE* (1901)

### Chapter X
### Fleeing from Self
### (Age 25 to 27)

In the fall of '96, my old teacher resigned the principalship of his school to the linguist and went away.

I was elected first assistant, and I now came as teacher where I had so long been a pupil.

As soon as I was separated from "My boy" in the preceding chapter, my lustful desires returned and with them the pressure on my brow.

When school opened I loved no one in particular, but I soon fell madly in love with one of my pupils, a boy about fifteen years of age.

This was the strangest affection I have ever felt.

I have never been able to decide whether it was love or lust, but I believe it was a mixture of the two.

I felt a deep interest in his welfare and progress in school, and at such times passion was dumb; at other times I yearned to clasp him in my arms and devour him with kisses, and these feelings were accompanied by erections.

I was always afraid of my love for him, and from the beginning felt guilty and unhappy, yet I could not give him up.

My love soon begot a kindred feeling in him for me.

At times he was calm and gentle in his affection, and again his face would flush to a deep crimson, and he seemed restless and uneasy.

Months passed by, and every day we loved each other more, yet we had never given expression to our love.

We met at church one afternoon, and I saw at a glance that his love or passion was unusually strong.

Mine was the same, and after services were over we instinctively lingered around the church door, waiting, one for the other.

When everyone was gone, we sat down upon the steps and talked for several moments.

We were both restless and uneasy, but I hardly knew why. At last he proposed going into the church and sitting down.

This we did, against my better judgment, for somehow I feared, for his sake, to be alone with him.

When we were seated side by side, a love stronger than I had ever felt for him before swept over me.

This was accompanied by that strange, drowsy, vaporous feeling that I had once before felt for "My boy," but now it was strongly colored with lust.

My face burned furiously.

I closed my eyes for a moment, and all was still.

During this moment the same feeling came over him, and throwing his arms around my neck, he kissed me with lips that burned with passion.

This was a warning, and we left the church at once.

After this I was very unhappy, for I feared, and still fear, that I had ruined his life; yet my love for him grew stronger every day, and I could scarcely resist his attempts to make me give it expression.

The weight on my head grew heavier till it was almost pain, and I feared I was losing my mind.

I went to the Insane Asylum and consulted the physicians in charge. I did not tell them my secret at first; but when they told me that unless I got immediate mental relief I would lose my mind, I told them the story of my life and my present love.

They did not understand my case at all, but told me I must give up my school and go away at once.

I asked them if nothing could be done for me, and they said they would search the records for a similar case, and if they could relieve me they would let me know.

I never heard from them, however, and when school closed I resigned and went to B—, a city nearby, to seek medical treatment, for I was becoming alarmed.

One Dr. A. was recommended to me as a nerve specialist, and he treated me for some time, without the least effect.

This same physician recommended sexual intercourse with women as a relief from my trouble, and I made up my mind to try it, though it was the most repulsive remedy ever offered me.

I went to a first-class house of prostitution, and selecting what I called the least repulsive of the lot, we went to her room together.

Well, I have parted from several of my molars, and if sacrificing another would have answered the same purpose—that of satisfying my physician—I would gladly have gone to the dentist's chair instead of to her bed.

I had it understood with her that, "No success, no pay," and after I had failed to sum up sufficient courage for the ordeal before me, she took the matter into her own hands, and so energetically did she [flaunt] her charms (?) before me, that I was completely disgusted.

It seemed that my already flaccid organs would shrivel up and disappear entirely.

I was in a dilemma, and on this especial occasion I was thankful for one feminine gift—a woman's wits in the time of embarrassment.

To relieve myself, I resorted to the following plan:

Closing my eyes so that I could not see the loathsome object beside me, I shut her from my mind and turned my thoughts to a very handsome man, with whom I was madly in love in a passionate way.

Ten minutes passed, and when all was over, she pronounced me a grand success, at the same time modestly (?) insinuating that her charms never failed to "bring 'em round."

Not wishing to wound her vanity, I did not undeceive her, but hastened out into the street with something of the feeling that one ends his first visit to a dissecting room.

This was my first and last sexual experience with a woman, and for several days after, I was almost sick with disgust.

I could see that my physician was greatly amused when I made my report, yet he had too much respect for my feelings to give vent to the mirth that shone in his countenance.

He did not advise me to repeat the experiment, for which I was most thankful.

I then consulted a spiritualist, who offered me much encouragement, but no relief.

As an excuse to my friends at home for my long stay in the city, as much as for the benefit it brought me, I took music and penmanship, and worked very hard.

The city was full of handsome men, and I burned with passion all the time.

I soon found that many others were suffering from a disease similar to my own, and while this knowledge gave me great relief, I was grieved to find the victims so numerous.

One night, while standing upon the sidewalk listening to a public speech, a very handsome and stylishly dressed man about thirty-five years of age, began a conversation with me.

I suspected him of course, for I could see that he labored under some nervous strain, and I decided to let him take his course.

We talked for some time, when he proposed that we go for a walk. I agreed and we walked on down to the river.

When we were in a quiet and dark spot, he placed his arms around my neck and kissed me several times.

Leaning forward, he whispered something in my ear. I had an idea what he meant, but was not sure.

Passion and curiosity tempted me sorely, and I did not repulse him.

Ten minutes passed.

A new experience had been added to my life, and a half slumbering desire awakened in my breast.

One night, several months later, when I was more lustful than usual, I went on the streets actually in search of some one with whom to gratify my maddening passion.

I was passing down a dimly lighted street, when I saw in front of me a man whose form was simply perfect.

I had not seen his face, but I was sure that he must be very handsome.

I quickened my pace, and in the act of passing him I glanced at his face.

One look was enough—too much.

He was all that my passionate soul could desire, and I could not pass him by without a word.

I begged his pardon, then asked him the way to some place that I knew to be in the direction he was going, and he kindly offered to show me the way.

He talked freely, but my own voice was so choked with passion, that I could scarcely answer him.

He soon took on my condition, and before we had gone another block, he had my hand in his and—we were in love.

We turned into a still darker street, for the city was not well lighted, and at that time we did not even have a moon.

He placed his strong arms about me, strained me to his great manly breast and kissed me again and again.

I lay perfectly still against his breast, for I was completely dazed with the sweet blissful feeling his caresses brought to my soul.

He too was aflame with passion, and placing his lips close to my ear, he made a request that I could not grant and I told him so.

He gently put me from him, told me I did not care for him and turned to leave me.

I put out my hand to detain him, and he repeated his request.

I hesitated a moment, and he again placed his arms about me.

I felt my resolution giving way, for oh, how I loved him and how I longed to please him—!

Placing his cheek against my own, he whispered: "Will you?"

At this moment reason returned, and springing from his arms, I firmly answered: "No, not if I die," and turning, I hurried away and left him.

I did not look back for some time, and when I did, he was gone, and I knew I had lost him.

I sat down upon a curb completely exhausted by the great strain under which I had been laboring.

I felt at that moment that I would grant any request if I only had him with me again.

I will not describe the rest of that wretched night in my room alone.

Suffice it to say that I met him again, and though men may curse me, I hope God will forgive me if I did *not* send him away.

He was a man sixty years of age, but he possessed a power, a fascination that I *could* not resist.

Even while writing these lines, my hand trembles and my face burns with passion when I remember those wild sweet moments we spent together.

Soon after this, I accidentally met a little man on the streets one night who was affected as I am. We spent the night together, and he seemed to love me very dearly.

My feeling for him was only passion and, after we separated, I gave him but little thought.

He wore a Van Dyke beard at that time, and I did not discover the beauty and sweetness of his face.

When I saw him several weeks later, I did not know him, for he had shaven, but recognizing me, he came at once and spoke to me.

Before I knew who he was, I was deeply in love with him, for without his beard he was beautiful as a dream and fascinating in every way.

We spent that night together, but sweet pure love had completely subdued my passion, and the same feeling soon came over him.

That was a night I shall never forget.

"Passion was dumb and purest love maintained its own dominion."

We lay in each other's arms all night and slept but little.

Our love was so sweet, so gentle, so tender and pure, that even wakefulness was a rest.

We talked of our dark lives, which were very similar, and tears were mingled freely.

We kissed each other a hundred times, and were so happy, the night stole by like a dream.

The next morning he went away, but I was not unhappy, for I knew we should see each other soon.

When he was gone, I fell down upon the bed where we had lain together and thanked God for this sweet pure love.

I began to improve at once.

My evil passion slunk away and hid itself, my conscience was at rest, and the great weight began to leave my forehead.

We corresponded all the time, and he told me in a letter that since our last night together, his passion for men was gone, and he loved no one but me.

I was sure he spoke the truth, for my feelings for him were the same.

He soon came to the city again, and we were so happy that we wept for joy.

He spent three nights with me, and we were so much in love that we almost forgot to take our meals.

I sought no more medical advice, for I did not need it now.

My physician was a man with a soul of love, my physic the love of his gentle soul, and I was well and happy again.

I at once began to take a new interest in life, and learning the merits of the B— schools, I determined to enter the University there in the fall.

This I did, and all went well for a time.

My beloved friend came often to see me, and life for us both was all joy and sunshine.

I was getting on nicely in school, and the days stole by on golden wings, and the Christmas holidays began. With them came a visit from my friend, and it seemed that we were never so happy before.

He was a Christian, and (smile if you wish) having a sweet musical voice, he would sing sad religious songs to me, which often brought tears to my eyes.

We would sit for hours with our arms about each other and talk of the dark, bitter life from which our love had saved us, and the happy future we were to spend together, but alas! for dreams of earthly joy.

The holidays passed and my friend went away.

From that day to this I have never seen or heard from him again. I wrote to him several times, but received no reply, and my pride, which has always been strong, whispered: "Leave him alone," and I obeyed. I believe he is dead, for he was never very strong physically.

I knew none of his people at all, and as I never signed my name to my letters to him, there was no possible chance for them to communicate with me in any way.

My love was lost, and now the days crept wearily by.

For a time, grief and anxiety mastered passion, but when hope gave place to despair, I again became an easy prey to lust, and I was miserable.

I burned with desire for my classmates and teachers, and could scarcely hold myself in check. My head began to trouble me again, and I could not sleep at night.

When I retired, it seemed that a weight of a hundred pounds was placed between my eyes, and when I slept at all, my dreams were hideous and terrible.

I remained in the city till April, when school closed, and then went back to my father's home in the country, where I at once began a summer school.

I was again adrift on the wild sea of an abnormal passion, without chart or rudder.

I had a little niece in school whom I had always loved very dearly, and I now turned my whole attention to her educational advancement.

My last disappointment had so discouraged me that I determined to give up all hope of love and recovery, and to make her welfare and happiness the one grand object of my life.

She was fifteen years of age, very beautiful and very intelligent, and I spared neither time nor expense in giving her every possible advantage.

I made a good salary, and had no one else to share it with me.

She advanced very rapidly, and I soon found myself living for her alone.

While the brotherly love I felt for her by no means subdued my passion for men, it to a great extent held me in check, and I was about as happy as I ever hoped to be.

My school continued until about the last of October, when it closed with a concert at night.

The entertainment consisted of music and a drama of my own composition, in which my niece was the heroine, and I the leading man.

The play was very sad, and gave excellent opportunity for good acting.

She took the part of my wife, and in a drunken frenzy I had murdered her.

Then followed my grief beside her coffin, the burial, and lastly, my lunacy behind prison bars.

I had always been a perfect failure as an actor, but I was not acting now.

In these scenes I found an opportunity to pour out before the world all the bitter anguish that had filled my life for almost eighteen years.

I forgot the play, the audience—everything, but the words of the drama, which were written to express the real feelings of my suffering soul.

The audience, I afterwards learned, was deeply moved.

The men were serious and thoughtful, and the women were all in tears.

After the play, a feeling of relief came over me that I cannot describe.

All the sorrow and suffering of my wretched life I had cried out before the world, yet no one knew my secret.

Compliments were showered upon me. I was called an actor and begged to go on the stage, at the absurdity of which I could but smile.

I knew my acting was over. I had told the world of my suffering, but I could not do it again; so I did not take to the stage.

After school closed, it was decided that Violet (my niece) should go for a long visit to an uncle in Texas, and preparations were at once begun.

I had not forgotten how to sew, and with the assistance of an experienced dressmaker, many beautiful gowns were planned and created.

After two weeks of preparation all was ready, and I bade her an affectionate farewell, and went back to the university, where I was to be graduated in the spring.

I had a letter from her every week. She had reached her uncle's in safety and was very happy.

Her letters were always full of affection and gratitude, and my heart welled up with pride when I thought of the future in store for her.

I was living for her sake, and determined to make her happy.

I slept, I dreamed, and for a time forgot that no hope of *mine* could ever materialize.

Friday came, the day for a letter from Violet.

Instead, there came a telegram, which simply read: "Violet is very low. Can't live."

The next day she died, and Sunday she was buried in a strange land, away from home and hearts that loved her.

I did not weep—no.

My heart simply collapsed, and sinking into a seat, I bowed my head, and the blackness of night closed again around my gloomy life.

> 'Twas ever thus from childhood's hour,
>    I've seen my fondest hope decay;
> I never loved a tree or flower,
>    But what 'twas first to fade away.[4]

# WILLA CATHER (1873–1947)

*Willa Cather is most closely associated with Nebraska, where she grew up and which figures in much of her writing. Her poetry, short stories, essays, and especially novels such as* O Pioneers *(1913),* My Antonia *(1918), and* Death Comes for the Archbishop *(1927) place her in the forefront of American fiction. A recurring theme with Cather was the struggle of artistic individuals in conflict with the narrowness of their surroundings. "Reviewing all artistic temperaments and aesthetic classes, we find that music and the dramatic stage present the greatest census of uranians (homosexuals)," says Edward Prime-Stevenson. Certainly the character of Paul displays an unusual obsession with décor and beauty and music, and this marks him as different: as Cather says of him, "He felt now that his surroundings explained him." A decade before this story was written, Oscar Wilde had become indelibly linked in the public eye with homosexuality and aestheticism. It seems likely that Cather, homosexual herself,[5] fully intends such subtext in any careful reading.[6] There are several markers for Paul's "difference" in this very popular story: his love of art and music and opera, his red carnation (Robert Hichens' 1894 satirical novel about Oscar Wilde,* The Green Carnation, *comes to mind), his lack of interest in women, and of course the story's subtitle. In meeting the same fate as Tolstoy's* Anna Karenina *(1877), Paul joins the many characters of this period who cannot reconcile their separateness with the society they live in.*

## "PAUL'S CASE: A STUDY IN TEMPERAMENT" (1905)

It was Paul's afternoon to appear before the faculty of the Pittsburgh High School to account for his various misdemeanors. He had been suspended a week ago, and his father had called at the Principal's office and confessed his perplexity about his son. Paul entered the faculty room suave and smiling. His clothes were a trifle out-grown, and the tan velvet on the collar of his open overcoat was frayed and worn; but for all that there was something of the dandy about him, and he wore an opal pin in his neatly knotted black four-in-hand, and a red carnation in his button-hole. This latter adornment the faculty somehow felt was not properly significant of the contrite spirit befitting a boy under the ban of suspension.

Paul was tall for his age and very thin, with high, cramped shoulders and a narrow chest. His eyes were remarkable for a certain hysterical brilliancy, and he continually used them in a conscious, theatrical sort of way, peculiarly offensive in a boy. The pupils were abnormally large, as though he were addicted to belladonna, but there was a glassy glitter about them which that drug does not produce.

When questioned by the Principal as to why he was there, Paul stated, politely enough, that he wanted to come back to school. This was a lie, but Paul was quite accustomed to lying; found it, indeed, indispensable for overcoming friction. His teachers were asked to state their respective charges against him, which they did with such a rancor and aggrievedness as evinced that this was not a usual case. Disorder and impertinence were among the offenses named, yet each of his instructors felt that it was scarcely possible to put into words the real cause of the trouble, which lay in a sort of hysterically defiant manner of the boy's; in the contempt which they all knew he felt for them, and which he seemingly made not the least effort to conceal. Once, when he had been making a synopsis of a paragraph at the blackboard, his English teacher had stepped to his side and attempted to guide his hand. Paul had started back with a shudder and thrust his hands violently behind him. The astonished woman could scarcely have been more hurt and embarrassed had he struck at her. The insult was so involuntary and definitely personal as to be unforgettable. In one way and another, he had made all his teachers, men and women alike, conscious of the same feeling of physical aversion. In one class he habitually sat with his hand shading his eyes; in another he always looked out of the window during the recitation; in another he made a running commentary on the lecture, with humorous intent.

His teachers felt this afternoon that his whole attitude was symbolized by his shrug and his flippantly red carnation flower, and they fell upon him without mercy, his English teacher leading the pack. He stood through it smiling, his pale lips parted over his white teeth. (His lips were continually twitching, and he had a habit of raising his eyebrows that was contemptuous and irritating to the last degree.) Older boys than Paul had broken down and shed tears under that ordeal, but his set smile did not once desert him, and his only sign of discomfort was the nervous trembling of the fingers that toyed with the buttons of his overcoat, and an occasional jerking of the other hand which held his hat. Paul was always smiling, always glancing about him, seeming to feel that people might be watching him and trying to detect something. This conscious expression, since it was as far as possible from boyish mirthfulness, was usually attributed to insolence or "smartness."

As the inquisition proceeded, one of his instructors repeated an impertinent remark of the boy's, and the Principal asked him whether he thought that a courteous speech to make to a woman. Paul shrugged his shoulders slightly and his eyebrows twitched.

"I don't know," he replied. "I didn't mean to be polite or impolite, either. I guess it's a sort of way I have, of saying things regardless."

The Principal, who was a sympathetic man, asked him whether he didn't think that a way it would be well to get rid of. Paul grinned and said he guessed so. When he was told that he could go, he bowed gracefully and went out. His bow was like a repetition of the scandalous red carnation.

His teachers were in despair, and his drawing master voiced the feeling of them all when he declared there was something about the boy which none of them understood. He added: "I don't really believe that smile of his comes altogether from insolence; there's something sort of haunted about it. The boy is not strong, for one thing. There is something wrong about the fellow."

The drawing master had come to realize that, in looking at Paul, one saw only his white teeth and the forced animation of his eyes. One warm afternoon the boy had gone to sleep at his drawing-board, and his master had noted with amazement what a white, blue-veined face it was; drawn and wrinkled like an old man's about the eyes, the lips twitching even in his sleep.

His teachers left the building dissatisfied and unhappy; humiliated to have felt so vindictive toward a mere boy, to have uttered this feeling in cutting terms, and to have set each other on, as it were, in the grewsome game of intemperate reproach. One of them remembered having seen a miserable street cat set at bay by a ring of tormentors.

As for Paul, he ran down the hill whistling the Soldiers' Chorus from *Faust,* looking wildly behind him now and then to see whether some of his teachers were not there to witness his lightheartedness. As it was now late in the afternoon and Paul was on duty that evening as usher at Carnegie Hall, he decided that he would not go home to supper.

When he reached the concert hall the doors were not yet open. It was chilly outside, and he decided to go up into the picture gallery—always deserted at this hour—where there were some of Raffelli's gay studies of Paris streets[7] and an airy blue Venetian scene or two that always exhilarated him. He was delighted to find no one in the gallery but the old guard, who sat in the corner, a newspaper on his knee, a black patch over one eye and the other closed. Paul possessed himself of the place and walked confidently up and down, whistling under his breath. After a while he sat down before a blue Rico[8] and lost himself. When he bethought him to look at his watch, it was after seven o'clock, and he rose with a start and ran downstairs, making a face at Augustus Caesar, peering out from the cast-room, and an evil gesture at the Venus of Milo as he passed her on the stairway.[9]

When Paul reached the ushers' dressing-room half-a-dozen boys were there already, and he began excitedly to tumble into his uniform. It was one of the few that at all approached fitting, and Paul thought it very becoming—though he knew the tight, straight coat accentuated his narrow chest, about which he was exceedingly sensitive. He was always excited while he dressed, twanging all over to the tuning of the strings and the preliminary flourishes of the horns in the music-room; but tonight he seemed quite beside himself, and he teased and plagued the boys until, telling him that he was crazy, they put him down on the floor and sat on him.

Somewhat calmed by his suppression, Paul dashed out to the front of the house to seat the early comers. He was a model usher. Gracious and smiling he ran up and down the aisles. Nothing was too much trouble for him; he carried messages and brought programs as though it were his greatest pleasure in life, and all the people in his section thought him a charming boy, feeling that he remembered and admired them. As the house filled, he grew more and more vivacious and animated, and the color came to his cheeks and lips. It was very much as though this were a great reception and Paul were the host. Just as the musicians came out to take their places, his English teacher arrived with checks for the seats which a prominent manufacturer had taken for the season. She betrayed some embarrassment when she handed Paul the tickets, and a *hauteur* which subsequently made her feel very foolish. Paul was startled for a moment, and had the feeling of wanting to put her out; what business had she here among all these fine people and gay colors? He looked her over and decided that she was not appropriately dressed and must be a fool to sit downstairs in such togs. The tickets had probably been sent her out of kindness, he reflected, as he put down a seat for her, and she had about as much right to sit there as he had.

When the symphony began Paul sank into one of the rear seats with a long sigh of relief, and lost himself as he had done before the Rico. It was not that symphonies, as such, meant anything in particular to Paul, but the first sigh of the instruments seemed to free some hilarious spirit within him; something that struggled there like the Genie in the bottle found by the Arab fisherman.[10] He felt a sudden zest of life; the lights danced before his eyes and the concert hall blazed into unimaginable splendor. When the soprano soloist came on, Paul forgot even the nastiness of his teacher's being there, and gave himself up to the peculiar intoxication such personages always had for him. The soloist chanced to be a German woman, by no means in her first youth, and the mother of many children; but she wore a satin gown and a tiara, and she had that indefinable air of achievement, that world-shine upon her, which always blinded Paul to any possible defects.

After a concert was over, Paul was often irritable and wretched until he got to sleep,—and tonight he was even more than usually restless. He had the feeling of not being able to let down; of its being impossible to give up this delicious excitement which was the only thing that could be called living at all. During the last number he withdrew and, after hastily changing his clothes in the dressing-room, slipped out to the side door where the singer's carriage stood. Here he began pacing rapidly up and down the walk, waiting to see her come out.

Over yonder the Schenley, in its vacant stretch, loomed big and square through the fine rain, the windows of its twelve stories glowing like those of a lighted card-board house under a Christmas tree. All the actors and singers of any importance stayed there when they were in the city, and a number of the big manufacturers of the place lived there in the winter. Paul had often hung about the hotel, watching the people go in and out, longing to enter and leave school-masters and dull care behind him for ever.

At last the singer came out, accompanied by the conductor, who helped her into her carriage and closed the door with a cordial *auf wiedersehen,*[11]— which set Paul to wondering whether she were not an old sweetheart of his. Paul followed the carriage over to the hotel, walking so rapidly as not to be far from the entrance when the singer alighted and disappeared behind the swinging glass doors which were opened by a negro in a tall hat and a long coat. In the moment that the door was ajar, it seemed to Paul that he, too, entered. He seemed to feel himself go after her up the steps, into the warm, lighted building, into an exotic, tropical world of shiny, glistening surfaces and basking ease. He reflected upon the mysterious dishes that were brought into the dining-room, the green bottles in buckets of ice, as he had seen them in the supper party pictures of the Sunday supplement. A quick gust of wind brought the rain down with sudden vehemence, and Paul was startled to find that he was still outside in the slush of the gravel driveway; that his boots were letting in the water and his scanty overcoat was clinging wet about him; that the lights in front of the concert hall were out, and that the rain was driving in sheets between him and the orange glow of the windows above him. There it was, what he wanted—tangibly before him, like the fairy world of a Christmas pantomime; as the rain beat in his face, Paul wondered whether he were destined always to shiver in the black night outside, looking up at it.

He turned and walked reluctantly toward the car tracks. The end had to come sometime; his father in his night-clothes at the top of the stairs, explanations that did not explain, hastily improvised fictions that were forever tripping him up, his upstairs room and its horrible yellow wallpaper, the creaking bureau with the greasy plush collar-box, and over his painted wooden bed the pictures of George Washington and John Calvin,[12] and the framed motto, "Feed my Lambs," which had been worked in red worsted by his mother, whom Paul could not remember.

Half an hour later, Paul alighted from the Negley Avenue car and went slowly down one of the side streets off the main thoroughfare. It was a highly respectable street, where all the houses were exactly alike, and where business men of moderate means begot and reared large families of children, all of whom went to Sabbath-school and learned the shorter catechism, and were interested in arithmetic; all of whom were as exactly alike as their homes, and of a piece with the monotony in which they lived. Paul never went up Cordelia Street without a shudder of loathing. His home was next to the house of the Cumberland minister. He approached it tonight with the nerveless sense of defeat, the hopeless feeling of sinking back forever into ugliness and commonness that he had always had when he came home. The moment he turned into Cordelia Street he felt the waters close above his head. After each of these orgies of living, he experienced all the physical depression which follows a debauch; the loathing of respectable beds, of common food, of a house permeated by kitchen odors; a shuddering repulsion for the flavorless, colorless mass of everyday existence; a morbid desire for cool things and soft lights and fresh flowers.

The nearer he approached the house, the more absolutely unequal Paul felt to the sight of it all; his ugly sleeping chamber; the cold bath-room with the grimy zinc tub, the cracked mirror, the dripping spiggots; his father, at the top of the stairs, his hairy legs sticking out from his nightshirt, his feet thrust into carpet slippers. He was so much later than usual that there would certainly be inquiries and reproaches. Paul stopped short before the door. He felt that he could not be accosted by his father tonight; that he could not toss again on that miserable bed. He would not go in. He would tell his father that he had no car fare, and it was raining so hard he had gone home with one of the boys and stayed all night.

Meanwhile, he was wet and cold. He went around to the back of the house and tried one of the basement windows, found it open, raised it cautiously, and scrambled down the cellar wall to the floor. There he stood, holding his breath, terrified by the noise he had made; but the floor above him was silent, and there was no creak on the stairs. He found a soap-box, and carried it over to the soft ring of light that streamed from the furnace door, and sat down. He was horribly afraid of rats, so he did not try to sleep, but sat looking distrustfully at the dark, still terrified lest he might have awakened his father. In such reactions, after one of the experiences which made days and nights out of the dreary blanks of the calendar, when his senses were deadened, Paul's head was always singularly clear. Suppose his father had heard him getting in at the window and had come down and shot him for a burglar? Then, again, suppose his father had come down, pistol in hand, and he had cried out in time to save himself, and his father had been horrified to think how nearly he had killed him? Then, again, suppose a day should come when his father would remember that night, and wish there had been no warning cry to stay his hand? With this last supposition Paul entertained himself until daybreak.

The following Sunday was fine; the sodden November chill was broken by the last flash of autumnal summer. In the morning Paul had to go to church and Sabbath-school, as always. On seasonable Sunday afternoons the burghers of Cordelia Street usually sat out on their front "stoops," and talked to their neighbors on the next stoop, or called to those across the street in neighborly fashion. The men sat placidly on gay cushions placed upon the steps that led down to the sidewalk, while the women, in their Sunday "waists," sat in rockers on the cramped porches, pretending to be greatly at their ease. The children played in the streets; there were so many of them that the place resembled the recreation grounds of a kindergarten. The men on the steps—all in their shirt sleeves, their vests unbuttoned—sat with their legs well apart, their stomachs comfortably protruding, and talked of the prices of things, or told anecdotes of the sagacity of their various chiefs and overlords. They occasionally looked over the multitude of squabbling children, listened affectionately to their high-pitched, nasal voices, smiling to see their own proclivities reproduced in their offspring, and interspersed their legends of the iron kings with remarks about their sons' progress at school, their grades in arithmetic, and the amounts they had saved in their toy banks.

On this last Sunday of November, Paul sat all the afternoon on the lowest step of his "stoop," staring into the street, while his sisters, in their rockers, were talking to the minister's daughters next door about how many shirt-waists they had made in the last week, and how many waffles some one had eaten at the last church supper. When the weather was warm, and his father was in a particularly jovial frame of mind, the girls made lemonade, which was always brought out in a red-glass pitcher, ornamented with forget-me-nots in blue enamel. This the girls thought very fine, and the neighbors joked about the suspicious color of the pitcher.[13]

Today Paul's father, on the top step, was talking to a young man who shift-ed a restless baby from knee to knee. He happened to be the young man who was daily held up to Paul as a model, and after whom it was his father's dear-est hope that he would pattern. This young man was of a ruddy complexion, with a compressed, red mouth, and faded, near-sighted eyes, over which he wore thick spectacles, with gold bows that curved about his ears. He was clerk to one of the magnates of a great steel corporation, and was looked upon in Cordelia Street as a young man with a future. There was a story that, some five years ago—he was now barely twenty-six—he had been a trifle "dissipated," but in order to curb his appetites and save the loss of time and strength that a sowing of wild oats might have entailed, he had taken his chief's advice, oft reiterated to his employees, and at twenty-one had married the first woman whom he could persuade to share his fortunes. She happened to be an angu-lar school-mistress, much older than he, who also wore thick glasses, and who had now borne him four children, all near-sighted, like herself.

The young man was relating how his chief, now cruising in the Mediter-ranean, kept in touch with all the details of the business, arranging his office hours on his yacht just as though he were at home, and "knocking off work enough to keep two stenographers busy." His father told, in turn, the plan his corporation was considering, of putting in an electric railway plant at Cairo. Paul snapped his teeth; he had an awful apprehension that they might spoil it all before he got there. Yet he rather liked to hear these legends of the iron kings, that were told and retold on Sundays and holidays; these stories of palaces in Venice, yachts on the Mediterranean, and high play at Monte Carlo appealed to his fancy, and he was interested in the triumphs of cash boys who had become famous, though he had no mind for the cash-boy stage.

After supper was over, and he had helped to dry the dishes, Paul nervous-ly asked his father whether he could go to George's to get some help in his geometry, and still more nervously asked for car-fare. This latter request he had to repeat, as his father, on principle, did not like to hear requests for money, whether much or little. He asked Paul whether he could not go to some boy who lived nearer, and told him that he ought not to leave his school work until Sunday; but he gave him the dime. He was not a poor man, but he had a worthy ambition to come up in the world. His only reason for allowing Paul to usher was that he thought a boy ought to be earning a little.

Paul bounded upstairs, scrubbed the greasy odor of the dish-water from his hands with the ill-smelling soap he hated, and then shook over his fingers a few drops of violet water from the bottle he kept hidden in his drawer. He left the house with his geometry conspicuously under his arm, and the moment he got out of Cordelia Street and boarded a downtown car, he shook off the lethargy of two deadening days, and began to live again.

The leading juvenile of the permanent stock company which played at one of the downtown theatres was an acquaintance of Paul's, and the boy had been invited to drop in at the Sunday-night rehearsals whenever he could. For more than a year Paul had spent every available moment loitering about Charley Edwards's dressing-room. He had won a place among Edwards's following not only because the young actor, who could not afford to employ a dresser, often found him useful, but because he recognized in Paul something akin to what churchmen term "vocation."

It was at the theatre and at Carnegie Hall that Paul really lived; the rest was but a sleep and a forgetting. This was Paul's fairy tale, and it had for him all the allurement of a secret love. The moment he inhaled the gassy, painty, dusty odor behind the scenes, he breathed like a prisoner set free, and felt within him the possibility of doing or saying splendid, brilliant things. The moment the cracked orchestra beat out the overture from *Martha*,[14] or jerked at the serenade from *Rigoletto*, all stupid and ugly things slid from him, and his senses were deliciously, yet delicately fired.

Perhaps it was because, in Paul's world, the natural nearly always wore the guise of ugliness, that a certain element of artificiality seemed to him necessary in beauty. Perhaps it was because his experience of life elsewhere was so full of Sabbath-school picnics, petty economies, wholesome advice as to how to succeed in life, and the unescapable odors of cooking, that he found this existence so alluring, these smartly-clad men and women so attractive, that he was so moved by these starry apple orchards that bloomed perennially under the lime-light.

It would be difficult to put it strongly enough how convincingly the stage entrance of that theatre was for Paul the actual portal of Romance. Certainly none of the company ever suspected it, least of all Charley Edwards. It was very like the old stories that used to float about London of fabulously rich Jews, who had subterranean halls, with palms, and fountains, and soft lamps and richly apparelled women who never saw the disenchanting light of London day. So, in the midst of that smoke-palled city, enamored of figures and grimy toil, Paul had his secret temple, his wishing-carpet, his bit of blue-and-white Mediterranean shore bathed in perpetual sunshine.

Several of Paul's teachers had a theory that his imagination had been perverted by garish fiction; but the truth was, he scarcely ever read at all. The books at home were not such as would either tempt or corrupt a youthful mind, and as for reading the novels that some of his friends urged upon him—well, he got what he wanted much more quickly from music; any sort of music, from an orchestra to a barrel organ. He needed only the spark, the indescribable thrill that made his imagination master of his senses, and he could make plots and pictures enough of his own. It was equally true that he was not stage-struck—not, at any rate, in the usual acceptation of that expression. He had no desire to become an actor, any more than he had to become a musician. He felt no necessity to do any of these things; what he wanted was to see, to be in the atmosphere, float on the wave of it, to be carried out, blue league after blue league, away from everything.

After a night behind the scenes, Paul found the school-room more than ever repulsive; the bare floors and naked walls; the prosy men who never wore frock coats, or violets in their buttonholes; the women with their dull gowns, shrill voices, and pitiful seriousness about prepositions that govern the dative. He could not bear to have the other pupils think, for a moment, that he took these people seriously; he must convey to them that he considered it all trivial, and was there only by way of a joke, anyway. He had autograph pictures of all the members of the stock company which he showed his classmates, telling them the most incredible stories of his familiarity with these people, of his acquaintance with the soloists who came to Carnegie Hall, his suppers with them and the flowers he sent them. When these stories lost their effect, and his audience grew listless, he would bid all the boys good-bye, announcing that he was going to travel for awhile; going to Naples, to California, to Egypt. Then, next Monday, he would slip back, conscious and nervously smiling; his sister was ill, and he would have to defer his voyage until spring.

Matters went steadily worse with Paul at school. In the itch to let his instructors know how heartily he despised them, and how thoroughly he was appreciated elsewhere, he mentioned once or twice that he had no time to fool with theorems; adding—with a twitch of the eyebrows and a touch of that nervous bravado which so perplexed them—that he was helping the people down at the stock company; they were old friends of his.

The upshot of the matter was, that the Principal went to Paul's father, and Paul was taken out of school and put to work. The manager at Carnegie Hall was told to get another usher in his stead; the doorkeeper at the theatre was warned not to admit him to the house; and Charley Edwards remorsefully promised the boy's father not to see him again.

The members of the stock company were vastly amused when some of Paul's stories reached them—especially the women. They were hard-working women, most of them supporting indolent husbands or brothers, and they laughed rather bitterly at having stirred the boy to such fervid and florid inventions. They agreed with the faculty and with his father, that Paul's was a bad case.

The east-bound train was ploughing through a January snow-storm; the dull dawn was beginning to show grey when the engine whistled a mile out of Newark. Paul started up from the seat where he had lain curled in uneasy slumber, rubbed the breath-misted window glass with his hand, and peered out. The snow was whirling in curling eddies above the white bottom lands, and the drifts lay already deep in the fields and along the fences, while here and there the long dead grass and dried weed stalks protruded black above it. Lights shone from the scattered houses, and a gang of laborers who stood beside the track waved their lanterns.

Paul had slept very little, and he felt grimy and uncomfortable. He had made the all-night journey in a day coach because he was afraid if he took a Pullman he might be seen by some Pittsburgh business man who had noticed him in Denny & Carson's office. When the whistle woke him, he clutched quickly at his breast pocket, glancing about him with an uncertain smile. But the little, clay-bespattered Italians were still sleeping, the slatternly women across the aisle were in open-mouthed oblivion, and even the crumby, crying babies were for the nonce stilled. Paul settled back to struggle with his impatience as best he could.

When he arrived at the Jersey City station, he hurried through his breakfast, manifestly ill at ease and keeping a sharp eye about him. After he reached the Twenty-third Street station, he consulted a cabman, and had himself driven to a men's furnishing establishment which was just opening for the day. He spent upward of two hours there, buying with endless reconsidering and great care. His new street suit he put on in the fitting-room; the frock coat and dress clothes he had bundled into the cab with his new shirts. Then he drove to a hatter's and a shoe house. His next errand was at Tiffany's, where he selected silver mounted brushes and a scarf-pin. He would not wait to have his silver marked, he said. Lastly, he stopped at a trunk shop on Broadway, and had his purchases packed into various travelling bags.

It was a little after one o'clock when he drove up to the Waldorf, and, after settling with the cabman, went into the office. He registered from Washington; said his mother and father had been abroad, and that he had come down to await the arrival of their steamer. He told his story plausibly and had no trouble, since he offered to pay for them in advance, in engaging his rooms; a sleeping-room, sitting-room and bath.

Not once, but a hundred times Paul had planned this entry into New York. He had gone over every detail of it with Charley Edwards, and in his scrap book at home there were pages of description about New York hotels, cut from the Sunday papers.

When he was shown to his sitting-room on the eighth floor, he saw at a glance that everything was as it should be; there was but one detail in his mental picture that the place did not realize, so he rang for the bell boy and sent him down for flowers. He moved about nervously until the boy returned, putting away his new linen and fingering it delightedly as he did so. When the flowers came, he put them hastily into water, and then tumbled into a hot bath. Presently he came out of his white bath-room, resplendent in his new silk underwear, and playing with the tassels of his red robe. The snow was whirling so fiercely outside his windows that he could scarcely see across the street; but within, the air was deliciously soft and fragrant. He put the violets and jonquils on the tabouret beside the couch, and threw himself down with a long sigh, covering himself with a Roman blanket. He was thoroughly tired; he had been in such haste, he had stood up to such a strain, covered so much ground in the last twenty-four hours, that he wanted to think how it had all come about. Lulled by the sound of the wind, the warm air, and the cool fragrance of the flowers, he sank into deep, drowsy retrospection.

It had been wonderfully simple; when they had shut him out of the theatre and concert hall, when they had taken away his bone, the whole thing was virtually determined. The rest was a mere matter of opportunity. The only thing that at all surprised him was his own courage—for he realized well enough that he had always been tormented by fear, a sort of apprehensive dread that, of late years, as the meshes of the lies he had told closed about him, had been pulling the muscles of his body tighter and tighter. Until now, he could not remember a time when he had not been dreading something. Even when he was a little boy, it was always there—behind him, or before, or on either side. There had always been the shadowed corner, the dark place into which he dared not look, but from which something seemed always to be watching him—and Paul had done things that were not pretty to watch, he knew.

But now he had a curious sense of relief, as though he had at last thrown down the gauntlet to the thing in the corner.

Yet it was but a day since he had been sulking in the traces; but yesterday afternoon that he had been sent to the bank with Denny & Carson's deposit, as usual—but this time he was instructed to leave the book to be balanced. There was above two thousand dollars in checks, and nearly a thousand in the bank notes which he had taken from the book and quietly transferred to his pocket. At the bank he had made out a new deposit slip. His nerves had been steady enough to permit of his returning to the office, where he had finished his work and asked for a full day's holiday tomorrow, Saturday, giving a perfectly reasonable pretext. The bank book, he knew, would not be returned before Monday or Tuesday, and his father would be out of town for the next week. From the time he slipped the bank notes into his pocket until he boarded the night train for New York, he had not known a moment's hesitation.

How astonishingly easy it had all been; here he was, the thing done; and this time there would be no awakening, no figure at the top of the stairs. He watched the snow flakes whirling by his window until he fell asleep.

When he awoke, it was four o'clock in the afternoon. He bounded up with a start; one of his precious days gone already! He spent nearly an hour in dressing, watching every stage of his toilet carefully in the mirror. Everything was quite perfect; he was exactly the kind of boy he had always wanted to be.

When he went downstairs, Paul took a carriage and drove up Fifth Avenue toward the Park. The snow had somewhat abated; carriages and tradesmen's wagons were hurrying soundlessly to and fro in the winter twilight; boys in woolen mufflers were shovelling off the doorsteps; the avenue stages made fine spots of color against the white street. Here and there on the corners whole flower gardens blooming behind glass windows, against which the snow flakes stuck and melted; violets, roses, carnations, lilies of the valley—somehow vastly more lovely and alluring that they blossomed thus unnaturally in the snow. The Park itself was a wonderful stage winter-piece.

When he returned, the pause of the twilight had ceased, and the tune of the streets had changed. The snow was falling faster, lights streamed from the hotels that reared their many stories fearlessly up into the storm, defying the raging Atlantic winds. A long, black stream of carriages poured down the avenue, intersected here and there by other streams, tending horizontally. There were a score of cabs about the entrance of his hotel, and his driver had to wait. Boys in livery were running in and out of the awning stretched across the sidewalk, up and down the red velvet carpet laid from the door to the street. Above, about, within it all, was the rumble and roar, the hurry and toss of thousands of human beings as hot for pleasure as himself, and on every side of him towered the glaring affirmation of the omnipotence of wealth.

The boy set his teeth and drew his shoulders together in a spasm of realization; the plot of all dramas, the text of all romances, the nervestuff of all sensations was whirling about him like the snow flakes. He burnt like a faggot in a tempest.

When Paul came down to dinner, the music of the orchestra floated up the elevator shaft to greet him. As he stepped into the thronged corridor, he sank back into one of the chairs against the wall to get his breath. The lights, the chatter, the perfumes, the bewildering medley of color—he had, for a moment, the feeling of not being able to stand it. But only for a moment; these were his own people, he told himself. He went slowly about the corridors, through the writing-rooms, smoking-rooms, reception-rooms, as though he were exploring the chambers of an enchanted palace, built and peopled for him alone.

When he reached the dining-room he sat down at a table near a window. The flowers, the white linen, the many-colored wine glasses, the gay toilettes of the women, the low popping of corks, the undulating repetitions of the *Blue Danube*[15] from the orchestra, all flooded Paul's dream with bewildering radiance. When the roseate tinge of his champagne was added—that cold, precious, bubbling stuff that creamed and foamed in his glass—Paul wondered that there were honest men in the world at all. This was what all the world was fighting for, he reflected; this was what all the struggle was about. He doubted the reality of his past. Had he ever known a place called Cordelia Street, a place where fagged looking business men boarded the early car? Mere rivets in a machine they seemed to Paul,—sickening men, with combings of children's hair always hanging to their coats, and the smell of cooking in their clothes. Cordelia Street—Ah, that belonged to another time and country! Had he not always been thus, had he not sat here night after night, from as far back as he could remember, looking pensively over just such shimmering textures, and slowly twirling the stem of a glass like this one between his thumb and middle finger? He rather thought he had.

He was not in the least abashed or lonely. He had no especial desire to meet or to know any of these people; all he demanded was the right to look on and conjecture, to watch the pageant. The mere stage properties were all he contended for. Nor was he lonely later in the evening, in his loge at the Opera. He was entirely rid of his nervous misgivings, of his forced aggressiveness, of the imperative desire to show himself different from his surroundings. He felt now that his surroundings explained him. Nobody questioned the purple; he had only to wear it passively. He had only to glance down at his dress coat to reassure himself that here it would be impossible for anyone to humiliate him.

He found it hard to leave his beautiful sitting-room to go to bed that night, and sat long watching the raging storm from his turret window. When he went to sleep, it was with the lights turned on in his bedroom; partly because of his old timidity, and partly so that, if he should wake in the night, there would be no wretched moment of doubt, no horrible suspicion of yellow wallpaper, or of Washington and Calvin above his bed.

On Sunday morning the city was practically snow-bound. Paul breakfasted late, and in the afternoon he fell in with a wild San Francisco boy, a freshman at Yale, who said he had run down for a "little flyer" over Sunday. The young man offered to show Paul the night side of the town, and the two boys went off together after dinner, not returning to the hotel until seven o'clock the next morning. They had started out in the confiding warmth of a champagne friendship, but their parting in the elevator was singularly cool. The freshman pulled himself together to make his train, and Paul went to bed. He awoke at two o'clock in the afternoon, very thirsty and dizzy, and rang for ice-water, coffee, and the Pittsburgh papers.

On the part of the hotel management, Paul excited no suspicion. There was this to be said for him, that he wore his spoils with dignity and in no way made himself conspicuous. His chief greediness lay in his ears and eyes, and his excesses were not offensive ones. His dearest pleasures were the grey winter twilights in his sitting-room; his quiet enjoyment of his flowers, his clothes, his wide divan, his cigarette and his sense of power. He could not remember a time when he had felt so at peace with himself. The mere release from the necessity of petty lying, lying every day and every day, restored his self-respect. He had never lied for pleasure, even at school; but to make himself noticed and admired, to assert his difference from other Cordelia Street boys; and he felt a good deal more manly, more honest, even, now that he had no need for boastful pretensions, now that he could, as his actor friends used to say, "dress the part." It was characteristic that remorse did not occur to him. His golden days went by without a shadow, and he made each as perfect as he could.

On the eighth day after his arrival in New York, he found the whole affair exploited in the Pittsburgh papers, exploited with a wealth of detail which indicated that local news of a sensational nature was at a low ebb. The firm of Denny & Carson announced that the boy's father had refunded the full amount of his theft, and that they had no intention of prosecuting. The Cumberland minister had been interviewed, and expressed his hope of yet reclaiming the motherless lad, and Paul's Sabbath-school teacher declared that she would spare no effort to that end. The rumor had reached Pittsburgh that the boy had been seen in a New York hotel, and his father had gone East to find him and bring him home.

Paul had just come in to dress for dinner; he sank into a chair, weak in the knees, and clasped his head in his hands. It was to be worse than jail, even; the tepid waters of Cordelia Street were to close over him finally and forever. The grey monotony stretched before him in hopeless, unrelieved years; Sabbath-school, Young People's Meeting, the yellow-papered room, the damp dish-towels; it all rushed back upon him with sickening vividness. He had the old feeling that the orchestra had suddenly stopped, the sinking sensation that the play was over. The sweat broke out on his face, and he sprang to his feet, looked about him with his white, conscious smile, and winked at himself in the mirror. With something of the childish belief in miracles with which he had so often gone to class, all his lessons unlearned, Paul dressed and dashed whistling down the corridor to the elevator.

He had no sooner entered the dining-room and caught the measure of the music, than his remembrance was lightened by his old elastic power of claiming the moment, mounting with it, and finding it all sufficient. The glare and glitter about him, the mere scenic accessories had again, and for the last time, their old potency. He would show himself that he was game, he would finish the thing splendidly. He doubted, more than ever, the existence of Cordelia Street, and for the first time he drank his wine recklessly. Was he not, after all, one of these fortunate beings? Was he not still himself, and in his own place? He drummed a nervous accompaniment to the music and looked about him, telling himself over and over that it had paid.

He reflected drowsily, to the swell of the violin and the chill sweetness of his wine, that he might have done it more wisely. He might have caught an outbound steamer and been well out of their clutches before now. But the other side of the world had seemed too far away and too uncertain then; he could not have waited for it; his need had been too sharp. If he had to choose over again, he would do the same thing tomorrow. He looked affectionately about the dining-room, now gilded with a soft mist. Ah, it had paid indeed!

Paul was awakened next morning by a painful throbbing in his head and feet. He had thrown himself across the bed without undressing, and had slept with his shoes on. His limbs and hands were lead heavy, and his tongue and throat were parched. There came upon him one of those fateful attacks of clear-headedness that never occurred except when he was physically exhausted and his nerves hung loose. He lay still and closed his eyes and let the tide of realities wash over him.

His father was in New York; "stopping at some joint or other," he told himself. The memory of successive summers on the front stoop fell upon him like a weight of black water. He had not a hundred dollars left; and he knew now, more than ever, that money was everything, the wall that stood between all he loathed and all he wanted. The thing was winding itself up; he had thought of that on his first glorious day in New York, and had even provided a way to snap the thread. It lay on his dressing-table now; he had got it out last night when he came blindly up from dinner,—but the shiny metal hurt his eyes, and he disliked the look of it, anyway.

He rose and moved about with a painful effort, succumbing now and again to attacks of nausea. It was the old depression exaggerated; all the world had become Cordelia Street. Yet somehow he was not afraid of anything, was absolutely calm; perhaps because he had looked into the dark corner at last, and knew. It was bad enough, what he saw there; but somehow not so bad as his long fear of it had been. He saw everything clearly now. He had a feeling that he had made the best of it, that he had lived the sort of life he was meant to live, and for half an hour he sat staring at the revolver. But he told himself that was not the way, so he went downstairs and took a cab to the ferry.

When Paul arrived at Newark, he got off the train and took another cab, directing the driver to follow the Pennsylvania tracks out of the town. The snow lay heavy on the roadways and had drifted deep in the open fields. Only here and there the dead grass or dried weed stalks projected, singularly black, above it. Once well into the country, Paul dismissed the carriage and walked, floundering along the tracks, his mind a medley of irrelevant things. He seemed to hold in his brain an actual picture of everything he had seen that morning. He remembered every feature of both his drivers, the toothless old woman from whom he had bought the red flowers in his coat, the agent from whom he had got his ticket, and all of his fellow-passengers on the ferry. His mind, unable to cope with vital matters near at hand, worked feverishly and deftly at sorting and grouping these images. They made for him a part of the ugliness of the world, of the ache in his head, and the bitter burning on his tongue. He stooped and put a handful of snow into his mouth as he walked, but that, too, seemed hot. When he reached a little hillside, where the tracks ran through a cut some twenty feet below him, he stopped and sat down.

The carnations in his coat were drooping with the cold, he noticed; all their red glory over. It occurred to him that all the flowers he had seen in the show windows that first night must have gone the same way, long before this. It was only one splendid breath they had, in spite of their brave mockery at the winter outside the glass. It was a losing game in the end, it seemed, this revolt against the homilies by which the world is run. Paul took one of the blossoms carefully from his coat and scooped a little hole in the snow, where he covered it up. Then he dozed a while, from his weak condition, seeming insensible to the cold.

The sound of an approaching train woke him, and he started to his feet, remembering only his resolution, and afraid lest he should be too late. He stood watching the approaching locomotive, his teeth chattering, his lips drawn away from them in a frightened smile; once or twice he glanced nervously sidewise, as though he were being watched. When the right moment came, he jumped. As he fell, the folly of his haste occurred to him with merciless clearness, the vastness of what he had left undone. There flashed through his brain, clearer than ever before, the blue of Adriatic water, the yellow of Algerian sands.

He felt something strike his chest,—his body was being thrown swiftly through the air, on and on, immeasurably far and fast, while his limbs gently relaxed. Then, because the picture making mechanism was crushed, the disturbing visions flashed into black, and Paul dropped back into the immense design of things.

# William Lee Howard (1860–1918)

*Dr. Howard was a well-regarded medical authority of his day. He wrote several popular books of advice for parents and children, as well as a novel ingenuously titled* The Perverts *(1904). This book was praised by* The Alienist & Neurologist *reviewer, who affirmed that "It is time that the erotopath and the sexual pervert of many kinds and the neuropath and psychopath among the criminal, the vicious, the crook, the crank and the inebriate, were more popularly and legally better comprehended." The two essays that follow are typical of the psychiatric thinking of the time.*

## "Effeminate Men and Masculine Women" (1900)

Weak physiological traits, like moral traits, can be increased or decreased by education, training, and example. Environment plays a most active and powerful role in this development. The child born of parents in the prime of physiological life, each one having strong sex characteristics, is apt to show these characteristics in its development and growth, regardless of environment and education. But not so the unfortunate child born of unstable parents; of those who have assumed the responsibility of parentage when life is on the wane, or whose physical or mental activities have been in channels far removed from anticipation and thoughts of married life. Such parents belong to the physiologically degenerate class. They forget that the tendency is, in all animal life, to degenerate rather than improve. This goes on, generation after generation, unless care is exercised to introduce improved blood on one side or the other.

When a child demonstrates in its acts and tastes an indifference to the natural preference and inclination of its sex, it should be strictly confined to the companionship of that sex. Its education should be along the same lines, and every encouragement given it to develop its normal attributes. An indifferent boy who grows up an effeminate man should be allowed to share the ridicule and contempt thrust upon him with his parents, the mother being given the major part. This same mother, who shields her son from physical harm, will bring him up in the nursery with embroidery; take the poor creature, dressed up in linens and velvet, to exhibit him to female admirers; shift him off to the nursery of her hostess, where he is left to dress dolls and have his hair curled by the female attendants, and sit down to a make-believe tea party with his little girl playmates.

He grows up psychically unsexed, detested by the vigorous male, utilized as a willing servitor by the society woman, and sternly admonished by a true

327

father if he finds him dancing attendance with all his mincing manners upon a daughter. The female with masculine ambition is always amusing and often pitiable; but the attenuated, weak-voiced neuter, the effeminate male: pity him, but blame his mother for the false training, and give scorn to the father for his indifference. Even the woman, when she meets such a man, should passionately and involuntarily exclaim: "*O! surgit amari aliquid.*"[16]

The female possessed of masculine ideas of independence; the viragint[17] who would sit in the public highways and lift up her pseudo-virile voice, proclaiming her sole right to decide questions of war or religion, or the value of celibacy and the curse of woman's impurity, and that disgusting antisocial being, the female sexual pervert, are simply different degrees of the same class—degenerates. These unsightly and subnormal beings are the victims of poor mating. When a woman neglects her maternal instincts, when her sentiment and dainty feminine characteristics are boldly and ostentatiously kept submerged, we can see an antisocial creature more amusing than dangerous. When such a woman marries, which she often does for the privileges derived from attaching Mrs. to her name, the husband is certain to be one she can rule, govern, and cause to follow her in voice and action. Should this female be unfortunate enough to become a mother, she ceases to be merely amusing, and is an antisocial being. She is then a menace to civilization, a producer of nonentities, the mother of mental and physical monstrosities who exist as a class of true degenerates until disgusted Nature, no longer tolerant of the woman who would be a man, or the man who would be a woman, allows them to shrink unto death.

The female who prefers the laboratory to the nursery; the mother quick with child who spends her mornings at the club, discussing "social statics," visiting the saloons and tenements in the afternoon, distributing, with an innocence in strange contrast to her assumptions, political tracts asking the denizens to vote her tickets, is a sad form of degeneracy. Such females are true degenerates, because they are unphysiological in their physical incompleteness. The progeny of such human misfits are perverts, moral or psychical. Their prenatal life has been influenced by the very antithesis of what the real woman would surround her expected child with. The child born of the "new woman" is to be pitied. If it could be taken away from its environments, kept from the misguidance of an unwilling mother, nurtured, tutored, and directed along the sex line Nature has struggled to give it, often would the child be true to its latent normal instincts and grow to respected womanhood or manhood. Unfortunate it is that this development does not take place. The weak, plastic, developing cells of the brain are twisted, distorted, and a perverted psychic growth promoted by the false examples and teachings of a discontented mother. These are the conditions which have been prolific in producing the antisocial "new woman" and the disgusting effeminate male, both typical examples of the physiological degenerate.

It is this class that clamors for "higher education" for the woman; that crowds public halls, shouting for the freedom of woman and demanding all the prerogative of the man. It is these female androids who are insulated in the dark umbrage of ignorance and delusion regarding their negative nature, who are faddist, "ism"-ites, and mental roamers. Ideally mobile, they go from the laboratory to the convent, ever restless, continuously discontented, morbidly majestic at periods, hysterically forcible at times. They form sects and societies regardless of sense or science.

They demonstrate their early perverted mental growth by their present lack of reasoning powers. They form the victims of shrewder degenerates. They claim to know more about the science of medicine without study than the men who have devoted their lives to that science. They walk broadcast, superciliously flaunting our health laws and hygienic regulations in the faces of the assumed intelligent masses, and shout their incomprehensible jargon and blasphemous voicings from the portals of their money-making mosques.

## "THE SEXUAL PERVERT IN LIFE INSURANCE" (1906)

[Read before the American Association of Medical Examiners at Boston, June 4, 1906.[18]]

The practical side of the study of sex perversions is all I shall attempt to speak about. The subject is a broad one and enters into the domains of sociology, penology, sexual ethics and Christian ethics. It is a study for men of broad minds and decided sex characteristics, and is being well investigated to-day by such men.

While certain forms of abnormal sexual activities have been known under the names of perversion and inversion, the true significance of these terms does not always seem clear to the general practitioner.

My remarks to-day will be confined to the Invert, or the passive and active aspects of algolagnia,[19] and how such individual should be considered by the life insurance examiner.

Let me make it clear at the commencement that my statements refer only to the congenital invert, and not to those forms of sexual perversions that are the result of mental disease, senility, alcoholism, satiety, vitiated sensuality, and those vicious practices that are the effects of isolation and segregation of one sex.

When I speak of an invert I refer to an individual whose sexual instincts turn apparently towards his or her own sex. I say apparently, because we shall see that while the secondary sexual organs, as I shall call the anatomical organs in this paper, decides the sex in popular judgment, the primary or real sexual determinants are situated in the brain and functuate in the mind. So you see that in the congenital invert what we observe is in reality a normal sexual instinct rising in the psychic sexual centers, while the mere body of the individual resembles that of the opposite sex.

As in the lower animals, so in man, instances of imperfect sex differentiation are found, and in man to-day there seems to be an increase of a disharmonious growth between the development of sex instincts and sex organs. Whether this is due to some deficiency of nutrition in the embryo, or of otherwise incomplete processes of gestation, is undecided in my mind. However, I have a little working hypothesis of the cause, but not until we know something tangible concerning ante-natal pathology can the problem be solved.

When the first two cells of the potential embryo divide and active proliferation of fission commences, differentiation of cells soon takes place. This is followed by the setting apart of groups of cells to finally harmoniously develop into the visible foetus.

Now let any one group of somatic cells become distorted, overgrown or poorly nourished, when the child is born we get some form of physical deformity: a club foot, blindness, or perhaps idiocy, depending upon the group of cells affected. These conditions are recognized as due to no fault or sin of the unfortunate, and measures are taken to remedy the defect if possible. If the victim of this sport of cellular growth has to go through life limping, or with the use of one arm only, or sightless, he receives sympathy and the help of his fellow men. Now, probably analogous conditions go on in the growth and development of the sexual cells in the cortex, and the child is born with a sexual deformity, or a true development of the opposite sex feeling to what is expected from his secondary sex organs, the penis and testicles. As the full development of sex feeling is the last instinct to be demonstrated, the child is brought up according as its external sex organs determine its sex; and when, later on, sexual instincts commence to be active and the individual seeks for gratification one of his, apparently, own sex, he is ostracized, perhaps imprisoned, and forever on this earth damned by all men. If my hypothesis is correct the congenital invert is not in reality an invert, paradoxically as this may seem, but a normal being wrongly adorned with organs that have no rapport with this individual's life.

I have had a large number of these unfortunate and misunderstood persons under personal care and observation. They have been mostly of the intellectual class and of vocations that did not call for much social contact with the virile element of our life. They were lawyers—but this class were office workers, not pleaders at the bar—ministers, artists and musicians. Many others are found in vocations suited to their true sex: dressmakers, milliners, valets to women, and negative writers—that is writers without force, virility or originality, but beautifully precise.

My experience has shown me that the congenital invert comes from a neurotic family with a vitiated heredity. Many of the families' histories are hidden in a fog of secrecy, or else conditions pregnant with important facts to the examiner, are not to be obtained if there has been the least consciousness on the female side of any sexual abnormality, secret vices or even an inordinate sexual craving, for remember, in our present state of civilization women have been taught to be ashamed of a normal physiological attribute, hence, in sexual matters all women are liars.

You must always bear in mind that the invert or pervert will never disclose his condition and sufferings unless he is certain that the physician will recognize his true deformity and not consider him a person to scorn and avoid as a moral leper. These unfortunate beings seem to realize that they were the last of a family of vitiated vitality, and that Nature, well knowing there was not enough energy to make a man or woman out of the started embryo, hesitated in sex determination after the anatomical growth had gotten well on its way, and either as a joke or as a lesson gave the centers in the brain a growth direction the antithesis of the sex organs. Possibly this abnormality may be one of Nature's methods of terminating a family and also presenting an object lesson.

Whenever we find this condition of non-correlation between the sexual system and its corresponding brain centers we should expect to find social habits and environments out of harmony with the rest of mankind.

The sexual invert lives a life alone, seldom having any male companions and only distrust for women. Active participation in sexual indulgence depends upon the physical and psychical temperament of each individual, opportunities and self-control, in fact, in these matters not differing from one whose brain centers and anatomical organs functuate harmoniously.

As the sexual inverts live a life apart from the rest of mankind they become morbid, introspective and suspicious. They read all the literature on sex matters possible to obtain, and many are better informed on this subject than the average physician. If the sexual desire is strong—and often it is impelling—they become the victims of blackmailers, sometimes form rabid and insane desires for a certain man, an hysterical form of sensuality where caution is inhibited and desire overpowers all sense of danger. The male invert only seeks the strong, virile male; the rough, muscular man, as we would expect from our studies of the cause of the apparent inversion. There are instances, not very frequent, where an invert forms the acquaintance of the individual who has the other sex inversion, the anatomical woman but the male brain, and these two live together.

The career of the invert is usually shortened by early death, suicide being the end of many and making up some of those sad terminations of life that are a puzzle to friends and family. The whole life of a congenital invert is one of fear and horror of exposure and the agonizing dread that the sexual impulse will at some fatal moment overpower them. This secretive life, this constant fear of self, grafted to an unstable, nervous organization soon develops mental morbidity and a peculiar form of melancholia. Frequently dipso-mania and other forms of narcotic mania demonstrate the congenital insta-bility. In these cases the individual loses his caution, exposure is inevitable and when the unfortunate realizes the horror of it all comes disappearance or suicide. Others struggle hard against Nature's insult and the suspicious jibes of casual associates. This latter class move on from town to town giving up lucrative positions without any apparent cause that the general public can discover. These are mostly those who have adopted the vocations of teaching, some reaching to eminent positions when they are suddenly placed in that category of "men who drop out of sight." These individuals seldom partici-pate in active or passive algolagny, but perhaps on account of this unnatural and abnormal abstinence with the fearful struggle they constantly maintain to suppress the woman in their bodies, they break down in health and at forty are on the physical decline, many dying from affections that a normal being would conquer. With the exception of this class, forty is the age where the normal man commences to do good brain work, and if he has spent the years up to forty in getting muscle and stamina the next twenty-five years of his life should be his mental harvest.

The man of fifty years of age requires special consideration, and the exam-ination in his case should be critical and prolonged. In addition to the dan-ger of arterio-sclerosis and its sequelae[20] is the potential danger that afflu-ence and the responsibility of some great business enterprise may induce unusual effort out of proportion to the applicant's power of endurance. There is also the danger that the abandonment of a business career for a life of leisure may favor dissipation with its attendant predisposition to excesses and its increased liability to venereal infection.

Much benefit to the company is derived if the medical examiner knows the applicant and his surroundings. On one occasion I refused to examine a gen-tleman who was to my knowledge subjected to serious business complications and who had had frequent attacks of some acute illness of variable duration, which incapacitated him for a week or so at a time. I knew no details but I knew the conditions under which he lived. He secured a policy of $50,000 in another company, and died of what was called angina pectoris[21] shortly after paying the second premium.

The medical examiner must be alert to the possibilities and if the chances of increased risk are apparent or probable his decision must be given with due reservation. He cannot be a detective but he can and must realize the meaning of increased liability. He must know what the moral hazard means, in all its relationships, and he must appraise its value in his estimation of the risk.

From what I have said you will all readily agree that physically the inverts are poor specimens of humanity. Their whole psychic life being feminine, muscular exercise is repugnant to them, hence at about forty years of age we find them with fat, flabby bodies that are unable to cope with the rush of strong, developed males, and as the anatomical conditions prevent the inverts from living and association with those of their real sex, moroseness and recklessness soon sends them on a career towards death.

The invert who does not meet with violent assaults or succumb to alcohol and other drugs develops some organic disease. These diseases are in no way directly connected with abnormal sexual life, but indirectly destroys the invert through that individual's physical inability to withstand any attack from invading bacilli or autotoxic material. Many of these cases die from tuberculosis.

What I say of the male invert applies in the reverse equally as well to the female invert.

What I have said concerning the male invert does not always hold true of the female invert. In the female invert mentally and psychically we have a man with all the powerful desires of a man; hence, while anatomically and socially we have a woman, the physical development will be such as to make the individual a good risk, and also, being classed as a female, however much her masculine tendencies may be objectionable, she is usually free from personal assaults, and the alcohol that she drinks seems to have a better physiological absorbing surface.

*Contemporary with Claude Hartland (see 303–10 above), Earl Lind's autobiography describes homosexual life at the turn of the century. Lind, however, was not so fortunate as to find a ready publisher, and his manuscript was not printed until 1918 by the* New York Medico-Legal Journal. *In 1922 he produced a sequel,* The Female-Impersonators. *Lind used other pseudonyms ("Ralph Werther," "Jennie June"), and even today his true identity—again, like Hartland's—has not been recovered. In a Jekyll–Hyde existence, he held a professional job by day but apparently haunted the New York underworld by night. This excerpt reflects the attitudes of the medical and religious institutions that he was up against, contrasting his acknowledged "femininity" with his bravery and candor in telling his story.*

## FROM *THE AUTOBIOGRAPHY OF AN ANDROGYNE* (1918)

[...] For several days following I suffered from shame and remorse. In order, if possible, to be cured of my abnormality, I now resolved to consult a specialist in venereal diseases, because at that time I believed my ailment came under that head. I was led to go to Dr. Prince A. Morrow, then the leading specialist in that line in New York City, who declared that either castration or marriage would be a sure cure for my abnormal passion! How many inverts have followed such advice of a physician, and seeking a cure in marriage, have been plunged into insanity or suicide, either on the eve of marriage, or soon after! Individuals like myself are women mentally. How is one woman to marry another, unless indeed one of the pair be a gynander,[22] when marriage *de facto*[23] often takes place. I could never think of tying myself to a wife until I felt myself to be a man.

Not satisfied, I immediately consulted another medical-college professor, this time an alienist,[24] Dr. Robert S. Newton. Both drugs and electrical stimulation of the brain and spinal cord were tried. Hypnotism was attempted unsuccessfully. During the first month of treatment, I excluded from my mind all thoughts of sexual admiration. Then, though I continued to struggle against them, they would occasionally be present in the stream of thought for a few days, when with a fresh dedication of myself to God and to a life of self-renunciation, I would again completely banish them for another half-month.

After several months' treatment, I was rendered almost a physical and nervous wreck by the powerful drugs administered, but my amorous desires showed no change. I now repeatedly appealed for castration. I argued that

Nature had designed me to be a fille de joie[25]—the worst fate possible as I then believed—and that castration alone could save me from it. But the answer was that I might in later years regret such a measure. I had recently read in a medical journal of a man similarly but not identically afflicted who was placed in possession of the normal procreative instinct through castration. During these months I had made diligent search at the library of the New York Academy of Medicine for light on my abnormality, and discovered a number of articles in American and foreign journals bearing on it.

During this course of treatment occurred one of the crises of my life. I had been appointed a delegate to a student's missionary convention in another city, and was assigned to a room with a rather athletic student from another college. The first night, after he had fallen asleep, I left the bed and lay on the floor, but was driven back by the cold. All possible alternatives were out of the question. Previous to that day, I had not known how I would have to pass the night. The chances were good that I would be assigned to a room alone, or else have an unattractive bed-fellow inasmuch as nine out of ten religious and studious adolescents were sexually repulsive, although highly esteemed as friends. Possibly I was cold to them because I myself am of a religious and studious disposition, as well as deficient in physical stamina, as they also are inclined to be.

I lay awake the whole night, but during the last half was in a sort of delirium. I partially yielded. The next morning, before several other students, my bed-fellow spoke sarcastically of me, evidently intending to visit on me what he considered to be deserved punishment. I was crushed by reason of shame, and they never saw me again, as I left by the next train. At the time I wrote in my diary:

"What have I ever done that God should make me suffer so? I feel that my abnormality bars me out of the ministry, the profession of my choice, and most likely out of all other professions. I feel that this passion is going to wreck my life, and never permit me to make any return to my parents for all they have done for me. I have no hope for the future. In the convention, while I would be singing, I was in thought hacking my body to pieces with a sword, or piercing my breast with a dagger. My continuous prayer was:

'Father, Father, hear my humble cry,
While on others thou art smiling,
    Do not pass me by!'

"The convention, to me, was a lesson in resignation. The other young men were divinely brought there to be inspired with the Holy Spirit, to be instructed in regard to missionary fields and methods, to be called to preach the

Gospel among those who sit in darkness; but I was brought there to learn the lesson of resignation in affliction, to experience the crushing to the earth by the mighty hand of God, to be tried like Isaac[26] to see whether I am willing to be morally slain in my youth in a way which seems inexplicable. I have been preparing myself to become a foreign missionary, having had this career in mind from childhood; but God and Nature have undoubtedly destined me to be a fille de joie. When a child of nine or ten years, although I had not learned that there were in the world such persons as fallen women, I often aspired to be a young woman, and to be a fallen one at that. I have resisted my fate with all the powers of my will and of my religious nature, but you cannot dam Niagara."

Not long afterwards I wrote: "Two ways open before me: one of sensual gratification, unrighteousness, falsehood, hypocrisy, dishonor; the other of blessing to the poor and the afflicted, a life which is holy and worthy of the good name given to it, a life which promises to my dear ones, on my account, more of health, happiness, and honor."

Shortly after writing the above, I brought the course of medical treatment to an abrupt termination. I would have continued longer if I had shown any improvement. I had lost all faith in the physician's ability to benefit me. Seeing that the science of medicine held out no hope, I felt more than ever that I was irresponsible for my abnormal sexual nature.

\*\*\*

Over five months after my previous visit, I again found myself on Mulberry Street, corner of Grand. I have always suspected that I was incited to this particular quest by an aphrodisiac. On or about that day, my physician administered a new drug. He probably hoped it would incite me to seek normal relations, but it acted along the line of my peculiar instincts.

Walking northward on the west side of the street, I encountered a mixed group of Italian and Irish "sports" of foreign parentage between sixteen and twenty-one years of age seated or standing around the portal of a warehouse. I timidly addressed them: "I am looking for a friend named Red Mike. Do any of you know him?"

One of them replied that he had just seen him up the street. Proceeding in that direction, I stopped occasionally to make the same inquiry of other adolescents. After walking several blocks in vain, I returned to the "gang" at the warehouse's portal, and asked: "Do you mind if I sit down to rest here? I am tired and lonesome. I have not been in the city long and don't know any one."

"Where did yez come from?"

"Philadelphia. I couldn't get any work there, so I came here."

It was not long before Red Mike happened to stroll by and recognized me even before I did him. An hour now passed, while they smoked and drank, hiding the beer-pail whenever a policeman went by. I had no desire to join in the drinking and smoking, and indeed up to my middle forties, when this autobiography goes to press, have never had any desire to learn to smoke, although having a few times put the lighted cigarette of a paramour in my mouth. I have always considered myself too feminine to smoke. Moreover, all my life I have been practically a total abstainer from alcoholic beverages.

But I reclined in the arms of one after another, covering face, neck, hands, arms, and clothing with kisses, while they caressed me and called me pet-names. I was supremely happy. For the first time in my life I learned about the fairie inmates of the lowest dives. They proposed to install me in one. I told them the story of my own life, only with such variations from the truth as were necessary for my own protection. We sang plantation songs, "Old Black Joe," "Uncle Ned," etc. These they had learned from Bixby's "Home Songs," published in that very neighborhood by the well-known shoe-blacking firm as an advertisement. I sang with them in the mock soprano or falsetto that fairies employ, trying to imitate the voice of a woman. Singing in this voice was not a novelty to me, as I had previously at times aped the warbling of a woman instinctively.

At the end of an hour, we adjourned down an alley, where the drinking and love-making continued even more intensely. After I had refused their repeated solicitations, one of them grasped my throat tightly to prevent any outcry and threw me down, while another removed part of my clothing, appropriating whatever of value he found in my pockets. With my face in the dust, and half-suffocated by the one ruffian's tight grip on my throat, I moaned and struggled with all my might, because of the excruciating pain. But in their single thought to experience an animal pleasure, they did not heed my moans and broken entreaties to spare me the suffering they were inflicting. For two months afterward I suffered pain at every step because of fissures and lacerations about the anus.

When finally released, terror-stricken and with only half my clothing, I rushed out through the alley and down Mulberry Street, and did not halt until I reached what I considered a safe refuge on brightly lighted Grand Street. Breathless and exhausted, I seated myself on the curb. "I am cured of my slumming," I said to myself. "God's will be done. It is His hand which has brought this about, in order to drive me back to the path of virtue. Truly the Lord ruleth in all things."

Because of my exhausted condition, I remained seated for several minutes. In the meantime, two of my assailants had followed me up, and expressed their regret that one of their number had stolen my cap and coat, promising to get them back, and assuring me of their friendly feelings. "You are only a baby," they said, "and so we will fight for you and protect you."

I was so touched by their gallantry, so enamoured of them, and so sure that the assault was not committed through malevolence, that I accompanied them back to our first meeting place on the warehouse steps. I still had great fear of violence at their hands—rape, not a beating—but I was powerfully drawn toward them. Fellatio was welcome; paedicatio, horrible to my moral sense, and physically, accompanied by excruciating pain. The "gang" received me kindly, petted and soothed me as one would a peevish baby, which I resembled in my actions, fretting and sobbing in happiness as I rested my head against their bodies. To lie in the bosom of these sturdy young manual laborers, all of whom were goodlooking and approximately my own age, was the highest earthly happiness I had yet tasted. With all my money gone, and cap and coat stolen besides, I finally had to walk home, a distance of several miles. Obtaining my keys in their hiding place, I succeeded in reaching my room without attracting attention.

The next day I wrote in my journal: "What a strange thing is life! Mephistopheles last night carried me through one of the experiences through which he carried Faust[27].... My carnal nature was aroused as never before. I groaned in despair. Never before in all my experience have I seen such a conflict between the flesh and the spirit.... How like an animal is man! Thus God has seen fit to make him."

A few days later I again wrote: "My present psychical state is most strange. I cannot yet repent of my conduct last Friday night, yet on the Sunday following I had one of the happiest experiences of nearness to God that I ever had. That afternoon I presented the Gospel in love for my Savior and for perishing souls. I have in my heart an intense desire to save from their lives of sin those in whose company I was Friday night, especially my Bill, so young, and yet so deep in sin. I want to rescue him, and make of him a strong educated champion for Christ. My heart yearns to carry blessings and peace to all those who are suffering in the slums of New York."

In a letter received shortly afterward from a venerable doctor of divinity and former pastor, whom for years I made my confidant, he expressed his judgment of my conduct as follows: "I believe God will overlook in you what He would not in others."

The judgment of the alienist, to whom also I confided the occurrences, was approximately as follows: "It was a physical impossibility for you to have withstood longer. The only thing for you to do is to follow out your instincts in moderation. If you do not, you will continue to be a nervous wreck, and may even become insane. The majority of men can live celibate lives without suffering in mind or body, but you are extraordinarily amorous, and celibacy with you is out of the question. Only don't go into the slums any more. Confide in some stalwart young man of your own class. You run great risk of being killed, or at least contracting disease, in running around after strangers in the slums." [...]

**Notes**

1   Thomas Sargent Perry was Peirce's student in 1863 and the two became lifelong friends. Later, as a Harvard professor, Perry corresponded with Symonds, and it was through Perry that Peirce's defense of homosexuality found its way into *Sexual Inversion*. For more, see Katz's revelatory *Love Stories: Sex between Men before Homosexuality* (Chicago: U of Chicago P, 2001), 308–16.

2   A physician accepted by a court of law as an expert on the mental competence of principals or witnesses; also an early name for psychiatrist.

3   *Alienist and Neurologist* 25.1 (Feb. 1904): 68.

4   From "The Fire-Worshippers" by Thomas Moore (1779–1852).

5   See Sharon O'Brien's well-written biography, *Willa Cather: The Emerging Voice* (New York: Oxford UP, 1987), which fully discusses the implications of Cather's homosexuality.

6   For a compelling interpretation of this idea, see Claude J. Summers' essay, "'A Losing Game in the End': Aestheticism and Homosexuality in Cather's 'Paul's Case,'" *Modern Fiction Studies* 36 (Spring 1990): 103–19.

7   Actually, Jean-François Raffaelli (1850–1924), a French artist whose drypoint engravings made him famous, particularly in his studies of Parisian life.

8   Martin Rico y Ortega (1833–1908), Spanish artist and engraver.

9   Augustus Caesar (63 BC–14 AD), Roman emperor, was represented by many busts; and the armless marble statue of the Venus di Milo (ca. second century BC) is one of the Louvre's most famous possessions. The implication here is that the gallery that Paul visits, with its "cast-room," is full of copies, not originals.

10  According to the classic *Arabian Nights*, a fisherman finds a bottle that contains an angry genie trapped inside. Facing imminent destruction, the fisherman is nonetheless granted a wish, whereupon he tricks the genie by asking how such a great genie could fit inside such a small container—whereupon the genie, trapped once again, must do as the fisherman bids.

11  Goodbye (German).

12  George Washington (1732-99) was the first president of the United States. John Calvin (1509–64) was the Protestant religious reformer whose ideas strongly influenced early American Puritans. Clearly both represent the culture Paul has been brought up in.

13  "Suspicious," perhaps because it is the color of wine.

14  *Martha* (1847) is a romantic comic opera by Friedrich Flowtow, and *Rigoletto* (1851) is a melodramatic opera by Giuseppe Verdi.

15  "By the Beautiful Blue Danube" (1867) is a famous Viennese waltz by Johann Strauss Jr. (1825–99).

16  Oh, he will grow up something to be loved! (Latin).

17  I.e., virago; a loud-voiced, scolding woman; a woman of masculine strength or spirit (archaic).

18 This essay appears in a badly printed version, rife with spelling errors and lines out of place. I have corrected obvious errors.

19 Sexual pleasure derived from enduring and inflicting pain, as in masochism or sadism.

20 Arterio-sclerosis is a chronic disease in which thickening, hardening, and loss of elasticity of the arterial walls results in impaired blood circulation. "Sequelae" refers to the pathological condition resulting from it.

21 Severe paroxysmal pain in the chest associated with an insufficient supply of blood to the heart.

22 Woman-man (Greek); i.e., any female exhibiting masculinization; a hermaphrodite.

23 In fact, in reality (Latin).

24 Psychiatrist.

25 Female prostitute (French).

26 In the Bible, God tests the faith of Abraham by asking him to sacrifice his son Isaac, and then stops Abraham before the boy is slain (Genesis 22).

27 The chief character in a medieval legend, represented as selling his soul to the devil (Mephistopheles) in exchange for knowledge and power.

# PART TWELVE

# MEN IN GROUPS

# JOSIAH FLYNT WILLARD (1869–1907)

*A self-titled tramp authority, Josiah Flynt Willard (nephew of Frances Willard, the noted temperance reformer) left college to live the wandering life of a hobo, tramping around America and Europe. He began writing about his experiences in 1893, publishing several short essays for popular magazines, and books which found wide readership, such as* Tramping with Tramps: Studies and Sketches of Vagabond Life *(1893),* The Little Brother: A Story of Tramp Life *(1902), and* The Rise of Ruderick Clowd *(1903). In contributing this essay to Havelock Ellis and John Addington Symonds's* Sexual Inversion *(1897; see above, Professor X, 301–02) he introduced a side of tramp life that had not been studied before, adding to the literature of men in groups as well as vagabondage (quite a different view from Bliss Carman and Richard Hovey's joyous description of this term [see 270–75, above]).*

## HOMOSEXUALITY AMONG TRAMPS (1897)

I have made a rather minute study of the tramp class in the United States, England and Germany, but I know it best in the States. I have lived with the tramps there for eight consecutive months, besides passing numerous shorter periods in their company, and my acquaintance with them is nearly of ten years' standing. My purpose in going among them has been to learn about their life in particular and outcast life in general. This can only be done by becoming part and parcel of its manifestations.

There are two kinds of tramps in the United States—out-of-works and "hoboes." The out-of-works are not genuine vagabonds; they really want work and have no sympathy with the hoboes. The latter are the real tramps. They make a business of begging—a very good business too—and keep at it, as a rule, to the end of their days. Whisky and *Wanderlust*,[1] or the love of wandering, are probably the main causes of their existence; but many of them are discouraged criminals, men who have tried their hand at crime and find that they lack criminal wit. They become tramps because they find that life "on the road" comes the nearest to the life they hoped to lead. They have enough talent to do very well as beggars, better, generally speaking, than the men who have reached the road simply as drunkards; they know more about the tricks of the trade and are cleverer in thinking out schemes and stories. All genuine tramps in America are, however, pretty much the same, as far as manners and philosophy are concerned, and all are equally welcome at the "hang-out."[2] The class of society from which they are drawn is generally the very lowest of all, but there are some hoboes who have come from the very highest, and these latter are frequently as vicious and depraved as their less well-born brethren.

Concerning sexual inversion among tramps, there is a great deal to be said, and I cannot attempt to tell all I have heard about it, but merely to give a general account of the matter. Every hobo in the United States knows what "unnatural intercourse" means, talking about it freely, and, according to my finding, every tenth man practices it, and defends his conduct. Boys are the victims of this passion. The tramps gain possession of these boys in various ways. A common method is to stop for a while in some town, and gain acquaintance with the slum children. They tell these children all sorts of stories about life "on the road," how they can ride on the railways for nothing, shoot Indians, and be "perfeshunnels" (professionals), and they choose some boy who specially pleases them. By smiles and flattering caresses they let him know that the stories are meant for him alone, and before long, if the boy is a suitable subject, he smiles back just as slyly. In time he learns to think that he is the favorite of the tramp, who will take him on his travels, and he begins to plan secret meetings with the man. The tramp, of course, continues to excite his imagination with stories and caresses, and some fine night there is one boy less in the town. On the road the lad is called a "prushun,"³ and his protector a "jocker." The majority of prushuns are between ten and fifteen years of age, but I have known some under ten and a few over fifteen. Each is compelled by hobo law to let his jocker do with him as he will, and many, I fear, learn to enjoy his treatment of them. They are also expected to beg in every town they come to, any laziness on their part receiving very severe punishment.

How the act of unnatural intercourse takes place is not entirely clear; the hoboes are not agreed. From what I have personally observed I should say that it is usually what they call "leg work" (intercrural), but sometimes *immissio penis in anum*,⁴ the boy in either case lying on his stomach. I have heard terrible stories of the physical results to the boy of anal intercourse.

One evening, near Cumberland, Pennsylvania, I was an unwilling witness of one of the worst scenes that can be imagined. In company with eight hoboes, I was in a freight car attached to a slowly moving train. A colored boy succeeded in scrambling into the car, and when the train was well under way again he was tripped up and "seduced" (to use the hobo euphemism) by each of the tramps. He made almost no resistance, and joked and laughed about the business as if he had expected it. This, indeed, I find to be the general feeling among the boys when they have been thoroughly initiated. At first they do not submit, and are inclined to run away or fight, but the men fondle and pet them, and after a while they do not seem to care. Some of them have told me that they get as much pleasure out of the affair as the jocker does. Even little fellows under ten have told me this, and I have known them to willfully tempt their jockers to intercourse. What the pleasure consists in I cannot say. The youngsters themselves describe it as a delightful tickling sensation in the parts involved, and this is possibly all that it amounts to among the smallest lads. Those who have passed the age of puberty seem to be satisfied in pretty much the same way that the men are. Among the men the practice is decidedly one of passion. The majority of them prefer a prushun to a woman, and nothing is more severely judged than rape. One often reads in the newspapers that a woman has been assaulted by a tramp, but the perverted tramp is never the guilty party.

I believe, however, that there are a few hoboes who have taken to boys because women are so scarce "on the road." For every woman in hoboland there are a hundred men. That this disproportion has something to do with the popularity of boys is made clear by the following case: In a gaol, where I was confined for a month during my life in vagabondage, I got acquainted with a tramp who had the reputation of being a "sod" (sodomist). One day a woman came to the gaol to see her husband, who was awaiting trial. One of the prisoners said he had known her before she was married and had lived with her. The tramp was soon to be discharged and he inquired where the woman lived. On learning that she was still approachable, he looked her up immediately after his release, and succeeded in staying with her for nearly a month. He told me later that he enjoyed his life with her much more than his intercourse with boys. I asked him why he went with boys at all, and he replied, "'Cause there ain't women enough. If I can't get them I've got to have the other."

It is in gaols that one sees the worst side of this perversion. In the daytime the prisoners are let out into a long hall, and can do much as they please; at night they are shut up, two and even four in a cell. If there are any boys in the crowd, they are made use of by all who care to have them. If they refuse to submit, they are gagged and held down. The sheriff seldom knows what goes on, and for the boys to say anything to him would be suicidal. There is a criminal ignorance all over the States concerning the life in these gaols, and things go on that would be impossible in any well-regulated prison. In one of these places I once witnessed the fiercest fight I have ever seen among hoboes; a boy was the cause of it. Two men said they loved him, and he seemed to return the affection of both with equal desire. A fight with razors was suggested to settle who should have him.[5] The men prepared for action, while the crowd gathered round to watch. They slashed away for over half an hour, cutting each other terribly, and then their backers stopped them for fear of fatal results. The boy was given to the one who was hurt the least.

Jealousy is one of the first things one notices in connection with this passion. I have known men to withdraw entirely from the "hang-out" life simply to be sure that their prushuns were not touched by other tramps. Such attachments frequently last for years, and some boys remain with their first jockers until they are "emancipated."

Emancipation means freedom to "snare" some other boy, and make him submit as the other had been obliged to submit when younger. As a rule, the prushun is freed when he is able to protect himself. If he can defend his "honor" from all who come, he is accepted into the class of "old stagers," and may do as he likes. This is the one reward held out to prushuns during their apprenticeship. They are told that some day they can have a boy and use him as they have been used. Thus hoboland is always sure of recruits.

It is difficult to say how many tramps are sexually inverted. It is not even certainly known how many vagabonds there are in the country. I have stated in one of my papers on tramps that, counting the boys, there are between fifty and sixty thousand genuine hoboes in the United States. A vagabond in Texas who saw this statement wrote me that he considered my estimate too low. The newspapers have criticized it as too high, but they are unable to judge. If my figures are, as I believe, approximately correct, the sexually perverted tramps may be estimated at between five and six thousand; this includes men and boys.

I have been told lately by tramps that the boys are less numerous than they were a few years ago. They say that it is now a risky business to be seen with a boy, and that it is more profitable, as far as begging is concerned, to go without them. Whether this means that the passion is less fierce than it used to be, or that the men find sexual satisfaction among themselves, I cannot say definitely. But from what I know of their disinclination to adopt the latter alternative, I am inclined to think that the passion may be dying out somewhat. I am sure that women are not more numerous "on the road" than formerly, and that the change, if real, has not been caused by them. So much for my finding in the United States.

In England, where I have also lived with tramps for some time, I have found very little contrary sexual feeling. In Germany also, excepting in prisons and workhouses, it seems very little known among vagabonds. There are a few Jewish wanderers (sometimes peddlars) who are said to have boys in their company, and I am told that they use them as the hoboes in the United States use their boys, but I cannot prove this from personal observation. In England I have met a number of male tramps who had no hesitation in declaring their preference for their own sex, and particularly for boys, but I am bound to say that I have seldom seen them with boys; as a rule they were quite alone, and they seem to live chiefly by themselves.

It is a noteworthy fact that both in England and Germany there are a great many women "on the road," or, at all events, so near it that intercourse with them is easy and cheap. In Germany almost every town has its quarter of "Stadt-Schieze"[6]—women who sell their bodies for a very small sum. They seldom ask over thirty or forty pfennigs for a night, which is usually spent in the open air. In England it is practically the same thing. In all the large cities there are women who are glad to do business for three or four pence, and those "on the road" for even less.

The general impression made on me by the sexually perverted men I have met in vagabondage is that they are abnormally masculine. In their intercourse with boys they always take the active part. The boys have in some cases seemed to me uncommonly feminine, but not as a rule. In the main they are very much like other lads, and I am unable to say whether their liking for the inverted relationship is inborn or acquired. That it is, however, a genuine liking, in altogether too many instances, I do not in the least doubt. As such, and all the more because it is such, it deserves to be more thoroughly investigated and more reasonably treated.

# MORRIS SCHAFF (1840–1929)

*Schaff was a soldier in the Civil War, after graduating from West Point in 1862. He didn't fight on the battlefield but served in ordnance behind the scenes. He wrote several distinguished books about the War, The Battle of the Wilderness (1910), The Sunset of the Confederacy (1912), and a life of Jefferson Davis (1912). Having had a Southern roommate at West Point certainly highlighted the anguish of the War that pitted "brother against brother." "The army-environment does not so shut in the soldier from general external influences, and from contact with women. Yet the soldier, whether a general or of the file, in number-less examples is instinctively indifferent toward feminine beauty," says Edward Prime-Stevenson in* The Intersexes. *"Day-by-day comradeship, the night-life of an army-corps, in peace or war, are pervaded with a vague similisexual ambient. It would seem that, being himself so robustly made, there is no place in a soldier's heart, or sexual impulse, for anything not vehemently manly. Here advances the theory of the Uranian as a super-virile, not sub-virile, sex."[7] As an example in contemporary writing, Prime-Stevenson pinpoints the "many delicate suggestions of the uranian emotion" in Morris Schaff's graceful and sympathetic reminiscence of life in 1858 West Point, first published as a series of sketches for* The Atlantic Monthly. *"Especially in its elegiac passages, it is eloquent of the homosexual thrill in young hearts that beneath uniforms can beat so passionally for each other."[8] How visible this is to the modern reader is an open question. Would Schaff have been scandalized or gratified by such a suggestion?*

## FROM *THE SPIRIT OF OLD WEST POINT* (1907)

[...] During the release from quarters, when the recitations of the day ended, some would take a stroll around Flirtation Walk—beautiful and solemnly elevating, as through trees and from open spaces the eye fell on the river in the fading light of day, on the snow-covered, skyward-tending landscape and the worshiping hills—all waiting in religious peace, for the coming of the night—how I should love to ramble along it once more!—a few would go over to the inspiriting silence of the library; a small number, poor victims of athletics, would wrestle with parallel bars, etc., in the gymnasium; but the larger number would congregate in the fencing-hall and dance to music by members of the band. How often I sat with Comly—for dancing was not among our accomplishments—and watched the mazing couples, Rosser and Pelham, "Cam" Emory and Ames, Chambliss and Hoxton, Kent and Beaumont, Haines and Cushing, Dearing and Gillespie, Dupont and Farquhar, and many, many others! Yes, that was the way we were passing the time in that January of 1861, on the verge of the Civil War. [...]

[...].Yes, I wish that my class might meet again, and, drawing the benches under the elms into a circle not far from the evening gun, be once more the happy boys we were,—I am sure the old flag on the staff over us would ripple out joyfully,—and should Hardee and Reynolds come along arm in arm, as I know they would, we would all rise and give them a right-hand salute. And should old Bentz, the bugler, reappear off across the Plain, on the walk which he always followed when he blew the calls for chapel, we would motion to him to come over and join us and we would shake the hand of the dear old soldier well.

And now, as so often happened with my Uncle Toby when he described his sieges and war experiences, the reunion has become a reality and about all of the boys of the class who entered in 1858 are present. Moreno of Florida, with his soft, liquid Castilian eyes,—Senator Mallory, Confederate Secretary of the Navy, married his sister,—has brought along his guitar and is singing once more the sweet little Spanish song, "Luego al instante"; Dearing is about to give us "Dixie"; but who are those coming across the Plain—and who is that at their head, swinging his cap? It is "Jim" Rollins of Missouri! the sun is shining on his golden hair, the dimple is in his cheek, affection is glowing in his handsome face, and on his brow is the same old seal of the gentleman. We throw our arms around him, for he was the darling of us all. And upon my soul! here comes Van Buren, with all of his courtly good manners, the same to one and all, and there is a general cheer for Van. And here come Drake and Riddle and little Wetmore, who, if he had stayed, would have graduated at the head of our class,—in about every way he was the most brilliant youth I ever saw,—and here comes George McKee. I have a little book in which some of the men who resigned wrote their names as they came to bid me good-by; in it is McKee's, whose Kentucky mother stopped his resignation just in time. It is written on the blade of a savage-looking bowie-knife, with "Good-by, Morris, God bless you!" over it. Mac takes his place as of old in the very centre of the class, his distinguished, handsome face and black eyes lit up with all the old-time fervor as he greets us all. And here come Joe Blount and Lovejoy and little Jim Hamilton and Clayton and Semmes, and we are all hands round the dear Southerners. And who is that drawing near with that natural sweet smile? some one cries out, perhaps it is Gillespie or Burroughs. "Why, boys, that's Jasper Myers; make way for dear old Jasper!" and there isn't a hand that hasn't a heart in it as all the Class of 1858 welcome him again. "Hats off, men!" commands Mackenzie, the ablest, the manliest, the most distinguished among us all, "here comes Sep Sanderson." Sanderson fell between his guns at Pleasant Hill; and with tears in our eyes we hug the dear fellow who is blushing like a girl with modesty. And now West, who is sitting between McCrea and myself on the same bench, turns to me and asks, "Morris, where is Murray?" And I lean over and say, in low tones, "John, don't you know that he was captured the day Hood made his attack on Sherman's left at Atlanta, the day McPherson was killed? He died in one of your Southern prisons—and, John, they say he died hungry." Whereupon my impulsive old roommate rises, and with his high tenor voice calls the class to attention: "Men, we are all here but little Murray, and Morris tells me that he died in one of our Southern prisons. I offer this hope for the sake of the name of Southerners, that in all future wars in which our countrymen are involved, there will be no Andersonvilles or Salisburys." But before he can go a word further, Sanderson exclaims, "Let me add, for the sake of the name of Northerner, West, that there will never be another Elmira with its horrible mortality"; and, "No more Camp Mortons," shout Beebe and Fred James. The writer, who with a pensive heart leaned more than once on the fence that enclosed the Confederate burial-ground at Rock Island, the little head-boards in weather-worn ranks rising pleadingly out of the matted grass,—there are two thousand of them who hear no trumpets now,—the writer said, "And may there be no more Rock Islands, John." "Allow me to finish, men," exclaims the Georgian. "Let us, the Class of 1858, assembled at West Point, under the flagstaff, and in the presence of all that is sacred to the Christian and to the honor of the soldier and the gentleman, let us beg our countrymen who are to follow us to see to it that all who fall into their hands, no matter who the enemy may be, black or white, civilized or uncivilized, shall be treated with mercy; and that no prisoner of war shall ever die for want of food, or clothing, or kindness. War is horrible enough at best, let us appeal to the higher nature of mankind for its redemption so far as it may be from barbarity and from a cold indifference to the unfortunate. I think I can pledge to such a prayer every one who followed the Confederate flag with me." And every Southerner present responds, "We stand by you, West, on that sentiment." And hardly have they uttered their hearty assent, when, behold! out of a cloud comes Murray himself, escorted by angels who for a moment sing, "Peace on earth, good will toward men," around us ere they rise. And who is this standing just outside the circle, with a band of heavenly light across her brow! Behold! it is the spirit of the little chapel. "Young gentlemen, I heard your voices and I thought I'd join you all once more." And off go our caps as to a sweetheart, and she is escorted to the very midst.

# ALEXANDER BERKMAN (1870–1936)

*Berkman was a lifelong revolutionary. During the nationwide strike for the eight-hour workday in May 1886 a mass meeting held in Chicago to protest police action resulted in an explosion and riot which led to several deaths: The Hay-market Tragedy was to strongly influence the young Berkman. When he learned of Henry Clay Frick's order to break a Carnegie Steel strike in 1891—an event which resulted in the wounding and deaths of hundreds of dissident workers—Berkman attempted to assassinate Frick. The gun misfired, and Berkman was sentenced to 22 years in maximum security. During the 14 years he actually served, Berkman made a fantastic transition from being an ignorant homophobe to an individual who willingly fell in love with other inmates. Though some might term "prison homosexuality" as situational in nature,[9] Berkman's writing helps to elucidate a facet of sexuality that was little recognized, much less understood, in 1912.*

## FROM *PRISON MEMOIRS OF AN ANARCHIST* (1912)

Love's Dungeon Flower

Late in the evening the young prisoners are relieved. But Johnny remains, and his apprehensions reawaken. Repeatedly during the night he rouses me from my drowsy torpor to be reassured that he is not in danger of the gallows, and that he will not be tried for his assault. I allay his fears by dwelling on the Warden's aversion to giving publicity to the sex practices in prison, and remind the boy of the Captain's official denial of their existence. These things happen almost every week, yet no one has ever been taken to court from Riverside on such charges.

Johnny grows more tranquil, and we converse about his family history, talking in a frank, confidential manner. With a glow of pleasure, I become aware of the note of tenderness in his voice. Presently he surprises me by asking:

"Friend Aleck, what do they call you in Russian?"

He prefers the fond "Sashenka," enunciating the strange word with quaint endearment, then diffidently confesses dislike for his own name, and relates the story he had recently read of a poor castaway Cuban youth; Felipe was his name, and he was just like himself.

"Shall I call you Felipe?" I offer.

"Yes, please do, Aleck, dear; no, Sashenka."

The springs of affection well up within me, as I lie huddled on the stone floor, cold and hungry. With closed eyes, I picture the boy before me, with his delicate face, and sensitive, girlish lips.

"Good night, dear Sashenka," he calls.

"Good night, little Felipe."

In the morning we are served with a slice of bread and water. I am tormented by thirst and hunger, and the small ration fails to assuage my sharp pangs. Smithy still refuses to drink out of the Deputy's hand; his doors remain unopened. With tremulous anxiety Johnny begs the Deputy Warden to tell him how much longer he will remain in the dungeon, but Greaves curtly commands silence, applying a vile epithet to the boy.

"Deputy," I call, boiling over with indignation, "he asked you a respectful question. I'd give him a decent answer."

"You mind your own business, you hear?" he retorts.

But I persist in defending my young friend, and berate the Deputy for his language. He hastens away in a towering passion, menacing me with "what Smithy got."

Johnny is distressed at being the innocent cause of the trouble. The threat of the Deputy disquiets him, and he warns me to prepare. My cell is provided with a double entrance, and I am apprehensive of a sudden attack. But the hours pass without the Deputy returning, and our fears are allayed. The boy rejoices on my account, and brims over with appreciation of my intercession.

The incident cements our intimacy; our first diffidence disappears, and we become openly tender and affectionate. The conversation lags: we feel weak and worn. But every little while we hail each other with words of encouragement. Smithy incessantly paces the cell; the gnawing of the river rats reaches our ears; the silence is frequently pierced by the wild yells of the insane man, startling us with dread foreboding. The quiet grows unbearable, and Johnny calls again:

"What are you doing, Sashenka?"

"Oh, nothing. Just thinking, Felipe."

"Am I in your thoughts, dear?"

"Yes, kiddie, you are."

"Sasha, dear, I've been thinking, too."

"What, Felipe?"

"You are the only one I care for. I haven't a friend in the whole place."

"Do you care much for me, Felipe?"

"Will you promise not to laugh at me, Sashenka?"

"I wouldn't laugh at you."

"Cross your hand over your heart. Got it, Sasha?"

"Yes."

"Well, I'll tell you. I was thinking—how shall I tell you? I was thinking, Sashenka—if you were here with me—I would like to kiss you."

An unaccountable sense of joy glows in my heart, and I muse in silence.

"What's the matter, Sashenka? Why don't you say something? Are you angry with me?"

"No, Felipe, you foolish little boy."

"You are laughing at me."

"No, dear; I feel just as you do."

"Really?"

"Yes."

"Oh, I am so glad, Sashenka."


In the evening the guards descend to relieve Johnny; he is to be transferred to the basket, they inform him. On the way past my cell, he whispers: "Hope I'll see you soon, Sashenka." A friendly officer knocks on the outer blind door of my cell. "That you thar, Berkman? You want to b'have to th' Dep'ty. He's put you down for two more days for sassin' him."

I feel more lonesome at the boy's departure. The silence grows more oppressive, the hours of darkness heavier. [...]

"Passing the Love of Woman"

[...] For a moment George pauses. The veins of his forehead protrude, as if he is undergoing a severe mental struggle. Presently he says: "Aleck, I'm going to speak very frankly to you. I'm much interested in the subject. I'll give you my intimate experiences, and I want you to be just as frank with me. I think it's one of the most important things, and I want to learn all I can about it. Very little is known about it, and much less understood."

"About what, George?"

"About homosexuality. I have spoken of the second phase of onanism.[10] With a strong effort I overcame it. Not entirely, of course. But I have succeeded in regulating the practice, indulging in it at certain intervals. But as the months and years passed, my emotions manifested themselves. It was like a psychic awakening. The desire to love something was strong upon me. Once I caught a little mouse in my cell, and tamed it a bit. It would eat out of my hand, and come around at meal times, and by and by it would stay all evening to play with me. I learned to love it. Honestly, Aleck, I cried when it died. And then, for a long time, I felt as if there was a void in my heart. I wanted something to love. It just swept me with a wild craving for affection. Somehow the thought of woman gradually faded from my mind. When I saw my wife, it was just like a dear friend. But I didn't feel toward her sexually. One day, as I was passing in the hall, I noticed a young boy. He had been in only a short time, and he was rosy-cheeked, with a smooth little face and sweet lips—he reminded me of a girl I used to court before I married. After that I frequently surprised myself thinking of the lad. I felt no desire toward him, except just to know him and get friendly. I became acquainted with him, and when he heard I was a medical man, he would often call to consult me about the stomach trouble he suffered. The doctor here persisted in giving the poor kid salts and physics all the time. Well, Aleck, I could hardly believe it myself, but I grew so fond of the boy, I was miserable when a day passed without my seeing him. I would take big chances to get near him. I was rangeman then, and he was assistant on a top tier. We often had opportunities to talk. I got him interested in literature, and advised him what to read, for he didn't know what to do with his time. He had a fine character, that boy, and he was bright and intelligent. At first it was only a liking for him, but it increased all the time, till I couldn't think of any woman. But don't misunderstand me, Aleck; it wasn't that I wanted a 'kid.' I swear to you, the other youths had no attraction for me whatever; but this boy—his name was Floyd—he became so dear to me, why, I used to give him everything I could get. I had a friendly guard, and he'd bring me fruit and things. Sometimes I'd just die to eat it, but I always gave it to Floyd. And, Aleck—you remember when I was down in the dungeon six days? Well, it was for the sake of that boy. He did something, and I took the blame on myself. And the last time—they kept me nine days chained up— I hit a fellow for abusing Floyd: he was small and couldn't defend himself. I did not realize it at the time, Aleck, but I know now that I was simply in love with the boy; wildly, madly in love. It came very gradually. For two years I loved him without the least taint of sex desire. It was the purest affection I ever felt in my life. It was all-absorbing, and I would have sacrificed my life for him if he had asked it. But by degrees the psychic stage began to manifest all the expressions of love between the opposite sexes. I remember the first time he kissed me. It was early in the morning; only the rangemen were out, and I stole up to his cell to give him a delicacy. He put both hands between the bars, and pressed his lips to mine. Aleck, I tell you, never in my life had I experienced such bliss as at that moment. It's five years ago, but it thrills me every time I think of it. It came suddenly; I didn't expect it. It was entirely spontaneous: our eyes met, and it seemed as if something drew us together. He told me he was very fond of me. From then on we became lovers. I used to neglect my work, and risk great danger to get a chance to kiss and embrace him. I grew terribly jealous, too, though I had no cause. I passed through every phase of a passionate love. With this difference, though—I felt a touch of the old disgust at the thought of actual sex contact. That I didn't do. It seemed to me a desecration of the boy, and of my love for him. But after a while that feeling also wore off, and I desired sexual relation with him. He said he loved me enough to do even that for me, though he had never done it before. He hadn't been in any reformatory, you know. And yet, somehow I couldn't bring myself to do it; I loved the lad too much for it. Perhaps you will smile, Aleck, but it was real, true love. When Floyd was unexpectedly transferred to the other block, I felt that I would be the happiest man if I could only touch his hand again, or get one more kiss. You—you're laughing?" he asks abruptly, a touch of anxiety in his voice.

"No, George. I am grateful for your confidence. I think it is a wonderful thing; and, George—I had felt the same horror and disgust at these things, as you did. But now I think quite differently about them."

"Really, Aleck? I'm glad you say so. Often I was troubled—is it viciousness or what, I wondered; but I could never talk to any one about it. They take everything here in such a filthy sense. Yet I knew in my heart that it was a true, honest emotion."

"George, I think it a very beautiful emotion. Just as beautiful as love for a woman. I had a friend here; his name was Russell; perhaps you remember him. I felt no physical passion toward him, but I think I loved him with all my heart. His death was a most terrible shock to me. It almost drove me insane."

Silently George holds out his hand.

**Notes**

1   The irresistible impulse to travel (German).
2   This is the home of the fraternity. Practically it is any corner where they can lay their heads; but, as a rule, it is either a lodging-house, a freight car, or a nest in the grass near the railway watering-tank [Flynt's note].
3   This term for a hobo's boy companion, the origin of which is obscure, also crept into prison and homosexual slang as well.
4   I.e., anal intercourse (Latin).
5   All hoboes carry razors, both for shaving and for defense. Strange to say, they succeed in smuggling them into gaols, as they are never searched thoroughly [Flynt's note].
6   This word is of Hebrew origin, and means girl (*Mädchen*) [Flynt's note].
7   *Intersexes*, 187.
8   *Intersexes*, 209–210.
9   See Regina G. Kunzel's essay "Situating Sex: Prison Sexual Culture in the Mid-Twentieth-Century United States," *GLQ: A Journal of Lesbian and Gay Studies* 8.3 (2002): 253–70.
10  Sexual self-abuse.

PART THIRTEEN

TO YOU ALONE

# Herman Melville (1819–1891)

*Melville is best known for his novels of the sea, starting with* Typee *(1846), his most popular work, and including the monumental* Moby-Dick *(1851), his masterpiece, which he dedicated to his friend Nathaniel Hawthorne. When he first met Hawthorne in the summer of 1850, Melville was as one struck by lightning. Recognizing the dark side of genius in the older, successful author, he developed an extremely close bond with Hawthorne—a "fraternity of feeling"—and they shared conversations, meetings, and letters over the course of several years. The friendship cooled about two years later, probably at Hawthorne's retreat from the younger man's intensity. There is some suggestion of this in Hawthorne's portrayal of the relationship between the two heroes in his novel* The Blithedale Romance *(1852), where Hollingsworth (Melville) and Coverdale (Hawthorne) face each other:*

> *It seemed his intention to say no more. But, after he had quite broken off, his deep eyes filled with tears, and he held out both his hands to me.*
>
> *"Coverdale," he murmured, "there is not the man in this wide world, whom I can love as I could you. Do not forsake me!"*
>
> *As I look back upon this scene, through the coldness and dimness of so many years, there is still a sensation as if Hollingsworth had caught hold of my heart, and were pulling it towards him with an almost irresistible force. It is a mystery to me, how I withstood it. But, in truth, I saw in his scheme of philanthropy nothing but what was odious. A loathsomeness that was to be forever in my daily work! A great, black ugliness of sin, which he proposed to collect out of a thousand human hearts, and that we should spend our lives in an experiment of transmuting it into virtue! Had I but touched his extended hand, Hollingsworth's magnetism would perhaps have penetrated me with his own conception of all these matters. But I stood aloof. I fortified myself with doubts whether his strength of purpose had not been too gigantic for his integrity, impelling him to trample on considerations that should have been paramount to every other.*

*There has been much speculation on the nature of this relationship.[1] We will never know for certain, but it is true that several of Melville's letters (none from Hawthorne survive) evoke the joy at finding what Edward Prime-Stevenson would later term "the friendship which is love, the love which is friendship." This has suggested to many readers an intensity beyond the adoration of romantic friendship—at least on Melville's part.*

# Two Letters to Nathaniel Hawthorne (1851)

July 22 1851

My dear Hawthorne:

This is not a letter, or even a note—but only a passing word said to you over your garden gate. I thank you for your easy-flowing long letter (received yesterday) which flowed through me, and refreshed all my meadows, as the Housatonic—opposite me—does in reality. I am now busy with various things—not incessantly though; but enough to require my frequent tinkerings; and this is the height of the haying season, and my nag is dragging me home his winter's dinners all the time. And so, one way and another, I am not yet a disengaged man; but shall be, very soon. Meantime, the earliest good chance I get, I shall roll down to you, my good fellow, seeing we—that is, you and I,—must hit upon some little bit of vagabondism,[2] before Autumn comes. Graylock—we must go and vagabondize there. But ere we start, we must dig a deep hole, and bury all Blue Devils, there to abide till the Last Day.

Goodbye, [his X mark].

November [17?] 1851

My Dear Hawthorne,—

People think that if a man has undergone any hardship, he should have a reward; but for my part, if I have done the hardest possible day's work, and then come to sit down in a corner and eat my supper comfortably—why, then I don't think I deserve any reward for my hard day's work—for am I not now at peace? Is not my supper good? My peace and my supper are my reward, my dear Hawthorne. So your joy-giving and exultation-breeding letter is not my reward for my ditcher's work with that book, but is the good goddess's bonus over and above what was stipulated—for not one man in five cycles, who is wise, will expect appreciative recognition from his fellows, or any one of them. Appreciation! Recognition! Is love appreciated? Why, ever since Adam, who has got to the meaning of this great allegory—the world? Then we pygmies must be content to have our paper allegories but ill comprehended. I say your appreciation is my glorious gratuity. In my proud, humble way,—a shepherd-king,—I was lord of a little vale in the solitary Crimea; but you have now given me the crown of India. But on trying it on my head, I found it fell down on my ears, notwithstanding their asinine length—for it's only such ears that sustain such crowns.

Your letter was handed me last night on the road going to Mr. Morewood's, and I read it there. Had I been at home, I would have sat down at once and answered it. In me divine magnanimities are spontaneous and instantaneous—catch them while you can. The world goes round, and the other side comes up. So now I can't write what I felt. But I felt pantheistic then—your heart beat in my ribs and mine in yours, and both in God's. A sense of unspeakable security is in me this moment, on account of your having understood the book. I have written a wicked book,[3] and feel spotless as the lamb. Ineffable socialities are in me. I would sit down and dine with you and all the gods in old Rome's Pantheon. It is a strange feeling—no hopefulness is in it, no despair. Content—that is it; and irresponsibility; but without licentious inclination. I speak now of my profoundest sense of being, not of an incidental feeling.

Whence come you, Hawthorne? By what right do you drink from my flagon of life? And when I put it to my lips—lo, they are yours and not mine. I feel that the Godhead is broken up like the bread at the Supper, and that we are the pieces. Hence this infinite fraternity of feeling. Now, sympathizing with the paper, my angel turns over another page. You did not care a penny for the book. But, now and then as you read, you understood the pervading thought that impelled the book—and that you praised. Was it not so? You were archangel enough to despise the imperfect body, and embrace the soul. Once you hugged the ugly Socrates because you saw the flame in the mouth, and heard the rushing of the demon,—the familiar,—and recognized the sound; for you have heard it in your own solitudes.

My dear Hawthorne, the atmospheric skepticisms steal into me now, and make me doubtful of my sanity in writing you thus. But, believe me, I am not mad, most noble Festus![4] But truth is ever incoherent, and when the big hearts strike together, the concussion is a little stunning. Farewell. Don't write a word about the book. That would be robbing me of my miserly delight. I am heartily sorry I ever wrote anything about you—it was paltry. Lord, when shall we be done growing? As long as we have anything more to do, we have done nothing. So, now, let us add Moby Dick to our blessing, and step from that. Leviathan is not the biggest fish;—I have heard of Krakens.[5]

This is a long letter, but you are not at all bound to answer it. Possibly, if you do answer it, and direct it to Herman Melville, you will missend it—for the very fingers that now guide this pen are not precisely the same that just took it up and put it on this paper. Lord, when shall we be done changing? Ah! it's a long stage, and no inn in sight, and night coming, and the body cold. But with you for a passenger, I am content and can be happy. I shall leave the world, I feel, with more satisfaction for having come to know you. Knowing you persuades me more than the Bible of our immortality.

What a pity, that, for your plain, bluff letter, you should get such gibberish! Mention me to Mrs. Hawthorne and to the children, and so, good-by to you, with my blessing.

Herman.

P.S. I can't stop yet. If the world was entirely made up of Magians,[6] I'll tell you what I should do. I should have a paper-mill established at one end of the house, and so have an endless riband of foolscap[7] rolling in upon my desk;

and upon that endless riband I should write a thousand—a million—billion thoughts, all under the form of a letter to you. The divine magnet is on you, and my magnet responds. Which is the biggest? A foolish question—they are *One.*

H.


P.P.S. Don't think that by writing me a letter, you shall always be bored with an immediate reply to it—and so keep both of us delving over a writing-desk eternally. No such thing! I sh'n't always answer your letters, and you may do just as you please.

# FRANCIS DAVIS MILLET (1846–1912)

*F.D. Millet was a painter renowned in his day, who enjoyed a distinguished and successful career. He was still a student in Italy, however, when he wrote these letters to Charles Warren Stoddard (see 93–103), with whom he lived in Venice through the winter of 1874–75. The fickle Stoddard left him there to continue his travel and writing, although Millet clearly wanted to continue their liaison. Millet later married but the friendship with Stoddard endured to the end of his life. Stoddard's papers included a sheaf of Millet's 38 letters, now in the possession of Syracuse University Library. They give us an intimate glimpse into the lives of two same-sex-loving men in the 1870s, offering a touching "close encounter" with a hidden side of the nineteenth century. Jonathan Ned Katz discusses these letters more fully in his revealing book* Love Stories. *Three years after Stoddard's death, Millet sailed on the maiden voyage of the* Titanic. *He was not one of the survivors.*

## LETTERS TO CHARLES WARREN STODDARD (1875)[8]

Ubi Bohemia Fuit[9]
Monday May 10 [1875]
Dear Old Chummeke:—
Mrs Harris and the perambulating corpse, the Dr, have just gone away and the old lady charged me to give you a scolding for not calling to say adieu. Please consider the scolding delivered. The time is 6 p.m. and 36 hours ago I was reading your letter from Pisa, having mailed previously one to you at Livorno enclosing an envelope from Paris directed to you in a feminine hand; all of which speriamo nella sanctissima[10] etc etc you will receive in due time.

Now I haven't got so doggoned much to say because I let out a bit in my first letter and can't possibly duplicate it, simply because I am once more a complete Venetian.

I have seen the Adamses several times. Donny is indignant because you neither left your photo, nor your adieux. Mrs A. is calm and collected. I told them that I had named the new dog Charles Warren Stoddard Venus, that it wasn't that kind of a dog but it was not a question of sex but of appropriateness. By the way, the pup has developed great natural talent for imitation. Whenever a bugle sounds or a whistle blows, he howls in the same key and does it splendidly.

"Listen to the Mocking Dog" etc etc

What do you suppose induced Mrs Harris to come down. She asks me to sit up tonight with a sick man. She doesn't consider that I have worked ten long hours today having transferred my cartoon to my canvas etc. But of course I cant well refuse to do such a service because I may sometime be in need myself—to look at it selfishly. She said she had never read anything of yours. I asked if she hadn't read the book[11] Eh..r..r..no. "Well you may take it"—"From what they say" she said "I don't think I should care to read it"—a maiden blush mantling her brow. I had given her the volume and she handed it back to me after a sly glance into it where she saw several naked figures dancing. She positively considers it immoral. Probably Miss Arbesser has put ideas in Mrs H's head.

Two women have been here today who are going to live [in] the house. They want to come in on the first of June and occupy our spare rooms. Can you believe that I refused this offer? I did 'pon honor. Tom sleeps in your place now and fills it all up—that is, the material space he occupies crowding me out of bed very often.

I've just had a letter from Jackson. He has seen your Padua letter and admires it. He is running the Herald office in London now. Call on him. Wetherbee has at last written. Both he, Chacu[?] and myself are refused of course. Sic transit gloria.[12]

If you see Joaquin[13] give him my love. I shall certainly be in Lunnun by July 10 or 15. & hope you will manage to stay.

Miss you? Bet your life. Put yourself in my place. It isn't the one who goes away who misses it is he who stays. Empty chair, empty bed, empty house. But nuf ced for tonight I hope to hear immediately on your arrival.

I call you chummeke diminutive of chum for you are already "chum" but have never been chummeke before. Flemish you know.

So, my dear old cuss, with lots of love I am thine—as you need not be told.

Frank.


Ubi Bohemia Fuit
May 26 1875
My dear Charlie:—
Your letter from Paris came safely and broke a long silence much to my joy. Your Anabasis[14] must have been full of interest in fact too much so for I'm sorry you failed to discover the wonders and beauties of Avignon. Paris with all the young artists sometimes comes up in my mind to tempt me to settle there and then I turn to my work and thank my stars that I am away from that motley crowd. You know there are so many fellows there I could not endure and would still have to meet that I should be in constant hot water all around. Nevertheless I shall pass one season there in the future. I'm glad you liked Woodward he and I are sympathetic—or were.

I'm writing this in a first class doublebarrelled thunderstorm and at the end of a terrible sciroco[15] day one of about 30 we have had in succession. I have been at work like a Trojan and have my big canvas covered up and in a fair way to be completed by July 1st. That's why I don't feel like writing. Have been posing two small cusses—the naked ones—together this p.m. and between the scirocco, the flash of lightning boys and the consciousness that in trying to paint the mercurial little cusses I have nearly ruined what good there was on the canvas before. This thunderstorm has just come in time to relieve me I wish you were here to tell me or at least make me feel that I have not done so awfully bad work today. A. doesn't do anything at all and I have to roll the ball alone which is a drag as you know it must be. Have never been more completely exhausted than some days the past week. And to cap the whole I've been watching with one of Mother Harris' sick men every night.

There is little to write about nor gossip to speak of except that Hunter does no work but spoons[16] with Miss Kellogg. Last eve. I was out with Ben in his Santolo. We went up to the Riva. I had on a white shirt and white vest and my coat was off. In the Adams' were the misses West. One remarked with "Oh my! Bohemia has got a white shirt on!" which was the text for much comment on the way we dressed in the winter. The narrowmindedness of these gals is beyond comprehension. "Donny" and I have had a squaring up. I spoke of the concert etc after she began it and told her exactly what I thought of her way of going off with one fellow and coming home with another. She put it all on to me and said I alone was touchy etc. I told her you agreed with me and then she seemed very anxious to beg my pardon etc which was not granted. Of course it was on your account she was sorry. She said Will Greene said to her that the reason why I was "gauming"[17] this winter was because I liked her and did not care to see another fellow go with her.

Mr Greene & my Klooter can make an acquaintance if they like. Does all this interest you? Donny wants that letter to Miss Fletcher, by the way. The Adams' send love—one and all. Mrs A is as lovely as ever, we were invited to dinner there Monday eve. and went in full dress, decorations & all. We found the two girls in white muslin. Mutual surprise at magnificence of costume etc. Arthur & I have been to Vicenza and Padua. I prayed to S. Antony.

By the way my boy, my plans are as follows. I'm going to carry my pictures up to Brussels on July 1st getting there about the middle of the month. Cant you come on & meet me there. We will then have the chance of seeing Brussels & Antwerp and perhaps Holland together. Do think it over. It is only a pound from London to Antwerp and an hour & a half further to Brussels. I shall have to be in these cities a few days to see to the framing of my pictures.

My dear old Boy, I miss you more than you do me and gaum constantly—after dark—why should one go and the other stay. It is rough on the one who remains.

Harry sends a wave of her tail and a gentle swagger of her body. Tom sends you his brightest smile and Venus wags his aimless tail in greeting.

Arthur encloses a little sketch. We have lost our six little chickens and bought five big ones and two crickets to sing in the evening. Otherwise all is as you left it. Bruce wrote me a funny letter about the furniture. He expects me to give him 600 francs for it. Write again soon and believe me with much love

thine, Frank.

Ubi Bohemia Fuit.
Venice May ~~29~~ 30 [1875]
My dear Old Boy:—
A rainy Sunday—blue gray—blue gray—that dismal stretch of water reminding me of the long dark Sundays of the past winter when we shivered over the stove and cursed Italy and all other cold countries. We were up at 4 this morning intending to go to Torcello. Ben Arthur Donaldson & myself were to go in a three oared gondola. But it blew & rained so it was useless to think of going and so we are gauming here at home—that is Arthur and I are.

I'm going to tell you how *I* sleep since you left. I haven't spoken of it before and I don't dare tell you why I haven't. Since we parted at Ferrara I haven't passed one good night. I always wake up in the middle of the night and in fact my whole sleep is but a succession of cat naps. At 4 a.m. I am wide awake, no difference how late I have been up or how tired I am, and by evening I am completely played out from want of sleep and rest. For a while I thought it was our old attic chamber that made me restless, so I suddenly ordered Giovanni to move all the stuff down into the improper room[18] and haven't been into our attic room since and don't intend to go. But change of room does not cure me I cant sleep there is no use trying, and this is a malady which is rare enough with me as you know. What is the matter? I know I miss you, my old chummeke, but isn't it reasonable that my other self[19] misses you still more and wont let me sleep because he wants your magnetism? I think it must be so.

Your London letter of May 24 came a day or two ago. I gave the messages to the Adams'. By the way I have told 'em that I hope you will come to Bruxelles to meet me and of course they want to hurry up and get there too. Mrs A. says, "if one man pays the $100 he owes and another *only* lets me have the $250 that's due I'll be there by the middle of July." I reply calmly "Madam, under these circumstances we shall not expect you." She is spooney on you, you know. We have been there to dinner twice this week. Didn't I write you how we went in full dress on Monday. Last night we were there in ordinary costume and Donny & I gaumed in the window all the evening. Her V.E. & F. Joseph letter is published in the Home Journal. I have never heard from any of mine. Bruce is playing me a scurvy trick. He expects me to give 600 frs for the stuff in the house—as I have told you—now he makes no reply to my letter asking for reasonable settlement but contents by walking off with 250 franks of mine and all I have is the rubbish. I have agreed to give it all to Giovanni for his last month's wages and shall give him no "buona mano"[20] besides. I wait patiently for some answer from Bruce, but still cant help cursing some because I have lost heaps of money on this old house. He evidently thinks I am cheating him.

Gossip:—

Hunter and Gildersleeve after a season of most unmitigated spooning with Miss Kellogg and Mrs Fish, have gone "Beechering" with the two ladies in Switzerland. Hunter gave no notice of his departure and none of them came to say "goodbye."

Mrs Ticknor & Miss Adams are not coming up having telegraphed Banker to that effect. He had engaged the rooms, had coolly cut the Wests and the Adamses and myself and was awaiting the sirens. Barker is now tout à fait desolé[21] and came down here late last evening to yell at me from a gondola; first attempt at recovery of position in Bohemia that was.

Will Greenes sister was drowned in the Schiller.

Mrs Harris has just returned from a weeks visit to Florence. I had previously purchased two strato fares[22] for the Adamses and presented them in our names. Mrs H. brought me two but Gildersleeve begged 'em away so I did not get them for myself as I had hoped.

Here endeth the Second Lesson. Am sorry to hear bad news of Miller. Am hoping to hear of your new book's success.

Bet your life, dear Boy, that it soothes me to learn that I am not the only one who misses his companion in arms.

Then with the wish that we may meet in six weeks in Belgium I am with all my heart and much love

Yours to put your finger on,

Frank.————

Tom's portrait shall come on.

P.S. Just recd letter from Bruce. Says the least he will take is 180 frs. Says I have stayed here rent free etc etc. That he is loser and that we have lived on him— or words to that effect. He insists that 600 francs was paid for the stuff, and don't believe a word, I say. I have given him your address if he wants any witness as to the truth of my assertions. I say we stayed here on his acct. and that if he had given up the house we would have been damned glad to go. That we did go away one month and then paid Giovanni 50 francs to take care of Bruce's furniture while we were gone. I have given all the stuff to Giovanni and wrote Bruce that if he was willing to come back on his written statements, I was not. That he had 231 francs of mine which makes rent of Jany & Feb'y 112 francs, highest price offered for furniture 70 francs total 182 francs there remains 50 francs which he can stick up as rent of his very valuable furniture.

Sic transit.

This business cuts down my travels and leaves me with precious little money to get home on.

F D M

Antwerp July 10 [1875]

My dear Charlie:—

I returned from the Harwich boat which I had been waiting for an hour in the rain with my heart as heavy as lead. No letter and no Charlie. I have already been here since Tuesday counting the hours till the boat should arrive and each day fearing to receive a letter from you that you wouldn't come. I had no letter so was sure you would be on hand. Imagine my disappointment! I returned to the house and in a few hours got yours fro Edinburgh saying you couldn't come now. It is a pity you didn't write a day or two sooner for I have lost much precious time on my pictures. I have the nigger[23] and the large one in Brussels waiting the exposition. Now that I have no need to wait in Antwerp I shall hurry to Brussels to work on them. Thursday they must be in the exposition. It is also a pity that you cant be here for Monday. There is an immense celebration in Malines such as is rarely seen here and you could make much money out of it because it is intensely Flemish and never been written up.

My plans are as follows. When you can make a quick and cheap trip through Holland starting from Antwerp about the 18th and returning in a week cost about 100-francs, or less. Then if I have money (I am pretty short, 500 francs goes slap for frames) I would like to take you to Ghent & Bruges. I must not travel much else I cant go home. I've only 1200 francs now. Passage will take 400 & frames 500 francs. Come on do, direct to Brussels via Ostend it is better for you since now I cannot come to Antwerp to meet you again. I cant possibly spare the time. If you have money come direct through to Brussels. At the station there get a cab to take you to the enclosed address where I now have a studio; Give the card to the coachman he will take you right there

If it happens to be evening & I am away, the woman will give you my address. that is my hotel. So I hope to see you there by Tuesday. I shall return here Thursday evening and stop at the Hotel du Nouveau Jardin in the Rue aux lits. So write me to the consulate or to the Hotel Nouveau Jardin Antwerp unless you come to Brussels before Thursday.

I am sorry not to see you today old boy but hope our meeting is only put off for a day or two.

 Yours in haste with very much love

  Frank

[enclosed handwritten card:

  François D. Millet

  artiste peintre

  No 25 Rue de la Charité

  Bruxelles

  chez M. Mommeus]

East Bridgewater
Aug 25, 1875
Most beloved Chummeke:—
A glorious sunset—it only wants the mood to make the evening perfect. But of course I cannot enjoy it, for two reasons. First:—the soul killing association with these good country people. Second:—the absence of the only one of my sex (or any other sex) with whom I could enjoy any beauties of nature or of art without the feeling that one or both of us was a porcupine with each quill as sensitive as a bare nerve.[24] If you were here, Charlie, I could, perhaps, be happy. When am I coming back? you ask in your letter just received. I have not changed the date yet. Immediately after Thanksgiving which comes on the last Thursday in November. I tell everybody that that is the time I am going back and everybody is making up their minds that on that date I leave the country & there is no manner of doubt about it at all, my boy, as I have already written two or three times. I have been home but very little as yet— only two weeks in the country, anyway, and the most of the time in Boston. I wrote you I think about my studio. We have just finished shingling the roof today. We work 12 hours a day and in a couple of days more it will be all done and painted inside. It is a jolly little room 20 x 15 with a great light. I shall carry my desk down there, stow away all my books and papers and be able to write at my ease there. It is only a temporary affair but a durable one so I can lock all my things up when I go away and give the keys to Father to keep the children out. Last Sunday I spent with the Adams in Quincy or rather we spent it down the harbour in his yacht and I passed the most peaceful 48 hours I have since I landed. Great house, plenty of servants, a good literary atmosphere, good dinners, good wine and good cheer. Mr A. who has been a good friend of mine says of course I must return in the fall. I have, of course, very many invitations. I refuse all I can. Since I have been in this town I have only been across the street once. Stick in my own dungeon all the time. I don't care a d— what my friends think. There is a first rate club in Boston composed of Bohemians, where I can plunge into all the magazines and newspapers. Fine rooms, the best I ever saw. There is Lippencotts. I read your "Sawdust Fairy" and Donny's "Saint Bernard." In the Overland is published her Provençal rhapsody. I also have seen in the Overland a poem of yours about Venice. Joaquin has changed his spots, at least I hear he has gone to Jersey or some other out of the way state. He is in for lectures on "New Rome & New Romans," "New Italy," "Afloat in Venice.["] The conceited ass! what does *he* know about the Italians or afloat in Venice? I'd like to hear the latter. Shall if I possibly can. Newspaper business is awfully dull. Can't get a painting to do or a cent for anything. It never has been so flat before. I had a little thing in the Courier which I send you. It is sort of funny I think even in dog days. Dog days are scirocco days and no discount. We have had nothing but dog days since I arrived and this and the mixed up state of my affairs makes

me write as I do. Hungry! I'd give all I possess if you were here to lie down under the pines on the river side and gaum with me for a season. But let us have patience and we shall meet again. In the same mail with yours (the last, containing the two letters of introduction for which many thanks) came one from Mrs Adams. A very good letter. I am really glad if there is nothing between Donny & Will Green—but I don't believe Mrs A. if she wrote you that. She may say so, but what I saw at St Elena in Donny's face told me quite a different story. How could she be so foolish. Oh I have had a letter from that creature. I returned it unopened and without a word. Mrs Adams who predicted great things may now be satisfied that I shall not return with Mrs Millet. I hope to hear from Donny soon. But it is late and I'll stop. Shall write once a week always, dear old boy and when we meet we'll have it out. With very much love I am always yours—Frank.

E. Bridgewater Dec 2nd
My dear Chummeke:-
A sigh from Capri reached me a few days ago and made more intense, if possible, my desire to be on the same continent with you. Since my last brief note great changes have taken place. I have been at work decorating the interior of a new church here which is more like an old Romanesque Catholic church than an Episcopal "tabernacle." The romantic and picturesque details of this enterprise I shall take keen delight in elaborating to you when we meet. I say "when we meet." Do you understand what that means? I am all packed up to go to Europe and am daily expecting to take passage, only awaiting for three reasons. 1st the completion of the church which is to be dedicated on Xmas day; 2nd a commission from the city of Boston to copy a portrait which must be done at the same time; 3rd the arrival of our teacher for the new drawing school (He sailed yesterday from Liverpool). The party is all made up to go and the others are waiting for me so there will probably be no reasonable doubt that we shall be in Paris by the middle of January. It is uncertain of course if we may stay there but our plan is now to take a flat there and keep house. Come up and gaum and work and know some of the most charming people you ever met! We changed our plan of going to Milan on account of some letters we received from there and are going to Paris first. Do come up to Paris, chummeke! now if you pass a winter in Italy dreaming or go into that hideous monastery I'll never forgive you so help me Moses! If you don't come wherever I am you will not show yourself either faithful, wise or at all devoted to your interests. *Come and work!* I am going to *work!* Fra idiot of Castello! don't you know you will never write half as good as you can unless you knuckle down to it? You don't use half your powers. Now I am in real earnest! Come up, Charlie, do! come and spoon and gaum and produce something. We will live again the old Bohemian in a different way; we will travel over Spain together, visit Brittany and Normandy and live as artists should in Paris. Do come!

Mark Twain came into the church the other day and we had a good talk about you and it was his idea that you intended to stay a year or more yet in Europe. This is what induces me to urge you to come to Paris and pitch in. He told me about your intention of publishing your travels and of the difficulty of making it go. You know you work better when you are with me. You know I must be as economical as yourself and that after one winter together in Venice we could endure any hardship together, so I repeat for the twentieth time: Do come and meet me!

I haven't anything to tell you except this. I am filled with it and running over. The church occupies all my time day and evening and my constant attention. Therefore I must not attempt to write you of a hundred things I want to talk to you about but continue to hope to meet you in six short weeks in the city of Paris. I shall write once more before we sail giving if possible my Paris address and shall expect you to come there. You will of course send me no more letters to America but reserve all to tell me in the long winter evenings when we hug once more our own stove and live again the days of our old Venetian existence in the little house in Castello. I haven't given up the idea of buying that nest yet. Mr Howells[25] sends you his compliments likewise Clemens who has asked me to come to Hartford and paint his portrait. I was obliged to decline because I am going away.

Yours always with very much love

Frank.

If you love me come and meet me!

*Some indications of homosexual feelings of past times occasionally surface, quite unexpectedly, in surprising places. Coy Ludwig, a personal friend of mine and retired art professor (with expertise on Maxfield Parrish [1870–1966]*[26]*), discovered this Christmas letter—written in careful cursive—totally by chance while rummaging through a Syracuse antiques shop in the 1970s and offered to share its contents for this anthology. In a different handwriting, apparently many years after the note had been sent, someone else had written "To Dad, from Bernard" on the envelope. There is no clue as to the identity of either man, or what the various relationships, long buried in the past, might be. The feelings such a carefully-written card conceal can only be guessed at by present-day readers. It reminds us that countless strong male–male relationships of the past have come and gone with no record of their existence.*

## "A MERRY CHRISTMAS" (1887)

A Merry Christmas
and A
Happy New Year.
Dec 24th 1887.

Dear *Ernest.*

What ever betide,
    No change of time
Can our true hearts divide.
    If thou in me,
        and I in thee
Shall trustingly confide.

your friend
*Bernard.*

# CLYDE FITCH (1865–1909)

*Clyde Fitch was a prolific playwright whose productions such as* Beau Brummel
*(1890),* Nathan Hale *(1899),* The Girl and the Judge *(1901), and* Captain
Jinks of the Horse-Marines *(1901) made him the toast of Broadway for many
years. He enjoyed a long correspondence with DeWitt Miller of Philadelphia, "a
middle-aged lyceum lecturer, who collected books and young men."*[27] *(Miller also
corresponded with Charles Warren Stoddard.) One letter in particular gives us
some insight into a subject taboo even to an impresario in the theater where, one
imagines, same-sex-loving men were a common occurrence.*[28]

## LETTER TO DEWITT MILLER (1891)

Jan. 2, 1891
58 West 57 St.
My dear Mr. Miller:
I sent off to you this morning acknowledging yr. kindness in sending me the
addition to my theatrical library (whose germ you generated, & whose soul
you seem to be) & for your thoughtfulness, & I now just remember, that in
my haste with a great quantity of mail I neglected to put on your address
merely sending the note to *Philadelphia!* What a muddled headed fellow I am!
Meanwhile your letter from Ohio, has just reached me. It is a shock & a surprise.

First let me say this,—Whittlesy has never influenced me about anybody or
anything & could not if he tried,—much less prejudice me. But I don't think
he ever tried to prejudice me against you—I will say that—we had one conversation once, about you,—of that, more later. Whittlesy & I are two very different men, a mutual appreciation of artistic coloring & things attracted us
into a friendship. I also admired what I believed to be his honesty, his great
& sweet good nature. We have not been very strong friends of late years. (Not
from being separated for two of the dearest friends I have, I haven't seen for
6 years, but always hear from & send to Xmas & Easter Days.) I am too much
of an enthusiast, I have stronger, perhaps wilder impulses than Whittlesy,
while Art is not my highest aim, Art with an ethical idea always is what I strive
for in my work.

For Whittlesy to make any "revelations" of my "private life" is absurd. He
never thoroughly knew me. We met, stopped a moment, & then passed each
other, in the youthful phase of life when happiness isn't serious. He had no
right, no rhyme nor reason, to make any "revelation." If you will remember

the conversation at lunch one Friday in Delmonico's, you will remember that *I did not know Whittlesy's inner life!*

It was about that conversation that you and I had that W— & I spoke. He gave me to understand differently—at least that is the impression left upon my mind now, we did not talk at length, & we did not talk plainly, we talked in *riddles* somewhat. The talk—to me at least—was unsatisfactory & ended in nothing. The only reason that I spoke of you at all was just in acknowledgment of your great thoughtfulness & touching generosity, 2nd I had been frightened by something you said & I tried to "pump" Whittlesy. You spoke of certain temperaments of men for the not ordinary sexual enjoyment, mentioned several names, & said you were going to write up the subject. Thinking it over afterward, I felt that it was something I did not at all approve of. I felt & feel you could have no right to do this, to expose what would ruin the reputation of many men living & dead who had fought hard against their temptations & done all in their power to make up for their secret life by those good & noble qualities that the best of them possess. I believe this temperament belongs to them, & they are answerable for it to God (who perhaps is *also* answerable to them) and not to the world. Who would condemn & damn them. Their family, their *mothers*, should be remembered.

This made an impression upon me of not liking you. This your innumerable kindnesses, your splendid letters, your many acts of unexpected thoughtfulness that went straight to my heart—& *stayed* there!—all these wore away this other impression until when I sent you my photograph, I had lost it, & in its place had come a real affectionate friendship for you. I mentioned if I hadn't misunderstood or if you hadn't been talking to *sound* me, or if [I] hadn't dreamed it! And lately I had forgotten all about it. I am proud of your friendship, grateful & happy in it. I want your affection. *The condition you make I acceded to before you made it.* I *will* be! and if anybody can write as good a letter as Johnson's, *you* can.

Yours faithfully
Clyde Fitch

I ask that you will *answer but* destroy this letter.

# George Sylvester Viereck (1884–1962)

*This letter congratulates Woodberry on the publication of his latest book of poetry, and says something about early networking between authors with homosexual sympathies.*

## Letter to George E. Woodberry (ca. 1912)[29]

202 Riverside Drive, Wednesday [undated, ca. 1912]
My dear Professor Woodberry:
I have just finished your wonderful book. The room above me is freezing with memories of Hellas[30] and Italia. I love many of the poems, especially "Comrades."[31] Some lines in others, such as

> "He stuck red cherries in his ears
> He smiled—and slew three thousand years"[32]

have indeed the glint of immortality. I wonder have you read my "Ballad of King David," "David and Jonathan" and "Ballad of the Golden Boy"? I have played with many fires, Greek fires and others. Just at present I have put them aside. But not altogether—Something always reminds me of the love passing the love of woman. Yet while Giovanni is still within call, like another Faust living at once through Acts I and II, full of the tragedy, I am in love with both Margaret and Helen.... Life is horribly complex. Or I am horribly complex. So complex that I have given up the hope of ever expressing in song what really stirs me and moves me. You have expressed much of that. There is a clean, sweet paganism in your book. But of course their [sic] must be many other chords, as you hint yourself, that you have not struck. Good luck and much joy to you for the rest of the journey. Believe me
truly *Sincerely* yours,
George Sylvester Viereck

## Notes

1   Much has been written on this subject. Michael Bronski's essay, "When Nathaniel Met Herman," published in *Z Magazine* (16.12, December. 2003), makes good observations. For a lucid summary of current thinking, see *ESQ: A Journal of the American Renaissance* which devoted an entire special issue to the Hawthorne-Melville relationship (Vol. 46.1/2, 2000).

2   The word-choice here is interesting. See Bliss Carman and Richard Hovey (above, 270–73).

3   *Moby-Dick* (1851).

4   When the governor accuses the proselytizing St. Paul that "too much study has made you crazy!" he receives the reply: "I am not insane, Most Excellent Festus. I am speaking the sober truth." Acts 26: 24–25.

5   Leviathan in the Old Testament is a great sea monster symbolizing evil [Hebrew]. Krakens are huge sea monsters in Norwegian legend.

6   I.e., Magi, wise men.

7   Printing paper.

8   Credit: Charles W. Stoddard Collection, Special Collections Research Center, Syracuse University Library.

9   Literally, Where Bohemia Was (Latin); i.e., Venice, where they shared an apartment together. Millet's use of the word Bohemia is a marker of difference, here a reference to his affair with Stoddard.

10   Hopefully, by all that is most holy (Italian).

11   Stoddard's *South Sea Idyls* (see above, 93–103).

12   Thus passes the glory of the world (Latin). The complete phrase is "Sic transit gloria mundi."

13   Joaquin Miller (1837–1913), American writer known as the "Poet of the Sierras."

14   I.e., journey, trek (Greek); from Xenophon's classic *Anabasis* [*March Up Country*] (386–377 BC).

15   Sirocco (Italian). Warm, oppressive southern winds from Africa bringing rain in its wake.

16   To "spoon" was to flirt, romance, have a crush on, etc.

17   The verb "gaum" appears often in Millet's letters and seems a slang term for idly passing time, staring into space vacantly, "mooning," or in modern parlance, "hanging out."

18   I.e., not fit for sleeping.

19   Millet's term for his homosexual side is a telling one. He sees his attraction to Stoddard as something that stands totally apart from his conventional, everyday self—something not explained by experience as he otherwise knows it.

20   Tip (Italian).

21   Entirely grieved (French).

22   Train fares.

23   Millet refers to a painting with a black model as its subject.

24   In spite of the implied suggestion that Stoddard was the only male who attracted him sexually, Millet would report in a later letter to Stoddard (29 June 1877) that he was "spooning frightfully with a young Greek here in Oltenitza."

25   William Dean Howells (1837–1920), the influential editor of *The Atlantic Monthly* and later styled the Dean of American Letters, was just beginning his career as a successful novelist.

26  Parrish was one of the most successful and widely-recognized commercial artists of his day. His dreamscapes—most often distinguished by their stunning shades of blue—decorated countless magazine covers, calendars, and American living room walls during the first half of the twentieth century.

27  Roger Austen, *Genteel Pagan*, 140.

28  This letter is reprinted with thanks from the Clyde Fitch Papers, Manuscripts and Archives Division, The New York Public Library, Astor, Lenox and Tilden Foundations.

29  Reprinted courtesy Houghton Library, Harvard University.

30  Hellas is the Greek name for Greece. Clearly Viereck associates Hellas with homosexuality, as he refers in this letter to homosexual poems that he himself has written (see above, 167–70).

31  See this poem under Woodberry (above, 284–85).

32  See Woodberry's "Flower of Etna" (286, above).

## PRIMARY SOURCES

Fone, Byrne R.S., ed. *The Columbia Anthology of Gay Literature: Readings from Western Antiquity to the Present Day.* New York: Columbia UP, 1998.

Hartland, Claude (pseud.). *The Story of a Life.* 1901. Amsterdam, The Netherlands: Fredonia Books, 2005.

James, Henry. *Beloved Boy: Letters to Hendrik C. Andersen, 1899–1915.* Ed. Rosella Mamoli Zorzi. Charlottesville: U of Virginia P, 2004.

———. *Dearly Beloved Friends: Henry James's Letters to Younger Men.* Ed. Susan E. Gunter and Steven H. Jobe. Ann Arbor: U of Michigan P, 2001.

Jolly, James, and Estelle Kohler, eds. *The Marginalia Book of Gay Letters.* London: Marginalia, 1995.

Katz, Jonathan Ned. *Gay American History.* New York: Thomas Y. Crowell, 1976.

Lind, Earl (pseud.). *Autobiography of an Androgyne.* 1918. New York: Arno, 1975.

Mitchell, Mark, and David Leavitt. *Pages Passed from Hand to Hand: The Hidden Tradition of Homosexual Literature in English from 1748 to 1914.* Boston: Mariner/Houghton Mifflin, 1997.

Nissen, Axel. *The Romantic Friendship Reader: Love Stories between Men in Victorian America.* Boston: Northeastern UP, 2003.

Prime-Stevenson, Edward. *Imre: A Memorandum.* 1906. Ed. James J. Gifford. Peterborough: Broadview, 2003.

———. *Mystically My Heart.* 1893. Ed. Tom Sargant. Pomfret VT: Elysium/Publishing Scoundrel, 2004.

———. *Those Restless Pilgrimages.* 1896; 1905. Ed. Tom Sargant. Pomfret VT: Elysium, 2002.

Roscoe, Will, ed. *Living the Spirit: A Gay American Indian Anthology.* New York: St. Martin's, 1988.

Senelick, Laurence, ed. *Lovesick: Modernist Plays of Same-Sex Love, 1894–1925.* New York: Routledge, 1999.

Stoddard, Charles Warren. *Cruising the South Seas.* Ed. Winston Leyland. San Francisco: Gay Sunshine, 1987.

———. *For the Pleasure of His Company: An Affair of the Misty City.* 1903. San Francisco: Gay Sunshine, 1987.

Symonds, John Addington. *The Memoirs of John Addington Symonds: The Secret Homosexual Life of a Leading Nineteenth-Century Man of Letters.* Ed. Phyllis Grosskurth. Chicago: U of Chicago P, 1984.

Whitman, Walt. *Leaves of Grass and other Writings.* Ed. Michael Moon. New York: Norton, 2002.

## Secondary Sources

Austen, Roger. *Genteel Pagan: the Double Life of Charles Warren Stoddard.* Ed. John W. Crowley. Amherst: U of Massachusetts P, 1991.

—. *Playing the Game: The Homosexual Novel in America.* Indianapolis: Bobbs-Merrill, 1977.

—. "Stoddard's Little Tricks in *South Sea Idyls.*" *Essays on Gay Literature.* Ed. Stuart Kellogg. New York: Harrington Park, 1985. 73–81.

Bergman, David. *Gaiety Transfigured: Gay Self-Representation in American Literature.* Madison: U of Wisconsin P, 1991.

Bode, Carl. "Introduction." *Ragged Dick and Struggling Upward.* By Horatio Alger, Jr. New York: Penguin, 1985. ix–xxi.

Borklund, Elmer W. *Howard Overing Sturgis: An Account of His Life and Writings Together with His Unpublished Works.* Unpublished Diss. U of Chicago, 1959. Ann Arbor: UMI, 1995. 4934.

—. "Howard Sturgis, Henry James, and *Belchamber.*" *Modern Philology* 58.4 (May 1961): 255–69.

Brodhead, Richard H. *The School of Hawthorne.* New York: Oxford UP, 1986.

Carbado, Devon W., Dwight A. McBride, and Donald Weise, eds. *Black Like Us: A Century of Lesbian, Gay and Bisexual African American Fiction.* San Francisco: Cleis, 2002.

Chauncey, George. *Gay New York: Gender, Urban Culture, and the Making of the Gay Male World 1890–1940.* New York: BasicBooks/HarperCollins, 1994.

Cohen, Ed. *Talk on the Wilde Side: Toward a Genealogy of a Discourse on Male Sexualities.* New York: Routledge, 1993.

Crain, Caleb. *American Sympathy: Men, Friendship, and Literature in the New Nation.* New Haven, Yale UP, 2001.

Crowley, John W. "Eden Off Nantucket: W.S. Bigelow and 'Tuckanuck.'" *Essex Institute Historical Collections* 109 (1973): 3–8.

—. *George Cabot Lodge.* Boston: Twayne/G.K. Hall, 1976.

—. "Howells, Stoddard, and Male Homosocial Attachment in Victorian America." *The Making of Masculinities: The New Men's Studies.* Ed. Harry Brod. Boston: Allyn and Unwin, 1987. 301–24.

Derrick, Scott S. *Monumental Anxieties: Homoerotic Desire and Feminine Influence in Nineteenth-Century U.S. Literature.* New Brunswick: Rutgers UP, 1997.

Duberman, Martin Bauml, Martha Vicinus, and George Chauncey Jr. *Hidden from History: Reclaiming the Gay and Lesbian Past.* New York: New American Library, 1989.

Ellmann, Richard. *Oscar Wilde.* New York: Vintage, 1987.

Féray, Jean-Claude. *Histoire du Mot* Pédérastie*: Grecques, les Moeurs du Hanneton?* Paris: Quintes-Feuilles, 2004.

—. "Une Mine de Données sur l'Homosexualité à la Belle Époque." *Du Similisexualisme dans les Armées et de la Prostitution Homosexuelle (Militaire et Civile) à la Belle Époque.* 1908. By Edward I. Prime-Stevenson. Ed. Jean-Claude Féray. Paris: Quintes-Feuilles, 2003. 1–8.

Fone, Byrne R.S. "This Other Eden: Arcadia and the Homosexual Imagination." *Essays on Gay Literature.* Ed. Stuart Kellogg. New York: Harrington Park, 1985. 13–34.

Foucault, Michel. *The History of Sexuality: An Introduction.* Trans. Robert Hurley. New York: Vintage, 1980.

Fuss, Diana, ed. *Inside/Out: Lesbian Theories, Gay Theories.* New York: Routledge, 1991.

Gertz, Elmer. *Odyssey of a Barbarian: the Biography of George Sylvester Viereck.* Buffalo: Prometheus, 1978.

Gifford, James. *Dayneford's Library: American Homosexual Writing, 1900–1913.* Amherst: U of Massachusetts P, 1995.

—. "Left to Themselves: The Subversive Boys Books of Edward Prime-Stevenson (1858–1942)." *Journal of American and Comparative Cultures* 24 (Fall/Winter 2001): 113–16.

Haeg, Larry. *In Gatsby's Shadow: The Story of Charles Macomb Flandrau.* Iowa City: U of Iowa P, 2004.

Haggerty, George E., and Bonnie Zimmerman, eds. *Professions of Desire: Lesbian and Gay Studies in Literature.* New York: Modern Language Association, 1995.

Halperin, David M. *How to Do the History of Homosexuality.* Chicago: U of Chicago P, 2002.

Hallock, John W.M. *Homosexuality and the Fall of Fitz-Greene Halleck.* Madison: U of Wisconsin P, 2000.

Hanson, Bert. "American Physicians' 'Discovery' of Homosexuals, 1880–1900: A New Diagnosis in a Changing Society." *Framing Disease: Studies in Cultural History.* Ed. Charles E. Rosenberg and Janet Golden. New Brunswick: Rutgers UP, 1992. 104–33.

Hatheway, Jay. *The Gilded Age Construction of Modern American Homophobia.* New York: Palgrave Macmillan, 2003.

Herrmann, Anne. *Queering the Moderns: Poses/Portraits/Performances.* New York: Palgrave, 2000.

The History Project. *Improper Bostonians: Lesbian and Gay History from the Puritans to Playland.* Boston: Beacon, 1998.

Jensen, Gerard E. *The Life and Letters of Henry Cuyler Bunner.* Durham: Duke UP, 1939.

Katz, Jonathan Ned. *Gay/Lesbian Almanac: A New Documentary.* New York: Harper & Row, 1983.

—. *Love Stories: Sex between Men before Homosexuality.* Chicago: U of Chicago P, 2001.

Koestenbaum, Wayne. *Double Talk: The Erotics of Male Literary Collaboration.* New York: Routledge, 1989.

—. *The Queen's Throat: Opera, Homosexuality and the Mystery of Desire.* New York: Poseidon Press, 1993.

Lewis, Lloyd, and Henry Justin Smith. *Oscar Wilde Discovers America: 1882.* New York: Harcourt, Brace, 1936.

Marra, Kim, and Robert A. Schanke, eds. *Staging Desire: Queer Readings of American Theater History.* Ann Arbor: U of Michigan P, 2002.

Martin, Robert K. "Bayard Taylor's Valley of Bliss: The Pastoral and the Search for Form." *The Markham Review* 9 (Fall 1979): 13–17.

—. *The Homosexual Tradition in American Poetry.* Austin: U of Texas P, 1979.

Packard, Chris. *Queer Cowboys: And Other Erotic Male Friendships in Nineteenth-Century American Literature.* New York: Palgrave/Macmillan, 2005.

Pilkington, John, Jr. *Henry Blake Fuller.* New York: Twayne, 1970.

Pronger, Brian. *The Arena of Masculinity: Sports, Homosexuality, and the Meaning of Sex.* New York: St. Martin's, 1990.

Robb, Graham. *Strangers: Homosexual Love in the Nineteenth Century.* New York: Norton, 2003.

Roscoe, Will. *Changing Ones: Third and Fourth Genders in Native North America.* New York: St. Martin's, 1998.

Scambray. Kenneth. *A Varied Harvest: The Life and Works of Henry Blake Fuller.* Pittsburgh: U of Pittsburgh P, 1987.

Scharnhorst, Gary, with Jack Bales. *The Lost Life of Horatio Alger, Jr.* Bloomington: Indiana UP, 1985.

Sedgwick, Eve Kosofsky. "The Beast in the Closet: James and the Writing of Homosexual Panic." *Sex, Politics, and Science in the Nineteenth-Century Novel: Selected Papers from the English Institute, 1983–84.* Ed. Ruth Bernard Yeazell. Baltimore: Johns Hopkins UP, 1984. 148–86.

—. *Between Men: English Literature and Male Homosocial Desire.* New York: Columbia UP, 1985.

—. *Epistomology of the Closet.* Berkeley: U of California P, 1990.

Seelye, John, ed. *Stories of the Old West: Tales of the Mining Camp, Cavalry Troop, & Cattle Ranch.* New York: Penguin, 1994.

Shand-Tucci, Douglass. *The Crimson Letter: Harvard, Homosexuality, and the Shaping of American Culture.* New York: St. Martin's, 2003.

Sinfield, Alan. *The Wilde Century: Effeminacy, Oscar Wilde and the Queer Moment.* New York: Columbia UP, 1994.

Sonstegard, Adam. "Performing the 'Unnatural' Life: America's First Gay Autobiography." *Biography* 25.4 (Fall 2002): 545–70.

Sox, David. *Bachelors of Art: Edward Perry Warren & The Lewes House Brotherhood.* London: Fourth Estate, 1991.

Stoneley, Peter. "Rewriting the Gold Rush: Twain, Harte and Homosociality." *Journal of American Studies* 30/2 (1996): 189–209.

Summers, Claude J. *Gay Fictions: Wilde to Stonewall: Studies in a Male Homosexual Literary Tradition.* New York: Continuum, 1990.

Thomsen, Dawn Fisk. "Skirted Men and Booted Ladies: Sexual Identity and Disguise in Nineteenth-Century American Detective Fiction." Paper presented at the Popular Culture Conference, San Antonio TX, 29 March 1997.

Watson, Charles. Introduction. *The Son of the Wolf: Tales of the Far North.* By Jack London. New York: Oxford UP, 1996. ix–xv.

Whitaker, Rick. *The First Time I Met Frank O'Hara: Reading Gay American Writers.* New York: Four Walls Eight Windows, 2003.

Whittle, Amberys R. *Trumbull Stickney.* Lewisburg: Bucknell UP, 1973.

Ziff, Larzer. *The American 1890s: Life and Times of a Lost Generation.* New York: Viking, 1966.

# Sources

I have made some occasional silent spelling changes for the sake of clarity; however, as the spelling and punctuation reflect their historical and cultural context, I have left many as in the original.

Aldrich, Thomas Bailey. *Marjorie Daw and Other People.* 1873. Boston: Houghton, Mifflin, 1891. 7–54.

Alger, Horatio Jr. *Charlie Codman's Cruise.* Chicago: M.A. Donohue, n.d. 172–78.

Atherton, Gertrude. "The Striding Place." 1896. *The Bell in the Fog and other Stories.* New York: Harper, 1905. 47–57.

Berkman, Alexander. *Prison Memoirs of an Anarchist.* New York: Mother Earth Publishing Association, 1912. 321–24; 437–40.

Bunner, H.C. "Our Aromatic Uncle." *Scribner's Magazine* 18 (July–December 1895): 169–82.

Carman, Bliss, and Richard Hovey. *Songs from Vagabondia.* Boston: Copeland and Day, 1894.

Cather, Willa. *The Troll Garden.* New York: McClure, Phillips, 1905.

Catlin, George. *Letters and Notes on the Manners, Customs, and Conditions of North American Indians.* Vol. 2. 1844. New York: Dover, 1973. 214–15.

Davis, Merrell R., and William H. Gilman, eds. *The Letters of Herman Melville.* New Haven: Yale UP, 1960.

Flandrau, Charles Macomb. *Harvard Episodes.* Boston: Copeland and Day, 1897. 70–76.

Flynt [Willard], Josiah. "Homosexuality among Tramps." In: Havelock Ellis and John Addington Symonds, eds., *Sexual Inversion.* London: Wilson & Macmillan, 1897. Appendix B, 252–57.

Fuller, Henry Blake. "Allisonian Classical Academy." Unpublished ms. The Newberry Library, Chicago, Special Collections. 7–10; 16–25.

—. "At Saint Judas's." *The Puppet-Booth: Twelve Plays.* New York: Century, 1896.

Haile, Berard. *Love-Magic and Butterfly People: The Slim Curly Version of the Ajitee and Mothway Myths.* Flagstaff: Museum of Northern Arizona, 1978. 83–84.

Halleck, Fitz-Greene. *Poems.* New York: T.Y. Crowell, [ca. 1898]. 86, 92, 131.

—. *The Poetical Writings of Fitz-Greene Halleck.* 1869. New York: AMS Press, 1969.

Harte, Bret. *The Luck of Roaring Camp and Other Stories.* Boston: Houghton, Mifflin, 1882. 135–46.

—. *Poems.* Boston: James R. Osgood, 1871.

Hartland, Claude (pseud.). *The Story of a Life.* 1901. Ed. Donald M. Allen. San Francisco: Grey Fox, 1985. 65–74.

Howard, Police Captain (pseud.) [Harry Enton]. "Young Sleuth, the Keen Detective; or, The Sharpest Boy in New York." *The Boys of New York: A Paper for Young Americans* 2.88 (23 April 1877): 1–2.

Howard, William Lee. "Effeminate Men and Masculine Women." *New York Medical Journal* 71 (5 May 1900): 686–87.

—. "The Sexual Pervert in Life Insurance." *The Medical Examiner and Practitioner* 16 (July 1906): 206–07.

James, Henry. "The Great Good Place." Vol. XVI. *The New York Edition: The Author of Beltraffio et al.* New York: Charles Scribner's Sons, 1907–09.

Johnson, James Weldon. *The Autobiography of an Ex-Colored Man.* Boston: Sherman, French & Company, 1912.

Johnson, Shirley Everton. *The Cult of the Purple Rose.* Boston: Richard G. Badger/The Gorham Press, 1902. 55–65.

Klah, Hasteen, and Mary C. Wheelwright. *Navajo Creation Myth: The Story of the Emergence.* Navajo Religion Series, Vol. 1. Sante Fe: Museum of Navajo Ceremonial Art, 1942. 39.

Lind, Earl (pseudo.). *The Autobiography of an Androgyne.* 1918. New York: Arno, 1975. 73–81; 251–59.

Lodge, George Cabot. "Moriturus." *Scribner's Magazine* 38.1 (July 1905): 42.

—. *Selected Fiction and Verse.* Ed. John W. Crowley. St. Paul: John Colet, 1976. 202, 222–23, 235.

London, Jack. "The White Silence." *Overland Monthly* 33 (February 1899): 138–42.

Loring, Fred.W. *Two College Friends.* Boston: Loring, 1871.

Peirce, James Mills [Professor X.]. *Sexual Inversion.* By Havelock Ellis and John Addington Symonds. 1897. New York: Ayer, 1994. 273–75.

Prime-Stevenson, Edward. "*Aquae Multae Non*—." In *Her Enemy, Some Friends, and Other Personages.* Florence: Obsner, 1913. 18–49.

—. [Xavier Mayne, pseud.] *The Intersexes: A History of Similisexualism as a Problem in Social Life.* 1908. New York: Arno, 1975. 376–77; 382–83.

Pyle, Howard. *The Merry Adventures of Robin Hood of Great Renown in Nottinghamshire.* 1883. Garden City, NY: Junior deluxe Editions, n.d. 113–24.

Raile, Arthur Lyon [Edward Perry Warren pseud.]. *Itamos: A Volume of Poems.* London: Grant Richards, 1903. 1, 17–18, 50–51, 60–62, 67, 84–88, 96–97, 107–09.

Riley, James Whitcomb. *Good-Bye, Jim.* New York: Grosset and Dunlap, 1913.

Santayana, George. *Sonnets and other Verses.* New York: Stone and Kimball, 1896. 60–63.

—. *Persons and Places: Fragments of An Autobiography.* Edited by William G. Holzberger and Herman J. Saatkamp, Jr. Cambridge: MIT, 1986. 357–60, 508–14.

Schaff, Morris. *The Spirit of Old West Point: 1858–1862.* Boston: Houghton Mifflin, 1907. 191–92; 238–42.

Stevenson, E. Irenaeus. *Mrs. Dee's Encore. Harper's Bazar* 29:7 (29 February 1896): 125–27.

Stickney, Trumbull. *The Poems of Trumbull Stickney.* Edited by George Cabot Lodge, William Vaughn Moody, and John Ellerton Lodge. Boston: Houghton, Mifflin, 1905.

Stoddard, Charles Warren. *South-Sea Idyls.* 1873. New York: Charles Scribner's Son, 1911. 132–53.

Sturgis, Howard Overing. *Belchamber.* New York: G.P. Putnam's Sons, 1905. 13–28.

Taylor, Bayard. *Poems of the Orient.* 3rd ed. Boston: Ticknor and Fields, 1855. 15, 124.

—. *The Poet's Journal.* Boston: Ticknor and Fields, 1863. 25–26.

—. *The Works of Bayard Taylor.* Eldorado ed. Vol. 3. New York: G.P. Putnam's Sons, n.d. 90–96.

Viereck, George Sylvester. *Nineveh and Other Poems.* New York: Moffat, Yard, 1908. 87, 88, 96, 133–36.

—. *The Candle and the Flame.* New York: Moffat, Yard, 1912. 19–28, 44, 49–50, 55.

Whitman, Walt. "The Child's Champion." *New World* 3.21 (20 November 1841): 321–22.

"Wilde in Utica." *The Utica [New York] Daily Observer,* 7 February 1882: 7.

Wilson, James Grant. *The Life and Letters of Fitz-Greene Halleck.* New York: D. Appleton, 1869. 73–82.

Woodberry, George Edward. *Selected Poems of George Edward Woodberry.* Boston: Houghton Mifflin, 1933. 52–56.